Romantic Love and Sexual Behavior

Perspectives from the Social Sciences

Edited by
VICTOR C. DE MUNCK

PRAEGER

Westport, Connecticut
London

Library of Congress Cataloging-in-Publication Data

Romantic love and sexual behavior : perspectives from the social
    sciences / edited by Victor C. de Munck.
        p.   cm.
    Includes bibliographical references and index.
    ISBN 0-275-95726-8 (alk. paper)
    1. Love—Cross-cultural studies.   2. Sexual behavior—Cross-
cultural studies.   3. Love.   4. Sexual behavior.   I. de Munck,
Victor C.
GT2630.R66   1998
306.7—dc21   97-26904

British Library Cataloguing in Publication Data is available.

Library of Congress Catalog Card Number: 97-26904
ISBN: 0-275-95726-8

First published in 1998

Praeger Publishers, 88 Post Road West, Westport, CT 06881
An imprint of Greenwood Publishing Group, Inc.

Printed in the United States of America

The paper used in this book complies with the
Permanent Paper Standard issued by the National
Information Standards Organization (Z39.48–1984).

10 9 8 7 6 5 4 3 2

Contents

SECTION III: EVOLUTIONARY AND INVESTMENT MODELS

SECTION IV: AIDS AND CULTURAL NARRATIVES

SECTION V: CROSS-CULTURAL STUDIES OF LOVE AND SEX

Preface

This volume is an interdisciplinary project that brings together anthropologists, psychologists, and sociologists who study romantic love and human sexuality. I first began to think of editing a volume like this in the summer of 1994 when I was attending a three-week National Science Foundation course on state-of-the-art methods for ethnographic fieldwork. There I met Elisa Sobo who was in the process of editing the galleys of her book *Choosing Unsafe Sex* (1995). Dr. Sobo said that she had found that romantic love was an important—perhaps the most important—cultural inhibitor for adopting safe sex practices. She also noted, to my surprise, that relatively little research had been done on the relationship between romantic love and sexual behavior. At the time, I had been coding and analyzing my field data on love and arranged marriage practices in Sri Lanka and wanted to show how Sri Lankans attempt to balance personal desires with social structural and economic requirements. Before my discussion with Dr. Sobo, I had assumed that there was a surfeit of studies on romantic love and sexual relations in the West.

I began to read the literature on romantic love and found, indeed, that there were numerous studies on romantic love and an equal number on sex, but hardly any that attempted to bridge the two. In fact, Rubin (1988:ix) noted that, at that time, there were almost no studies on the relationship between romantic love and sex. Since then, scholars have begun to research this relationship and write up their findings. Most of this research is bifurcated, with one camp of scholars motivated by funding and concern over the AIDS pandemic; their focus is specific to the issues of how romantic love influences sexual risk behavior. Such studies are intended to address a specific situational problem (e.g., how do you get couples to use condoms for penetrative-receptive sex?) rather than study romantic love and sexual behavior writ large. The second camp moves to the beat of the sociobiologists and evolutionary psychologists. Evolutionary psychologists view romantic love as a strategy for mate selection (i.e., sex) that varies both across gender and within gender, depending on cultural markers for success or attractiveness. For the AIDS researchers, romantic love tends to be viewed as an independent variable that influences decisions about sexual behaviors, and for the evolutionary psychologists, romantic love is viewed as a dependent variable shaped by the motive to optimize individual reproductive success in a given cultural milieu.

As a result of my intensive reading of this literature, my views on romantic love and sex began to change. I had assumed that sex was a "byproduct" of love and that love led to marriage and marriage legitimated love and that this cultural script was, more or less, culturally universal. Re-examining my own work, I recognized that the triadic relation of romantic love, marriage, and sex, and the conceptualization of this triad are different in significant ways in Sri Lanka and the United States. Thus, the relationship between romantic love and sexual practices is problematic and variable both within and between cultures. What is not problematic is that there is always a relationship between the two, even if that relationship is one that prohibits sexual contact between lovers or love between sexual partners. I also realized that there were strong disciplinary boundaries in this field of research. Anthropologists tended to speak to their own, as did psychologists and sociologists. In the midst of this whirlwind of ideas and interests, I became interested in putting together an interdisciplinary volume that, in the sense that any one volume can, bridged the moats between disciplines and, like rays of sunlight, showed the range of approaches that can be used to shed light on this universal, complex, and important relationship.

Acknowledgments

To put together a volume, you need three things: a coherent theme that gives reason and rhyme to the chapters that make up the volume; authors that are doing significant work and are willing and responsible participants in the project; and a compassionate and competent editor. I have been lucky enough to have all three. My job has been made much easier by the contributing authors, all of whom have written multiple drafts of their chapters without complaint and have been encouraging and supportive from the beginning. Specifically, I want to thank Elisa Sobo for starting me thinking about this project; John Alan Lee for his words of wisdom and reminder that life is more than work; Dorothy Tennov for her willingness to take a risk on an upstart; and Pamela Regan for all her enthusiasm and reassurances. Timothy Perper and Martha Cornog have provided encouragement and ideas that are still ripening. I am indebted to Alan Beals, David Kronenfeld, and Steve Reyna for reading portions of this volume and providing useful comments and criticisms. Acknowledgments are a pleasure to write when one can mention those people "behind the scenes" who are as necessary to the creation and successful completion of this enterprise as the authors, editor, and publisher. Mrs. Luci Plourde has worked fiercely and finely on the thankless and laborious tasks of collating the endnotes and bibliography and formatting this manuscript. Trini Garro, my wife, makes me wish that everyone was in love and profoundly deepens my belief that love is the answer to Freud's question "What do human beings want?" Finally, I dedicate this volume to my mother, Mechelina, without whom it could not have been written.

Introduction

It is taken for granted that love leads to sex and then to marriage or, for some, to marriage and then sex. Couples, heterosexual and homosexual, do have sex without love and, on occasion, marry without mutual love. But such sexual acts and marriages, we assume, are less legitimate, less worthy, and less complete than those catalyzed by and enveloped in love. This causal relationship has not always been a cultural axiom in the West, nor do we expect it to be true in the non-Western world where marriages are arranged on the basis of familial interests rather than the affective bond of the couple. Yet we cannot help believing that somehow the deep and intense emotions of being "in love" must be universal and that these emotions, when they are mutual, must find their way into a sexual and probably marital relationship. Is romantic love a cultural universal? Does it inevitably lead to the marriage bed, or any bed, for that matter? If love legitimates sex, will individuals motivated by "love" view sex differently from those who are not? Do males and females view love in the same way? Does love diminish the risks of unsafe sex? Are there different sex styles as well as different love styles? Is the enthrallment in which a charismatic leader hold his or her followers the same as "being captive to love?" Although love feels like an unmeasurable quality, can we analyze it as a measure of investment in another person?

These are some of the questions the authors in this volume examine. This volume represents the first interdisciplinary collection of studies that explores the many ways romantic love and sexual relationships may be understood and related to one another. Included are historical and cultural constructionist views that present love and sex as potentially separate spheres of interest and motivation; utilitarian perspectives that show how individuals weigh the costs and benefits of their mate relative to their ideal or potential alternative mates; evolutionary approaches that view romantic love as a cultural means to a biological end; prototype approaches that recognize a universal sexual and emotional core to love layered by cultural norms for reckoning and expressing attraction; and applied studies that indicate how conceptions of love influence sexual behaviors. In each study, the authors use their particular expertise to describe and explain how, and if, love (and here "love" is used as a default for romantic/passionate love styles rather than familial love or love of objects and ideas) and sex are related. In this introduction I present a review of the literature on this relationship as well as a summary of the chapters that this volume comprises.

HOW ARE LOVE AND SEX RELATED?

In 1988 Rubin wrote that although there are a plethora of studies on love and an equal number on sex, almost none have been published on the relationship between love and sex. He also noted the absence of a "common vocabulary" of love that would facilitate discussion among scholars. This, he remarked, was an indication of the "immaturity" of love as an area of study (1988:ix).[1] Eight years later, Berscheid and Meyers (1996:20) and Noller (1996:97) noted a lack of scholarly agreement on "what love is," and Dion and Dion (1996:2) observed that remarkably few studies examine the relationship between love and sex.

The relationship between love and sex has been studied from an evolutionary perspective in which love is part of a more global mating and caretaking strategy (Buss 1988, 1994; Fisher 1992, 1995). A few have sought to study love in terms of "optimal biasing" (Weinstein 1982) or risk-taking strategies (Fullilove et al. 1990, Sobo 1995) associated with studies of the AIDS pandemic. The last two studies identify romantic love as akin to a culturally constructed "master motive" (D'Andrade 1995:126). A master motive is a goal that members of a culture—regardless of class, gender, ethnic or other social distinctions—share and have internalized and strive toward.

Although there is little agreement about "what love is" and whether it is a biologically or culturally constituted motive for behavior, little controversy exists over the biological basis of sexual behavior. Sexual motives and practices need not be attached to love. Sex is typically perceived as a biological drive akin to hunger (e.g., Freud [1929] 1961; Murray 1938). Buss (1988), Bogaert and Fisher (1995), and countless researchers have noted the seemingly inherent, hence acultural, disposition to promiscuity by the human male and the converse tendency to monogamy by the human female. Bogaert and Fisher propose that males adopt one of two sexual strategies: if they are dominant and sought-after, they adopt low-attachment maximal partner strategies, whereas if they are subordinate males, they adopt high-attachment monogamous strategies.

Studies by Perper (1985), Holland and Eisenhart (1990), and Holland and Skinner (1987) argue for a more integrated biocultural approach in which culture is not merely the means for a biological end but that promotes an interweaving between nature and nurture. Perper (1985) uses ethological, observational methods to study how the "biology of love" is woven into a culturally interpreted process of courtship. Holland and Skinner (1987) report how female college students in the United States are more likely to engage in sexual intercourse (and in a shorter span of time) with high-prestige men than with low-prestige men. Such studies argue for the cultural universality and temporal constancy of the sex drive as a determinant of male-female relationships interacting with a culture's ideologies and symbols of romantic love. The cultural symbols and ideals are then molded around a biological (one can't help thinking "molten") core. Dorothy Tennov's chapter on limerence (Chapter 3) and Robert Moore's chapter on romantic love in China (Chapter 11) are excellent examples of this perspective.

Recent research (Liebowitz 1983; Fisher 1995:24–25; Money 1980) suggests that there is a real sexual "chemistry" to love. Lovers become literally addicted to one another, and this addiction spans approximately seven years before it loses its potency—the period most critical to child-rearing and also the year when men get the renowned "seven-year itch." In such studies, love is one possible cultural expression of deep-rooted chemical processes triggered by sexual attraction.

In this volume, Charles Lindholm provides an important critique of the evolutionary approach (Chapter 1). First, he argues that in much of the world, societies arrange pair-bonding so that love, and hence, chemistry, are factored out of the sexual and parental equation. Second, he notes that only in the West is romantic love the desire on which marriages are cast and that Western nations have lower population densities and rates of growth than societies where marriages are arranged. If, as evolutionary psychologists argue, romantic love is a byproduct of sexual strategies, then why doesn't it correlate with historical and contemporary population demographics? If love is not a necessary condition for keeping parents together or for child-rearing, as Lindholm suggests, then we need to consider more culturally premised approaches to studying love as distinct from sex. One could counter that we were foragers for approximately one and a half million years (if we go back to *Homo erectus*) before we were horticulturalists and that romantic love seems to be a motive for pair-bonding in foraging societies (Shostak 1983).

Biology may not be a necessary antecedent condition for romantic love, but it is certainly a sufficient condition for arousing and shaping feelings of romantic love, even if indirectly. Since love is neither a necessary condition for sexual reproduction nor a universal criterion for self-selecting the most inclusively fit humans to reproduce, then we must open the theoretical doors and examine the possible kinds of relationships that can exist between love and sex. Both the cultural constructionist and evolutionary psychologist views postulate (opposing) a priori conditions: that of independence in the former and that of interdependence in the latter.

MODELING THE RELATIONSHIP BETWEEN LOVE AND SEX

In a summary of different theories of the relationship between love and sexuality, Aron and Aron (1991) proposed four relational models: (1) sex as primary and love as a sublimation or reformulation of sex (Freudian theories); (2) sex as primary and love as a secondary consequence (e.g., evolutionary psychologists and attachment theorists); (3) sex and love as distinct and separate constructs (e.g., Lindholm, this volume; Grant 1976); and (4) love as primary and sex as a minor component of love (e.g., Sternberg 1988).

Debates over which model is king and which is a "pretender to the throne" are futile precisely because love is a polysemous concept that varies in salience and experience across individuals and cultures. Furthermore, the relationship between love (a "thought-feeling" concept) and sex (an act) is, in practice, "relativized to context."[2] For example, one may believe one is going to remain a virgin until marriage—until one falls madly and utterly in love. Fehr (1988, 1994), Fehr and Russell (1991), and Soble (1990) have used different approaches to argue for the multiple ways that individuals use the term "love." One can love cheesecake, a car, a cat, a nation, an idea, God, one's family, friends, spouse, or lover. One's love for an individual can wax and wane. Love researchers have not reached a consensus on either a definition or a vocabulary of love. This elusiveness is a source of frustration for many researchers (Noller 1996). Arguments that love is a cultural universal are based on a reductionist and romantic proposition that love, despite its various manifestations, is ultimately rooted in a single emotive seed. The polysemous argument—that love has many meanings—suggests that love is an umbrella term that covers a range of conjunctive feelings and thoughts, so that its meaning is in its use rather than in some molten bio-semantic core that gave "birth" to the term. Tennov's (1979) term "limerence" provides a particular carving up of the semantic domain of love that seems a good place to start in locating and examining a prototypical core. Lee's (1976) definitions of "lovestyles" and his insistence that, like colors, there are a multitude of permutations from the primary lovestyles and, like colors, lovestyles are a matter of taste and preference rather than arrayed along an absolute hierarchy provides another avenue for clarifying what we mean by love. Love, as used colloquially, is often, as I noted, "relativized to context." This has the practical advantage that in "real life" we need not be clear about what we mean by love.

If sex is "hardwired" as a drive to reproduce and erotic love is "softwired," then in the context of reproduction, erotic love is an adaptation to sex. Sex as a drive is indiscriminate, whereas love provides one criterion for mate selection. However, outside the context of reproduction, the motives for erotic love may be cloudy. Certainly, we see erotic love as an intrinsic good, valuing it for its own sake—the feeling is its own reward. Second, we value erotic love because it implies a feeling directed toward someone else and the potential for the reciprocation of that feeling. Erotic love, in this case, fulfills the Platonic ideal of completing two halves of an otherwise incomplete person. The romantic ideal of transcendental unity with the beloved is a conscious rejection of love as "lust in lamb's clothing." Freud argues that the romantic ideal is merely sex sublimated. But the voices of Singer (1994), Lindholm (1995 and this volume), poets, and my students who vociferously and unanimously reject the idea of love as lust disguised (see also Hendricks and Hendricks 1986, 1988) cannot be ignored or merely cast aside as a variant of false consciousness. I argue that we can do both: reduce love and sex to either their cultural or biological scaffolds or accept that the relationship is both cultural and biological. The point is not to offer a tower of Babel and let noise reign, but to be clear about the model we are using and to recognize that more than one good model is available.

The attempt to build a unified vocabulary and an agreed-upon model is a bit like looking for a grand unified theory of the universe. The more physicists attempt to decipher the forces and particles that compose the universe, the more precise they get about particular aspects of the whole and the more mysterious the whole becomes. The concept of love is a bit like that—the more we become experts at understanding a facet of love, the more we become aware of the complexity of the whole. Ultimately, the answers will reside not in what researchers think but in what they find out about what people actually think, feel, and do. Biology may shape culture to fit "its" needs, but it is also possible for biology to be shaped by culture to fit "its" needs. I am thinking of Scheper-Hughes' monograph (1992) of Brazilian mothers who develop a strategy of "mortal selective neglect" in which attachment to their infants is delayed for a year or more until they reckon the infant is likely to survive. The maternal instinct to bond with and nurture a child is surely as "hardwired" in humans as romantic love, but in this case it is voluntarily and consciously stalled. If social realities can stifle maternal love, certainly they can also shape or inhibit love. For this reason, I would guess that we will find that cores of truth and insight reside in evolutionary and constructionist models. The argument will not be which model is "right" but how good is the model "of" description and "for" analysis?

HOW THIS BOOK IS ORGANIZED

This volume is organized in five sections: (I) theory; (II) psychological models of romantic love and sexual desire; (III) investment and evolutionary models; (IV) AIDS and gender narratives of love and sex; and (V) cross-cultural studies of love and sex. Theoretical and thematic threads wend through these sections. For example, Robert Moore uses Tennov's idea of limerence to lock onto a particular universal expression of love (Chapter 11); Michael Strube and Larry Davis's analysis (Chapter 7) of black males' lower commitment to relationships than black females' complements Elisa Sobo's study (Chapter 9) that suggests that poor black women are reluctant to use condoms because they symbolize sex and promiscuity rather than love and loyalty.

Section I: Theory

The first three chapters are theoretical pieces. Lindholm, an anthropologist, asks what the future of love is in an increasingly rationalized and impersonal world. Using cross-cultural data, he demonstrates convincingly that love and sex are independent motivations and states. If love and sex are not genetically intertwined, then the question becomes, under what conditions are they connected or separated? Lindholm then asks how contemporary socio-cultural processes shape love and sex. He contrasts his perspective with that of Giddens' (1992) post-structural notion of "confluent love" in which individuals are liberated from socio- or psycho-structural constraints and can satisfy their emotional and sexual needs en passant, so to speak. Lindholm, using a Weberian-Freudian perspective, argues that romantic love is a cultural shaping of a transcendental impulse to eternal unity. It is not the same as sex, and it springs from different motivations. Westerners feel more compelled to enter a passionate, transcendental love relationship as the social world becomes more impersonal and bureaucratized. Thus, he argues that people will be more motivated to seek love as both refuge from an uncaring world and as a fund for meaning. He suggests that there are two sources for love: one in a dyadic, coupled relationship, and the other, as a devotee to a charismatic leader. The two are inversely related, so that one is either in a romantic love relationship or has embraced a charismatically based movement, but not both. A cheery thought.

Reading Lee's chapter is the mental equivalent of white-water rafting: full of energy, all over the place, and thrilling. He is best known for his book *The Colours of Love* (1976) in which he develops his multidimensional theory of lovestyles as analogous to colors. In this chapter, he introduces his color theory of love and how it has been adopted and validated by many subsequent studies. He harangues scholars who insist on a unidimensional or "one true" type of love. He then identifies sexstyles associated with his six primary lovestyles and provides a brief account of "taboo sex styles." But, as I see it, the central issue of his chapter is how ideology, power, and class shape constructions of love and sex. He criticizes the default cultural ideology that romantic love means heterosexual love and sex. He shows that the origins of romantic love stem from twelfth-century French knights attempting to legitimate their new status by rejecting social considerations for marriage and sex and legitimating individual attraction. Romantic love is seen as emerging in a capitalist clime where individuals, rather than groups, can be upwardly mobile. From there he discusses how love and sex have become, in post-modern society, "consumer goods" and examines how personal ads are written so as to define oneself and a potential partner in terms of parts and services. By incorporating new technologies and resources, the arena where lovers meet and how they meet has shifted from local to global and from face-to-face to monitor-to-monitor. Lee demonstrates in very pragmatic prose and examples how the ideology of the marketplace and new technologies have invaded and altered love and sex, often transforming intimacies into commodities, and that this is confluent with the spread of a marketplace culture.

Tennov is a psychologist who coined the term "limerence," which refers to feelings of obsessive love. She argues that limerence is a cultural universal but is not present in every individual. Those who are disposed to limerence find themselves overwhelmed by intrusive and obsessive feelings of love toward a person from whom they desperately desire some sort of reciprocation but are simultaneously fearful of expressing their affection for that person (the limerent object).

Section II: The Psychology of Love and Sexual Desire

This section consists of two studies: Pamela Regan's and Duncan Cramer and Dennis Howitt's. Both contributions focus on the definitional complexities of love and sex as they influence individual behavior. Regan uses "prototype" experiments and discourse analysis to show that sexual desire is a key diacritic that distinguishes passionate love from other types of love. She begins with a brief but fairly extensive review of the social psychological literature of studies that have neglected and those that have incorporated sex into their analyses of romantic love. Following Hatfield and her colleagues, Regan verifies the importance of sexual desire as a component of romantic love in Western culture in two prototype studies. Beyond demonstrating that sexual desire is a part of love, Regan concludes by noting how sexual intercourse linguistically framed as romantic love may be manipulated by a person to "legitimize" the use of force and that movie audiences are also more likely to interpret forced sex as "making love" rather than rape.

Cramer and Howitt ask to what extent romantic love plays a part in sexual fantasy. They state that romantic love does not necessarily "coexist" with sexual desire and that, while romantic love is always viewed as positive and warm, sexual fantasies may be callous and negative. Thus, sexually callous imagery can be used between two people in love, and, conversely, romantic imagery may be used by a rapist. The purported objective of sexual fantasies, whether romantic or callous, is to enhance sexual activity. Cramer and Howitt show that the vast majority of men (90%) and women (75%) fantasize during masturbation and during intercourse (60% of men and 57% of women). The content of fantasies differs significantly across gender, however, with 80% of females incorporating romantic love into their fantasies and only 57% of the men doing so. Furthermore, while force was a relatively common feature of male fantasies (25%), it was extremely rare for women (3%). Cramer and Howitt's purpose is to show that the relationship between sexual experience, romantic or conjugal love, and erotic fantasies is complex and that current dogma regarding rape as not having a sexual component or true love not having a callous component confuses and simplifies complex and important issues.

Section III: Evolutionary and Investment Models

These three chapters rely on a cost-benefit formal analysis of relationship to explain divorce and commitment to a relationship. Todd Shackelford applies an evolutionary psychological perspective to analyze infidelity as a cause for divorce. Six kinds of infidelities are arrayed along a continuum of severity from "flirting with someone else" to "a serious affair." Husbands and wives of 207 newlywed couples were interviewed separately and asked to evaluate how upset they would be and how likely various infidelities and other types of issues would eventuate in divorce. Shackelford comes to a number of conclusions, three of which are (1) that the anticipated probability of divorce increases with the severity of the infidelity for both men and women; (2) that women who are assessed as having a greater mate value or attractiveness rating than their husbands are more likely to divorce for the same kinds of infidelities than women who have lower mate values or are of equal or less attractiveness than their husbands; and (3) that men are more likely to divorce a wife if she had been unfaithful previously than if she had not. The argument is based on a cost-benefit analysis of reproductive costs. Shackelford's conclusions support Buss's strategic interference model for divorced people based on the interplay of kinds of infidelities, relative mate value, and other criteria of distress.

Morrow and O'Sullivan use Rusbult's Investment Model to analyze how the discrepancy between one's idealized mate and actual mate influence one's investment in staying in a relationship. As with Shackelford, Morrow and O'Sullivan rely on a cost-benefit analysis to assess the durability of a relationship. Instead of reproductive costs, however, the authors rely on the more imagined costs that accrue in terms of the discrepancy between one's ideal partner and one's current partner. This is referred to as the "comparison level" component in the Investment Model and has been relatively neglected because of the difficulty of measuring this gap. They find that "security/trust" and "satisfaction" are the most important predictors of commitment to a relationship.

Strube and Davis point out that marriage rates for blacks have decreased disproportionately to those of whites so that, for example, two-thirds of all black adults are single compared to one-third of all white adults and that "as many as 25% of black women will never marry." They argue that the difference between blacks and whites can be explained in terms of Rusbult's Investment Model rather than as a direct result of cultural factors. Because of the sex imbalance of available black men, "a good man is hard to find." Because black men know they are "in demand," they are less inclined than white men to marry or stay married.

Comparing two samples of twenty white and black couples, they found that the only significant ethnic difference was that satisfaction was a better predictor of commitment for white males than black males. They suggest that this is due to the black males' knowledge that there are more "alternatives" out there for them. In a second study of single black professionals, they found that satisfaction was, as opposed to the college sample of black males, a significant predictor of commitment. They hypothesized, somewhat along the evolutionary lines described by Buss (1988; 1994), that males' satisfaction is related to their ability to invest in the woman. Therefore, satisfaction and commitment are positively correlated for professional males but not for college-aged males who do not have the money to make "serious" investments in a mate. They also suggest that since comparatively few black males become professionals, the ones that do view the resources that they have to invest in a relationship as particularly "precious." At the same time, because males have and view themselves as having more "alternatives" outside the relationship than females, a man is likely to be less committed to the relationship than a woman, though both are equally satisfied with it. This fits in with the predicament of Sobo's poor black women who attempt to construct their relationship with their man as "committed" and therefore are unwilling to request that condoms be used in penetrative sexual encounters.

Section IV: AIDS and Cultural Narratives

Elisa Sobo, Susan Moore and Doreen Rosenthal all argue that cultural models of love and gendered models of sex influence condom use among black women in Cleveland and Australian adolescents, respectively.

Sobo asks why some inner-city women practice unsafe sex with their male partners. In her work with heterosexual black women in Cleveland, Sobo uses interviews, focus groups, content analysis, and questionnaires to examine their explanations for their sexual practices. Sobo notes that explanations based on poverty obscure how American cultural ideals are internalized and influence the sexual decisions of these women. From her interviews she concludes that her informants clearly reject instrumentally motivated, economically driven, sex. Instead they have internalized a model of the conjugal ideal constructed through television soap operas, songs, and women's magazines that is of a loving, monogamous, and "germ-free" partner. Sobo states that many women "actively" seek to attain this ideal through practicing "unsafe sex" as a symbol of monogamy, trust, and the germ-free status of themselves and their mate and that condoms, in contrast, symbolize distrust and divisiveness within a relationship. In terms of this complex of symbolic tensions, inner-city women construct "Wisdom" and "Monogamy" narratives. The first narrative signals that the woman is wise enough to choose a "good" germ-free man, and the second signals that he is to be trusted and is faithful. In this way, both narratives work together to produce an idealized image of their partner and themselves that both enhances their self-esteem and their status in the community. Sobo shows how mainstream cultural ideals are salient forces shaping the way inner-city black women think about themselves and their partner and how they act.

Moore and Rosenthal tackle the way adolescents in Australia triangulate the relationship between love, sex, and concerns over sexually transmitted diseases. Their chapter is similar in spirit to Sobo's because the focus is on how romantic ideals shape and motivate sexual behavior and disguise the assessment of sexual risk. Their study differs from Sobo's in that it is less culturally explicit and focuses on gender differences. Using interviews in conjunction with other studies on adolescent sexual behavior, Moore and Rosenthal present a rather conservative view of adolescent culture in which sex is legitimated within the context of romantic love. However, they note a number of important gender differences: women are more likely to be monogamous than males; promiscuity is more stigmatized for females than males, and males tend to separate sex from love and to describe sex as a biological drive whereas females view sex as an emotional tie with a partner. They conclude by incorporating their findings in Hollway's three types of male-female discourse: the male sex drive discourse; the have/hold discourse; and the permissive discourse. They argue that the last of these discourses is most amenable to sex education programs because it takes a pragmatic and gender-neutral approach to sexual activity. However, they warn that romantic ideals concerning sex are internalized at an early age and are not easily dislodged.

Section V: Cross-Cultural Studies of Love and Sex

Robert Moore combines attachment and schema-prototype theory to analyze changes in sexual attitudes and behaviors among Chinese mainland college youths. He integrates cognitive-constructionist and psycho-evolutionary theories of love to examine how a universalist, limerent core of romantic love is shaped by other interacting Chinese cultural norms, specifically filial piety. Thus, he examines how a "fixed" emotion is molded by cultural norms and processes. Moore compares "Westernized" Chinese courtship patterns with "traditional" courtship patterns in order to tease out and describe both the uniquely Chinese cultural and the universalist features of romantic love.

de Munck's chapter challenges our ethnocentric view of arranged marriage practices and shows that, in Sri Lanka, love influences mate selection practices. In developing his argument, he shows that love and arranged marriages are not mutually exclusive categories but that Western culture foregrounds or, more technically, figures, one complex of values and variables that serve as ground to the other culture, and vice versa. de Munck shows how various social practices in Sri Lanka work to direct the course of love to a categorically and structurally "correct" other so that structure, love, and sexual desire are harmonized. de Munck and Moore show that the manner in which romantic love is conceptualized and how it bridges over to sex and marriage is culturally shaped. In both China and Sri Lanka, romantic love may be important in mate selection, but it must be publicly muted and subordinated to family interests to a much greater degree than in the West.

NOTES

1. In his 1970 dissertation, Rubin developed the Likert scale for measuring love and this work is frequently cited as the beginning of the empirical study of romantic love.

2. The term "thought-feeling" was coined by Wilkan (1989). "Relativized to context" is a phrase used by Quinn (1985:294).

REFERENCES

Aron, A. "Relationship Variables in Human Heterosexual Relationships." Doctoral dissertation, University of Toronto, 1970.

Berscheid, E., and S. A. Meyers. "A Social Categorical Approach to a Question about Love." *Personal Relationships* 3:19–44, 1996.

Bogaert, A. F., and W. A. Fisher. "Predictor of University Men's Number of Sexual Partners." *The Journal of Sex Research* 32:119–130, 1995.

Buss, D. "Love Acts: The Evolutionary Biology of Love." In R. J. Sternberge and M. L. Barnes (eds.), *The Psychology of Love*. New Haven, Conn.: Yale University Press, 1988, pp. 100–118

————. *The Evolution of Desire*. New York: Basic Books, 1994.

D'Andrade, R. *The Development of Cognitive Anthropology*. Cambridge: Cambridge University Press, 1995

Dion, K. K., and K. L. Dion. "Cultural Perspective on Romantic Love." *Personal Relationships* 3:5–18, 1996.

Fehr, B. "Prototype Analysis of the Concept of Love and Commitment." *Journal of Personality and Social Psychology* 55:557–579, 1988.

————. "Prototype-Based Assessment of Laypeople's Views of Love." *Personal Relationships* 1:309–331, 1994.

Fehr, B., and J. A. Russell. "The Concept of Love Viewed from a Prototype Perspective." *Journal of Personality and Social Psychology* 60:425–438, 1991.

Fisher, H. *Anatomy of Love: The Natural History of Monogamy, Adultery, and Divorce*. New York: W. W. Norton, 1992.

————. "The Nature and Evolution of Romantic Love." In W. Jankowiak (ed.), *Passionate Love*. New York: Columbia University Press, 1995, pp. 57–71.

Freud, S. *Civilization and Its Discontents*. New York: W. W. Norton [1929], 1961.

Fullilove, M.; R. Fullilove; K. Haynes; and S. Gross. "Black Women and AIDS Prevention: A View Towards Understanding the Gender Rules." *Journal of Sex Research* 27:47–74, 1990.

Giddens, A. *The Transformation of Intimacy: Sexuality, Love and Intimacy in Modern Societies*. Stanford: University of California Press, 1992.

Grant, V. W. *Falling in Love: The Psychology of the Romantic Emotion*. New York: Springer Publishing, 1976.

Hendrick, C., and S. Hendrick. "A Theory and Method of Love." *Journal of Personality and Social Psychology* 50(2):392–402, 1986.

Hendrick, C., and S. S. Hendrick. "Lovers Wear Rose Colored Glasses." *Journal of Personality and Social Psychology* 54:161–183, 1988.

Holland, D., and M. Eisenhart. *Educated in Romance: Women, Achievement, and College Culture.* Chicago: University of Chicago Press, 1990.

Holland, D., and D. Skinner. "Prestige and Intimacy: The Cultural Models Behind American's Talk about Gender Types" In D. Holland and N. Quinn (eds.), *Cultural Models in Language & Thought.* Cambridge: Cambridge University Press, 1987, pp. 78–111.

Lee, J. A. *Colours of Love.* Toronto: General, 1976.

Liebowitz, M. *The Chemistry of Love.* Boston: Little, Brown, 1983.

Lindholm, C. "Love as an Experience of Transcendence." In W. Jankowiak (ed.), *Passionate Love.* New York: Columbia University Press, 1995, pp. 57–71.

Money, J. *Love and Love Sickness: The Science of Sex, Gender Difference, and Pair Bonding.* Baltimore, Md.: Johns Hopkins University Press, 1980.

Murray, H. A. *Explorations in Personality.* New York: Oxford University Press, 1938.

Noller, P. "What Is This Thing Called Love?" *Personal Relationships* 3:97–115, 1996.

Perper, Timothy. *Sex Signals: The Biology of Love.* Philadelphia: ISI Press, 1985.

Quinn, N. "'Commitment' in American Marriage." In Janet W. D. Dougherty (ed.), *Directions in Cognitive Anthropology.* Urbana: University of Illinois Press, 1985, pp. 291–320.

Rubin, Z. Preface. In R. J. Sternberg and Michael L. Barnes (eds.), *The Psychology of Love.* New Haven, Conn.: Yale University Press, 1988, pp. vii–xii.

Scheper-Hughes, N. *Death Without Weeping: The Violence of Everyday Life in Brazil.* Berkeley: University of California Press, 1992.

Shostak, M. *Nisa: The Life and Words of a !Kung Woman.* New York: Vintage, 1983.

Singer, I. *The Pursuit of Love.* Baltimore, Md.: Johns Hopkins University Press, 1994.

Soble, A. *The Structure of Love.* New Haven, Conn.: Yale University Press, 1990.

Sobo, E. J. *Choosing Unsafe Sex: AIDS Risk Denial Among Disadvantaged Women.* Philadelphia: University of Pennsylvania Press, 1995.

Sternberg, R. J. *The Triangle of Love.* New York: Basic Books, 1988.

Tennov, D. *Love and Limerence.* New York: Stein and Day, 1979.

Wienstein, N. "Unrealistic Optimism about Susceptibility to Health Problems." *Journal of Behavioral Medicine* 5(1):441–460, 1982.

Wikan, U. "Managing the Heart to Brighten Face and Soul: Emotions in Balinese Morality and Health Care." *American Ethnologist* 16(2):294–312, 1989.

SECTION I

THEORY

1

The Future of Love

Charles Lindholm

Is romantic love eternal, or is it destined to disappear? And if it does disappear, what are the consequences? For most Americans, these might seem to be strange questions indeed. Certainly, the songs, poems, novels, and films of our society have portrayed love as life's ultimate value: overwhelming, ecstatic, uniquely blissful. Love, our cliches tell us, makes the world go around, nothing is impossible for lovers, love knows no boundaries, life without love is not worth living, and love is forever.[1]

Despite the subjective sensation of lovers that their love is timeless and boundless, it is nonetheless true that romantic love has a past and exists within a particular cultural context. For most theorists, our present notion of love developed out of a European premodern culture wherein the sexual passion we regard as central to falling in love was portrayed instead as a dangerous compulsion that could draw young people into inappropriate and dangerous liaisons, dissolve arranged marriages, and cause untold conflict and misery. To protect against these threats, mechanisms such as child betrothal, chaperonage, institutionalized prostitution, and so on, were developed in order to maintain corporate group control over reproduction either by suppressing wayward erotic desire or by channeling it to a sphere entirely separate from marriage.[2]

According to many historians, an intense erotic attraction toward another individual was transformed into idealization of the beloved and linked to marriage only when traditional society began to disintegrate as a result of industrialization and nascent capitalism. The collapse of

the old order corresponded with the appearance of a new type of reproductive unit that was not bound together by the group obligations
characteristic of earlier times.[3] As Howard Gadlin writes, "intimate
relationships, as we understand them today, emerged during the early
decades of the nineteenth century. . . with the self conscious bourgeois
individual whose life is torn between the separated worlds of work and
home. Individualism and intimacy are the Siamese twins of modernization."[4] The triumph of modernization created a fluid social world
where, (as the philosopher Robert Solomon puts it) an "extraordinary
emphasis in the concept of individuality and individual self-identity (as
well as) a high degree of mobility and flexibility in relationships in
general." Correspondingly, there was an increased emphasis on "personal choice at the core of mating and marrying rituals."[5]

Increased personal choice and individuality, along with a new emphasis on intimacy, meant that marriage was now constituted not by
interest or duty, as in previous generations, but by the mutual idealization of romantic love. Love marriage has usually been portrayed by
sociologists—following Parsons[6]—as a necessary functional aid to the
integration of a fragmented modern world. As Gideon Sjorberg writes,
"the romantic love ideology may be seen as appropriate, even necessary,
in a society where the external pressures on permanent unions through
kinship are largely absent."[7] From this point of view, falling in love
provides individuals in a fluid and atomistic environment with a means
of establishing relationships that draw them away from adolescence
into the married life of adulthood.

Besides its association with marriage, romantic idealization has
other distinctive features that mark it off from pure erotic desire. As
Anthony Giddens tells us, the modern type of love is unique in its "one
and only" and "forever" qualities, and in its insistence on the beloved as
the source of a mystical sense of completion for the lover. Overwhelming sexual desire, predominant in the passionate love of earlier
social worlds, has become etherialized in romantic attraction and
integrated into a larger narrative of a shared life course made
meaningful by love. As Giddens says, "romantic love is made of amour,
passion, a specific cluster of beliefs, and ideals geared to transcendence;
romantic love may end in tragedy and feed upon transgression, but it
also produces triumph, a conquest of mundane prescriptions and
compromises."[8]

Like Parsons, Giddens credits romantic love with serving a purpose
during the beginnings of capitalism. Then it gave isolated people in an
alienating environment some kind of meaning to their lives, and it also
provided a legitimate means for society to reproduce itself. But unlike
Parsons, Giddens does not believe that romantic idealization is required
to bind modern society together. Rather, he is dismayed by the ideal-

izing and unrealistic aspects of romantic love, which he portrays as a delusion that enmeshes people in destructive fantasy relationships while preventing them from any serious exploration of personal freedom and sexual variety. "Romance," he says, "is the counterfactual thinking of the deprived."[9]

According to Giddens, however, in the self-reflexive and self-actualizing world of today we no longer require such counterfactual delusions. Romance has lost its purpose and is bound to die out. It will be replaced, he argues, by a new, pragmatic, non-transcendental form of relationship that looks very much like the frank erotic desire so carefully controlled by traditional societies, but without the intensity or danger. Giddons calls this new form of erotic tie "confluent love" (although romantic lovers would certainly not recognize it as love at all). It is active, contingent, and, above all, based on each partner's calculating maximization of erotic satisfaction; confluent love "makes the achievement of reciprocal sexual pleasure a key element in whether the relationship is sustained or dissolved," and it is predicated on the "acceptance on the part of each partner, 'until further notice', that each gains sufficient benefit from the relation to make its continuance worthwhile."[10] Confluent love, Giddens says, is a "pure relationship" without entangling ideals, commitments, or moral obligations. Instead, it is based on a freely negotiated contractual agreement between two free agents acting for themselves in an open market for the realization of their desires. Love has now become a wholly utilitarian matter.[11]

The appearance of confluent love, Giddens argues, is an inevitable result of increased sexual plasticity, the breakdown of distinctions between male and female identity, and a heightened reflexive awareness among modern individuals, who, like improvising actors, now feel free to construct their own selves from a panoply of possible roles. It is praised as a positive development—one that enables active, self-aware, pleasure-seeking agents in a fluid world to make their own choices and negotiate with one another openly and with self-awareness of their sexual needs, rather than being trapped in delusory, unhappy, and addictive "co-dependent" relationships. The result, Giddens believes, will be greater personal autonomy, increased sexual experimentation, heightened pleasure, and even a more pluralistic, democratic society as individuals learn, through practice in sexual negotiation, how to participate in more public forms of presenting and affirming their interests.

Giddens' picture of the demise of romantic love is not new. In his argument, he largely recapitulates, in updated garb and with significant moral differences, the cultural history of love and romance originally formulated by Max Weber. Like Giddens, Weber contended that the historical processes of capitalist organization and technical rationalization would necessarily oblige men and women to enter into competitive and calculating relations with one another as they pursue their instrumental goals of achieving profits and position. This situation, Weber argued, must undermine the comforting beliefs and supportive communities characteristic of traditional culture and result in what he called the disenchantment of the world. In this new environment, human relationships would be governed by purely instrumental efforts to maximize pleasure and minimize pain, without the masking provided by illusory transcendental motives. Under such conditions, love of all sorts would have no place. As he writes: "The routinized economic cosmos, and thus the rationally highest form of the provision of material goods which is indispensable for all worldly culture, has been a structure to which the absence of love is attached from the very root."[12]

The erosion of romantic love is not Weber's major concern, however. Rather, his focus is on the destruction of any sense of participation in a transcendent community. For Weber, this participatory experience is originally based on the "acosmism of love"[13] that blossoms when a charismatic prophet is possessed by the gods in an ecstatic trance that arouses his audience into a responsive frenzy. Weber paints the attraction of the group to the charismatic as irrational, compulsive, emotional, and grounded in the belief that the leader is a conduit of the divine. It is also closely connected to sexual arousal. As Weber writes, "sexual intercourse was very frequently part of magic orgiasticism or was an unintended result of orgiastic excitement,"[14] and he notes several times that the orgy was the original state of religious intoxication.

Weber argued that ecstatic charisma offers a serious threat to all hierarchical clerical and state systems. To maintain stability and structure, complex social organizations naturally develop more restrained, coherent and lasting solutions to existential problems of suffering, so that the orgies inspired by the magical charismatic are gradually supplanted by systematic and tranquil ceremonies organized by devout clerics. In time, according to Weber's theory, these rituals too are replaced by the calculating ethic of capitalism and by the accompanying impersonal bureaucratic rules of the modern state, where efficiency and control are the sole virtues.

In Weber's view, the historical development of salvationist and ethical monotheism split the social from the natural, de-emphasized ecstatic engagement, and anesthetized the body in favor of etherealizing the soul. But even though Weber argued that experiences of religious rapture, like experiences of romantic idealization, have become largely impossible within the technically businesslike and disenchanted world of competitive entrepreneurs and systematizing clerks, this did not mean a diminution of the importance of sexuality.

On the contrary, Weber argued that as magical experiences of charisma and communal ecstasy are de-legitimized, sexuality is detached from its previous position as an expression of possession by the gods. Instead, sexuality is increasingly perceived as, in Weber's words: "The royal road away from the impersonal or supra-personal 'value' mechanism, away from enslavement to the lifeless routines of everyday existence and from the pretentiousness of unrealities handed down from on high . . . a sphere claiming its own 'immanent' worth in the most extreme sense of the word."[15] In the modern world, according to Weber, erotic experience has been gradually transformed into a democratic form of experienced redemption—an ersatz ecstatic religion immediately available to all, one that does not require of the faithful any knowledge of dogma or any form of institutional intervention by a de-legitimized church or a coercive state. All that is required is the discharge of one's sexual energy.[16]

Giddens substantially agrees with Weber's prophecy that sexuality is the modern replacement for religion. He notes that "ecstasy, or the promise of it, has echoes of the 'ethical passion' which transcendental symbolism used to inspire—and of course cultivated eroticism, as distinct from sexuality in the service of reproduction, has long been associated with religiosity." For contemporary men and women, sexual passion is the only thing that can allow contact with "all that has been foregone for the technical security that day-to-day life has to offer."[17]

But while Giddens cheerily greets the new centrality of sexuality as "a prerequisite for recognizing the other as an independent being, who can be loved for her or his specific traits and qualities; and it also offers the chance of release from an obsessive involvement with a broken or dying relationship,"[18] Weber has a more jaundiced view. For him the veneration of sexual pleasure removed from all transcendent moorings has no binding significance for the community at large. Instead, the sacred love of the community of believers for the charismatic or the romantic lovers for one another is transmuted into the meaningless lust of individuals who view others as mere objects upon whom they can vent their desire. As Margareta Bertilsson writes: "There is a Kantian warning in Weber's text, that when religion is dead we will become each other's means rather than ends. . . . The process of rationalization in the end turns into its opposite, and modern man's escape from religious superstition results in him losing both a sense of meaning and freedom."[19]

How much are these visions, which agree in their substantive conclusions despite their vast moral differences, correct? The argument about the increasing centrality of freely negotiated eroticism in the modern world does seem to be borne out by the ubiquity of sexual messages in the media and by the positive attitudes of ordinary North Americans toward sexual orgasm as the best of all possible goods, to be pursued and enjoyed whenever possible by men and women alike. In this world of "confluent love," the ideal is to rapidly substitute other, more gratifying sexual relationships for those that have proven to be too demanding and not pleasurable enough. As a result, "the search for *open* relationships, which is not simply restricted to the sexual realm, slides into the search for *interchangeable* relationships."[20] Under these circumstances, the sense of eternity, idealization, and commitment characteristic of romantic love become less and less possible.

An example of the modern attitude is to be found in Michael Moffat's study of the sexual mores of American undergraduates at Rutgers, who were unanimous in their praise of sexual intercourse, which they portrayed as an unmitigated and absolute pleasure. Despite the fact that these young people had a wide variety of sexual histories ranging from celibacy to promiscuity, none argued that sexual desire was a problematic or perilous urge, or favored chastity as a positive experience.[21] Similarly, the omnipresent sexual surveys and how-to-do-it books cited by Giddens assume without question that sexuality is an absolute good; the major problems they address are discovering what form of erotic play is most enjoyable, and the difficulty of finding an attractive and willing partner.

So it seems, then, that we have returned to the pre-modern image of love as purely erotic desire, though in our individualistic universe we need no longer fear its disruptive quality. Although this positive attitude toward erotic pleasure—summed up by Woody Allen's comment about sex as the only thing on earth which is good even when it's bad—may seem to be self-evidently true to my readers, it is worth recalling that cross-culturally and historically sexual intercourse has often been viewed very differently. For instance, proper public Victorian middle-class morality portrayed sexual desire as a degrading animalistic intrusion on reason, to be resisted and controlled by men and denied completely by women. Nor is this unusual. In South Asia, men fear debility from semen loss while Chinese are terrified of being afflicted by koro (the withdrawal of the penis into the body) as the result of excessive sexual activity. Fear of sexuality often correlates with a social configuration in which chastity is inordinately valued, as among the Dugum Dani of New Guinea, who practice almost complete abstinence.[22]

In fact, Melanesia is the *locus classicus* of the antipathy toward erotic pleasure, where the sexual act is generally viewed as polluting, dangerous, and repellant, to be avoided except under the most extraordinary circumstances. For instance, in Manus, as described by

Margaret Mead, sexual intercourse is a distasteful, perilous, and shameful business. When Manus men and women are drawn into extramarital liaisons, these "illicit love affairs, affairs of choice, are, significantly enough, described as situations in which people need not have sex if they do not wish to, but can simply sit and talk and laugh together. . . . The wonderful thing about lovers is that you don't have to sleep with them."[23]

Comparatively, then, it does seem that the unambiguous pursuit of sexual pleasure has assumed an inordinately predominant and highly valued place in the modern psyche. Yet, even if Americans generally believe sexual orgasm to be an absolute good in itself, a debate nonetheless remains over the issue of when sex should properly be enjoyed, and this debate centers around the issue of romantic attachment. As Moffat reports, a significant number of the students he interviewed claimed sex and romantic involvement ought to be united, although others said romance was not a necessary precondition for sexual pleasure. The relationship between sexuality and romantic love as articulated by these young people indicates that for many sexuality has not yet been freed from the old aura of commitment and idealization. And even those who did cognitively separate romance and sex still generally believed that marriage should ideally be to someone with whom one is "in love."

Are these beliefs in romance simply residues, soon to be replaced by a calculated weighing up of the possible pleasures a sexual partner has to offer? One argument against this possibility was made by Schopenhauer, who believed that romantic idealization is required as the impetus that compels human beings to reproduce and to care for their children. As he writes, lovers desire a "fusion into a single being, in order then to go on living only as this being; and this longing receives its fulfillment in the child they produce"; or, put more prosaically: "if Petrarch's passion had been satisfied, his song would have been silenced from that moment, just as is that of the bird, as soon as the eggs are laid."[24] For Schopenhauer, romantic idealization, as a strategy of the Will, must be universal and everlasting, except for the few philosophers or mystics who manage to see through the illusion and achieve detachment.

Schopenhauer's argument has been dressed in modern garb by sociobiologists who assert that romantic love is a genetically innate mechanism serving to offset the male's natural tendency to maximize his gene pool through promiscuity. Idealization of his mate ties the wandering male to a particular female, and the enhanced pair-bonding that results serves the evolutionary purpose of increasing the overall rate of survival for human children. It therefore must be eternal, although culture can have an enhancing or dampening effect on its expression.

But as I have argued elsewhere,[25] the very ubiquity and success of cultural institutions for the control of sexuality demonstrate that Schopenhauer and the sociobiologists are in error. For instance, even though it is a fact that in almost every known culture married couples produce and raise the vast majority of children, it is also a fact that the correlation between romantic idealization and marriage characteristic of the contemporary West is rare indeed. Instead, it is far more usual, cross-culturally, for romantic attraction to be reserved for those whom one does not and cannot marry, while marriage itself is generally a prosaic affair based on contracts between lineages and other corporate groups.

Furthermore, if idealization of one's mate is assumed to correlate with reproductive success, one would expect that the West, which has one of the world's most elaborated ideologies of romance, would also have one of the highest birth rates. But, the converse is the case. Cultures in which marriages are between unloving strangers and are arranged for political and economic benefit by parents have always produced far higher birth rates than the love marriages of the West.[26] So, if romantic love is the means that nature uses to ensure human reproduction, then culture has been made a fool of by nature, since an absence of romance correlates positively with population growth. The sociobiological point therefore appears to be an instance of cultural projection, rendering universal and natural what is in truth very much a Western phenomenon.

Instead of trying to fall back on genetic explanations, a defense of romantic idealization requires a return to the definition of love itself, which can be reconsidered within a larger comparative and structural perspective. In our culture, the content of love appears to be at right angles to ordinary experience, which is, we generally believe, characterized by a weighing up of means and ends by rational actors who pursue pleasure and avoid pain. In contrast, the prevailing love ideology asserts that selfishness is the antithesis of romantic love, while self-sacrifice is its highest value, if that sacrifice gives pleasure to or protects the beloved one. Rational planning is as great a sin against romantic love as selfishness, since calculation requires a weighing and measuring of the advantages and disadvantages of a relation that is felt to be unique, absolute, and beyond such pragmatic considerations.

The contrast between romance and daily life is most marked in the belief that the experience of falling in love is felt to dissolve individual separateness. As the young Hegel wrote, in the heat of romantic attraction "consciousness of a separate self disappears, and all distinction between the lovers is annulled."[27] In this state of merger, as

Francesco Alberoni writes, "the possible opens before us and the pure object of eros appears, the unambivalent object, in which duty and pleasure coincide, in which all alienation is extinguished."[28] Structurally speaking, romance then is a reversal of the individualistic and competitive self-seeking that is characteristic of the mundane world, offering instead self-loss in merger with the idealized beloved. In short, love is an experience of transcendence.

Sexual intercourse is a natural expression of the lovers' state of ecstatic merger because it offers human beings their most potent physical sensation of self-loss—the "little death" of the orgasm. Our culture then can plausibly conflate sexual experience with the mystical aspects of romantic attraction, since the two have an "elective affinity" for one another; orgasm gives the bodily experience of the disintegration of boundaries that romantic love demands. But it is a mistake to assume, as Schopenhauer and the sociobiologists do, that romantic love is simply a dressing up of the sexual urge. It is equally a mistake to assume that romantic idealization is somehow less "real" than the sexuality that is associated with it and can therefore be easily displaced.

Despite their apparently natural association in modern Western thought, sexuality need not be connected at all with romantic idealization and may instead stand in opposition to it. A well-known example is the tradition of courtly love in which, in a transformation of the cult of the Virgin Mary, the courtier worshiped his beloved as a pure angel above the realm of earthly lust, not to be sullied in thought or deed.[29] This form of chaste love does not require a complex court society. A similar, perhaps ancestral, tradition is found in the non-sexual love of the seventh-century Yemeni tribe of the Banu Udhra, who believed that a divine spirit was embodied in the beloved, which could be internalized only through avid and devout contemplation, so that eventually the two would become one.[30] In the same vein, Middle Eastern romantic poems usually end in the death of the lovers, who never consummate their passion but always remain pure. Even if offered the opportunity, the lover rejects the embrace of the beloved, preferring to continue wasting away. For Middle Eastern poets, only a love that remains on the level of profound yearning has the spiritual dimension that renders it worthy of retelling.

Such behavior patterns and idealizations are hardly unusual even today, although the structure of the love relationship may vary considerably. For example, the Marri Baluch, a patrilineal desert people of Pakistan and Iran, have a highly elaborate romantic love complex. Men and women, married for political and economic purposes, long to participate in secret and highly dangerous illicit love affairs. These passionate relationships are hugely valued in Marri culture, and are the subject of innumerable poems and songs.

According to the Marri, when lovers meet, they exchange tokens of mutual affection and talk heart to heart, without dissimulation. In marked contrast to the elevation of the lady in courtly love, and in marked contrast as well to the reality of male domination in Marri society, Marri lovers regard one another as equals. For this reason, the lovers should be chaste: sexuality, culturally understood as an expression of male power, imposes an element of oppression and subordination that the cultural ideal of mutuality and respect between lovers cannot permit.[31] How many of these relationships are indeed sexless is impossible to say, but chastity is what the Marri believe to be characteristic of the deepest forms of love between men and women; to suppose that this belief is a falsehood is to do them and their culture an injustice by assuming that we know the truth behind their ideals.

And if all this seems too unfamiliar, we need look back in time no further than our own Victorian forebearers. The familiar split between whore and virgin was a reality for the Victorians, and sexual desire was, as much as possible, divorced from middle-class marriage, since women of culture were assumed not to have demeaning sexual impulses. Men demanded virginal purity in the women they married, while wives appear, from their own accounts, to have often managed to live up to the ideal. Sexual contact between a husband and his beloved wife was regarded as an unfortunate necessity of marriage, to be engaged in as a duty; men overcome by sexual passion were expected to spend themselves in the company of prostitutes, whom they certainly did not love. This characteristic Victorian division between love and sexuality is a mode of feeling that must be taken on its own terms.[32]

It seems, then, that instead of seeing the experience of falling in love as a repressed form of sexual desire, it is more useful to conceive it as one possible response to the human existential condition of contingency and self-consciousness. In response to this unbearable but inescapable dilemma, human beings everywhere search for ways to escape the burden of loneliness while avoiding confrontation with a cold and indifferent cosmos. One of the ways this escape can be attained is in the experience of falling in love, where the feeling of being over-whelmed, the sense of merger, the willingness to embrace self-sacrifice, and the idealization of the other are closely akin to the charismatic devotion that Weber saw as the source of religion and community. Both states are characterized by a fear of loss of the idealized other, and suicidal despair if that loss occurs; and both have a strong tendency toward rationalization. (Charismatic groups become bureaucracies; romantic lovers become companionate couples.) Thus, Francesco Alberoni can reasonably write that "the experience of falling in love is the simplest form of collective movement."[33]

The course of romantic love can therefore be seen as running parallel to charismatic religion.[34] Because of the complete adoration demanded in each setting, the two experiences are also mutually exclusive. The hostile disjuncture between charismatic group and personal romantic relationships is clear in the actual working of charismatic communities where a consistent effort is made to devalue and break any dyadic bonds and to increase the focus of the followers on the leader.[35] To accomplish this end, groups have often obliged followers to maintain celibacy, or else have enforced promiscuity. But whatever the mechanisms employed, it seems clear that an inclusive charismatic group is intrinsically "hostile toward the couple in love, since two lovers form the smallest social unit capable of defying it,"[36] and that the charismatic leader will attempt to serve as the focus of all the love of the followers.

It is hardly surprising that charismatic groups are especially attractive to those who have been disappointed in love, and who consequently seek solace by losing themselves in the arms of the all-embracing community and love of the leader. Popular wisdom has it that the traditional refuges for unhappy lovers are the communal environments of the army and the nunnery. Accounts of conversion to cults demonstrate this same sequence. The opposite pattern also holds true, as members of charismatic groups gain the courage to leave the group as a result of establishing a romantic relationship.

If charisma and romance are opposed but subjectively equivalent expressions of a deep desire for an ecstatic transcendence of the self in merger with the beloved other, and if romance has been the dominant escape from the cold grip of rationality in the modern world, then we have to ask what will happen if romantic idealization is destined to be devalued in favor of an absence of commitment and as "the fail-safe ability to disengage entirely—quickly, effectively, efficiently—is cultivated, refined and treasured?"[37] For Weber and Giddens, as we have seen, the answer is simple. Human beings, increasingly disinclined to give up their valued autonomy for the sake of what are perceived to be unwanted and unnecessary chains of responsibility, will simply lose their fantasies and negotiate for pleasure in a world of utilitarian sexual contractors.

We have already seen that Weber had deep reservations about a society in which a sexuality bereft of love would reign, since placing sexual sensation at the center of life reduces and dehumanizes the desired other to an object while turning the pleasure seeker into an automaton driven by a desire that has no purpose beyond its own satisfaction. Unlike Giddens, Weber saw that the retreat to irrational ecstasies of sexuality did not challenge the public hegemony of instrumental reason, but left human beings alone in the face of the "polar night of icy darkness and hardness" that he so feared as our fated destiny.[38]

Unhappily, Weber's view of human character left little room for resistance to this depressing fate. Humankind could, he believed, be reduced to automatons, or soulless ghosts, by the inexorable grinding of instrumental rationality and the gradual secularization of the world. But, as I have argued elsewhere,[39] a more psychologically adequate vision of human character—based on Freud's faith that human beings cannot, under any conditions, be transformed into termites, and on the premise that the desire for an escape from solipsism is an existential part of our condition—would mean that the triumph of instrumental reason and the consequent unwillingness of individuals to give themselves up to the risky business of falling in love will necessarily have its counter in a heightened pressure toward self-loss and identificatory merger in alternative forms of ecstatic relationships. This pressure will increase as experiences of participation in communion are increasingly lacking in the world at large because of the greater competitiveness, diversification, and fluidity of the work environment implicit in the process of modernization. Many of these alienated persons may numb their feelings of emptiness with tranquilizers and television, or in a compulsive search for sexual fulfillment. For others, self-transcendence, no longer found in intimate personal relationships and long absent in the central institutions of the society, will be sought in other arenas. The question is: Where?

We can certainly expect that expressive public arenas of sport, art, entertainment, and consumption will be more and more important in people's lives if the potential for dyadic identification fades. And we can expect greater fusion between individual and the personalized nation as well. However, such diffuse and distant symbolic forms are only pale substitutes for the immediacy of the actual physical presence of the other. Of course, the reader will recognize that sensations of loneliness, meaninglessness, and disillusionment are a precondition for the intensity offered by the older sibling of romantic love: charismatic involvement. Thus, we might suggest that the deep desire for an ecstatic escape from the boundaries of the self, in the absence of the intimate expression of such needs in romantic attachments, and in the absence of other emotionally gratifying communal alternatives, will not be satisfied by the relatively abstract, impersonal, and distanced expressions presently available. Instead, the erosion of idealized love is likely to correspond with a proliferation of religious-political-therapeutic charismatic groups that offer the follower the sense of commitment and selfless belonging that cannot be found elsewhere.

To conclude, I have argued that the repudiation of intense and idealized personal romantic relationships in favor of pragmatic ties of mutual sexual satisfaction may have unforeseen consequences. A lack of commitment in love, within the modern context in which alternative forms of idealized attachment are weak or absent, may lead not to self-actualization (whatever that amorphous term may mean) but to a pervasive feeling of isolation, depression, and insignificance. This state of mind in turn is conducive to the loss of the self in the anonymity of the group—a loss that may be rationalized by any number of intell-ectual superstructures, but that really gains its appeal because it offers the sensation of transcendence that is absent in the world at large and no longer to be found in romantic idealization.

NOTES

1. Some theorists have argued that this imagery is simply the empty symbolism of advertising. It is true that Hollywood and advertising make use of the fantasies, fears, and hopes of its audience for their own mercantile purposes, but this usage does not falsify the desire for the experience itself which the media plays upon. Dismissing love as a myth does not get us any closer to understanding why the imagery of love should have such a hold on the popular consciousness.

2. See Goode, "The Theoretical Importance of Love," for an argument on the relationship between social structure and the regulation of erotic desire, which he considers to be the equivalent of romantic love. The historical process is, of course, hugely complex. See Hunt, *The Natural History of Love*, for one history of romantic involvement, and Singer, *The Nature of Love* (3 vols.), for a synopsis of some changing philosophical and artistic presentations of love.

3. See Stone, "Passionate Attachments in the West," and Shorter, *The Making of the Modern Family,* for representative statements of this argument. In contrast, MacFarlane, *Marriage and Love in England*, argues convincingly that the ideal of romantic love was not a product of the Industrial Revolution, but rather was one of its most important preconditions. See Lindholm, "Love as an Experience of Transcendence," for a review and critique of this and other literature on love.

4. Gadlin, "Private Lives and Public Order," p. 34.

5. Solomon, *Love, Emotion, Myth and Metaphor*, p. xxvii.

6. Parsons, "The Social Structure of the Family."

7. Sjoberg, *The Preindustustrial City, Past and Present*, pp. 139–140.

8. Giddens, *The Transformation of Intimacy*, p. 45.

9. Ibid., p. 45.

10. Ibid., pp. 62–63.

11. Many other authors agree, though they are far from approving this development. For instance, as Swidler writes: "the partners in a relationship remain autonomous and separate, each concerned about what he will have gained, what he will take away when the relationship is over." See Swidler, "Love and Adulthood in American Culture," p. 137.

12. Weber, *From Max Weber*, p. 355.

13. Ibid., p. 330.

14. Ibid., p. 343.

15. Quoted in Green, *The Von Richthofen Sisters*, pp. 170–171.

16. Here Weber offers a strong contrast to Freud, who imagined that modern conditions must necessitate ever greater sexual repression.

17. Giddens, *The Transformation of Intimacy*, pp. 180, 197.

18. Ibid., p. 93.

19. Bertilsson, "Love's Labour Lost?," p. 23.

20. Zablocki, *Alienation and Charisma*, p. 171.

21. Moffat, *Coming of Age in New Jersey*.

22. See Heider, *The Dugum Dani*.

23. Mead, *New Lives for Old*, pp. 361, 405.

24. Schopenhauer, *The World as Will and Representation*, pp. 536, 557.

25. Lindholm, "Love as an Experience of Transcendence."

26. Of course, the success rate of child-raising is another question, and one could argue that the strong emotional investment of parents romantically involved in their own relationship might heighten the possibility of their children reaching reproductive maturity, since the loving couple will stay together, protecting and nurturing their children. However, one could also make the opposite argument—that is, that those who are romantically involved will not wish the distraction of children—and will not reproduce at the same rate as those who are married for more pragmatic reasons.

27. Hegel, *Early Theological Writings*, p. 307.

28. Alberoni, *Falling in Love*, p. 23.

29. See Boase (1977) for a comprehensive review of this literature.

30. See Massignon, *The Passion of al-Hallaj*, pp. 348–349, for an account. The chaste ideal of sexless merging later degenerated into an esoteric practice among some Sufis who sought mystical communion by gazing at beautiful boys. The notion that romantic love must be heterosexual is not part of the Middle Eastern view of love, and some of the great classics of Medieval romantic literature concern love between men—the most famous being the love of King Mahmud of Ghazna for his Turkish slave Ayaz.

31. See Pehrson, *The Social Organization of the Marri Baluch*.

32. See Lindholm, "Love and Culture."

33. Alberoni, *Falling in Love*, p. 7.

34. For extended versions of this argument, see Lindholm, "Lovers and Leaders," and Lindholm, *Charisma*.

35. Zablocki, *Alienation and Charisma*, p. 131.

36. Alberoni, *Falling in Love*, p. 158.

37. Pope, "Defining and Studying Romantic Love," p. 22.

38. Weber, *The Protestant Ethic and Spirit of Capitalism*, p. 22.

39. Lindholm, *Charisma*.

REFERENCES

Alberoni, Francesco. *Falling in Love*. New York: Random House, 1983.

Bertilsson, Margareta. "Love's Labour Lost? A Sociological View." *Theory, Culture and Society* 3:19–35, 1986.

Boase, Roger. *The Origin and Meaning of Courtly Love*. Manchester: Manchester University Press, 1977.

Gadlin, Howard. "Private Lives and Public Order: A Critical View of the History of Intimate Relations in the United States." In George Levinger and Harold Raush (eds.), *Close Relationships: Perspectives on the Meaning of Intimacy*. Amherst: University of Massachusetts Press, 1977.

Giddens, Anthony. *The Transformation of Intimacy: Sexuality, Love and Intimacy in Modern Societies*. Stanford: Stanford University Press, 1992.

Goode, William. "The Theoretical Importance of Love." *American Sociological Review* 24:38–47, 1959.

Green, Martin. *The Von Richthofen Sisters: The Triumphant and the Tragic Modes of Love*. New York: Basic Books, 1974.

Hegel, G. *Early Theological Writings*. Chicago: University of Chicago Press, 1948.

Heider, Karl. *The Dugum Dani: A Papuan Culture in the Highlands of New Guinea*. Chicago: Aldine, 1970.

Hunt, Morton. *The Natural History of Love*. New York: Alfred Knopf, 1959.

Lindholm, Charles. "Lovers and Leaders: A Comparison of Social and Psychological Models of Romance and Charisma." *Social Science Information* 16:3–45, 1988.

———. *Charisma*. Oxford: Basil Blackwell, 1990.

———. "Love as an Experience of Transcendence." In William Jankowiak (ed.), *Romantic Love: A Universal Experience?* New York: Columbia University Press, 1995.

———. "Love and Culture." *Theory, Culture and Society*. In press.

MacFarlane, Alan. *Marriage and Love in England: 1300–1840*. Oxford: Blackwell, 1986.

Massignon, Louis. *The Passion of al-Hallaj: Mystic and Martyr of Islam: Vol. 1. The Life of al-Hallaj*. Princeton, N.J.: Princeton University Press, 1982.

Mead, Margaret. *New Lives for Old: Cultural Transformation Manus, 1920–1953*. New York: William Morrow, 1956.

Moffat, Michael. *Coming of Age in New Jersey*. New Brunswick, N.J.: Rutgers University Press, 1989.

Parsons, Talcott. "The Social Structure of the Family." In Ruth Nanda Anshen (ed.), *The Family: Its Function and Destiny*. New York: Harper and Brothers, 1949.

Pehrson, Robert. *The Social Organization of the Marri Baluch*. Chicago: Aldine, 1966.

Pope, Kenneth. "Defining and Studying Romantic Love." In K. Pope (ed.), *On Love and Loving*. San Francisco: Jossey-Bass, 1980.

Schopenhauer, Arthur. *The World as Will and Representation*, Vol. 2. New York: Dover, 1966.

Shorter, Edward. *The Making of the Modern Family*. New York: Basic Books, 1977.

Singer, Irving. *The Nature of Love. Vol. 1: Plato to Luther*. Chicago: University of Chicago Press, 1984a.

———. *The Nature of Love. Vol. 2: Courtly and Romantic*. Chicago: University of Chicago Press, 1984b.

———. *The Nature of Love. Vol. 3: The Modern World*. Chicago: University of Chicago Press, 1987.

Sjoberg, Gideon. *The Preindustrial City, Past and Present*. Glencoe, Ill.: Free Press, 1960.

Solomon, Robert. *Love, Emotion, Myth and Metaphor*. Garden City, N.J.: Anchor Books, 1981.

Stone, Laurence. "Passionate Attachments in the West in Historical Perspective." In W. Gaylin and E. Person (eds.), *Passionate Attachments*. New York: Free Press, 1988.

Swidler, Anne. "Love and Adulthood in American Culture." In N. Smelser and E. Erikson (eds.), *Themes of Work and Love in Adulthood*. Cambridge, Mass.: Harvard University Press, 1980.

Weber, Max. *From Max Weber: Essays in Sociology*. New York: Oxford University Press, 1946.

———. *The Protestant Ethic and the Spirit of Capitalism*. New York: Scribner's, 1958.

Zablocki, Benjamin. *Alienation and Charisma*. New York: Free Press, 1980.

2

Ideologies of Lovestyle and Sexstyle

John Alan Lee

A NEW ROMANTIC AGE

It's no accident that the lush romantic novels of Jane Austen (1775–1817) are back in vogue. Postmodern society is on the verge of a new age of love. The first Romantic era (about 1770–1870) was ushered in by the profound changes of the Industrial Revolution. Goethe, Coleridge, and Carlysle were linked to the decline of rural life and cottage industry, and the rise of a new industrial ideology of work (Hoefnagel 1978:265, 1979:36). Yet, what is obvious to anyone watching the Jane Austen movies is that all the important characters do no work. They pass their idle days in the pursuit of love.

The new millennium will bring a mirror image of the Austen households. The new overclass will work hard but constitute perhaps 20% of the population. The great underclass will experience The End of Work (Rifkin 1994). For two centuries, the lifelong job or career was the focus of human life in the Western world. Now that window on history is closing.

A small overclass of highly skilled and highly paid technicians will enjoy the delights of worldwide computer links and the illusions of "virtual reality," but these adult toys will be beyond the means of the great masses of unemployed and underemployed. Lest they grow restless and entertain thoughts of revolution, the underclass will require absorbing diversions. What is more amusing, distracting, even obsessive, than love?

Love may be listed on the stock exchange, alongside oil wells, computers, and mutual funds. Love may attract and amuse more players than any casino or lottery—and produce more profit. On the individual level, love is a relatively cheap distraction, but love as mass amusement could generate more gross national product than oil or electronics.

Both material differentiation and personal individuation in a global market economy will offer postmodern men and women a vast array of methods for interpenetrating each other's lives. Adventures in various styles of love will become as popular as adventure travel, theme parks, and computer games. The great underclass could be kept preoccupied with cycles of obsessive, self-defeating romance while the overclass enjoys the pleasures of playful, non-committal love.

Post-modern society is multiplying at an astonishing rate the means by which impersonal (corporate, technical and consumer) relationships can be conducted: fax, speed-dial phones, conference calls, e-mail, Internet, and the World Wide Web. But this new technology could also be used to greatly multiply "the opportunities for more intense personal relationships" (Luhman 1986:12).

SOCIAL SCIENCE DISCOVERS LOVE

For most of the twentieth century, social scientists have treated love as a topic not worth serious investigation. Curtin (1973) reports that in all the volumes of the *Annual Review of Psychology* up to 1973, there are many studies of dating but no mention of research on love. Then things changed. In 1980, Murstein observed a decline in research on dating and the emergence of a new focus of research on "love . . . with a preoccupation with theory" (Murstein 1980:777). One of the new theories Murstein noted was my typology of love.

In England in 1970, I created the first scientific (that is, replicable by experiment with other samples) method for distinguishing and measuring different kinds of love, using the analogy of the color wheel (a method for distinguishing colors). The empirical methods I used are reported in Lee 1970, 1973, 1974, 1976 and 1988. The kinds of love I proposed are constructed ideal types, as originally conceived by Max Weber in his ideal types of capitalism and the Protestant Ethic.

As Weber did with capitalism and religion, I set out to deconstruct and demythologize the Western myth of love. I began with heterosexual relationships, but further research showed that the same typology of love works with homosexual experience—not surprisingly, since gay men and lesbians are socialized in much the same romantic culture as heterosexuals.

People live life in different ways. The contemporary name for these different approaches is lifestyles. I argue that there are also different notions about the nature of "true love," and I call these "lovestyles."

There are also different approaches to sexuality, ranging from lifetime celibacy to "having sex" as often as possible. I call these notions "sexstyles." This chapter is about three things: lovestyles, sexstyles, and an analysis of the different ways we think about lovestyles and sexstyles. Sociologists call these different ways of thinking ideologies.

THE LOVESTYLES: A BRIEF DESCRIPTION

Think of a package of crayons. The cheapest package contains eight colors, but you can purchase packages with more than one hundred colors. Yet all these colors have a structure. There are primaries (such as red) and secondaries (such as orange, a mix of red and yellow). In the same way, my theory of lovestyles argues that there are certain basic or primary kinds of love, and various secondaries. Just as you find the most common colors in a package of only eight crayons, some of the kinds of love are more common than others. In our culture, the six most important lovestyles are the primary kinds, Eros, Ludus, and Storge, and the secondaries, Mania, Pragma, and Agape (Fig. 2.1). Modern languages lack names for different kinds of love, so I revived these names from ancient languages. (The ancient Greeks named sixteen different kinds of love!) The essential features I described for each lovestyle (Lee 1973) have been confirmed since, in numerous studies (see references).

Eros is a conception of love centered on an expectation of intense emotional and physical attraction to the beloved. Even before meeting a partner, the lover has a mental image of what the ideal beloved will look like. The hopeful lover can describe this image in detail—or sort the preferred image from a large set of photographs. There is excited recognition as soon as an example of the ideal is encountered, and there is an eagerness to become familiar with that person.

Keen disappointment occurs if the would-be lover discovers that the love object has some repellent physical attribute. Excessive body hair, hidden at first by clothing and later revealed, is a common example. Erotic images are individual but culturally shaped; our contemporary culture tends to emphasize a smooth, hairless male body in advertising and modeling. Thus, more American women are now consciously looking for a hairless male body. Similarly, more men are looking for the very slim female body featured in media and advertising.

If the would-be erotic lover is going to succeed in this lovestyle, he or she must have a high level of self-assurance. Otherwise, the lover is likely to slip into a manic lovestyle.

Figure 2.1
Lovestyles

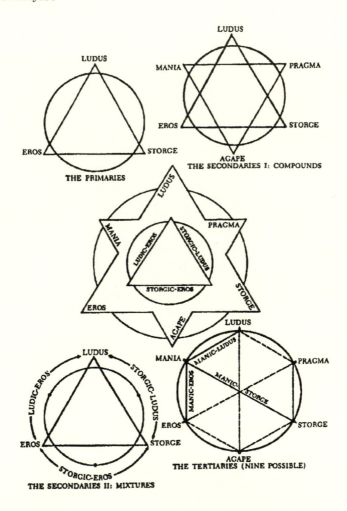

LUDUS

EROS   STORGE

THE PRIMARIES

LUDUS

MANIA   PRAGMA

EROS   STORGE

AGAPE
THE SECONDARIES I: COMPOUNDS

LUDUS

MANIA   PRAGMA

LUDIC-EROS   STORGIC-LUDUS

STORGIC-EROS

EROS   STORGE

AGAPE

LUDUS

LUDIC-EROS   STORGIC-LUDUS

EROS   STORGE

STORGIC-EROS

THE SECONDARIES II: MIXTURES

LUDUS

MANIA   MANIC-LUDUS   PRAGMA

MANIC-EROS   MANIC-STORGE

EROS   STORGE

AGAPE
THE TERTIARIES (NINE POSSIBLE)

Storge (pronounced stor-gay) is the ancient Greek conception of a quiet and friendly attachment, lacking in intensity but deep and calm in its affection. It's the sort of love that grows between longtime school chums or childhood neighbors whose affection for each other has deep roots. There is little passion in storge. Self-disclosure comes slowly and shyly, but with an expectation of long-term commitment. The storgic lover usually avoids thoughts of "being in love" and expressions such as "I love you."

No particular physical image is sought for or recognized. A storgic lover has great difficulty in sorting a "preferred type" from photographs. Told to choose the "person you would most like to date," the respondent will ask questions about the character and activities of each photographed subject, in an effort to "become acquainted."

Ludus (lew-dus) comes to us from the Latin (play or game) and was first described by the ancient Roman poet Ovid. This style views love as a game governed by rules (which vary with the culture). The lover expects the beloved to understand and play by the rules. It is a love without jealousy, or commitment to a single partner. For the ludic lover, love should be fun, not anxiety or suffering.

The ludic lover thinks of love as rather like alcohol: enjoy it but don't become dependent upon it. Love as a game may be played with a variety of players at the same time (a different date for each night of the week) or in series, one affair after another. The expression of emotions is controlled, and the ludic lover recovers easily from each breakup, moving on to the next partner. Style, not sincerity, is the hallmark of ludus. Just because ludus is a playful love does not mean that it is easy; it requires at least as much knowledge of the rules and skill in strategy as a game of chess. As with eros, the player of ludus who lacks sufficient ability is likely to slip into mania.

The most important secondaries are mania, pragma, and agape. Mania (may-nee-a) is a combination of eros and ludus, just as orange is a mix of red and yellow. It combines the intensity of eros with the efforts to control of ludus, but, in the process of mixing, excludes the self-confidence of eros and the freedom from jealousy found in ludus. The manic lover feels a strong need to be loved, yet manic lovers often choose socially incompatible partners who are almost guaranteed not to return their love.

Mania is an obsessive, possessive, over-intense, anxious approach to love. The lover becomes mentally preoccupied with thoughts of the beloved but is unskilled in showing affectionate attachment. Manic love is often "self-defeating," thriving on obstacles and (often imagined) injuries. The lover is in desperate need of repeated reassurances of love, but even if these reassurances are offered, the manic lover cannot believe them.

Pragma (prag-ma) is the ancient Greek root of pragmatic. This ideology defines love as a practical matter of finding a compatible partner for a relationship (whether short-term or lifelong). The pragmatic lover has a shopping list of qualities sought in the partner and is able to specify these in an advertisement.

The qualities are not those recognized on sight (as in the case of eros), but tend to be demographic and personality qualities, such as race, religion, social class, and/or athletic or artistic activities. The pragmatic lover has a sensible assessment of his or her "market value" on the "meet market" and knows what realistic exchange of assets can be hoped for and, likewise, who is "out of my league." This ideology of love is easily facilitated by introduction agencies and computer-dating networks. In my typology, pragma is a secondary, combining selected qualities of ludus and storge. It consciously "arranges" a friendship when the ordinary circumstances of life have not thrown the two people together.

Agape (a-ga-pay) combines aspects of eros and storge. Agape is altruistic, intense, and friendly love, guided more by reason than by emotion. Agape is the ancient Greek term for a kind of loving adopted by the early Christians as their ideological ideal (and used by St. Paul in his famous description of perfect love in his letter to the early Christians of the city of Corinth). As a choice of lovestyle for dating and mating, agape is not common in Western society, but researchers testing my typology in other cultures have found greater evidence of it (Cho and Cross 1995:285).

There are other lovestyles in my typology, other mixtures of primary colors of love: ludic eros, storgic eros, storgic ludus, manic ludus. Because most scholars want to simplify their research, especially when using paper-and-pencil tests, these other lovestyles have been neglected. This is especially unfortunate in the case of ludic eros, which I predicted in 1973 would become one of the most fashionable of American lovestyles.

The ludic-erotic lover is a "collector" of love experiences (Lee 1973:110), moving cheerfully (in a ludic style) from one erotically attractive partner to the next, collecting "exes." It is a highly adaptive ideology of love in an age when existentialism combines with serial monogamy. Each marriage or affair is intensely enjoyed while it lasts (eros) but it is not expected to endure, and the lover moves on (ludus) to the next joyful love.

MIXING AND MATCHING LOVESTYLES

Due to oversimplification, some scholars leave the impression that I identify only six types of love. Obviously, that is not the case. Also, it must be understood that the theory of lovestyles is not a kind of zodiac. One is not born ludic or erotic, or whatever. With sufficient skill and experience, any lover can practice any lovestyle. It may be convenient to describe a person as a "pragmatic lover," but what is meant is "a lover who at the time, with the partner being considered, is attempting to practice the pragmatic lovestyle."

It is quite possible to enjoy relationships of different lovestyles at the same time, or one after the other (see confirmation by Hendrick and Hendrick 1986:401). For example, you might love one partner in a friendly way (storge) and be passionately attracted to another's beauty (eros). Obviously, some lovestyles do not combine well (for example, mania and ludus). Few lovers are pure examples of any given lovestyle. As with choices of colors for clothing or decoration, most people mix and match lovestyles. After all, any of these lovestyles is available in our media.

Many lovers will find one lovestyle easier to practice than the others, just as you would find some political or religious beliefs easier to practice than others. Choices of lovestyle are often influenced by personality traits. I first suggested this in 1970, arguing that manic lovers I interviewed were more likely to be lonely and unhappy people in family life and workplace, or that erotic and ludic lovers were more likely to have high self-esteem (Lee 1970, 1973, 1976).

Research since then has established that each choice of lovestyle tends to be correlated with distinctive personality traits (for example: Mallandain and Davies 1994:557; Taraban 1995:453). This is true not only of "positive" traits such as high self-esteem, but also of "negative" traits such as "feeling lonely" (Rotenberg and Korol 1996:537) or a self-defeating attitude toward life and love (Feeney and Nolle 1990:281; Williams and Schill 1994:31).

Therefore, you are not equally free to choose one lovestyle or another. Given your personality traits, some styles will come more easily than others.

THE RECENT SURGE OF INTEREST IN STUDYING LOVE

Consult the PsychLit Index or SocioFile Index and you'll discover the enormous amount of research published about love in recent years. This surge of interest is often dated from Rubin's article, "The Measurement of Romantic Love" (Rubin 1970).

Rubin accepted the dominant ideology of American society that there is only one kind of true love. By dominant ideology, I mean the "set of closely related beliefs accepted as fact or truth in a particular culture" (Plamenatz 1970:15). This ideology is expressed in language that, to people in that culture, is nothing more than "common sense" which "everyone knows," and which "goes without saying." For example, the notions that people fall in love or have sex are the words of an ideology that we take for granted. We swim in this language, and we do not question it any more than fish question water. But do people really fall in love, or do they jump? You can have dinner, but can you have sex?

The dominant form in our culture treats love as one thing, to be acquired in amounts. Look at our everyday words: How much do you love me? As much as I love you? Do you love me more than you loved your "ex"? Why don't you love me as much as you used to? Rubin never got out of this "taken for granted" about love in American society, so he defined love as a single "attitude." He created a paper-and-pencil test that measured this attitude on an intensity scale, the way a thermometer measures heat. Other researchers soon adopted Rubin's scale. Rubin-type scales ask a subject a series of questions, and the answers are "scored" to determine how much the person loves someone. Thus, these scales assume that love is unidimensional.

Soon after I published my scientific theory of multidimensional love (Lee 1973), two American sociologists, Thomas and Marcia Lasswell (1976), simplified my four-hour interview method into a half-hour paper-and-pencil test. Over the next four years they replicated six major lovestyles in samples totaling more than one thousand respondents (Hatkoff and Lasswell 1979; Lasswell and Lasswell 1976; Lasswell and Lobsenz 1980).

In 1986, two Texas psychologists, Susan and Clyde Hendrick, adopted my theory and published a new paper-and-pencil test for measuring the six most commonly understood lovestyles. With large samples and test-retest verifications, they demonstrated that each of six different styles can be clearly distinguished from the others. The Hendricks preferred to simplify their tests by concentrating on the three primary lovestyles and three secondaries, leaving out the additional styles such as ludic eros, but their research (summarized in Hendrick and Hendrick 1992) confirms my theory that lovestyles are interrelated like colors. They found that eros has a strong negative correlation with ludus, but a strong positive correlation with mania and agape. As I predicted, the Hendricks found that storge is strongly correlated with pragma and agape.

The Hendricks' paper-and-pencil test has become more popular than the Lasswells', and there are now numerous replications in America and around the world. A few examples are England: Mallandain and Davies 1994:557; Portugal: Neto, 1994:613; Mexico: Leon, 1994:307 and 1995:527; Germany: Klein and Bierhoff, 1991:189 and Bierhoff and Klein 1991:53; Japan: Nakamura, 1991, and Matsui, 1993:335; and China: Cho and Cross, 1995:283. In 1990, Borello and Thompson published a definitive test of "the validity of Lee's typology of love" and confirmed that factor analysis supported the lovestyles.

Some Scholars Still Insist on One True Love

At least one hundred studies have now validated the multi-dimensionality of love, so it is hard to believe that some scholars still insist on "one true love." For example, Murstein (1980:780) was so ideologically committed to one kind of love that he could actually say: "One approach that has ignored [!] love's unidimensionality is Lee." In 1988, between the same book covers as myself, Murstein asked, "Is there a single general factor we call love, or are there at least nine types of love as Lee has claimed?" He insisted that studies available at that time supported a single factor, except for the Hendricks, whose work he dismissed in a footnote questioning their methods. Murstein then repeated his article of faith: "There is only one major factor of love that includes a wide variety of behaviors, feelings and attitudes. This factor encompasses all the good things one can think about another" (1988:31). Some reactions to the notion of multidimensionality of love would be amusing if they were not so infuriatingly inconsistent. Hatfield and Walster's *A New Look at Love* (1978) is fully cognizant of my theory: pages 38 to 44 of their book accurately report my lovestyles. However, these pages form part of a chapter titled "Understanding Passionate Love." Several of my lovestyles described in these pages are not "passionate" at all!

In 1996, Hatfield collaborated with Richard Rapson in a new book, *Love and Sex: Cross Cultural Perspectives.* This book insists that people are torn between two definitions of love: passionate love and companionate love, but only one of these is true love. Passionate love is "infatuation, love sickness, or obsessive love" while companionate love is "affectionate love, tender love, true love and marital love" (Hatfield and Rapson 1996:63–64).

Some scholars pretend to support a multidimensional approach but sneak unidimensionality in the back door by labeling the kinds of love so that only one of them is truly love; the rest are pretenders to the throne. Sternberg (1986, 1988:122–129) developed a "triangular theory" of love which ostensibly recognizes different loves according to combinations of three basic components: intimacy, passion, and commitment. The result is "liking" (intimacy without passion or commitment), infatuation (automatically a pejorative label), empty love (even more so), romantic love (intimacy and passion but no commitment), companionate love (no passion), fatuous love (!!!—no intimacy), and consummate love (all three components). How many true loves are there here?

Instead of thinking of lovestyles as ideologies, most scholars have retained Rubin's conception of love as an attitude. Two of the most consistent supporters of my theory, Clyde and Susan Hendrick, have entirely rejected Rubin's bipolar scale and have generously credited me with inventing the idea of lovestyles. Nevertheless, they named their instrument for measuring differences in lovestyles the Love Attitudes Scale (Hendrick and Hendrick 1986:326, 1990:239).

Some scholars reject or ignore my lovestyles in favor of a "cross-cultural approach" that recognizes different cultural definitions of love (for example, Dion and Dion 1993a; Sprecher and Metts 1989; Shaver et al. 1992). The ideological nature of these definitions is recognized, yet the authors remain within their own culture when defining love. For example, Dion and Dion (1996:8) understand the ideological contrast of collectivistic versus individualistic cultures and yet are able to speak of "romantic love" as if it were one kind.

I am not taken in by my own propaganda; I fully realize that the color theory of lovestyles is also an ideological platform. I just happen to think that its adoption would be more beneficial for both societies and individuals than the continued belief in one or another kind of love as the one true love. I am not wedded to any number of lovestyles, such as the six often used in replications. How many colors are there? Would there be any point in trying to count them? There is already evidence that cultures differing from the Western tradition contain similar lovestyles but combine the primary colors of love in different ways than we do. For example, a "style where eros is combined with agape" has been identified as a favorite in Chinese culture (Cho and Cross 1995:283).

There is no point in defining color, but it is useful to accurately define each hue (as a paint store must do in producing another can of exactly the same color you ran out of last week while painting your living room walls). Similarly, what is important is not to define love, but to establish a social awareness of the marvelous range of experiences available to each lover. A lover who finds that one style does not bring happiness may change to another (Philbrick and Leon 1991:912).

SEXSTYLES

Sexual styles of language and behavior (sexstyles) are generally better understood than lovestyles. Since the earliest religious thinkers, certain sexual practices and the slightest hints of them in language have been banned or severely punished. St. Paul thundered that total chastity was the true Christian way of life. If a believer could not control the sex drive, the only alternative was a single, sexually faithful lifetime marriage. Such a marriage, from which you could never be divorced, was better than total chastity only because, St. Paul conceded, it is "better to marry than to burn" (I Corinthians:7). Two thousand years later, and in modern ideological language, some Christians still argue that the best way young people can avoid sexually transmitted diseases is not to have sex until after they fall in love and get married.

It is less controversial to argue multidimensionality in the case of sexstyles than of lovestyles (Hendrick and Hendrick 1987:505). The popular culture has often assumed "one true love," but it has always recognized different sexstyles. Powerful institutions such as the Roman Catholic Church have made aggressive moves to establish one dominant sexstyle based on premarital chastity and marital sexual fidelity, but these efforts have never succeeded, even among the clergy themselves.

Separation of lovestyle from sexstyle is a useful device for analysis but does not happen in real life. Any analysis of lovestyle eventually leads to what Luhman calls "incorporation of sexuality" (1986:109). For example, in mania the words or actions of sexual jealousy or posses- siveness are automatically understood as evidence of the depth and sincerity of the lover's attachment: "I need you so much that I could never share you with another." Numerous love songs in this style speak of one person making another "mine alone."

But in ludus such jealous behavior instantly evokes annoyance, if not anger and flight. In pragma, sexual fidelity is a practical issue, not a question of proving your love. Each partner may have discreet sexual affairs from time to time, but these must not be allowed to interfere with marriage and family life. Once a would-be lover understands his or her lovestyle and that of the potential partner, an assessment of the appropriate sexstyle for that relationship easily follows (Lee 1973:25–29).

Each society in history has developed a dominant ideology of sexstyle. For example, Victorian society in Europe and America applied the famous double standard. The ideal sexual behavior for a woman was virginity and chastity before marriage and lifelong sexual fidelity to her spouse after marriage. The ideal sexual behavior for a young male was chastity before marriage, but he was allowed to enjoy limited and discreet sexual experience with women of the kind he would never choose to marry. After marriage, the ideal male sexstyle was fidelity, but, again, the double standard was more likely to forgive discreet affairs by husbands than by wives. The dominant Victorian sexstyle did not accept certain sexual acts at any time, even within marriage (e.g., fellatio) and banned others with severe penalties (e.g., sodomy). The dominant Victorian sexstyle, says Luhman (1986:145), was "the ideo- logy of reproduction."

Like lovestyles, sexstyles go through cultural changes, becoming or ceasing to be the dominant ideology. Sometimes the changes are gradual as in the Victorian era (Hendrick and Hendrick 1992:41). Sometimes the changes are as revolutionary as the Reformation in religion or the Bolshevik Revolution in politics. The Kinsey Report was said to have caused a "sexual revolution" (Hotchner 1978:350). Among the profound shock tremors of modern sexuality are changes in technology and modern medicines for STDs, the feminist movement, and gay liberation. Stephen O. Murray's comprehensive overview, *American Gay,* specifically distinguishes a "gay ideology" from sexstyles of the "dominant culture" (Murray 1996:174–175). Profound changes in religion or politics create great difficulty in choosing a political or religious ideology. Similarly, the successive waves of change in sexual ideology over the past half-century have enormously complicated anyone's choice of sexstyle.

Social conflicts rage around some of the distinctively new sexstyles. For example, the issue of public recognition of gay and lesbian relationships has divided the American Senate down the middle, 49 to 50. There is angry debate about public legitimation of gay and lesbian marriages. There are also new bisexual, "transgender," and "transsexual" patterns. For more ordinary lovers, there is respectability for several marriages in a lifetime or living together without getting married. Only a few decades ago "common law" relationships were stigmatized and disadvantaged in both law and popular opinion. Another sexstyle change is that fewer young lovers now insist that their partner be a "virgin."

Each of these changes is linked with changes in lovestyles. For example, the widespread respectability of prophylactics in sex makes it much easier to be a ludic or ludic-erotic lover. It is now possible to have one love affair after another, or several at the same time, with less fear of lasting consequences such as STDs, unwanted pregnancy, or a shotgun marriage.

The difficulty of introducing a new sexstyle without concomitant changes in lovestyle ideology is well illustrated by recent campaigns for safer sex. Research suggests that these educational campaigns are not having sufficient effect among the young. That a lover should take "time out of wooing" to put on a condom is a notion that fits easily with a pragmatic or storgic definition. It badly disrupts the delight of eros and ludus, where maintaining a sense of heightened excitement is essential (in the vernacular, being "hot"). We're having trouble designing condoms that are "hot."

TABOO SEXSTYLES

There is no space here to discuss in detail the special connections between lovestyles and various socially proscribed sexstyles such as homosexuality or sadomasochism. Correlational research is already uncovering some of these links (e.g., Gosselin 1991:11; Sarwer 1993:265). I have already published extensively on the social psychology of slave and master scenarios in sexstyle (Lee 1979).

Slave and Master sex (which is a more sociologically accurate translation of SM than sadomasochism) is essentially a sexual game that can be most safely played in certain lovestyles—ludus in particular—and is most dangerous in certain other lovestyles—mania in particular. Good SM play for both partners requires that both be in firm control of their emotions. SM's inherent structure of inequality (dominance and submission) makes it quite unsuitable for storge; friendship is built on equality.

Ironically, joyful and safe SM requires mutual trust, an element central to storge (but not at all essential to playful ludus), so the storgic-ludus lovestyle is one of the best matches with SM play. The eros-style lover is limited in potential enjoyment of SM scenarios to those where the partner meets the lover's ideal physical image. The less picky ludic style allows for a wide range of partners, as long as each partner can "play the game," or in the lingo of SM, "knows the ropes."

The ludic lovestyle also stretches the imagination more, and a capacity for fantasy contributes greatly to enjoyment of SM sex, at least on a scene-by-scene basis. But (and this is a lovely paradox!) if a lover wishes to enjoy a series of SM scenarios over time with the same partner—even if the two are merely making love, not living together as a couple—there is a great advantage in the partners going through a "debriefing" process after each scenario. The caring, agapic quality of this debriefing helps to restore the social equality of the partners until it is voluntarily converted to dominance-submission in the next scenario.

Thus, Slave and Master sex is a tightrope act of balancing various lovestyles. If it becomes part of the sexual repertoire of a long-term couple seeking variety in their sexual expression of love, it becomes the sexual equivalent of the playful, joyful imagination found in the ludic-erotic lovestyle. Of course, it is possible to play SM games simply as sex. As one more way of having sex, it is outside the ideological concerns of this chapter.

I haven't said anything yet about power. Slave and Master sex is all about the theater of power plays, the sort of power games inimical to storge and agape over the long run, because they take love and life seriously. SM is safe only if it is not taken seriously. With such a complex structure, it's little wonder that talking about SM frightens most people—let alone admitting to enjoying it personally. Our dominant political ideology of "equality" does not admit the theatrical playfulness or the open power games of SM.

UNDERSTANDING LOVE AS AN IDEOLOGY

Like everyone else, Americans think ideologically; they just don't like to call it that. Societies cannot exist without the production of ideology any more than they can exist without the production of material goods (Sinfield 1992:32). Ideology is especially important in times of change. The Industrial Revolution went hand in hand with the age of Romanticism, but it also generated new ideologies of politics (utopianism, socialism, fascism), as well as economics, religion, education, and science.

When social scientists correctly use the term, ideology is a neutral concept. It is simply the "value or belief system accepted as fact or truth by some group." In popular usage, ideology often suggests extreme systems of thought or propaganda such as Marxism, fascism, or fundamentalism. An example of this confusion may be found in a current college text. Speaking of cross-cultural comparisons of love, Hatfield and Rapson (1996:19) state: "One must not be ideological, but ruthlessly truthful." To these authors, ideology "verges on propaganda" (1996:19).

To consider love as ideology is not merely a matter of intellectual or scientific interest. Every day, people "look for love" and enter "relationships" because they believe they have found love, or they leave relationships because they believe they have "lost" love. Most do not stop to notice that this is not merely an attitude change but an ideological conversion, much the same as converting to a new religion in search of "faith" or joining a new political party or "becoming a feminist."

Many researchers have ignored these larger implications of lovestyles and sexstyles. Instead of pursuing an ideological analysis, scholars have concentrated on that hobgoblin of psychology: the correlation of X with Y. The typical research question is: "Which X (lovestyle) is correlated with which Y?" The list of Y correlates is now a long one and has thoroughly distracted researchers from the larger problems of love and sex.

Roseham (1978) first asked the obvious question: "Which lovestyles are correlated with men or with women?" and also found that women were better able to distinguish lovestyles than men. There has been a steady flow of these correlational studies for two decades. They include Snead (1980), Sandor (1982), Prentice (1983), Prasinos and Bennett (1984), C. and S. Hendrick (1987, 1989), Richardson et al. (1988), Collins and Read (1990), Adler and Hendrick (1991), Gosselin (1991), Tancy and Bergloss (1991), Feingold (1992), Cramer (1993), Cimbalo and Novell (1993), Leon (1994, 1995), Morrow (1995), Rotenberg and Korol (1996), and numerous others (see References).

These studies have correlated lovestyles with a bewildering array of variables. The following list is hardly exhaustive:

1. Various personality dimensions, such as self-esteem.
2. Durability of sexual satisfaction in relationships.
3. Durability of general satisfaction with a love partner.
4. Sexual attraction over a large gap in the age of partners.
5. The practice of sadomasochistic sex.
6. Sexual aggressiveness in loveplay.
7. The early or late introduction of sex in a love relationship.
8. Belief in eternal love versus existential worldviews.
9. Degrees of concern with social compatibility of the partner.
10. Risk-taking and "sensation seeking."
11. The degree of concern with the physical appearance of partner.
12. Variations in the screening of potential partners.
13. Variations by lovestyle in the experience of loneliness.
14. Varying concern to get to know partners first before sexual intimacy.
15. Religious background of the lover.
16. Variations in life satisfaction scores by lovestyle.
17. Different levels of concern about safer sex and use of condoms.
18. Varying developmental stages of love by lovestyle.

Surely, this correlational research has at least settled the debate about whether there are different kinds of love! Yet some scholars still insist love is unidimensional. Such "true believers" are the best proof that "true love" is a question of ideological bias. As for the general population, the publication of numerous scholarly studies has made hardly any impact on the way ordinary people think about love.

That is not surprising. Four centuries have passed since Copernicus turned the contemporary ideologies of church and state upside down by showing that the earth goes around the sun. We are not a special creation. Yet every day humans continue to behave as a special creation and continue to talk about the sun rising and setting. We have seen films of "earthrise" on the moon, yet our language still does not admit that the sun has never gone around Earth in the four billion years of this planet's existence. Perhaps someday we will accurately say "the Earth turned toward dawn," just as we say our plane landed—not "the earth rose toward us." Old ideas die hard.

THE ADVANTAGES OF AN IDEOLOGICAL ANALYSIS

I appreciate the concern to convert my theory of lovestyles into practical scales and paper-and-pencil tests for measuring and achieving more compatible and enduring relationships. Many feel that ours is an era of pandemic "breakdown" of marriage and love relationships, an "emotional depression" comparable, in economics, to the Great Depression (Page 1988:5). In sexual ideology, we face a similar crisis. In times like these, most people are not much concerned about understanding the competing ideological systems of sex and love. They want to know WHAT TO DO.

Mere correlative research will not provide us with the *PRACTICAL* understanding of love we need and yearn for. What are the practical implications of continuing to think and behave as if there is only one kind of true love, or two at best? The answer to that question is clear, once we consider the practical implications of similar monolithic thinking in other areas of life, such as politics and religion.

Whenever American foreign policy insisted that all communist governments were the same, all part of one evil empire, the results were inflexible and self-defeating policies and initiatives. But whenever American policy recognized that Communism A is not equal to Communism B, actions were taken which eventually broke apart whatever unity the communist countries attempted (examples: the recognition that Tito's Yugoslavia was not the same Communism as East Germany's or, later, Nixon's initiatives with Communist China). Eventually, multidimensional thinking precipitated the breakup of the "empire"—including the Soviet Union itself. In religion, we need hardly elaborate the consequences of insisting that there is only one true Christianity.

THE CONFLICT OF COMPETING IDEOLOGIES

It is when ideologies are in conflict, and *CONTRADICT* each other, that we begin to notice that there are ideologies that we otherwise take for granted (Dollimore 1991:87). In Mannheim's classic *Ideology and Utopia* (1936), ideology is separated into the "particular" and "the total." That is, an ideology may be partial or comprehensive.

A partial ideology is the specific set of ideas that the occupant of a given social status uses to justify and explain actions. For example, an employer may argue that it is "fair" to throw thousands of employees out of work because management has "a responsibility to the shareholders to make as large a profit as possible." A partial ideology tends to affect only some aspects of our daily life (Plamenatz 1970:18). For example, "Monetarism" affects mainly economic policies.

A "total" or "comprehensive" ideology develops when partial ideologies combine into larger and more pervasive systems of ideas. For example, "feminists" began with a fairly limited concern about inequality in gender relations, but have rapidly expanded into issues of economics and politics and recently have advocated changes in religion, such as God as "she" and a revival of interest in goddess religion. Certain religious and political ideologies have grown to include beliefs about all aspects for life—for example, "Christianity" or "Islam" or "Communism" or "the American way of life." These comprehensive ideologies are often called "worldviews."

In the case of lovestyles and sexstyles, a partial ideology may affect only relationships with a specific individual. For example, I may have a ludic relationship with one partner and a storgic relationship with another. I may arrange to be sexually monogamous with the partner I have now, after having had an "open marriage" with my "ex."

On a broad social scale, however, a lovestyle or sexstyle may become dominant in that society and enforced by—or forbidden by—a church, state, or other social institution. For example, a polygamous sexstyle was originally advocated by the Mormon Church but banned by the federal state; a manic, adulterous, individualistic style of loving (usually called "courtly love") was widely advocated by Renaissance poet-singers (troubadours) but firmly opposed by the Catholic Church. The playful erotic lovestyle that I call "ludic eros" has become the comprehensive ideology of contemporary Hollywood films, but fundamentalist Christians accuse the film producers of "undermining family values" and even threaten boycotts if a sitcom character is scripted to "come out" (change sexstyle) as a gay person. Family values is now becoming one of Mannheim's "total ideologies" and includes beliefs not only about love and sex, but also about appropriate gender roles, child–parent relations, and many other social arrangements.An ideology is not merely a set of ideas; it includes a persuasive element that is not found, for example, in a science or an art. There is a commitment to this set of ideas, because these ideas are considered to be in the best interest of the believers. An ideology always involves a story with a moral (Feuer 1975:5, Plamenatz 1970:76). Powerful social institutions are called into action to "sell" this story as a plausible explanation of ordinary life. People are encouraged to "believe in" this story, and dissent from this story is discouraged and punished (Sinfield 1992:33).

The story is the easiest way to tell and learn the ideology. The story of Jesus is the heart of Christianity, of whatever denomination. Some version of the "log cabin to White House" story is at the core of Ameri- can democracy, whatever the political party, or the reality that pre- sidents (e.g., Roosevelt, Kennedy) are as likely to come from the elite. de Rougemont (1940) correctly noted the important role of the Tristan and Iseult legend in the ideological development of "romantic love," no matter what the original intention of that legend. When this legend is updated as Eric Segal's *Love Story*, it is the same old story.

Ideology involves goal-directed behavior, part of Talcott Parsons' "integrative" functions of the social system that bind and legitimize social action. Ideologies distort any totally "objective" approach to life and society because the goals of any one ideology exclude or oppose the goals of other ideologies (Parsons 1951:354). Lovestyles vary in the degree to which they distort everyday life: mania distorts to the extreme, pragma least of all, which is why the first is popularly called "romantic" and the latter "realistic."

To embrace an ideology is to make an act of faith in the essential truth about life contained in the fantastic story—whether the story is that of Christ's resurrection or the magical adventures of Tristan and Iseult. Feuer (1975) argues that as an ideology develops, certain mythical ideas become "sacred." Each new believer makes a leap from the mythical ideas to a sacred truth—what Feuer calls the ideological leap.

For example, people who believe the ancient story (first set in writing in Plato's *Symposium*) that each person has a "soulmate" will continue to search for Mr. or Ms. Right in spite of one disappointment after another. A competing (ludic) ideology makes fun of such "romantic" believers and reminds us that "there are plenty of fish in the sea" (which recent ecological disasters remind us is also a myth).

THE SOCIAL CONSTRUCTION OF LOVESTYLES

The notion that lovestyles are socially constructed ideologies made no sense to most of my readers three decades ago. Today this idea has growing support in the social sciences (Beall 1995). In the next millennium, it will be as much part of everyday language as the term "significant other"—once a term of specialized sociological jargon.

Each newly constructed ideology comes into conflict with existing ideologies and survives through compromise. Consider the belief that a marriage must begin with and retain "true love." At one time this ideology, known then as courtly love, was a quite new idea in society was opposed by many important people. When Ann Paston, a daughter of an English squire in the fifteenth century, fell in love with her father's bailiff and wanted to marry him instead of her father's choice of a "suitable" partner, she was packed off to the bishop for a stern lecture (Bennett 1922:45). When she still refused, her father locked her up!

The historical development of competing ideologies of love is well documented by Luhman (1986), including the relationship between each stage and its relevant social class. Lantz (1980) also showed how the advance of ideologies of romantic love was interconnected with changes in other ideological systems such as modernization and market economy. Slowly, over time, and with gains and reversals, the notion that "marriage must be for love" won out over the opposing ideology of a marriage of parental convenience. The conflicts between these competing ideologies are well illustrated by the novels and theatrical comedies of the seventeenth and eighteenth centuries.

The notion of the ideologies of love is not new. An English anthropologist with the unlikely name of Finck wrote about it in the nineteenth century (Finck 1889). Some American sociologists have discussed the "theoretical importance of love" while avoiding the word ideology (Goode 1959; Reiss 1960). Pitirim Sorokin devoted much research to a sociology of love but avoided ideological concepts. He never managed to get out of his own "taken for granted"—the assumption that what he called "altruistic love" is the only true love.

As for sexstyles, there is a long history of ideologies of sex, although the word "ideology" is generally avoided. From Havelock Ellis to Vern Bullough (1976), there are numerous arguments between conflicting sets of beliefs about sex. I contributed my own theoretical model of different possible arrangements of lovestyle and sexuality in 1978. I called it "A Chart of Intimate Unions" (Table 2.1) (Lee 1978:278). I argued that sexuality, like love, was multidimensional. When the variations of each are combined, at least *twenty* different combinations are possible. I located and interviewed people living in each one of these twenty relationships.

The twenty variations combine three kinds of sexuality with two kinds of living arrangements (couples, or groups of more than two), two kinds of goal for the duration of the relationship (long term, short term) and two kinds of commitment to partner(s): exclusive and open. In exclusive unions, the partners have intimate exchanges only with other members of the union. (As with colors of love, I am not suggesting that only twenty arrangements are possible; I simply want to show that "there are many rooms" in the mansions of lovestyle and sexstyle.) The traditional long-term, sexually exclusive heterosexual marriage is not the only available combination of love and sex (Lee 1978:279). It is obvious that only one of these arrangements has been ideologically dominant for long periods of time in various societies, Christian or otherwise. Although most Islamic societies permit a man to have more than one wife, the great majority of men live in the same long-term, sexually exclusive couple that is still ideologically dominant in Christian societies. However, many of the other arrangements have been widely tolerated. There is even evidence of discreet unofficial tolerance of homosexual unions in medieval Christian societies (Boswell 1980:54).

IDEOLOGY, POWER, AND SOCIAL CLASS

Ideology may have a bad reputation, but we cannot deconstruct and demystify systems of thought without ideological analysis. Such analysis exposes both the structure of the reality we take for granted,

Table 2.1
A Chart of Intimate Unions*

Sexuality	Couple or Group	Intended Duration			
		Long Term		Short Term	
		Exclusive	Open	Exclusive	Open
Hetero-sexual	Couple	1 Traditional Christian marriage	2 Open marriage	3 Short-term renewable contract marriage	4 Traditional affair and contract cohabitation
	Group	5 Corporate family	6 Communes	7 Senior polygyny	8 Group sex
Same Sex	Couple	9 Traditional gay marriage	10 Gay open marriage	11 Same-sex affairs	12 Prison relationships
	Group	13 Gay family of choice	14 Gay commune	15 Gay triads	16 Gay threesomes and orgies
Mixed	Group	17 Long-term bisexual arrangements	18 Mixed-sex communes	19 Bisexual threesomes and triads	20 Short-term bisexual arrangements

* Consult *Getting Sex* (Lee 1978) for details on some of the less familiar arrangements. Generally speaking, human societies have been sexist; thus more lovestyle/sexstyle options (more boxes in the chart) have been open to men than to women.

and the social powers that endorse and promote that structure by making their chosen ideology the dominant, taken-for-granted way of thinking (Giddens 1979:69).

In other words, we must ask who benefits and who suffers from the social construction of different ideologies of love and sex. For example, how did the notion of romantic love come to be constructed as always involving persons of the opposite sex, so that even scholars sometimes use the term "heterosexual love" as if it were synonymous with romantic love? College texts on love and sex can discuss these topics for hundreds of pages without mentioning love between homosexual partners. Gay and lesbian students in the classroom are made invisible by these texts.

An ideology is always linked, at least in its origins, with a social class. Some links are clear enough: Communism is linked to the working class or proletariat. Fascism is commonly linked with the frustrated and dispossessed petit bourgeoisie. Other links are widely understood but controversial—for example, Frederick Nietzsche's arguments linking the origins of Christianity with the Roman slave class.

An ideology has its origins in a social class, but it does not stop there. People in other social classes can embrace an ideology once it has become a competitive set of ideas about how to understand life. Some millionaires have become Communists. Many—despite the parable of the camel and the eye of the needle—have become Christians.

Social class is about power and politics. I define politics as the decision-making process for the distribution of resources in any social system. Thus, a family has its politics about space, money, and other resources in the home. The way social classes are structured has a great deal to do with power, which I define as the ability to use the system's politics to get and keep more than your proportionate share of resources in that system.

Each social class has a vested interest in using politics to increase its share of power at the expense of others in the system, so it follows that social classes with opposing vested interests will have opposing ideologies. Capitalism versus Communism does not imply that Communism is supported only by workers, or capitalism only by bosses. What I mean is that a particular ideology is addressed to the interests—especially the historical and economic interests—of a particular social class. Feuer (1975) calls this the "chosen" social class; Marx called it the "oppressed" class.

Each social class will attempt to advance its own cause in history and, in particular, its place in the social stratification of society, compared with other classes, by enacting the appropriate ideology. Communism is offered to the proletariat in its struggle with capitalism.

The modern ideology of feminism is offered to the "oppressed" women of society in their struggle with "sexist men."

But what has all this to do with Love- and Sexstyles? Exactly! The great majority of studies about love and sex completely ignore issues of politics, power, resources, and vested interests of classes. In other topics, such as sexism or gender, there is now ample research and theory about power and politics (Davis et al. 1991). Artists are often ahead of social scientists in their sensitive observations of social reality, and Tennessee Williams was a prime example. In *Sweet Bird of Youth*, he makes one of the most astute observations about love, sex, power, and social classes: "The world is not divided into rich and poor, or weak and powerful. It is divided into those who enjoy the delights of love, and those who do not."

Little research has been done to link the origins of any specific ideology of love or sex with the powers of competing social classes. That was the puzzle I set out to solve in "The Romantic Heresy" (Lee 1975). I started with the work of Denis de Rougemont (1940).

Denis de Rougemont was well aware of the link between love and class. After tracing the great myth of Tristan and Iseult through history, he linked it to "a conflict between chivalry and feudal society . . . a conflict between two kinds of duty, and even between two 'religions.'" (1940:33). Not being a sociologist, he was not interested in class, and after a brief reference that "courtly love arose as a reaction to the brutal lawlessness of feudal manners" (1940:33) he returned to his focus, the discrediting of romantic love as a heresy. In 1975 I asked:

How did the notion of romantic love become so widely accepted in Western society as a legitimate basis of mate selection? This notion was not an important element of marriage in the European society of ancient and medieval times. It has not been important to marriage in traditional oriental society (Mace 1959:128; Blood 1967:26). It is "diametrically opposed, point by point" to the definition of loving relationship taught by the Christian religion. (Aubert 1965: 454) "Courtly love" or the lovestyle I call mania, replaced the medieval Christian doctrine of parental control over marriage, because mania has all the persuasive power of a religion, and this new religion was more favorable to the interests of a new and ambitious social class than the traditional love ideology of Christianity, which was supported by the ruling elites (compare Protestantism and capitalism in Weber).

I can only summarize my arguments here (see Lee 1975). The troubadours of twelfth-century Provence are the "starting point for all subsequent manifestations of romantic love" (Henriques 1959:84). In the troubadour poetry, the ideology of love I call "mania" ceased to be a misfortune and became defined instead as the ultimate life experience to be sought after (rather than Christian "salvation"). As a modern song puts the troubadour message, "You're nobody until somebody loves you" and the somebody had to be another human, not a deity.

Mania had enormous appeal as an ideology for a newly emerging social class in late medieval Europe: the knights of the courtly society (castle or feudal society), which developed to defend Europe against invaders. Except for the commanders, knights were usually socially displaced single men recruited as boys from the peasant or serf classes, and drawn into an ambivalent social status in the castles or "courts." They did not wish to marry beneath their new rank (by choosing peasant wives), but could not marry upward by choosing wives from the nobility of the castle.

The new doctrines of mania (courtly love as defined especially by Andreas, chaplain of Marie de Champagne) gave the knights a legitimate opening for class advancement: secret courtship with daughters of the nobility. Mania legitimated love and sexual trysts which ignored social considerations of family, class, and state and instead legitimated acts of individual attraction. This quality of mania and its quasi-religious power to overcome social norms is still true today (Dion and Dion 1996:8; Lee 1973).

The state and the upper classes fought this new doctrine, as did the Catholic Church. That battle is immortalized in the great love tragedies, of which Romeo and Juliet is probably more familiar to most than, say, Tristan and Iseult. But rebel youth had some allies. In Romeo and Juliet, both the Nurse and the Friar are of lower social class origin and on the lovers' side. More important, mania had highly effective propagandists-traveling troubadours, poets, and soon, novelists and playwrights.

Pragma was the love ideology of the elite five centuries ago, and it still is, among the "high society" of Western democracies. "Love matches" are frowned on and even forbidden, whenever the match will endanger the family or corporate fortune. Secret love and sex are especially forbidden (they produced bastard children). And still today, pragma is the favored ideology of those college texts (e.g., Hatfield and Rapson 1996) that attempt to persuade students to believe in "realistic" love.

Pragma is the traditional teaching of the churches about marriage, which the Catholic Church attempted to solidify by making it a "sacrament" in the seventeenth century. This family of ideas includes institutionalized monogamy, premarital chastity followed by lifetime marital fidelity, mate selection guided by parents and other adult authorities, social rituals of approval of this choice ("showers," engagement, banns of marriage, a white wedding), and the focus on "family values" such as raising of children.

In "The Romantic Heresy" (1975) I demonstrated the ideological structure of love. "The Romantic Heresy" disappeared like a stone in quicksand, never to be cited in subsequent decades of research. In the *Personality and Social Psychology Bulletin* (Spring 1977: 173–182), I argued that "each lovestyle is an ideology." This article stimulated much "X is correlated with Y" research but only one ideological study (Prasinos and Bennett 1984).

They have never been cited again. Once more, in Sternberg's widely read summary of love research (1988:41–42), I insisted that lovestyles are ideologies. No one paid any attention.

LOVE AND SEX AS CONSUMER GOODS

We have considered some of the broader social aspects of ideologies of lovestyle and sexstyle, but it is important to remember that ideologies affect the personal fate of individuals. The ideology of feminism stimulates the everyday behavior of feminists. Some ideologies can be quite intolerant of others. Fortunately, most modern ideologies of lovestyle and sexstyle are fairly tolerant; we do not burn "sodomites" or brand "adulteresses" any more. Today a believer can be, for example, a capitalist, a Protestant, a feminist, and a lesbian at the same time. However, some ideologies do not make comfortable bedfellows. It is not easy to be a Christian fundamentalist and a homosexual (but there are some!)

Important questions arise out of the interplay of larger ideological belief systems with the daily choices of personal behavior. Except for a few topics such as abortion, the great majority of scientific studies have tended to ignore the issues of politics, power, strategies, and vested interests, which come into play when ideologies are linked with personal choices.

For example, what kind of social class structure facilitates or discourages a ludic lovestyle, or what is the institutional power behind the continuing popularity of manic love? These are research questions worth asking. Or, what are the chances of a would-be lover trapped in poverty and ill health finding and enjoying a ludic-erotic experience? What are the chances of an overworked and underpaid single mother using modern technologies—print ads, telephone personals, computer networks—to find a new lover? What choices and strategies are involved when gay men choose to "out" a prominent but closeted politician or general? (This topic has had some very recent and exciting discussion—but not by social scientists!)

A successful lover cannot merely choose a lovestyle and its associated sexstyle. He or she must learn how to practice the ideologies involved, just as Christians or communists must know how to practice their ideologies. It has also been demonstrated that your choice is more important in affecting the outcome of a relationship than your partner's choice (Morrow 1995:363).

In our consumer society, love is becoming a prime consumer good. Sex already is. There is evidence of the ways in which singles are being manipulated by the language and procedures of dating agencies, phone lines, and print ads (Adelman 1991). At one time, searching for a love or sex partner in the personal ads was regarded as a "deviant activity" to be hidden from all but one's closest friends (Darden 1988). Today advertising is increasingly popular, and users in any major city number in the tens of thousands.

One effect of this increased use is greater tension between the search for erotic experience (which requires visual screening), ludic multiple experiences of love before "making a commitment," and the search for "compatible" partners based on pragmatic demographic variables. For example, some users of a voice mail system, seeking an eros style, will insist on meeting first ("I won't know if I like you until I see you"). Others, of a more pragmatic style, want personal background information first, before agreeing to meet ("What do you do for a living?"). If you don't understand these differences in love ideology, you will simply be confused.

In past centuries a lack of literacy and technology, and the power of a few social institutions such as the church (which censored books), made it difficult for most ordinary people to be aware of a variety of options when choosing a love partner. Most "settled" for whatever reasonably decent match was available to them. Today universal literacy, popular media, and easy access to technology encourage most people to "shop around" for the best possible partner according to their varying definitions of "true love" and "good sex." But since most people are not yet equipped with the ability to distinguish between love and sexstyles, it's rather like the color-blind trying to shop for clothes.

WRITING AN AD FOR A LOVESTYLE/SEXSTYLE

You have only to read or listen to ads by those seeking a love partner to observe the ideological confusion most people suffer as they attempt to describe themselves and the partner they seek. We could compare the difficulties faced by Europeans in choosing their brand of religious ideology between the Reformation and the Counter-Reformation. That choice could mean life or death in the religious wars of the sixteenth century. Finding a lover is hardly a matter of life or death, but making a mistake can result in years of unhappy consequences.

Consider the confusion of someone who advertises for a partner who is "goodlooking." Looks are not merely in the eye of the beholder! The concept of what is "beautiful" varies with the lovestyle. For example, an overweight storgic lover will ask partners to look beneath "skin" and see the person "I really am inside." But the erotic seeker will reply, "I'm sorry, but it doesn't matter what you're like inside. I don't like fat bodies" or beards, or a shaved head, or whatever "skin deep" qualities the erotic lover detests.

On the other hand, we know that an advertiser has an exacting erotic lovestyle when the ad specifies detailed body requirements: "between age 28 and 32, at least 5'10" tall, with blond hair . . ." and so on. Or the seeker may have a clear pragmatic choice of lovestyle: "must be a professional, in an upper income bracket, and never previously married." Or a tactful ludic style: "Married man seeks casual but continuing discreet relationship with a well-established career woman."

Dominant ideologies in other sectors of life naturally influence the way we word our ads. People with traditional religious convictions cannot easily run a ludic ad. Those who share the dominant Western ideology that we call "the belief in progress and technology" will tend to believe that perfectibility is also possible in love. Their ads define the desired partner so narrowly that there may be only one person in a million who fits the bill.

Worst off are the seekers with PIGs—perfectly incompatible goals. This is much the same as the employer who wants an applicant with ten years' experience in the business but who is only 25 years old. A common PIG in search for a partner is "someone who is young and lovely, but with the life experience of an emotionally mature older person." Or a beautiful and clever young woman who is content to be a housewife.

MERMAIDS, CENTAURS: WHAT CAN BE IMAGINED MUST EXIST!

Strange social phenomena have developed around the booming business of advertising for a love partner. In the old days, kings told ambassadors what kind of princess to seek in foreign courts, but the ambassador might bring the king back to reality: "I'm most humbly sorry, your majesty, but if you want a princess to link the Crowns of England and Spain, then she won't be pretty. The daughters of King Charles are notoriously ugly." A typical marriage broker could say much the same things to parents who could afford his services: "Considering your daughter's plain looks, I cannot arrange a handsome match unless you offer a handsome dowry."

Today, most people are writing their own Internet or newspaper ads or voice messages on telephone networks. A tendency has developed to select the desirable qualities from perhaps a half dozen former affairs and roll them all into one person. I'd like Bill's hunky body, Arthur's witty mind, and Jim's love for foreign travel. Since the advertiser has actually experienced all these desired qualities in real people, he or she concludes that somewhere there must be someone who combines them. Fish exist, women exist, why not mermaids?

If this imagined person must exist somewhere, my problem is merely to conduct a search and find this partner. Having written the ad, the would-be lover begins to think the ideal person must exist. Conversely, reading someone else's ad containing my key requirements, I immediately imagine that the advertiser must be the one I am looking for. What disappointment on the blind date! Candidates who "come close" are passed over, because the true soulmate might be just around the corner. This "romantic perfectionism" is similar to what Marx called false consciousness among working-class people who voted for political parties run by employers, a vote clearly not cast in the worker's own class interests. Lovers often use search methods that are not in their own best interest.

Another strange phenomenon arises from the advertising search process. The ad-responder becomes aware that there are "thousands" of other people seeking love, and slips into a "better dealing" mode, withholding more than token commitment to any new partner just in case a more interesting candidate appears in the ads or on the phone network. Since no relationship can "take off" and "go into orbit" without a certain minimum acceleration, the responder to my ad must give me the impression that she or he is definitely interested in me, even while scanning the ads for a better candidate.

Thus, it is entirely possible to find myself believing, after a series of dates, that my search is over and I have found my mate. All that remains is to build up the new relationship. Suddenly and almost without notice, my new partner will break off, because she or he has found someone new in the meet market. After several such experiences, even the most sincere seeker is likely to protect herself by having another date to "fall back on." In a traditional network of friends and townspeople who know each other, such double-dealing is impossible. The cheats quickly develop a bad reputation. But in the anonymous and almost anomic world of the phone and print meet markets, reputations do not stick. No one can be brought to account for their double dealing. It's love in a Teflon world.

So far I haven't included sex in the search, but most would-be lovers have had some sex experience, and naturally want the particular kinds of sexuality they like in their sought-for partner: the smooth skin of A, but the sexual skill-in-bed of B, and the tenderness of C. That makes it all the less likely that one person will be found who is all the desired qualities rolled into one—and what are the chances that this paragon of virtues is already "taken?" Even more disheartening, suppose you meet this person and she or he is free, but YOU do not meet the other's requirements?

As changing economics and technology create whole new social classes (such as the high-tech occupations, or the new class of clerks who work at home with a computer and modem), the choices of love-style will change accordingly. For example, those whose work and lifestyle already predispose them to spend hours at a computer screen find it easy to slip into a modern ludic lovestyle. They shop the Internet for cyberlove and cybersex, and send romantic or sexy e-mail in all directions. Once a visual hookup is generally available, would-be lovers will be able to see the alleged appearance of the respondent—but you'll never be sure if it's a digitally doctored image until you meet.

Perhaps an easier future awaits the pragmatic seeker who "does not expect too much," finds a reasonably suitable partner after a short search, and settles down to "work things out." Asked years later: "How did you know that he was Mr. Right for you?" she replies, with a mix of contentment and resignation: "Who says George was Mr. Right? He was Mr. Stop Here."

LAUNCHING A RELATIONSHIP

Eventually, a relationship must be put in motion, from first encounter to eventual commitment, or break off. Implementing a chosen ideology of love and sex can require more skill today than was exercised by the most successful matchmakers of bygone eras. Amateur wooing and courtship is as obsolete in the modern meet market as amateur business skills are in the global marketplace.

Each kind of lover must assemble particular resources or fail for their lacking. For example, a successful erotic lover (always recalling that in another partnership the same person could be pragmatic or storgic) must have a high level of self-confidence (Lee 1973:44; Mallandain and Davies 1994:557). If things don't go well in a newly launched relationship, this self-confidence is in danger of being deeply shaken. If the seeker meets a partner who is lovely to behold, but does not feel a reciprocal attraction, or finds the longed-for sexual intimacy postponed, the erotic lover may slip into manic fixation. You'd better have good friends and enjoyable work ready to prevent obsessive pre-occupation with thoughts of the beloved.

As various social forces (such as the market, education, and migration) differentiate the resources and powers of individuals, the role of resources in implementing a love relationship becomes critical. Most working-class people of America in 1900, to use an example, had roughly the same limited resources for finding a partner. A single new invention could alter those resources. Prior to the general availability of the automobile, only those who owned a horse and carriage could easily contemplate courtship of a partner more than a day's walk away.

In a multicultural, highly technological society, it is possible to consider potential partners many miles distant and from social backgrounds (race, religion, language, and so on) very different from one's own. Regardless of the most kindly intentions, newly encountered lovers are frequently pitched into a competition of resources. Peter Blau (1964:76ff.) first showed us that any successful love relationship involves negotiations between rival powers, but power is still a topic few lovers tackle head on.

For example, Blau agreed with Waller (1951) that "the partner who has the least interest in the continuation of the relationship has the most power over its direction." Thus, it is always wise for a would-be lover not to "come on too strong . . . the lover who does not express unconditional affection early has the advantage" (Blau 1964:78). Unfortunately, Blau thought of love as only one kind, and the contest for control actually varies greatly with the lovestyle and its associated sexstyle.

Perhaps the condom comes to mind as the most obvious example of a device that can affect success in practicing an ideology such as ludus, but there are less obvious examples. Consider "call display." In the old days, a ludic lover could make numerous phone calls to a partner who was playing "hard to get". Numerous calls suggests more intense interest in the partner than the ludic lover would wish to admit. But his persistence is not given away, as there is no way of proving who is making the unanswered calls. Today, call display reduces the lover's control over evidence of interest in the beloved. Imagine what visual-display phones will do to the erotic lovestyle! The lover will have to shave, or put on makeup, just to make a phone call!

Lovers who can afford these new resources will have advantages over those who cannot—if they understand how to exploit the resources for various lovestyles. Ironically, Fein and Schneider's recent bestseller, *The Rules* (1997), which time-tested secrets for capturing the heart of Mr. Right, tells young women to abandon feminism and go back to grandma's power-plays, but like almost all guides, it still treats love as if it were only one kind!

No wonder Nate Penn and Lawrence Rose have already published *The Code, Time-tested Secrets for Getting What You Want from Women Without Marrying Them* (1997). In these last years of the twentieth century, the power struggle of conflicting ideologies of love/sex is reaching fever pitch in the bars and bedrooms!

THE MARKET VALUE OF MANIA

Manic love keeps the thoughts and even the body of the lover very busy. As the mind becomes more obsessed and jealous, the body becomes sleepless and indifferent to food. The lover waits for the phone to ring or calls again if the partner has not returned a message in a short time. Mania consumes enormous amounts of personal energy. The manic lover actually enjoys being miserable. "I love you so much I'm glad to be sad over you."

I argued in "The Romantic Heresy" (1975) that mania was at least as influential over the everyday actions of young people in Western societies as science or religion or politics or other ideological systems. All the replication research on my lovestyles shows that there are impressive amounts of manic thinking among the samples.

Of course, mania is an equal color of love with the others, and there are advantages in experiencing a manic relationship. The lover is drawn out of him or herself into a world of feelings probably never known before. For the first time, the lover discovers just how deeply she or he is capable of feeling for another person. Mania rouses full expression of emotional capacity. It can be good to know you are capable of such intense feeling for another person.

For those who control the resources of a society, there are also advantages in keeping the underclass preoccupied with their feelings of love rather than their resentment at getting less than a fair share of consumer goods. For the deeply engulfed manic lover, a feeling of pain and even despair is reassurance of still being alive.

As modern societies are polarized into overclass and underclass, those who understand the resources required for each lovestyle will be tempted into schemes for the social engineering of love. Just as the elite class of the supposedly classless Soviet Union manipulated ideology to persuade the masses not to revolt against the great privileges enjoyed by the Commissars, so the new technological elite will be tempted to use the centralized control of television, publishing and film, and even the new corporatist universities, to captivate the underclass with visions of love. It may even become possible for ordinary people to enjoy "virtual love" by cheap Internet connections, but the real joy of person-to-person love connections will be as restricted to the elite, as holiday resorts were to deserving Commissars.

One innovation would be lotteries where the prize is not a great sum of money, but an opportunity for great love. (Some TV love-game programs have already provided a model.) The resources of commerce and technology could be put at the disposal of the lottery winner, to help him or her find their perfect beloved, in the same way that contemporary lotteries allow the poor a chance for riches.

Would-be erotic lovers would be encouraged to believe that "true love" can overcome all. The myth of fated love will become reality with the resources of global communication in the control of elites. The elites will be able to actualize such love whenever they wish, by travel and the most sophisticated computer-matching of partners. Even as I write, a billionaire has a staff of Boston "matchmakers" screening hundreds of women in my city and many others to find his perfect mate (*Toronto Star*, February 1997). The planet does not have the resources to provide such happiness for all, so lotteries could throw the underclass an occasional "big win."

RELATIONSHIPS: THE WATER WE SWIM IN

The word "relationship" has been used numerous times in this chapter, but the way it is used on the eve of the millennium is not the way it was used in former times. Our grandparents, and generations before them, did not "have a relationship" with their spouses; they courted, engaged, and wed—for better or worse. Today, we marry for better or else; and we are just as likely to "live with" someone as to marry. The term "my ex" would have baffled a Victorian but is quite commonplace today, and many of us have several "ex's." Not only do we have TV programs where people meet and "rate the date," but we have programs where couples break up their relationship in front of both a live and broadcast audience!

The use of "relationship" as a serious, meaningful term in the language of love, rather than as a joke, came into our culture during the Second World War. At that time, countless engagements and marriages had to be "put on hold for the duration." The word "relationship" was then more of a comic term than a serious way to describe a commitment leading to marriage. Today relationship has become the serious term, and the new comic term is love connection (as in the TV program of that name).

In the hit Hollywood movie, *Ball of Fire* (Samuel Goldwyn, 1942), Gary Cooper plays a naive professor who falls in love with a gangster's girlfriend. *Ball of Fire* was one of the last of a genre of Hollywood films that dated back to the Keystone Cops, a genre that did not survive the war: the screwball comedy. In this movie, Cooper presents his unlikely new girlfriend with a cheap engagement ring, with the professorial words "It's time we clarified our relationship."

Since those comic days, the term "relationship" has taken on a pseudoserious meaning, but only "for the duration." If "our relationship does not work out" then, as comics now put it, "I'm out of here" and on to the next. My students talk about the Big C word. They don't mean Cancer. They mean Commitment.

WHAT HOPE FOR GENERATION X?

One of the major social issues of the coming decades will be the question of who will be allowed to fully understand and implement the theory of lovestyles. If social forces move us toward a more egalitarian society, then most young people will be educated in lovestyles and provided with sufficient resources to pursue their chosen style(s). The currently blossoming facilities for love connections will expand and become cheaper, available to the masses. If the contrary trend continues—toward a more polarized society—then the relatively cheap facilities now available will probably remain in place, but efforts to clarify lovestyles and teach youngsters how to act on them will be suppressed. Instead, the confusing one-kind-of-love propaganda of the Hatfields and Rapsons (1996) will flourish in the media and in education, assuring that happy love relationships become increasingly rare. Sophisticated facilities that might assist lovers will be available only to those who can command the necessary consumer power.

Consider those facilities. In your city as in mine, tens of thousands of men and women may be already enrolled in various telephone networks that offer categories from "Casual sex" to "Long-term re-lationships" to "Kinky times." Check your local Yellow Pages directory. In mine, there are more pages listing "escorts" than there are listing lawyers. Local newspapers run "personal ads" under numerous cate-gories by sex, age, and even "seeking the same." In your local bookstore, count the books under "Self-help" that offer to help you find true love, or get over your last partner and move on to the next. At last count I found 120 titles, ranging from *If I'm So Wonderful Why am I Still Single?* to *Fifty Ways to Find a Lover* to *Are You the One for Me?* to *How to Fall Out of Love.*

As would-be young lovers attempt to navigate their way through this welter of facilities, their repeated unsuccessful efforts (or those that succeed only for months rather than years) will keep them busy—and poor in both happy love and spending power. The costs of some of the existing facilities, running to $3.00 per minute on the phone, or $100 for a print ad, are already impressive. It is not unusual to find high school students who have become addicted to the search process and saddled with staggering telephone bills for using 976 lines.

The demythologizing of love could help reduce the suffering of all those who have moved along the assembly line of child socialization in our notoriously dysfunctional families, directionless schools, and mindless, sound-bite/photo-op media. Millions of young men and wo-men are seeking to repair their "wounded child" (Hendrix 1992:12; Sills 1993:5) by seeking assurance that they are lovable in a "relationship." One attempt after another fails with accelerating speed. The expected duration of living together or being married is now to the point where couples celebrate their first year! The injured crawl out of the trash and try again, seeking love from each hopeful new encounter.

Can an analysis of lovestyles and sexstyles address this aggravating social problem and widespread personal trouble (Mills 1959:1)? I believe it can, first, by reminding the unhappy combatants in the battlefields of sex and love—the singles bars and the personal columns, the telephone networks, introduction agencies and Internet listings—that there are competing choices of ideologies as well as partners. These ideologies have been constructed and mystified into the taken-for-granted; you can demystify and deconstruct them. When your partner asks, "Do you really love me?" you can ask, "In which love and sex style do you intend that really to apply?"

THE PROBLEM OF THE POOL

If ordinary people, and not only the elite, are to benefit from the possible miracles of technology in providing real opportunities for love of the varied kinds each individual lover may seek, then technology must be applied to solve the problem of the pool. This will not only be costly—thus reducing the disproportionate riches of the overclass—it will also be contrary to the vested interests of the overclass.

What is the problem of the pool? Many adults have long forgotten their high school arithmetic, especially permutations and combinations. They forget that if you roll one die, the chances of getting a six are one in six. If you roll two, the chances of getting two sixes are 6 multiplied by 6, or 1 in 36. Roll five dice, and the chance of five sixes is 1 in 7,776. Add just one more 6, and your chances of six sixes are now 1 in 46,656! The odds rise geometrically against you, with each die you add.

Similar odds face a lover seeking uncorrelated qualities in a partner, when each occurs in only one in every N persons in the population. For example, suppose you seek a partner who is between the ages of 25 and 30, is slim and blond, has a college degree in Management, and loves wilderness canoeing. There are measurable odds for each of these requirements. Check any clothing store to find what proportion of young males or females are the waist size you consider slim. A hairstylist can tell you the approximate proportion of blonds in the population. Federal or state statistics will tell you about education levels, and the population that is single and age 25–30. Trade magazines such as Canoe and Kayak will give you a reasonable estimate of avid canoeists.

There is a weak connection between some of the requirements—slim people are more likely to be canoeists than fat people—but no particular connection between slim/fat and a degree in Management, or blond and college-educated. We can treat your five requirements as essentially independent of each other, like the roll of five fair dice. If the odds for the five requirements are 1 in 5, 1 in 3, 1 in 10, 1 in 4, and 1 in 20 (only a tiny part of the population is into wilderness canoeing), then finding that wonderful man or woman of your dreams is a chance of the multiple of these odds, or 1 in 12,000. In your city there are perhaps ten or twenty candidates for your affection!

Suppose you add just one more "requirement," such as a partner who is a Catholic. Being a dedicated Catholic is not connected to being blond, or slim, or a graduate in Management, or a canoeist; there is a weak negative correlation to age. Suppose in your town one-quarter of the population is Catholic. Now you want a Catholic aged 25–30 who is slim and blond, holds a degree in Management, and loves wilderness canoeing. Your odds just jumped from 1 in 12,000 to 1 in 48,000 (12,000 x 4; see Hendrix 1992:14; Lee 1973:3; Wolf 1992:13).

The potential of modern computer systems such as the Internet to create large pools for lovers to draw from is patently obvious. But will it be in the interests of those controlling such systems to apply them in this way? Who would bear the costs? Only a society that collectively resolved that finding enjoyable love relationships was as important to the public good as, say, building billion-dollar B-2 airplanes, would allocate the resources necessary to solve the problem of the pool.

LOVE AND SEX AT THE LEVEL OF "GRAND THEORY"

Considerable research has been done on the history and social construction of sexual styles (ranging from Bullough 1976 to Michel Foucault 1978–1988). Yet, so far, there is a great reluctance to deal with sexstyles in terms of class, politics, and power, in the same way as we use those tools of analysis on other ideological systems such as Communism or Christianity. For example, few scholars are investigating the vested interest certain corporations have in maintaining chastity and monogamy along with an agapic or storgic lovestyle, while the sales and profits of other corporations benefit from promoting ludic love and sexual permissiveness.

One of the few theories in this field is Wilkinson's "sexual blockage theory" a narrowly focused theory that argued that social norms artificially limit sexual satisfaction, resulting in increased interest in "romantic" notions (Wilkinson 1978). In *Getting Sex* (1978), I noted that the theoretical supply of sex partners is immense, yet society has constructed numerous barriers so effective that the majority of the population may never enjoy as much sexual pleasure as they want. In the same year, Betzold (1978) built on Freud to show how marriage is socially constructed to confine and restrain libido and contribute productive work instead.

"Personal best" in American culture may be defined in terms of career success, or in sports or the arts, or in any field where there are contests and awards, ceremonies and honors for achievement. But it is rare indeed for our culture to celebrate a person who has achieved his personal best in a lovestyle. Indeed, such honors are reserved almost exclusively for the winners in agape, like Mother Teresa. We remember Lord Bertrand Russell for his mathematical genius or his peacemaking, but he wanted to be remembered for his achievements in love (Russell 1967:1). "Of all the forms of caution, caution in love is the most fatal for human happiness," Russell warned.

UTOPIA OR DYSTOPIA OF LOVE?

A comprehensive theory to link language, behavioral norms, and ideology across love, sex, and productive work in a capitalist society was the goal of Herbert Marcuse. His *Eros and Civilization* (1955) opens with the "politics" of love. When I read Marcuse in 1969, I began playing in the margins with his paradigms, matching storge, ludus, and mania with various formulations of his pleasure and reality principles. Marcuse helped me to break out of the conventional wisdom of one true love.

His schematic analyses of love and sex helped me to realize that love was structured as primaries and secondaries. I realized that mania, despite its pervasive influence in our society, is a secondary, not primary, form of love. Although Marcuse does not identify and name different styles of loving, it was clear to me, once I had identified ludus and storge, that they are the styles that serve as Marcuse's "restraints." They prevent eros from breaking out and disrupting civilization. The results of such restraint are also anticipated in Marcuse. Mania is madcap love when eros is restrained unsuccessfully by ludus; agape is compassionate love when eros is serenely restrained by storge.

Marcuse was optimistic about the future of eros. He believed that eros would break its bonds as modern society developed the technology to facilitate more and more "phantasies" of "polymorphous sexuality"—literally, imaginative thoughts about many kinds of sexual loving. I, too, was a sixties optimist, and I scribbled on page 54 of my copy of *Eros and Civilization*: "There will be no further need for bitter lessons about love out of control—no more ideology of manic love, once eros is freed."

Marcuse believed that the "sexual revolution" of the sixties for the first time in history permitted "phantasy-making" on a wide social scale. Until then, it had been the exclusive preserve of a tiny privileged class of people with the leisure to enjoy their fantasies (1955:119). This expansion of fantasy would finally restrain "one of the most protected values of modern culture—that of productivity."

Marcuse was deeply opposed to the ideology of the "work ethic" and "productivity" in our culture. He believed this ideology not only limited our opportunities in the economic sphere; it also devastated our opportunities for love. Marcuse demonstrated just how pervasive was the hegemony of the productivity ethic, by noting that the other most important ideologist of love and sexuality in his time, Erich Fromm, actually defined his "true love" as productive love (Fromm 1963:18).

Although Marcuse thinks in terms of reaction to Freudian paradigms, his schema of love and sex is ideological at root—including his analysis of the underlying myths that energize any ideology (in his case, Orpheus and Narcissus: 1955, 132 ff). But for all his imagination and optimism, Marcuse, like Fromm, remained stuck in the notion that there is only one kind of "true love." He recognized that our culture contains other ideologies of love, but only one kind was really love. For Marcuse, it was a love that demands "enduring and responsible relations" founded on "a union of sexuality with affection."

Locked into a unidimensional concept of "true love," he hoped for a transformation of this true love into a "fuller Eros" (1955:139)—a true love that is truer than true! This fuller Eros would "eroticize the entire personality" (1955:164) breaking free of the restraints of a repressive, production-centered civilization. Marcuse held so firmly to the notion that there can only be one love that he concludes that "Eros and Agape" will be one and the same in his new utopia, when Eros breaks free of the "repressive definition of Eros" first introduced into Western culture by Plato (Marcuse 1955:169).

We are in an age of global economies, not expanding playful and erotic fantasies, except to the extent that corporations are able to expropriate fantasy away from individual lovers, produce it in mass versions, and sell it back to the lovers as consumers. Individual lovers in the market economy are told by the dominant global market ideology that they must work faster and harder than ever, to compete with the dragons of the Pacific Rim.

If these productive people fulfill their market calling, they are permitted to enjoy a few hours a week consuming fantasies that have been expropriated from their imaginations and packaged as discos with fabulous lighting, video pornography stocked with luscious models, colorful romantic movies from Merchant and Ivory, thousands of sex workers in every large city, and the semblance of intimate conversation on the Internet.

The resulting hunger for intimacy is obvious everywhere. For many, the slaking of erotic imagination by adult toys and games is no better than drinking salt water to quench thirst.

THE VICTORY OF THE MARKET ECONOMY

The dominant stream of ideology in love and sex today seems to be exactly the same as in politics and economics: the market economy, in which one looks for the best possible deal and measures love by its outcome, and especially, by its "productivity," not its existential pleasure. Most popular guides (James and Schlesinger 1987; Page 1988) include exercises and charts to enable the reader to sort their choices and rate potential partners. You are guided to list specific compatibilities, as well as to rate the priority of each, and then to "score" your partner, perhaps with a 1 for low and a 5 for high, on each item.

As for sexstyles, no one has yet (to my knowledge) proposed an equivalent rating scheme to help users of the constantly expanding singles' meet-markets and sexworker services in large cities. No doubt, an appropriate market service will soon be available to guide consumers to the most promising service providers.

Stumbling toward practical solutions without concern for ideology, entrepreneurs are now developing dating agencies for busy people. "We'll do the searching for you." There are fifty-five such agencies in my province of Canada. Recruiting a large enough pool is a prime goal (for reasons already explained), and every technology is now being bent to the task-computer tabulating, videotaped profiles of clients, categorizations by major type selectors, and circulation by e-mail of information on each new addition to the pool, who just might, at long last, be the love you're waiting for.

CONCLUSION

Many would like to think that the battle between the ideologies of Communism and capitalism is over now that the Cold War has ended. Whether or not that is true, it is certainly the case that the battle stemming from medieval times, between competing ideologies of love and sex, has continued into modern times and will continue into the next millennium.

Indeed, this contest of ideologies has become ever more complex and is fought on more and more fronts, now that we have new ideas about sexism and sexual harassment, about women's liberation and gay liberation and even "singles liberation," about "safe sex," "family values," and "the homosexual agenda." The fact that some of these ideas must be put in quotation marks emphasizes the new complexity of the conflict that rages in politics and church and school and home.

In spite of the length of this chapter, I have barely begun to discuss the specifics of lovestyles and sexstyles, such as the connection of mania and pragma to a safer sexstyle or to computer arrangements for casual sex. And that's only a contemporary specific—there's a vast field of research for lovestyle-sexstyle patterns in ancient, medieval and early modern societies, and an equally vast field of cross cultural studies. Many existing studies need to be repeated to get rid of the idea of a single true love.

Anxious lovers in the next millennium await our best scientific efforts to understand this most beautiful and essential of human activities.

REFERENCES

Ackerly, J. R. *My Father and Myself*. New York: Harcourt, Brace, 1968.

Adelman, M. B. "Mediated Channels for Mate Seeking." *Critical Studies in Mass Communication* 8(3):273-289, 1991.

Adler, N. L., and S. S. Hendrick, "Relationships Between Contraceptive Behavior and Love Attitudes, Sex Attitudes and Self-esteem." *Journal of Counseling and Development* 70:302-308, 1991.

Aubert, Vilhelm. *The Hidden Society*. London: Bedminster Press, 1965.

Bailey, W.; C. Hendrick; and S. S. Hendrick. "Relationship of Sex and Gender Role to Love, Sexual Attitudes, and Self-esteem." *Sex Roles* 16:637–648, 1987.

Beall, A. E. "The Social Construction of Love." *Journal of Social and Personal Relationships* 12(3):417–438,1995.

Bennett, H. S. *The Pastons and Their England*. Cambridge: Cambridge University Press, 1922.

Berger, Peter, and T. Luckmann. *The Social Construction of Reality*. New York: Doubleday, 1965.

Betzold, Michael. *Sexual Scarcity: The Marital Mistake*. Detroit: Human Press, 1978.

Bierhoff, H., and K. Klein. "Dimensions of Love: Development of a German Scale for Measuring Love Styles." *Zeitschrift fur Differentielle und Diagnostische Psychologie* 12(1):53–71, 1991.

Blau, Peter. *Exchange and Power in Social Life*. New York: John Wiley, 1964.

Blood, Robert. *Love Match and Arranged Marriage*. Glencoe, Ill.: Free Press, 1967.

Blumstein, P., and P. Kollack. *Annual Review of Sociology* 14:467–490, 1988.

Booth-Butterfield, M. "Attributional Patterns for the Expression of Love." *Communication Reports* 7(2):119–129,1994.

Borello, G. M., and B. Thompson. "A Note on the Validity of Lee's Typology of Love." *Journal of Psychology* 124(6):639–44, 1990.

Borscheid, Peter. "Romantic Love or Material Interest: Choosing Partners in 19th Century Germany." *Journal of Family History* 11(2):157–168, 1986.

Boswell, John. *Christianity, Social Tolerance and Homosexuality*. Chicago: University of Chicago Press, 1980.

Bullough, Vern. *Sexual Variance in Society and History*. New York: John Wiley, 1976.

Burns, David. *Intimate Connections*. New York: Signet, 1985.

Carnelley, K., and R. Janoff. "Optimism About Love Relationships." *Journal of Social and Personal Relationships* 9(1):5–20, 1992.

Casler, Lawrence. "Toward a Re-evaluation of Love." In M. E. Curtin (ed.), *Symposium on Love*, 1973, pp. 1–36.

Cho, W., and S. Cross. "Taiwanese Love Styles and Their Association with Self-esteem and Relationship Quality. *Genetic, Social and General Psychology Monographs* 12(3):283–309, 1995.

Christensen, Jerome. "The Romantic Movement at the End of History." *Critical Inquiry* 20:3: 452–476, 1994.

Cimbalo, R., and D. O. Novell. "Sex Differences in Romantic Love Attitudes of College Students." *Psychology Reports* 73:15–18, 1993.

Clark, M. S., and H. T. Reis. "Interpersonal Processes in Close Relationships." *Annual Review of Psychology* 39:609–672,1988.

Collins, N. L., and S. J. Read. "Adult Attachment, Working Models, and Relationship Quality in Dating Couples." *Journal of Personality and Social Psychology* 58:644–663, 1990.

Cramer, D. "Dimensions of Romantic Love in British Female Adolescents." *Journal of Social Psychology* 133:411–413, 1993.

Curtin, M. E. *Symposium on Love.* New York: Behavioral Publications, 1973.

Darden, D. K. "Using the Personal Ads: A Deviant Activity?" *Deviant Behavior* 9(4):383–400, 1988.

Davis, K. E., and H. Latty-Mann. "Love Styles and Relationship Quality: A Contribution to Validation." *Journal of Social and Personal Relationships* 4:409–428, 1987.

Davis, K.; M. Leijenaar; and J. Oldersma (eds.). *The Gender of Power.* Newbury Park, Calif.: Sage, 1991.

De Angelis, Barbara. *Are You the Right One for Me?* New York: Dell, 1992.

de Rougemont, Denis. *Love in the Western World.* New York: Pantheon, 1940.

Dion, K., and K. Dion. "Individualistic and Collectivistic Perspectives on Gender and the Cultural Context of Love." *Journal of Social Issues* 49(3):53–69, 1993a.

———. "Gender and Ethnocultural Comparisons in Styles of Loving." *Psychology of Women Quarterly* 17(4):463–473, 1993b.

———. "Cultural Perspectives on Romantic Love." *Personal Relationships* 3:5–17, 1996.

Dollimore, John. *Sexual Dissidence.* Oxford: Clarendon Press, 1991.

Domhoff, G. W., and H. B. Ballard. *C. Wright Mills and the Power Elite.* New York: Free Press, 1968.

Feeney, J. A., and P. Noller. "Attachment Style as a Predictor of Adult Romantic Relationships." *Journal of Personality and Social Psychology* 58(2):281–291, 1990.

Fehr, B. "A Prototype Analysis of the Concepts of Love and Commitment." *Journal of Personality and Social Psychology* 55:557–579, 1988.

Fein, E., and S. Schneider. *The Rules: The Time-tested Secrets for Capturing the Heart of Mr. Right.* New York: Warner, 1997.

Feingold, A. "Gender Differences in Mate Selection Preferences." *Psychological Bulletin* 112:123–139, 1992.

Feuer, Lewis. *Ideology and the Ideologists.* Oxford: Blackwell, 1975.

Finck, H. T. *Primitive Love and Love Stories.* New York: Scribner's, 1889.

Foucault, Michel. *The History of Sexuality.* New York: Hurley, 1978–1988.

Fromm, Erich. *The Art of Loving.* New York: Bantam, 1963.

Fukuyama, Francis. *The End of History*. New York: Free Press, 1992.

Giddens, Anthony. *Central Problems in Social Theory*. London: MacMillan, 1979.

Goode, W. "The Theoretical Importance of Love." *American Sociological Review* 24:38–47, 1959.

Gosselin, C. C. "Personality and Sexual Differences in Sado-masochistic Women." *Personality and Individual Differences* 12:11–16, 1991.

Greenfield, Sidney. "Some Sociological Consequences of Proposed Alternatives to Romantic Love." In M. E. Curtin (ed.), *Symposium on Love*, 1973, pp. 53–67.

Guerrero, L. K. "Patterns of Touch and Touch Avoidance Across Romantic Relationship Stages." *Journal of Nonverbal Behavior* 18(2):137–153, 1994.

Harris, M. B. "Is Love Seen as Different for the Other?" *Journal of Applied Social Psychology* 20:1209–1224, 1990.

Hatfield, E. "Passionate and Companionate Love." In R. J. Sternberg (ed.), *The Psychology of Love*, 1988, pp. 191–217.

Hatfield, E., and R. L. Rapson. "Passionate Love, Sexual Desire." *Archives of Sexual Research* 16:259–278, 1987a.

———. "The Relationship of Sex and Gender Roles to Love, Sexual Attitudes and Self Esteem." *Sex Roles* 16:637–648,1987b.

———. *Love and Sex: Cross Cultural Perspectives*. Toronto: Allyn and Bacon, 1996.

Hatfield, E., and G. W. Walster. *A New Look at Love*. New York: University Press of America, 1978.

Hatkoff, T. S., and T. E. Lasswell. "Male-Female Similarities and Differences in Conceptualizing Love. International Conference on Love and Attraction." In M. Cook and G. Wilson (eds.), *Love and Attraction*. Oxford: Pergamon, 1979, pp. 221–227.

Hazan, C. and P. Shaver. "Romantic Love as an Attachment Process." *Journal of Personality and Social Psychology* 52:511–524, 1987.

Hendrick, C., and S. Hendrick. "A Theory and Method of Love." *Journal of Personal and Social Psychology* 50:392–402, 1986.

———. "Multidimensionality of Sexual Attitudes." *Journal of Sex Research* 23:502–526, 1987.

———. "Research on Love—Does It Measure Up?" *Journal of Personality and Social Psychology* 56:784–794, 1989.

———. "A Relation-Specific Version of the Love Attitudes Scale." *Journal of Social Behavior and Personality* 5(4):239–254, 1990.

———. *Romantic Love*. Newbury Park, Calif.: Sage, 1992.

Hendrick, S. "Romantic Relationships, Love, Satisfaction and Staying Together." *Journal of Personality and Social Psychology* 54:980–988, 1988.

Hendrix, H. *Keeping the Love You Find*. New York: Pocket Books, 1992.

Henriques, Fernando. *Love in Action*. London: Panther, 1959.

Hobart, C. W. "Incidence of Romanticism in Courtship." *Social Forces* 5:361–365, 1958.

Hoefnagel, A. "The Impact of the Industrial Revolution on the Ideas of the English Romantic Movement: The Case of Samuel Coleridge." *Sociologische Gids* 25(4):262–272, 1978.

————. "The Impact of the Industrial Revolution on the Ideas of the English Romantic Movement: The Case of Thomas Carlysle." *Sociologische Gids* 26(5):34–53, 1979.

Holleran, Andrew. *Nights in Aruba.* New York: New American Library, 1983.

Hotchner, B. "Contemporary American Sex Shocks." International Conference on Love and Attraction, Wales, pp. 347–351, 1978.

Hunter, M. S. "A Scale to Measure Love Addiction." *Psychological Reports* 48:582, 1981.

Illorz, E. "Reason Within Passion—Love in Women's Magazines." *Critical Studies in Mass Communication* (3):231–248, 1991.

James, John, and Ibis Schlesinger. *Are You the Right One for Me?* New York: Addison-Wesley, 1987.

Jankowiak, W. R., and E. F. Fischer. "A Cross-Cultural Perspective on Romantic Love." *Ethnology* 31:149–155, 1992.

Kelly, G. A. *The Psychology of Personal Constructs.* New York: Norton, 1956

Klein, R., and H. Bierhoff. "Lee's Lovestyles and Their Relationship to the Concrete Content of a Relationship." *Gruppendynamik* 22(2):189–206, 1991.

Lantz, H. R. "Romantic Love in the Pre-modern Period." *Journal of Social History* 15(3):349–370, 1980.

Lasswell, M. E., and N. M. Lobsenz. *Styles of Loving.* New York: Doubleday, 1980.

Lasswell, T. E., and M. E. Lasswell. "I Love You but I'm Not in Love with You." *Journal of Marriage and Family Counseling* 30:638–642, 1976.

Le, M. "Lovestyles and Attachment Styles Compared." *Journal of Social and Personal Relationships* 5(4):439–471, 1988.

Leak, G. K. "Relationship Between Religious Orientation and Love Styles, Sexual Attitudes and Sexual Behaviors." *Journal of Psychology and Theology* 21(4):315–318, 1993.

Lee, J. A. "A Typology of Love." Unpublished thesis, University of Sussex, 600 pp., 1970.

————. *Colours of Love.* Toronto: New Press, 1973.

————. "The Styles of Loving." *Psychology Today* October, 1974.

————. "The Romantic Heresy." *Canadian Review of Sociology and Anthropology* 2(4):514–528, 1975.

————. *Colours of Love.* Toronto: General, 1976.

————. "A Typology of Styles of Loving." *Personality and Social Psychology Bulletin* 3(2):173–182, 1977.

————. *Getting Sex.* Toronto: General, 1978.

————. "Social Organization of Sexual Risk." *Alternative Lifestyles* 2(1):69–100, 1979.

————. "Lovestyles." In R. J. Sternberg (ed.), *The Psychology of Love,* 1988, pp. 38–67.

Leon, J. J. "Love Styles Among University Students in Mexico." *Psychological Reports* 74(1):307–310, 1994.

————. "Love Styles Among Latino Community College Students in Los Angeles." *Psychological Reports* 77(2):527–530, 1995.

Luhman, Niklas. *Love as Passion: The Codification of Intimacy.* Cambridge: Cambridge University Press, 1986.

Mace, David, and Vera Mace. *Marriage East and West*. New York: Doubleday, 1959.

Mallandain, I., and M. Davies. "The Colors of Love: Personality Correlates of Love Styles." *Personality and Individual Differences* 17(4):557–560, 1994.

Mannheim, Karl. *Ideology and Utopia*. New York: Harcourt Brace, 1936.

Marcuse, Herbert. *Eros and Civilization*. New York: Doubleday, 1955.

Mathes, E. W. "Nine Colors of Romantic Love?" *Psychological Reports* 47:371–376, 1980.

Matsui, Y. "Love Styles and Developmental Stages in Romantic Love." *Japanese Journal of Psychology* 64(5):335–342,1993.

Mendelson, S. H. "Marriage in the Upper Gentry Family in 17th Century England." *Past and Present* 85:126–135, 1979.

Mills, C. W. *The Sociological Imagination*. New York: Oxford University Press, 1959.

Morrow, G. D. "Individual and Partner Love Styles." *Journal of Social and Personal Relationships* 12(3):363–387, 1995.

Murray, Stephen O. *American Gay*. Chicago: University of Chicago Press, 1996.

Murstein, B. I. "Mate Selection in the 1970s." *Journal of Marriage and Family* 42:777–792, 1980.

———. "A Taxonomy of Love." In R. J. Sternberg (ed.), *The Psychology of Love*. New Haven, Conn.: Yale University Press, 1988, pp. 13–37.

———. "Lovestyles in the United States and France: A Cross Cultural Comparison." *Journal of Social and Clinical Psychology* 10(1):37–46, 1991.

Nakamura, M. "Determinants of Love Styles and Relational Evaluations in Heterosexual Involvement of College Students." *Japanese Journal of Experimental Social Psychology* 31(2):132–146, 1991.

Neto F. "Love Styles Among Portuguese Students." *Journal of Psychology* 128(5):613–616, 1994.

Page, Susan. *If I'm So Wonderful Why Am I Still Single?* New York: Bantam, 1988.

Parsons, Talcott. *The Social System*. New York: Free Press, 1951.

Penn, N., and L. Rose. *The Code, Time-tested Secrets for Getting What You Want from Women Without Marrying Them*. New York: Simon and Schuster, 1997.

Philbrick, J. L., and J. J. Leon. "Change in College Students' Love Styles." *Psychological Reports* 69(3):912–914, 1991.

Pistole, C. "College Students' Ended Love Relationships: Attachment Style and Emotion." *Journal of College Student Development* 36(1):53–60, 1995.

Plamenatz, John. *Ideology*. New York: Macmillan, 1970.

Poplawski, W. T. "Adult Altruism." *Psychologia* 29:197–213, 1986.

Prasinos, S., and I. T. Bennett. "The Existential Context of Lovestyles." *Journal of Humanistic Psychology* 24(1):95–112, 1984.

Prentice, D. S. "Romantic Attitudes of American College Students." *Psychological Reports* 53:815–822, 1983.

Raciti, M., and S. S. Hendrick. "The Relationship Between Eating Disorders and Love and Sex Attitudes." *Sex Roles* 27:553–564, 1992.

Reiss, I. L. "Toward a Sociology of the Heterosexual Love Relationship." *Marriage and Family Living* 22:139–145, 1960.

———. "Some Observations on Ideology and Sexuality in America." *Journal of Marriage and the Family* 43(2):271–283, 1981.

Rejai, Mostafa. "Ideology." In P. P. Winer (ed.), *Dictionary of the History of Ideas*. New York: Scribner's Sons, 1973, pp. 552–559.

Richardson, D. R.; N. Medvin; and G. Hammock. "Lovestyles, Relationship Experience and Sensation Seeking, a Test of Validity." *Personality and Individual Differences* 9:645–651, 1988.

Rifkin, J. *The End of Work*. New York: Scribner's Sons, 1994.

Rimmer, Robert. *Proposition 31*. New York: Signet, 1973.

Roseham, M. F. "Liking, Loving and Styles of Loving." *Psychological Reports* 42:1243–1246, 1978.

Rotenberg, K., and S. Korol. "The Role of Loneliness and Gender in Individuals' Love Styles." *Journal of Social Behavior and Personality* 10(3):537–546, 1996.

Rubin, Z. "The Measurement of Romantic Love." *Journal of Personality and Social Psychology* 16:265–273, 1970.

———. *Liking and Loving*. New York: Holt Rinehart, 1973.

Russell, Lord Bertrand. *Autobiography*. New York: Bantam, 1967.

Sandor, D. "Love, An Investigation." Unpublished thesis, Department of Psychology, University of Melbourne, 1982.

Sarwer, D. "Sexual Aggression and Love Styles—An Exploratory Study." *Archives of Sexual Behavior* 22(3):265–275, 1993.

Shaver, P. "A Biased Overview of the Study of Love." *Journal of Social and Personal Relationships* 5(4):473–501, 1988.

Shaver, P.; S. Wu; and J. C. Schwartz. "Cross-cultural Similarities and Differences in Emotion." *Review of Personality and Social Psychology* 13:175–121, 1992.

Sills, Judith. *Excess Baggage*. New York: Viking, 1993.

Simmons, C. H. "A Comparison of German, Japanese and American Romantic Attitudes." *Journal of Social Psychology* 126(3):327–336, 1986.

———. "Differences in Attitudes Toward Romantic Love of French and American College Students." *Journal of Social Psychology* 129(6):793–800, 1989.

Simon, Robin. "The Development of Feeling Norms Underlying Romantic Love Among Adolescent Females." *Social Psychology Quarterly* 55(1):29–46, 1992.

Sinfield, Alan. *Faultlines*. Oxford: Clarendon Press, 1992.

Snead, H. "Multidimensional Analysis of Styles of Love." Unpublished thesis, Department of Psychology, Catholic University of America, 1980.

Sorokin, Pitirim. *The Ways and Power of Love*. Chicago: Henry Regnery, 1967.

Sprecher, S., and S. Metts. "Development of the Romantic Beliefs Scale." *Journal of Social and Personal Relationships* 6:387–344, 1989.

Sternberg, R. J. "A Triangular Theory of Love." *Psychological Review* 93:119–135, 1986.

———(ed). *The Psychology of Love*. New Haven, Conn.: Yale University Press, 1988.

Tancy, G., and S. Bergloss. "Love Styles and Life Satisfaction." *Psychological Reports* 68:883–890, 1991.

Taraban, C. B. "Personality Perception Associated with Six Different Styles of Love." *Journal of Social and Personal Relationships* 12(3):453–461, 1995.

Waller, Willard. *The Family*. New York: Dryden, 1951.

Wilkinson, M. L. "Romantic Love and Sexual Expression." *Family Coordinator* 27(2):141–148, 1978.

Williams, D., and T. Schill. "Adult Attachment, Love Styles, and Self-defeating Personality Characteristics." *Psychological Reports* 75(1):31–34, 1994.

Wolf, Sharyn. *50 Ways to Find a Lover.* Holbrook, Mass.: Bob Adams, 1992.

———. *Guerrilla Dating Tactics.* New York: Plume, 1992.

Yancy, G., and S. Bergloss. "Love Styles and Life Satisfaction." *Psychological Reports* 68(3):883–890, 1991.

3

Love Madness

Dorothy Tennov

... love, is nothing but a blind instinct ... an appetite which
directs us toward one object rather than another without our
being able to account for our taste.

—Ninonde L'Enclos
(Seventeenth Century)

Love is like a fever that comes and goes quite independently
of the will.

—Stendhal

The disease that is love brings into conflict our conscious
intelligence and our basic will.

—Andre Maurois

Another aspect of the pattern is that one falls in love not by
design and conscious choice, but according to some accident of
fate over which the victim has no control.

—Sidney M. Greenfield

The idea that human beings are unique among creatures is so fully
accepted that most people think of either people or animals, not people
and other animals. The absence of "missing links," either in the anthropological record or in existence at present, is increasingly explained
as resulting from a human tendency to destroy closely related species.
With a logic and persistence similar to that which finds human beings
special and superior, we have also tended to view ourselves as free of
such constraints as are genetically imposed on other species. In con-

trast with the beast moved by "blind instinct," human beings are rational and free, acting through our individual inclinations and not because of a wired-in animal necessity uninfluenceable by experience.

If it were experience alone that makes us what we are, then even the extended time available for human development after birth seems insufficient to produce the complex emotional and behavioral repertoires shared by humans, whatever their culture. Granting that human beings do not operate through full-blown instincts in the old-fashioned sense of a complex pattern fully prewired, it is still hard to believe that human beings do not at least have built-in reactions in their basic natures that make the learning of significant strategies for biological survival (evolutionary development) easier than if culture operated on the proverbial blank slate. The conception that some aspects of mental life are analyzable as special-function brain mechanisms, or modules, has confirmatory evidence. Furthermore, if any human reactions are under the direct influence of the genes, surely those related to reproduction are likely candidates.

LIMERENCE DEFINED

The subjective experience identified by the term "limerence" as revealed in personal testimonies contains the following elements: intrusive thinking about the person who is the object of desire (the limerent object or LO); acute longing for reciprocation from LO; dependency of mood on LO's actions, or more accurately, interpretation of LO's actions with respect to the probability of reciprocation; inability to react limerently to more than one person at a time; some fleeting and transient relief from unrequited limerent passion through vivid imagination of action by LO from which reciprocation can be inferred; fear of rejection and shyness in LO's presence, especially in the beginning and whenever uncertainty strikes; intensification through adversity (at least, up to a point), acute sensitivity to any act or thought or condition that can be interpreted favorably; extraordinary ability to devise or invent "reasonable" explanations for why the neutrality or even rejection that the disinterested observer might see in LO's behavior is in fact a sign of hidden passion; an aching of the "heart" (a region in the center front of the chest) when uncertainty is strong; buoyancy (a feeling of walking on air) when reciprocation seems evident; a general intensity of feeling that often leaves other concerns in the background; and a remarkable ability to emphasize what is truly admirable in LO and to avoid dwelling on less favorable characteristics.[1]

Limerence theory holds the following: (1) The underlying mechanism is universal. (2) The state of limerence comes into being automatically when barriers[2] to receptivity are down and a likely person appears. As limerence takes hold, certain laws of operation apply. What happens thereafter depends on how strongly it seems that the hoped-for reciprocation will indeed occur. This is largely, though perhaps not entirely, a matter of LO's actions. Small doses of attention from LO increase the intensity of the limerence experience. (3) Reciprocation leads to euphoria, followed by a union that might be stable or unstable, and that might or might not endure.

THROUGH THE EYES OF HUMAN EVOLUTION

Similarity of experience among diverse persons as well as involuntariness suggests that limerence is well rooted—whatever the culture and lifestyle—in the very nature of humanness (Harris 1995). In many species, mates form attachments that aid the survival of resulting offspring. But by what mechanism are we humans guided toward our partners? Those who were our ancestors mated successfully and also avoided inbreeding (mating with very close relatives) by overlooking those nearest (genetically) and dearest. The "dearest" are recognized from a complex mix of inborn inclinations, reason (meaning foresight and figuring), learning (consciously or otherwise), and selection (Calvin 1996; Cziko 1996) at various stages.

Many have seen being in love as a madness.[3] Not everyone considers it illogical or abnormal, but even so strong an advocate as the nineteenth-century writer Stendhal spoke of it as a disease. Recovered former limerents among interviewees often agreed. Those whose limerence was replaced by affectional bonding with the same partner might say, reminiscing about the wonderful, ecstatic, honeymoon days that were gradually replaced by a satisfactory—affectionate and companionable—partnership, "We were very much in love when we were married; today we love each other very much." How often and under what conditions limerence is followed by satisfactory companionship is a subject for future research. The point is that it is a state a person is either in or not in, and, if in, then a lot of what is happening is not under voluntary control. That is what is meant by "madness."

A hallmark of limerence is that if it is limerence, there is only one LO (at a time). When that one person fails to reciprocate, the result may be long hours of sustained lovesickness that is relieved, and then only slightly, by achieving the limerence goal in imagination. There may come a time when the sufferer has had enough and wants to end the painful prepossession, when all bases for hope have been exhausted and it is time to abandon ship, only to find—and this is the madness of it—that these thoughts cannot be turned off and on at will as can most thoughts. Scarlett O'Hara (who said she would think about it "tomorrow") might have been over-optimistic, or she might have mainly been suffering loss of pride and fear of being left alone in her old age. If limerent, she would not have been able to stop thinking about Rhett, and she would probably go back to alcohol in an attempt to stop the anguish. The intrusions and literal aches of unfulfilled desire, and the precious lost moments of life during which the mind travels relentlessly down a dead-end course, force recognition that there are limits to our ability to control our thoughts and feelings. Limerence is not something a person does, any more than is the common cold. The multitudinous contradictions in what has been said about love suggests that it is capable of appearing in numerous guises depending on time, circumstance, and persons.[4]

What I found instead is ubiquitous sameness across diverse situations. I was also attracted to ideas that had begun to emerge from the biological sciences, especially from the study of hereditary mechanisms and genetic theories, and from evolutionary disciplines that cross traditional barriers between psychology and biology. Scientists consider the possibility that over the course of biological history, certain social behavioral tendencies have evolved along with more readily observable physiological features (Barash 1975).

The relationship between inborn tendencies and environmental influences is complex, even chaotic (Maynard Smith and Szathmary, 1995). In many species, learning appears to be involved in the development of basically instinctive reactions (Wilson and Nias 1976). Very few complex behavioral reactions are fully programmed in the nervous system. Although the mere existence of a reaction, even if universal, does not imply that it is inborn, the evidence suggests a clear genetic base for certain traits. For example, in a survey of sculpture and paintings from various parts of the world and different historical eras, it was found that roughly 93% were rendered with the right hand, a proportion maintained regardless of historical era or culture (Coren and Porac 1977), such evidence favors the theory of a genetic predisposition.

Limerence can be seen as a normal and usual feature of the human species, and my approach is basically that of the ethologist who observes and analyzes the behavior of animals in natural settings from an evolutionary perspective (Bateson and Hinde 1976). A main difference is that the observations I gathered came by means of self-reports. Any pattern observed, whether it be salmon migration, the retrieval of pups that stray from the maternal rat's nest, courtship displays by certain birds, or limerence in humans, can be considered in the light of how the specific behavior is adaptive. Evolution is not an ever-upward drive toward perfection. This is not to say that it is a totally random process. If it were, there would be no evolving. The environment selects. In the variations that chance throws out for selection, the process is highly constrained, and often bungling, inefficient, and cruel (Dawkins 1976). Yet the fundamental principle is disarmingly simple. The inherited you (or genotype) is the product of a "selection" of traits that run in a continuous line back from your parents to theirs and on through all the organisms that were your progenitors to the primordial substance in which the spark of life first began on this isolated planet.

Step by minute step across eons of incredible duration, life proliferated and changed through the single essential principle of selection. If a behavior or a state is genetically programmed, it is one that either enhanced or in no way diminished the "fitness" of organisms carrying its controlling gene or genes (Williams 1966). Courtship, mating, the nature and duration of the pair bonds (if any) that exist between partners, sexual behavior, and child-rearing have been the focus of many sociobiological studies (e.g., Symons 1979).

DISADVANTAGEOUS REMNANTS

Evolutionary thinking can also explain the existence of less desirable traits. Treisman (1977) noted that vomiting induced by motion had been viewed as an evolutionary anomaly. Evolutionary theorists speculate about hidden advantages, perhaps from a former time, with vestigial carry over. Treisman's evolutionary hypothesis is that motion sickness is an accidental byproduct of the organism's response to certain head and eye movements that occur in the case of food poisoning but unfortunately also in the case of certain types of motion. Thus, evolutionary thinking assists the scientific process of theorizing in more complex ways than simply conjecturing about "survival value."[5] The force behind the way a particular trait functions to permit its own survival through a continual supply of individuals who carry the genes for it is known as the ultimate cause of the adaptive process. The specific way the trait functions is known as the "mechanism" or proximate cause.[6] For what ultimate cause might the state of limerence be a proximate cause? In other words, why were people who became limerent successful, maybe more successful than others, in passing their genes on to succeeding generations back a few hundred thousand or million years ago when heads grew larger and fathers who left mother and child to fend for themselves were less "reproductively successful"—in the long run, that is (Morgan 1993). Did limerence evolve to cement a relationship long enough to get the offspring up and running?

To explain why the environment of our ancestors "selected" limerence, we might consider the behavior it induces. Some limerence-inspired actions are socially undesirable, even socially disruptive. Limerence intrudes, deflecting interest from affairs of business, of state, even of family. In the midst of battle, the soldier's despair over a letter of rejection from LO is not forgotten. A king gives up his crown. An artist's career languishes. But such visible disadvantages should not constitute the sole basis of judgment. The most consistent result of limerence is mating, not merely sexual interaction but also commitment, the establishment of a shared domicile in the form of a cozy nest built for the enjoyment of ecstasy, for reproduction, and for the rearing of children.

Limerence also frees the young from too strong and too enduring an attachment to parents. In human beings, it does not ensure the kind of permanent monogamy sometimes found in other species, but its duration of several years allows a female to become pregnant, bear a child, and begin the new family (Money and Ehrhardt 1972). Voluntary testimony suggests that a lower limit might be as long as three years, at least among mature adults, and that there is no upper limit.

Not that limerence is the only mechanism in the human system to help offspring on their way in life. There is, for example, an inborn response to the characteristics of infants perceived as "cute," characteristics such as large eyes low in a head somewhat out of proportion, at least out of adult proportion, to the rest of the body—a set of characteristics shared by most mammalian young (Wickler 1973). Human beings are not the only animals to respond favorably and protectively to these features, and some species have actually capitalized on the reaction (think giant panda). Many animals also form pair bonds, and in some species partners remain monogamous for life; others are monogamous for only a season. The type of pair bond formed, if any, is related to the species' overall reproductive pattern ("strategy"). In some, by the time the young emerge from egg or pupa, the parents have long since departed, and the generations never even meet except perhaps by remote chance. The new generation fends for itself from the outset. The interspecies range of pair-bonding types and the duration of pair-bonding is wide. Wickler (1973) described the behavior of the native European bird, the *Panurus biamicus* (the bearded tit):

The partners spend their whole lives in very close permanent monogamy and can only be separated by force. . . . Two or three days after the male has concentrated his attention on a particular female and she has tolerated it willingly, the matter is decided, and the two sleep closely clumped together at night and not with [their] brothers and sisters as before. During cleaning and drinking, foraging, bathing, and sleeping, the one will hardly leave the side of the other, and they continually preen each other's ruffled feathers. If one flies a grass blade farther away, the other will land beside it a moment later. If one loses sight of the other, it will call loudly until they have found each other again. Although two months later the call alone is enough . . . so that they can tolerate a separation of a few meters. But the marital partners sleep close together throughout their life. If one dies, the other will fly around excitedly, searching and constantly calling and becoming extremely agitated the moment it hears the call of another bearded tit or a sudden rustling in the bushes, as though hoping that at last its partner was about to land beside it. (pp. 95–96)

The duration of a typical sustained pairing in humans is proportionately shorter than the lifelong attachment of these little birds. On the other hand, who can say that what the bearded tit feels for its mate is not basically the same as what the human limerent feels for LO? The outward actions look very similar. Among geese, Konrad Lorenz, founder of ethology, noted that "Such a bond may arise explosively, almost before one has realized it, joining two individuals together for life. We say then . . . that the two have fallen in love" (Lorenz 1966).

THE ETHOLOGY OF LIMERENCE

The term "imprinting" refers to a kind of fast exposure learning in which young birds follow in the wake of whatever it was that appeared in their visual field at a certain critical period during early development. Under natural conditions, that stimulus would be the mother bird; in the laboratory, chicks and ducklings have picked up and taken after red rubber balls, and experimenters.[7] This phenomenon is a good example of built-in potential for adapting to a particular environment. If something happened to the mother, the animal would come to "love" the father, foster mother, or whoever happened to be around at the time (even a predator, I presume, but that would be a short-lived love affair).

The vision of geese hopping along in the wake of an experimenter (Lorenz in a famous photograph) excited the imagination of many behavioral scientists, some of whom attempted, with varying degrees of success, to detect the phenomenon in other species and at other points in the life span. One investigator (Salk 1962) reported prenatal imprinting of the human infant to the mother's heartbeat, which he felt might predispose the child to certain musical tempos in later life. Others contended that imprinting, when it occurred, was limited to visual, not auditory stimuli. Controversy broke out in the scientific journals concerning appropriate use of the term when some seemed ready to apply the label wherever the faintest degree of resemblance appeared (Sluckin 1974).

Although there may be controversy in the details, evidence is abundant that environmental conditions, at a certain time of life, affect the organism thereafter. It ranges from prenatal susceptibility to certain substances during the first weeks of gestation to language learning, and to the types of attachments that develop among family and group members. Inevitably, someone wondered whether falling in love could be classified as imprinting. Utilizing findings in genetics, embryology, endocrinology, neuroendocrinology, psychology, and anthropology in an analysis of gender identity focusing on the interactions of heredity and environment, Money and Ehrhardt (1972) describe romantic love to include prepossession and emotional dependency on the actions of the loved person, descriptions that are consistent with limerence theory. Also consistent with the findings of the limerence research, they do not, for example, find falling in love to differ particularly as a function of gender, and they assume that it is both involuntary and largely genetically determined. Although the first limerence experience may precede or follow the onset of hormonal puberty, Money and Ehrhardt clearly assume a biological basis for falling in love. Imprinting implies a certain time during development when the effect can occur. Limerence more closely resembles another ethological concept, that of the "fixed action pattern." At a certain point during the transition from nonlimerence to limerence, an event takes place that Stendhal called "crystallization" in which the mind fashions an image of "perfections" from LO's actual attractive features. The process of redefining LO in the best light usually is one of emphasis rather than complete invention.

An impressive case for a kind of negative imprinting and for the role of involuntary and unconscious factors is provided by the findings on mate selection in Israeli kibbutzim (Talmon 1964). Kibbutzim children reared together in the same infants' houses during their first five years did not, in later life, "regard each other as erotically desirable." Despite parental preferences to the contrary, data on 2,769 marriages that took place in second-generation offspring of kibbutzim dwellers indicate that not one occurred between persons reared together uninterruptedly during the first five years. It appears that intimacy during early childhood left an "imprint" that prevented limerence. This finding of an automatic mechanism in which an animal responds with a complex reaction that is, however, universal within the species, is consistent with the idea that limerence is a human "universal" (Brown 1991) rather than the result of a culture "saturated" with romantic love in its stories and songs.

Anti-incest imprinting has value, for too-close relatives tend to have inferior offspring when they mate. (Observations of higher primates reveal a disinclination toward mating on the part of mothers and male offspring.) The element of arbitrariness regarding the object of limerent fixation promotes matings among persons outside the immediate group. Cultures have differed in their reactions to limerence, in their approval or disapproval, as well as in relation to who is and is not an acceptable marriage partner or whether the selection is made by the individuals or by their elders. The kibbutzim finding does not rule out cultural influence over some aspects of the limerent reaction, but it clearly supports the notion that limerence is at least partly governed by forces outside the influence of social, as well as conscious, control.

PHYSICAL ATTRACTIVENESS

Because physical features contribute heavily to attractiveness, persons attempting to elicit reciprocation in LO become very concerned about their own attractiveness. As one interviewee put it, "They will alter their posture and try to hide baldness or what they believe to be their unattractive facial features. Some develop nervous gestures designed to distract the viewer from the 'ugly sight.'"

The role of physical attractiveness[8] is an aspect of romantic attachment and human courting behavior that has been researched with some thoroughness by psychologists and sociologists. In study after study, the result was the same: the better-looking people had the advantage. That appearance is of importance is itself reflected in the intense concern those who are limerent feel about their own attractiveness. Hair dyes, makeup, attire, diet, and exercise regimens are regularly featured in popular magazines because they make the user feel more able to stimulate the limerent reaction in LO. When limerence is intense, no aspect of living is as important as is the hope of achieving the persistently envisioned goal of reciprocation. Surely it is no accident that the time of life during which, by group consensus, human beings are most attractive—post-adolescence and early adulthood—is also the time at which most reproductive matings are initiated.

Physical attractiveness and youth are rough indications of good health and other attributes that relate to breeding capability and thus genetic fitness. Sex differences in the importance of physical attractiveness to human beings is also well documented (e.g., Buss 1995). But isn't it wasteful for standards of physical attractiveness to be universal within a society? Isn't one of the biggest problems of living that of trying to meet standards that can only be achieved by a few at the top? Wouldn't transmission of the most favorable genetic material to future generations be better served by a mate selection process that did not depend so much on stereotypes of appearance but rather depended on assessment of a possible mate's aptitudes and capabilities? In other words, wouldn't producing healthy and desirable children be more likely if it did not depend on superficial physical traits when other features might be of greater importance?

The answer might be that the large role physical attractiveness plays in mate selection permits traits uncorrelated with beauty to be selected randomly. That is, there may be greater genetic benefit from not allowing individuals to choose mates by conscious, rational means. What appears to be a good match by "rational" criteria might in fact have amounted to a genetically unfit form of inbreeding. Physical attractiveness draws individuals to a mate who may be unlike themselves in other respects. The ability of the culture to shift specific standards of beauty seems to occur only within a certain range. That it can occur at all suggests interplay between external influence and genetic makeup, something scientists have found in abundance wherever they have looked. Whatever factors cause an individual to "select" a specific person as LO, limerence cements the reaction and locks the emotional gates against competitors. This exclusivity weakens the effect of physical attractiveness, since the most beautiful individual in the world cannot compete with LO once limerence has taken hold. Thus, persons across a wide range of physical appearances are able to secure mates.

When I gave the first paper on my research on romantic love, as I called it then, a man in the audience reacted with indignation over the idea of putting a sacred subject under the cold light of science. In the two decades since *Love and Limerence* (1979) was published, I have had the opportunity to witness reactions to the idea of falling in love as "falling" into an automatic, involuntary condition in which one's happiness is under the control of another. Some, misunderstanding, assumed that by "limerence" I referred to an extreme reaction. While it is true that limerence can lead to extreme feelings and action, that is not the definition. The definition of limerence is of a state in which the Laws of Limerence are operative.

NOTES

1. For a description of the original research and findings, see Tennov (1979). This chapter is partly an adaptation of Chapter Seven.
2. A 750-word magazine article about limerence research using the term "love madness" rather than "limerence" brought a response of several hundred letters from people who wrote much the same kinds of things as did readers of *Love and Limerence*. And several of those said they didn't even wait to finish the book. The implication? That the condition is well known.
3. The general attitude is that love is so complicated and so individual that anything said about it is probably true for some people, or under some conditions (e.g., Wilson and Nias 1976).
4. For other sources of information concerning the unfortunate leavings of prior adaptations, see Morgan (1993) and Nesse and Williams (1995).
5. The term "proximate" case can refer to mechanisms at any lower level. Limerence theory focuses on the level of experience. There has been much speculation, but, as yet, few definitive conclusions have been reached regarding the physiological level (Fisher 1992).
6. The social, ethical, as well as scientific, implications of limerence theory are dealt with elsewhere (see Tennov 1986).

7. Of course, it isn't that simple. For a discussion of imprinting research, see Bateson (1987).

8. "Attractiveness" is one of several concepts in limerence theory that are without unequivocal referents. (Others in this category are "reciprocation" and "unrequited.") Because these terms are currently without objective referents, limerence theory can rightly be said to lack some attributes of a scientific theory. But I concur with Calvin (1996) and others who see speculation as an integral part of the scientific process, the only constraint being that known facts are not violated.

REFERENCES

Bach, George R., and Ronald M. Deutsch. *Pairing.* New York: Avon Books, 1971.

Barash, David P. "Behavior as Evolutionary Strategy." *Science* 190:1084–1085, 1975.

———. *Sociobiology and Behavior.* New York: Elsevier North-Holland, 1977.

Bateson, P.P.G., and R. A. Hinde. *Growing Points in Ethology.* New York: Cambridge University Press, 1976.

———. "Imprinting." In Richard L. Gregory (ed.), *The Oxford Companion to the Mind.* Oxford: Oxford University Press, 1987, pp. 355–357.

Bloom, Martin. "Toward a Developmental Concept of Love." *Journal of Human Relations* 15:246–263, 1967.

Brown, Donald E. *Human Universals.* New York: McGraw-Hill, 1991.

Buss, David. *The Evolution of Desire.* New York: Basic Books, 1995.

Calvin, William H. *The Cerebral Code: Thinking a Thought in the Mosaics of the Mind.* Cambridge, Mass.: MIT Press, 1996.

Coren, Stanley, and Clare Porac. "Fifty Centuries of Right-handedness: The Historical Record." *Science* 198:631–632, 1977.

Cziko, Gary. *Without Miracles: Universal Selection Theory and the Second Darwinian Revolution.* Cambridge, Mass.: MIT Press, 1996.

Dawkins, Richard. *The Selfish Gene.* Oxford: Oxford University Press, 1976.

Dennett, Daniel C. *Darwin's Dangerous Idea.* New York: Simon and Schuster, 1995.

Fisher, Helen. *Anatomy of Love: The Natural History of Monogamy, Adultery, and Divorce.* New York: W. W. Norton, 1992.

Greenfield, Sidney M. "Love and Marriage in Modern America." *The Sociological Quarterly* 6:363–364, 1965.

Harris, Helen. "Rethinking Heterosexual Relationships in Polynesia: A Case Study of Mangaia, Cook Island." In William Jankowiak (ed.), *Romantic Passion: A Universal Experience?* New York: Columbia University Press, 1995.

Hunt, Morton M. *The Natural History of Love.* New York: Alfred A. Knopf, 1959.

Kirkpatrick, Clifford, and Theodore Caplow. "Emotional Trends in the Courtship Experience of College Students as Expressed by Graphs, with Some Observations on Methodological Implications." *American Sociological Review* 5:619–626, 1945.

Lorenz, Konrad. *On Aggression.* London: Methuen, 1966.

Maurois, Andre. *Seven Faces of Love.* New York: Didier, 1944.

Maynard Smith, John, and Eors Szathmary. *The Major Transitions in Evolution.* New York: W. H. Freeman, 1995.

Money, John, and Anke A. Ehrhardt. *Man and Woman, Boy and Girl: The Differentiation and Dimorphism of Gender Identity from Conception to Maturity.* Baltimore, Md.: Johns Hopkins University Press, 1972.

Morgan, Elaine. *The Scars of Evolution: What Our Bodies Tell Us about Human Origins.* New York: Oxford University Press, 1993.

————. *The Descent of the Child: Human Evolution from a New Perspective.* New York: Oxford University Press, 1995.

Nesse, Randolph M., and George Williams. *Why We Get Sick: The New Science of Darwinian Medicine.* New York: Times Books, 1995.

Riegel, Michelle Galler. "Monogamous Mammals: Variations of a Scheme." *Science News* 112:76–78, 1977.

Salk, Lee. "Mother's Heartbeat as an Imprinting Stimulus." *Transactions of the New York Academy of Science* 24:753–763, 1962.

Salzen, Eric. Introduction to the Routledge edition of *On Aggression* by Konrad Lorenz. New York: Routledge, 1996.

Sluckin, W. "Imprinting Reconsidered." *Bulletin of the British Psychological Society* 27:447–451, 1974.

Stendhal. *Love.* Translated by Gilbert Sale and Suzanne Sale; Introduction by Jean Stewart and B.C.J.C. Knight. Middlesex, England: Penguin Books, 1975.

Symons, Donald. *The Evolution of Human Sexuality.* Oxford: Oxford University Press, 1979.

Talmon, Yonina. "Mate Selection in Collective Settlements." *American Sociological Review* 29:491–508, 1964.

Tennov, Dorothy. "Sex Differences in Romantic Love and Depression Among College Students." *Proceedings of the 81st Animal Convention of the American Psychological Association,* Montreal, Canada, 8:421–422, 1973.

————. *Psychotherapy, the Hazardous Cure.* New York: Doubleday/Anchor, 1975.

————. *Super Self: A Woman's Guide to Self-Management.* New York: Jove, 1978.

————. *Love and Limerence.* New York: Stein and Day, 1979.

————. "The Limerence Retreat." Unpublished (but widely distributed), 1986.

————. "Limerence and Human Nature Science" (work in progress).

Treisman, Michel. "Motion Sickness: An Evolutionary Hypothesis." *Science* 197:493–495, 1977.

Washburn, Sherwood L. "Human Behavior and the Behavior of Other Animals." *American Psychologist* 33:405–418,1978.

Wickler, Wolfgang. *The Sexual Code.* Garden City, N.J.: Anchor Press/ Doubleday, 1973.

Williams, George C. *Adaptation and Natural Selection.* Princeton, N.J.: Princeton University Press, 1966.

Wilson, Glenn, and David Nias. *The Mystery of Love: How the Science of Sexual Attraction Can Work for You.* New York: Quadrangle, 1976.

SECTION II

THE PSYCHOLOGY OF LOVE AND SEXUAL DESIRE

4

Romantic Love and Sexual Desire

Pamela Regan

INTRODUCTION

Love has been the subject of much speculation throughout the ages. For example, Shakespeare was not the first to note that love is blind —Chaucer said it almost two hundred years earlier in *The Canterbury Tales* 1387–1400, and he certainly will not be the last. Poets, playwrights, and authors alike have attempted to specify the nature of love, in the process composing sonnets, singing odes, and writing ballads that alternately glorify and vilify this most elusive of human experiences. This interest in love—in its features, antecedents, and consequences—shows no signs of diminishing today, as psychologists and other social and behavioral scientists continue to grapple with the question, "What is love?" Numerous taxonomies that specify types or varieties of love (e.g., romantic love, companionate love, altruistic love) have been proposed (e.g., Hendrick and Hendrick 1992; Sternberg and Barnes 1988). Such typologies generally include a variety of love referred to as romantic, passionate, or erotic love. This particular type of love has assumed special importance in interpersonal relationships research and in theoretical discourse on love for a number of reasons: Romantic love is generally sought after by individuals and exalted in Western culture; romantic love has become the *sine qua non* of the marriage contract; and the absence of romantic love may be a factor in marital dissolution (e.g., Berscheid 1985; Burgess and Wallin 1953; Goode 1959; Kazak and Reppucci 1980; Kephart 1967; Simpson, Campbell, and Berscheid 1986; Spaulding 1971). In addition, not only is romantic love intricately associated with these and other significant individual and interpersonal events, but also current social psychological discourse on romantic love suggests that sexuality is one of the dimensions that differentiates romantic love from other types and varieties of love. This chapter explores the social psychological discourse on romantic love and sexuality and then presents empirical evidence that romantic love is most closely associated with one particular aspect of sexuality, namely, sexual desire.

SOCIAL PSYCHOLOGICAL DISCOURSE ON ROMANTIC LOVE AND SEXUALITY

The type of linkage, if any, that exists between sexuality and (not necessarily romantic) love has been the focus of a great deal of theoretical debate. Aron and Aron (1991), for example, divide the many theories that have touched upon love or sexuality into five general categories, including (1) theories of sexuality that ignore love or consider love to be one result of sexuality (e.g., Freud, sociobiological approaches); (2) theories that emphasize sexuality and consider love to be a minor feature of sexuality (e.g., Bowlby); (3) theories that consider love and sexuality to be separate (e.g., Reiss); (4) theories that emphasize love and view sexuality as a minor part of love (e.g., Sternberg, Lee, Rubin); and (5) theories that ignore sexuality or consider sexuality to be one result of love (e.g., Dion and Dion, Maslow, object relations theory). As this review illustrates, there is little consensus among social scientists about the nature of the association between sexuality and love. Nonetheless, as Aron and Aron and others have noted (e.g., Hendrick and Hendrick 1992), our own culture seems to link sexuality and *romantic* love quite closely.

Sexless Romantic Love

Theorists have not always followed suit. For many years social psychologists interested in romantic love assumed that this type of love was nothing more than a form of intense interpersonal attraction, a sort of liking run wild. The determinants of romantic love were therefore thought to be simply more intense versions of the antecedents of liking, and the principles of reinforcement that neatly explain why we prefer or like certain persons over others were assumed to explain the reasons we fall in love with one individual and not another. Because sexuality was not hypothesized to be one of the major determinants of liking, those social psychologists who utilized the conceptual framework associated with liking and interpersonal attraction presented a view of romantic love that was remarkably devoid of sex. For example, noted attraction and love researcher Rubin (e.g., 1970, 1973) was one of the first individuals to attempt to operationalize and empirically distinguish between romantic love and related phenomena such as liking, or interpersonal attraction, and the love between children and parents, an individual and God, and close friends. He argued that romantic love, defined as "love between unmarried opposite-sex peers, of the sort which could possibly lead to marriage" (1970:266), is associated with a physical or emotional need, "a passionate desire to possess and to be fulfilled by another person" (1973:213). However, he chose to interpret this "love-need" as a nonsexual attachment similar to the bonds formed between infants and their parents; it is not surprising, then, that the thirteen items on Rubin's romantic love scale reflect affiliative and dependent needs, the predisposition to help the partner, and nonsexual feelings of exclusiveness, absorption, and possessiveness. None of the scale items could be considered even remotely sexual. The most sexually charged item states, "When I am with ——, I spend a good deal of time just looking at him (her)" (1970:267). Rubin's romantic love scale is moderately correlated with the scale he developed to measure liking (e.g., Mathes 1984; Rubin 1970), suggesting that the two may reflect essentially the same nonsexual, affection-based construct.

Other researchers and theorists concerned with romantic love have similarly ignored or downplayed the sexual aspects of the phenomenon in their conceptualizations and measures. For example, the questionnaire designed by Dion and Dion (e.g., 1973) to assess the "intense, mysterious, and volatile" (p. 51) phenomenon of romantic love is noticeably sexless. This measure included a list of such stereotypic romantic love "symptoms" as feelings of euphoria and depression, agitation and restlessness, daydreaming, sleep difficulties, and decreased ability to concentrate. Items designed to assess attitudes toward romantic love are similarly lacking in sexual content, and the only remotely sexual dimensions included on a series of romantic love adjective rating scales are "sensual-intellectual" and "spiritual-physical" (p. 54).

Driscoll, Davis, and Lipetz (1972) distinguish between romantic love, defined as "a distinct form of interpersonal attraction that occurs between opposite-sex partners under specifiable social conditions" (p. 1), and what they called "conjugal love," or the trusting, loyal, appreciative love found between mature adults and close friends. Interestingly, these authors expanded their conceptualization of romantic love to include feelings of passion and physical attraction, but their four-item love scale only assesses general feelings of love, caring, need, and the importance of the relationship. No items related to sexual feelings toward the partner are included.

Similarly, items included on Bardis's (1971) "erotometer" were ostensibly selected to represent eighteen aspects of "heterosexual love"

(p. 71). Like Driscoll et al. (1972), Bardis clearly associated the physical aspect of this variety of love with the sexual elements of the love relationship (see p.72) and thus at least tipped his theoretical hat to the connection between romantic love and sex. However, an examination of the fifty items composing his scale reveals nothing explicitly or implicitly sexual in nature or tone (the most sexual items read "Longing to do things together" and "Enjoying just being together").

More recently, Brehm (1988) has argued that passionate (romantic) love is an intense and not particularly sexual experience that represents the combination of imagination and emotion and that serves to motivate human beings to construct a vision of a better world. Critical aspects or consequences of passionate love include the emotional experiences of joy, frustration, aridity (feelings of being dry, barren, and unresponsive that signal emotional exhaustion), and terror; the motivation to act in ways that promote closeness to the beloved; and detachment from other people and things that are not directly related to the beloved. Although Brehm recognizes that romantic or passionate love may have sexual consequences, she nonetheless concludes that sex has very little to do with the experience:

It may seem strange that, in this discussion of passionate love, I have given so little attention to sex. Passionate love does, of course, often focus on a potential or existing sexual partner, and desired or actual sexual activity with that partner can be a major source of heightened emotional experience. I do not, however, regard sexuality as a necessary component of passionate love . . . it is a serious mistake to regard all forms of passionate love as essentially sexual in origin or purpose. Just as one can have a highly active sexual life without a trace of passionate love, so one can be passionately in love independent of one's sexual drives. (p. 257)

Certainly, it is possible to feel desire for, become aroused by, and engage in sexual activities with individuals for whom we feel little or no romantic love. However, the assertion that romantic love exists independently of sexuality has come under attack in recent years.

Sexualized Romantic Love

Now, many social psychological theorists argue that sexual phenomena ought to be included in conceptualizations and measures of romantic love (e.g., Berscheid 1988; Hatfield 1988; Hatfield and Rapson 1987). For example, Elaine Hatfield (then Walster) and Ellen Berscheid (1971; Berscheid and Walster 1974)—among the first contemporary researchers to conduct a dialogue on the nature of love—conceptualized passionate or romantic love as an exotic variety of interpersonal attraction. According to these researchers, this fragile, temporary, intense phenomenon blossoms only when an individual is extremely aroused physiologically and when situational or contextual cues indicate that "passionate love" is the appropriate label for that arousal. Such emotional experiences as fear, rejection, frustration, hatred, excitement, and sexual gratification, which are all associated with physiological arousal, can be instrumental in producing and enhancing passionate feelings. Berscheid and Walster quite explicitly provide a place for such sexual phenomena as arousal and gratification in their elegant and thorough discussion. They posit, for example, that the inhibition of sexual satisfaction and the sexual challenge provided by "hard-to-get" men and women will increase the romantic feelings of erstwhile admirers.

A good portion of Hatfield and Walster's (1978) discussion of passionate love derives from earlier work conducted with Berscheid and similarly emphasizes the sexual aspects of romantic love. For example, we learn that passionate love consists of a wild confusion of tender, sexual, painful, anxious, altruistic, and jealous feelings, and that feelings of passion and romance are promoted by such physiologically arousing states as anxiety, anger, fear, loneliness, and sexual deprivation that often heighten sexual attraction and subjective and physiological sexual arousal (also see Hatfield 1988). In contrast to the affectionate, companionate love often seen between old friends or long-married couples, passionate love is described as a short-lived state, dying quickly once sexual aims are satisfied, and the novelty of sexual activity with the heretofore unattainable object inevitably degenerates into routine sex with a no-longer-exciting partner.

Other authors also recognize that romantic love contains a sexual element. Like Berscheid, Hatfield, and Walster, Lee (e.g., 1973, 1988) devoted considerable energy to an examination of different types of love, and in the process developed a novel approach in which different styles of loving are likened to primary or secondary colors (hence the title of his 1973 book, *Colours of Love*). Eros, one of the primary colors or styles of loving, is an intensely emotional experience that is similar to the passionate love described by Berscheid, Hatfield, and Walster. According to Lee, the erotic lover is "turned on" by a particular physical type, is prone to fall instantly and completely in love with a stranger ("love at first sight"), rapidly becomes preoccupied with pleasant thoughts about that individual, experiences an intense need for daily contact with the beloved, and wishes the relationship to remain exclusive. Like passionate love, erotic love has a sexual component. For example, not only does the erotic style of loving always begin with a strong physical attraction, but also the erotic lover always seeks some form of sexual involvement early in the relationship. Indeed, in profiling the typical erotic lover, Lee writes that he or she is "eager to get to know the beloved quickly, intensely—and undressed" (1988:50).

Originally fascinated by the oftentimes devastating emotional aftermath of broken love relationships, Tennov (1979) set out to characterize the agony and ecstasy of the individual experience of being "in love." In her fascinating (1979) book, *Love and Limerence*, she coined the now-famous term *"limerence"* to describe the state of what others have called erotic, passionate, or romantic love. Limerence is an intense mental state or cognitive obsession characterized by persistent, intrusive thought about the object of passionate desire (called the limerent object or LO), acute longing for reciprocation, mood fluctuations, intense awareness of the LO's actions, fear of rejection, shyness, physical reactions (i.e., "heartache"), emotional highs and lows depending on the LO's perceived reciprocity, and idealization of the LO's positive qualities. Limerence is not the same as sexual attraction, and sexual activity is not enough to satisfy the limerent need. However, Tennov strongly believed that sexual feelings are a necessary part of the limerent experience. She wrote:

I am inclined toward the generalization that sexual attraction is an essential component of limerence. This sexual feeling may be combined with shyness, impotence or some form of sexual dysfunction or disinclination, or with some social unsuitability. But LO, in order to become LO, must stand in relation to the limerent as one for whom the limerent is a potential sex partner. Sexual attraction is not "enough," to be sure. Selection standards for limerence are, according to informants, not identical to those by which "mere" sexual partners are evaluated, and sex is seldom the main focus of limerence. Either the potential for sexual mating is felt to be there, however, or the state described is not limerence. (pp. 24–25)

Limerence generally fades after a period of time, although it may be supplanted by a more genuine form of love based on support, care, and concern that is similar to the companionate love described by Berscheid and Walster (1974).

Intimacy, decision/commitment, and passion form the vertices of Sternberg's more recent triangular theory of love (e.g., 1986, 1988). The intimacy component refers to feelings of warmth, closeness, and connection in the love relationship; the decision/commitment component represents both the short-term decision that one individual loves another and the longer-term commitment to maintain that love; and the passion component refers to "the drives that lead to romance, physical attraction, sexual consummation, and the like in a loving relationship" (1988:120). According to Sternberg, all forms of love (specifically, eight) can be conceptualized as combinations of one or more of these components. For example, romantic love derives from the combination of the intimacy and passion components of love, and thus can be viewed as liking or friendship supplemented by physical or sexual attraction.

Similarly, Branden's (1988) conceptualization of romantic love—defined as a "passionate spiritual-emotional-sexual attachment between two people that reflects a high regard for the value of each other's person" (p. 220)—contains sexual elements. Arguing that romantic love allows people to satisfy the psychological need for sexual fulfillment, he notes that individuals who are in love not only view the loved one as critically important to their sexual happiness, but they also tend to express their love physically, via sexual encounters. According to Branden, a relationship cannot be viewed as romantic if it lacks a strong sexual attraction.

Like Sternberg and Branden, Murstein's (1988) conceptualization of romantic love also includes an emphasis on passion. This theorist argues that there are three stages of love: Passionate love or physical attraction, which involves intense arousal and has a strong sexual base; romantic love, which resembles passionate love but is more focused on the idealization of the beloved; and conjugal or companionate love, which is characterized by liking and trust. Although Murstein contends that romantic love is a less explicitly sexual experience than passionate love, he maintains that it does have a physical or sexual element.

Shaver, Hazan, and colleagues conceptualize romantic love as a biological process that has been designed by evolution to facilitate the attachment between adult sexual partners (e.g., Hazan and Shaver 1987; Shaver and Hazan 1988; Shaver, Hazan, and Bradshaw 1988). These researchers note that the key features of infant–caregiver attachment are remarkably similar to those of adult romantic love. For example, an infant seeks to maintain proximity and contact with his or her primary caregiver by engaging in such behaviors as holding, touching, kissing, clinging, and smiling. Romantic lovers also seek to spend time with and maintain physical contact with the loved object; specifically, they hold, touch, caress, kiss, make love with, and smile at the partner. However, adult romantic love differs from infant–caregiver attachment in two important ways: Not only do adult romantic partners engage in reciprocal caregiving, but sexual attraction and sexual behavior are an important part of romantic love. Thus, Shaver and colleagues argue that adult romantic love involves the integration of three independent behavioral systems: attachment, reciprocal care-giving, and sexuality (described as an innate system consisting of a cycle of desire and arousal followed by sexual behavior and orgasm). Although different romantic love relationships involve different mixtures of these components (e.g., one-sided "crushes" and nonsexual romantic relationships), these researchers contend that prototypical adult romantic love contains all three elements.

Buss (e.g., 1988) also takes an evolutionary approach to romantic love, arguing that the key consequences of this phenomenon center around reproduction. Specifically, he hypothesizes that the acts or behaviors that fall in the category of "love" have evolved to achieve such proximate goals as sexual intimacy and reproduction, among others. In fact, Buss proposes that sexual intimacy is the *sine qua non* of "heterosexual love," described as the state of being "in love." Love acts of sexual intimacy, which include engaging in sexual intercourse, losing one's virginity to the loved one, and being "sexually open" with one's partner, serve to seal the bond between lovers and may result in conception.

The increasing attention given to sexual phenomena in theoretical discourses on the nature of romantic love has gradually permeated the empirical literature in social psychology. For example, Critelli, Myers, and Loos (1986) created their measure of romantic love by supplementing existing love scales constructed by Rubin (1970) and Driscoll, Davis, and Lipetz (1972) with items designed to reflect feelings of sexual arousal, physiological arousal, passion, excitement, romance, and physical attraction; Pam, Plutchik, and Conte (1975) included items related to the physical and sexual attractiveness of the romantic partner in their measure of "being in love" (p. 83); and Swensen (1961) and Swensen and Gilner (1963) placed a physical expression category (containing items concerned with sexual behaviors such as hugging, kissing, "necking," "petting," and sexual relations) among the other varieties of love expression assessed by their particular measure. Like Critelli et al. (1986), Hendrick and Hendrick (1986) recognized that erotic love contains elements of "strong physical preferences, early attraction, and intensity of emotion" (p. 400). Of the seven items designed to assess this particular love style, three directly relate to sexual attraction, behavior, and satisfaction. Specifically, the final version of the scale contains items assessing the extent to which the participant believes that he or she and the partner experienced immediate mutual attraction, have the right physical "chemistry" between them, and engage in very intense and satisfying lovemaking.

All of the aforementioned theorists and researchers seem to agree that romantic love contains a sexual component that differentiates it from other types or varieties of love. Where they lack consensus is in the specification of the precise nature of that sexual component. That is, many of the existing theoretical conceptualizations and empirical measures of romantic love contain an interesting mixture of sexual phenomena, including *physical and/or sexual attraction* (e.g., Critelli et al. 1986; Hatfield 1988; Hatfield and Walster 1978; Hendrick and Hendrick 1986; Lee 1973; Pam et al. 1975; Shaver and Hazan 1988; Sternberg 1988; Tennov 1979), *sexual excitement* (e.g., Critelli et al.

1986; Hatfield and Walster 1978), *physiological and/or sexual arousal* (e.g., Critelli et al. 1986; Hatfield and Sprecher 1986; Hatfield and Walster 1978; Shaver et al. 1988), *sexual deprivation* (e.g., Hatfield and Walster 1978), *sexual satisfaction and/or gratification* (e.g., Berscheid and Walster 1974; Hendrick and Hendrick 1986; Shaver et al. 1988; Walster and Berscheid 1971), *sexual involvement* (e.g., Hendrick and Hendrick 1986; Lee 1973, 1978), and *sexual activity* (e.g., Buss 1988; Swensen 1961; Swensen and Gilner 1963; Shaver and Hazan 1988). These phenomena do not represent the same, or in some instances even similar, concepts.

SEXUAL DESIRE: AN ESSENTIAL FEATURE OR ROMANTIC LOVE?

This state of affairs is changing, however. Researchers who prior to this time were content to view the sexual component of romantic love as an undifferentiated construct encompassing anything from sexual deprivation to sexual feelings to sexual arousal to sexual activity are now beginning to recognize that not all sexual phenomena are created equal and that different sexual experiences may have decidedly different consequences for romantic love. In particular, it is *sexual desire* (i.e., a subjective, psychological experience that can be understood broadly as an interest in sexual objects or activities, or as a wish, need, or drive to seek out sexual objects or to engage in sexual activities; e.g., Bancroft 1988; Kaplan 1979; Regan and Berscheid 1995, 1996)—and not *sexual arousal* (i.e., a state of reflex activation that involves the sex organs and nervous system; e.g., Masters, Johnson, and Kolodny 1982) or *sexual activity* (e.g., masturbation, intercourse)—that is the experience most closely associated with romantic love.

For example, Berscheid (1988) ended her comments on the state of social psychological theory and research with respect to romantic love with the following admonition:

My third, and final, conclusion (to which I've already alluded) is that the role of sexual desire and experience has been neglected in contemporary discussions of romantic love. It is all very well to look down one's nose at Sigmund Freud's cursory analysis of romantic love as repressed, suppressed, or frustrated sexual desire, but, for me at least, Freud seems to have gotten smarter as I've gotten older. And, surely, it is no accident that the wisest of the romantic love theorists, Theodore Reik, entitled his classic book *Of Love and Lust* (1941) (and not, by the way, *Of Love and Liking*. (p. 372)

Others have taken a similar stance. Hatfield and her colleagues no longer view passionate love as an amorphous amalgamation of un-differentiated "tender and sexual feelings" (Hatfield, Traupmann, and

Sprecher 1984: 109), but now argue that passionate love, "the desire for union with another," and sexual desire, "the desire for *sexual* union with another," have much in common and can in fact be explained by the same paradigm (Hatfield and Rapson 1987:259). Specifically, Hatfield and Rapson (1987) believe that both passionate love and sexual desire are fueled by and thrive under the "right conditions"—in this case, a mixture of both intensely positive and intensely negative emotional experiences such as delight, security, anger, anxiety, and jealousy (also see Hatfield 1988).

Indeed, Hatfield and Sprecher's (1986) Passionate Love Scale represents perhaps the best measure of romantic love currently available. Drawing on past theoretical conceptualizations, previously developed romantic love measures, and in-depth personal interviews, these researchers carefully crafted a series of items designed to represent the cognitive, emotional, and behavioral components of the passionate love experience. Subsequent administration and revision of this original set of items resulted in a 30-item scale that reliably discriminates between feelings of passionate versus companionate love. Of particular interest is the fact that the scale contains a number of items that are directly and indirectly relevant to the sexual aspect of passionate love, including the following:

   3. Sometimes my body trembles with excitement at the sight of ———.
   4. I take delight in studying the movements and angles of———'s body.
11. I want ———physically, emotionally, mentally.
13. I melt when looking deeply into ———'s eyes.
17. I sense my body responding when ——— touches me.
24. I eagerly look for signs indicating ———'s desire for me.
27. In the presence of ———, I yearn to touch and be touched.
29. I possess a powerful attraction for ———.

Items 27 and 29, and perhaps items 11 and 24, seem in particular to capture the essence of sexual desire.

Romantic love *is* different from the other types of love that have been labeled and discussed over the years, and I think that Berscheid and Hatfield have correctly surmised wherein that difference lies: Sexual desire is a distinguishing feature and a prerequisite of the romantic love experience. The proof, however, is in the pudding. The remainder of this chapter, then, examines empirical evidence, some conducted by myself and my students, that speaks to the question of whether sexual desire is in fact related to the experience of romantic love.

EMPIRICAL EVIDENCE FOR THE ASSOCIATION BETWEEN SEXUAL DESIRE AND ROMANTIC LOVE

Indirect Evidence

Indirect empirical support for the association between sexual desire and romantic love is provided by several sources. Therapists with years of clinical experience find that the waxing and waning of sexual desire in a relationship corresponds to how well a couple is functioning in other, nonsexual relational areas (e.g., how well they communicate, their level of emotional intimacy, the ways in which they deal with conflict, how power is distributed in the relationship; e.g., Arnett, Prosen, and Toews 1986; Kaplan 1979; LoPiccolo 1980; Pietropinto 1986; Schover 1986; Stuart, Hammond, and Pett 1987; Verhulst and Heiman 1979). In addition, some clinicians argue that sexual desire is enhanced by feelings of romantic love. For example, Kaplan (1979) proposes that "love is the best aphrodisiac discovered so far" (p. 61), as does Levine (1982). These clinical observations are based on case studies and unsystematic observations of troubled marriages and persons. Nonetheless, they provide indirect support for a relationship between sexual desire and romantic love.

A moderate amount of non-clinical, albeit still indirect, evidence for this association also exists. For example, during the process of scale validation, Hatfield and Sprecher (1986) gave their Passionate Love Scale (PLS) and a battery of various other measures to students involved in dating or more serious relationships. These researchers found that scores for both men and women on the PLS scale correlated significantly with self-reported satisfaction with the sexual aspect of the current relationship, as well as with several ratings of current desire for physical interaction with the partner. Specifically, higher PLS scores were associated with an increased desire to be held by the partner, to kiss the partner, and to engage in sex with the partner. Individuals who are very passionately in love, then, experience more sexual desire for their partner than people who are less passionately in love.

Similar results were found earlier by Pam et al. (1975). These researchers administered their thirty-item love scale to a group of unmarried male and female college students who were reportedly either in love, dating but not in love, or merely friendly with another individual of the opposite sex. Results indicated that the "in love" group and the "friendship" group scored essentially the same on the respect subscale and significantly higher than the "dating" group, implying that respect is as important an aspect of romantic relationships as it is of friendships. However, when a comparison of means was made for the physical attraction subscale (this subscale contained items assessing the perceived physical and sexual attractiveness of the partner), the "in love" group had a significantly higher mean score than either the "dating" or "friendship" group. It thus appears that the sexual desirability of the partner is a vital component of a romantic relationship.

Direct Evidence

None of the above research was specifically designed to assess the relationship between sexual desire and romantic love. Thus, the results, though suggestive, provide at best only weak support for that association. However, a growing number of social psychologists have attempted to examine this relationship explicitly.

A series of studies conducted by Berscheid and colleagues provides a provocative and convincing examination of the sexual desire–romantic love connection. These researchers argue that the experience of "love" is fundamentally different from the experience of being "in love," and they present evidence that romantic or passionate love ("in love") is characterized by a greater amount of sexual attraction than "love." For example, Meyers, Ridge, and Berscheid (1991) asked a sample of undergraduate men and women whether they believed that a difference existed between the experience of being in love with and that of loving another person: Fully 87% emphatically claimed that there was a difference between the two experiences. In addition, when asked to specify the nature of that difference in an open-ended response format, participants were more likely to cite sexual attraction (i.e., sexual desire) as descriptive of the "in love" experience.

More recently, using what they term a "social categorical method," Meyers and Berscheid (1996; also see Berscheid and Meyers 1996) asked a large sample of undergraduate men and women to list the initials of all the people they currently love[d], the initials of all those with whom they were currently in love, and the initials of all those toward whom they currently felt sexual attraction/desire. For each individual respondent, the authors calculated the probability that persons named in the "sexually desire" category were also named in the "in love" and "love" categories. These sets of probabilities were then averaged across respondents. The results indicated that 85% of the persons listed in the "in love" category were also listed in the "sexually desire" category, whereas only 2% of those listed in the "love" category (and not cross-listed in the "in love" category) were listed in the "sexually desire" category. Thus, the objects of respondents' feelings of romantic love (but not of their feelings of love) also tended to be the objects of their desire.

My own research also provides evidence that romantic love is a qualitatively different experience from such other varieties of interpersonal attraction as loving and liking, and that sexual desire in particular is one of its essential components. For example, Elizabeth Kocan, Teresa Whitlock and I became interested in how people conceptualize the state of being in love. Essentially, we wanted to determine what features spontaneously enter people's minds when thinking about romantic love. If sexual desire is indeed an important or central feature of romantic love, as theory suggests, then one of the features people should report being characteristic of the state of romantic love is sexual desire or attraction. To investigate this hypothesis, we conducted a prototype study (Regan, Kocan & Whitlock, in press). The prototype approach is a standard social cognition paradigm used to investigate how people organize or represent a concept—like romantic love—in their cognitive systems. It allows researchers to determine the central (highly distinguishing or essential) and peripheral (less distinguishing or essential) features of a concept (e.g., Rosch 1975). We asked 120 undergraduate men and women to list in a free response format all of the features they considered characteristic or prototypical of the state of romantic love. We reminded them that these features could include emotions, feelings, thoughts, behaviors, actions, or events, and, in addition, could range from positive to negative. Two raters then compiled a verbatim list of all the specific features generated by our participants, and we then grouped these features into relatively larger categories to eliminate redundancies. This resulted in a list of 119 features of romantic love. Finally, two additional raters coded each participant's free response for the presence or absence of these features.

Table 4.1 illustrates the most commonly generated features. Out of 119 features spontaneously generated by our participants, sexual desire received the second highest frequency rating. In other words, when thinking of romantic love, the majority of our participants automatically thought of sexual attraction. In addition, this feature was viewed as more significant to the romantic love concept than kissing (cited by only 10% of participants), touching/holding (cited by 17.5%), and sexual activity (cited by 25%). These results support the notion that subjective, psychological sexual phenomena are more essential to the romantic love experience than behavioral sexual events, at least in the minds of young adults.

Two recent person perception experiments provided additional support for these prototype results (Regan in press). Person perception experiments are commonly used in social psychological research and essentially involve manipulating people's perceptions of a relationship and then measuring the impact of that manipulation on their subsequent evaluations and beliefs. In Experiment 1, a sample of sixty undergraduate men and women were given two self-report questionnaires ostensibly completed by "Rob" and "Nancy," a student couple enrolled at the same university. The members of this couple reported experiencing no sexual desire for each other or a high amount of sexual desire for each other, and were currently engaging in sexual activity with each other or were not sexually active. Thus, the design was a 2 (Sexual desire: Present, absent) x 2 (Sexual activity: Present, absent) factorial. Participants then estimated the likelihood that the partners experienced romantic love as well as a variety of other relationship events. The results indicated that both men and women believed that dating partners who experienced sexual desire for each other were more likely to be romantically in love with each other than dating partners who do not desire each other sexually, regardless of their current level of sexual activity. Specifically, on a 1–9 point scale, participants felt that it was highly likely that the couple who desired each other would also be in love (7.00 on the scale on average) and that it was significantly less likely that the desireless couple was in love (2.23 on the same scale).

Table 4.1
Features of Romantic Love

Rank	Feature	Frequency*
1	Trust	80.0
2	**Sexual attraction/desire**	65.8
3	Acceptance/tolerance	50.8
4	Share thoughts/secrets	44.2
5	Spend time together	44.2
6	Honesty	40.0
7	Personal sacrifice	40.0
8	Companionship/friendship	39.2
9	Jealousy	37.5
10	Communication	36.7
...		
18	**Sexual activities**	25.0
...		
25	**Touching/holding**	17.5
...		
55	**Kissing**	10.0
...		

*Percentage of respondents who spontaneously cited each item in their free response definitions of the concept of romantic love.

A second study, a conceptual replication of the first, confirmed these results. Here, 48 men and women received information about the members of a heterosexual, dating "student couple" who ostensibly reported that they were currently romantically in love with each other, that they loved each other, or that they liked each other. Using 1–9 point scales, participants then estimated the likelihood that the members of the couple experienced sexual desire for each other and the amount of desire that they felt for each other (i.e., a 2 [Participant Gender] x 3 [Relationship Type: Romantic love, loving, liking] between-participants factorial design). Analyses revealed that participants perceived couples who were romantically in love as more *likely* to experience sexual desire than couples who loved each other (7.81 vs. 5.94 on the scale) or who liked each other (7.81 vs. 4.81 on the scale). Similarly, couples who were romantically in love were believed to experience a greater *amount* of sexual desire for each other than couples who loved each other or who liked each other (7.31 vs. 4.87). Interestingly, sexual desire was believed to be no more likely in a "loving" relationship than in a "liking" relationship, and greater amounts of sexual desire were not believed to occur in loving relationships than liking relationships. Again, it seems that sexual desire is viewed, at least by young men and women, as an important feature or component of romantic love relationships—and not of relationships characterized by feelings of love and/or liking.

I have argued that sexual desire is necessary for the experience of romantic love. Certainly, the studies presented earlier suggest that young adults perceive sexual desire to be an important feature of that experience. However, it is also important to recognize that sexual desire may not be sufficient for romantic love. Other feelings and events, including affection and tenderness, no doubt must be present before the majority of individuals reach the conclusion that they are "in love." Similarly, this discussion is not meant to imply that sexual desire cannot occur in the absence of romantic love or that sexual desire is the sole property of romantic love relationships. Sexual desire no doubt occurs in relationships characterized by liking and loving, although it is probably less likely to be present in those relationships than in relationships characterized by romantic love.

In sum, sexual desire is the ingredient that puts the "romantic" in romantic love. A person who does not sexually desire his or her partner may like, love, care for, or even altruistically be willing to die for that individual, but he or she is not likely to be romantically in love with that person.

CONCLUSION: CONSEQUENCES OF BELIEFS ABOUT THE SEXUAL DESIRE–ROMANTIC LOVE LINK

Over the course of conducting my research, I have grown increasingly dissatisfied with simply exploring whether sexual desire and romantic love are associated. Rather, I have begun to think that it might be more important to examine whether there are implications or consequences to this perceived association between desire and love. For example, does the fact that most young adults seem to link sexual desire and romantic love have implications for understanding the dynamics of sexual interactions, including those that result in date rape or harassment? I suspect that it does, and this is why I think that it is so important to study cognitions—beliefs, thoughts, expectations—about sexual desire and romantic love. We know that such cognitions are associated with behavior. The sexuality literature provides at least two demonstrations that beliefs and attitudes about sexual phenomena parallel actual sexual behavior in romantic relationships. For example, research on sexual standards has identified a set of widely held beliefs about the male and female role in heterosexual sexual interaction (i.e., men initiate sexual activity, women respond to male initiation with refusal or acceptance; e.g., Reiss 1981). These beliefs closely match the actual behavior of men and women in both dating (e.g., O'Sullivan and Byers 1992) and marital relationships (e.g., Byers and Heinlein 1989). Similarly, researchers interested in sexual aggression and rape have delineated a set of stereotypic beliefs or "rape myths" (e.g., women have an unconscious wish to be raped) that is not only commonly endorsed by the American population (e.g., Burt 1980) but that also predicts sexually aggressive behavior among young men in their ongoing dating relationships (e.g., Christopher, Owens, and Stecker 1993; Malamuth et al. 1991).

In short, whatever their origin and whether they have basis in fact, the beliefs that men and women hold about sex and love undoubtedly have direct implications for their interpersonal behavior and for their relationships with actual and potential sexual and romantic partners. And it is precisely this topic that I have turned to in the past few years. In a recent person perception experiment (Regan 1997), I hypothesized that, because romantic love is assumed to reflect sexual desire, an expression of love during a sexual interaction may significantly alter perceptions of that interaction. To explore this hypothesis, I asked 80 college students to read one of two versions of a scenario involving an interaction between a heterosexual, dating couple, whom I called "Bob" and "Cathy." In each scenario, the couple has rented a movie and returned to the man's room in order to view the video; during the movie, Bob expresses an interest in sexual activity to Cathy. Half of the participants read a scenario in which Bob's request is romantically phrased (i.e., "Cathy, I'm in love with you. I'd like to show you how I feel by making love to you"). The other half of the participants read a sexual request that is simply stated as such (i.e., "Cathy, I find you very attractive. I want to have sex with you"). Both scenarios continue with Bob proceeding to initiate sexual activity. This action is followed by a verbal refusal from Cathy in which she states that she does not feel that the couple should engage in intercourse and adds that she herself is not ready for this experience. Participants were then told that the date ends in sexual intercourse. Thus, the two scenarios differed only in the manner in which Bob phrased his request for sexual intercourse. I then asked the participants to make several inferences about the partners and their interaction, using 9-point scales.

There were three noteworthy results. The first indicated that the nature of Bob's sexual request to Cathy (love or sex) indeed did affect perceptions of the couple and of their interaction. Specifically, when Bob expressed his feelings of romantic love for Cathy, he was perceived as less likely to have sexually assaulted (3.85 vs. 5.98) and coerced (4.30 vs. 6.18) her, and as less responsible for the occurrence of intercourse (4.97 vs. 6.55) than when he expressed his sexual interest in her. Conversely, when Cathy received a verbal declaration of love from Bob, she was viewed as more likely to have experienced sexual desire (6.05 vs. 3.70) and to have wanted sexual intercourse (4.20 vs. 2.30)—despite her clearly stated unwillingness—than when she received an expression of sexual interest. Finally, the sexual interaction was perceived as significantly more consensual (i.e., reflecting the mutual desires of the partners; 4.88 vs. 3.40) when Bob professed love than when he professed sexual intent.

The second finding was that these perceptions of the male and female target were associated with the perceived likelihood of consensual sex. That is, a series of correlational analyses revealed that three beliefs about Cathy—the likelihood that she experienced sexual desire, wanted to engage in intercourse with the male target, and was responsible for the occurrence of intercourse—were positively correlated with the perceived likelihood that the couple's sexual activity was consensual. (In other words, the more sexual desire that Cathy was believed to experience, the more responsible she was assumed to be for the sexual episode.) One belief about Bob—the likelihood that he was responsible for the occurrence of intercourse—was negatively associated with the perception that the couple's sexual activity was consensual (i.e., the more responsible he was assumed to be, the less consensual the sexual episode was believed to be).

The major result was that Cathy's perceived sexual desire level—and there were two items that tapped this—*mediated* the effect of Bob's sexual request style (romantic vs. sexual) on the perceived likelihood of consensual sex. To test this hypothesis, I followed Baron and Kenny's (1986) analytic approach. First, the independent variable (the style of Bob's sexual request) was found to be correlated with the dependent variable (perceived likelihood of consensual sex). This independent variable was also correlated with the proposed mediators (perceived likelihood that Cathy experienced sexual desire; perceived likelihood that Cathy wanted to engage in sexual intercourse). Third, three regression equations were estimated. In Equation 1, each presumed mediator was regressed on the independent variable; this analysis confirmed that Bob's request style significantly predicted the perceived likelihood that Cathy felt sexual desire and the perceived likelihood that Cathy wanted to engage in sex. (Remember that we knew this from the correlational analyses I mentioned earlier.) Equation 2 involved regressing the dependent variable (likelihood of consensual sex) on the independent variable (Bob's sexual request style), I found that request style did significantly predict perceived likelihood of consensual sex, which we also already knew from the correlational analyses. Finally, in Equation 3 the dependent variable was regressed on both the independent and mediator variables. This analysis revealed that the effect of request style on the perceived likelihood of consensual sex dropped to non-significance when the mediators were added into the equation. The results from these three equations establish mediation according to Baron and Kenny's (1986) guidelines.

So, in plain English, what does all this mean? Well, this type of mediational analysis provides an indirect test for the hypothesis that beliefs about the association between sexual desire and romantic love may contribute to sexual miscommunication and poorly coordinated sexual interactions. Specifically, my results demonstrate that, by providing people with varied information about a male target's sexual request style, their perception of a female target's level of desire was altered. As a consequence, beliefs about the nature of the targets' sexual interaction were also altered. This suggests at least a partial explanation for how external events—like a man's sexual request style, or the degree of resistance offered by a rape victim—come to take on psychological significance and thereby affect subsequent assumptions about the nature of a sexual interaction. An expression of romantic love by a male target significantly increases the likelihood that a subsequent sexual interaction with an unwilling partner is labeled "consensual" *because perceivers assume that this expression has caused sexual desire in that partner* (and not because they attribute greater responsibility to the male or female partner, for instance).

These findings suggest that beliefs about desire and love may contribute to sexual dynamics, communication, and miscommunication; may influence the labels we place on sexual interactions; and may even result in sexually inappropriate behavior. For example, a male partner may express feelings of love, intimacy, and commitment in an attempt to excite his partner's feelings of sexual desire and to increase the likelihood of sexual activity. Moreover, assuming that sexual desire in women is inevitably triggered by declarations of love and commitment, he may view these "romantic" events as adequate justification for the occurrence of forcible sexual activity. Conversely, a woman who believes that she ought to experience desire upon receiving an expression of intimacy or love from a dating partner may be uncertain as to how to interpret, and consequently less likely to report, a sexually violent encounter.

In short, beliefs and assumptions about the relation between sex and love matter. It is my hope that future researchers will continue to explore cognitions about desire and love, and will begin to delineate the ways in which men and women allow their behaviors to be guided by these beliefs and expectations in their actual, ongoing interactions.

REFERENCES

Arnett, J. L.; H. Prosen; and J. A. Toews. "Loss of Libido Due to Stress." *Medical Aspects of Human Sexuality* 20: 140–148, 1986.

Aron, A., and E. N. Aron. "Love and Sexuality." In K. McKinney and S. Sprecher (eds.), *Sexuality in Close Relationships*. Hillsdale, N.J.: Erlbaum, 1991, pp. 25–48.

Bancroft, J. "Sexual Desire and the Brain." *Sexual and Marital Therapy* 3: 11–27, 1988.

Bardis, P. D. "Erotometer: A Technique for the Measurement of Heterosexual Love." *International Review of Sociology* 1: 71–77, 1971.

Baron, R. M., and D. A. Kenny. "The Moderator-Mediator Variable Distinction in Social Psychological Research: Conceptual, Strategic, and Statistical Considerations." *Journal of Personality and Social Psychology* 51: 1173–1182, 1986.

Berscheid, E. "Interpersonal Attraction." In G. Lindzey and E. Aronson (eds.), *The Handbook of Social Psychology*, 3rd ed., Vol. 2. New York: Random House, 1985, pp. 413–484.

———. "Some Comments on Love's Anatomy: Or, Whatever Happened to Old-fashioned Lust?" In R. J. Sternberg and M. L. Barnes (eds.), *The Psychology of Love*. New Haven, Conn.: Yale University Press, 1988, pp. 359–374.

Berscheid, E., and S. A. Meyers. "A Social Categorical Approach to a Question About Love." *Personal Relationships* 3: 19–43, 1996.

Berscheid, E., and E. Walster. "A Little Bit About Love." In T. L. Huston (ed.), *Foundations of Interpersonal Attraction*. New York: Academic Press, 1974, pp. 355–381.

Bowlby, J. *Attachment and Loss. Vol. 1, Attachment*. New York: Basic Books, 1969.

Branden, N. "A Vision of Romantic Love." In R. J. Sternberg, and M. L. Barnes (eds.), *The Psychology of Love*. New Haven, Conn.: Yale University Press, 1988, pp. 218–231.

Brehm, S. S. "Passionate Love." In R. J. Sternberg and M. L. Barnes (eds.), *The Psychology of Love*. New Haven, Conn.: Yale University Press, 1988, pp. 232–263.

Burgess, E. W., and P. Wallin. *Engagement and Marriage*. Philadelphia: Lippincott, 1953.

Burt, M. R. "Cultural Myths and Supports for Rape." *Journal of Personality and Social Psychology* 38: 217–230, 1980.

Buss, D. M. "Love Acts: The Evolutionary Biology of Love." In R. J. Sternberg, and M. L. Barnes (eds.), *The Psychology of Love*. New Haven, Conn.: Yale University Press, 1988, pp. 100–118.

Byers, E. S., and L. Heinlein. "Predicting Initiations and Refusals of Sexual Activities in Married and Cohabiting Heterosexual Couples." *The Journal of Sex Research* 26: 210–231, 1989.

Chaucer, G. *The Canterbury Tales*. In F. N. Robinson (ed.), *The Works of Geoffrey Chaucer*, 2nd ed. Cambridge, Mass.: Riverside Press, 1957, pp. 17–265. (Original work written 1387–1400.)

Christopher, F. S.; L. A. Owens; and H. L. Stecker. "Exploring the Darkside of Courtship: A Test of a Model of Male Premarital Sexual Aggressiveness." *Journal of Marriage and the Family* 55: 469–479, 1993.

Critelli, J. W.; E. J. Myers; and V. E. Loos. "The Components of Love: Romantic Attraction and Sex Role Orientation." *Journal of Personality* 54: 354–370, 1986.

Dion, K. L., and K. K. Dion. "Correlates of Romantic Love." *Journal of Consulting and Clinical Psychology* 1: 51–56, 1973.

Driscoll, R.; K. E. Davis; and M. E. Lipetz. "Parental Interference and Romantic Love: The Romeo and Juliet Effect." *Journal of Personality and Social Psychology*, 24: 1–10, 1972.

Goode, W. J. "The Theoretical Importance of Love." *American Sociological Review* 24: 38–47, 1959.

Hatfield, E. "Passionate and Companionate Love." In R. L. Sternberg and M. L. Barnes (eds.), *The Psychology of Love*. New Haven, Conn.: Yale University Press, 1988, pp. 191–217.

Hatfield, E., and R. L. Rapson. "Passionate Love/Sexual Desire: Can the Same Paradigm Explain Both?" *Archives of Sexual Behavior* 16: 259–278, 1987.

Hatfield, E., and S. Sprecher. "Measuring Passionate Love in Intimate Relationships." *Journal of Adolescence* 9: 383–410, 1986.

Hatfield, E., and G. W. Walster. *A New Look at Love*. Reading, Mass.: Addison-Wesley, 1978.

Hatfield, E.; J. Traupmann; and S. Sprecher. "Older Women's Perceptions of Their Intimate Relationships." *Journal of Social and Clinical Psychology* 2: 108–124, 1984.

Hazan, C., and P. Shaver. "Romantic Love Conceptualized as an Attachment Process." *Journal of Personality and Social Psychology* 52: 511–524, 1987.

Hendrick, C., and S. Hendrick. "A Theory and Method of Love." *Journal of Personality and Social Psychology* 50: 392–402, 1986.

Hendrick, S., and C. Hendrick. *Liking, Loving, & Relating*, 2nd ed. Pacific Grove, Calif.: Brooks/Cole, 1992.

Kaplan, H. S. *Disorders of Sexual Desire and Other New Concepts and Techniques in Sex Therapy*. New York: Simon and Schuster, 1979.

Kazak, A. E., and N. D. Reppucci. "Romantic Love as a Social Institution." In K. S. Pope (ed.), *On Love and Loving*. San Francisco, Calif.: Jossey-Bass, 1980, pp. 209–227.

Kephart, W. M. "Some Correlates of Romantic Love." *Journal of Marriage and the Family* 29: 470–474, 1967.

Lee, J. A. *Colours of Love*. Toronto: New Press, 1973.

———. "Love-styles." In R. J. Sternberg and M. L. Barnes (eds.), *The Psychology of Love*. New Haven, Conn.: Yale University Press, 1988, pp. 38–67.

Levine, S. B. "A Modern Perspective on Nymphomania." *Journal of Sex & Marital Therapy* 8: 316–324, 1982.

LoPiccolo, L. "Low Sexual Desire." In S. R. Leiblum and L. A. Pervin (eds.), *Principles and Practice of Sex Therapy*. New York: Guilford Press, 1980, pp. 29–63.

Malamuth, N. M.; R. J. Sockloskie; M. P. Koss, and J. S. Tanaka. "Characteristics of Aggressors Against Women: Testing a Model Using a National Sample of College Students." *Journal of Consulting and Clinical Psychology* 59: 670–681, 1991.

Maslow, A. H. *Motivation and Personality*. New York: Harper, 1970.

Masters, W. H.; V. E. Johnson; and R. C. Kolodny. *Human Sexuality*. Boston: Mass.: Little, Brown, 1982.

Mathes, E. W. "Convergence Among Measures of Interpersonal Attraction." *Motivation and Emotion* 8: 77–84, 1984.

Meyers, S., and E. Berscheid. "The Language of Love: The Difference a Preposition Makes." *Personality and Social Psychology Bulletin,* 1996.

Meyers, S.; R. D. Ridge; and E. Berscheid. "'Love' vs. 'In Love.'" Unpublished manuscript, University of Minnesota, Department of Psychology, Minneapolis, 1991.

Murstein, B. I. "A Taxonomy of Love." In R. J. Sternberg and M. L. Barnes (eds.), *The Psychology of Love*. New Haven, Conn.: Yale University Press, 1988, pp. 13–37.

Pam, A.; R. Plutchik; and H. R. Conte. "Love: A Psychometric Approach." *Psychological Reports* 37: 83–88, 1975.

Pietropinto, A. "Inhibited Sexual Desire." *Medical Aspects of Human Sexuality* 20: 46–49, 1986.

O'Sullivan, L. F., and E. S. Byers. "College Students' Incorporation of Initiator and Restrictor Roles in Sexual Dating Interactions." *Journal of Sex Research* 29: 435–446, 1992.

Regan, P. C. "Of Lust and Love: Beliefs about the Role of Sexual Desire in Romantic Relationships." *Personal Relationships*, in press.

———. "The Impact of Male Sexual Request Style on Perceptions of Sexual Interactions: The Mediational Role of Beliefs about Female Sexual Desire." *Basic and Applied Social Psychology*, 19: 519–532, 1997.

Regan, P. C., and E. Berscheid. "Gender Differences in Beliefs about the Causes of Male and Female Sexual Desire." *Personal Relationships* 2: 345–358, 1995.

———. "Beliefs about the State, Goals, and Objects of Sexual Desire." *Journal of Sex & Marital Therapy* 22: 110–120, 1996.

Regan, P. C.; E. R. Kocan; and T. Whitlock. "Ain't Love Grand! A Prototype Analysis of Romantic Love." *Journal of Social and Personal Relationships* (in press).

Reiss, I. L. "Some Observations on Ideology and Sexuality in America." *Journal of Marriage and the Family* 43: 271–283, 1981.

Rosch, E. "Cognitive Representations of Semantic Categories." *Journal of Experimental Psychology: General* 104: 192–233, 1975.

Rubin, Z. "Measurement of Romantic Love." *Journal of Personality and Social Psychology* 16: 265–273, 1970.

————. *Liking and Loving: An Invitation to Social Psychology*. New York: Holt, Rinehart, and Winston, 1973.

Schover, L. R. "Sexual Dysfunction: When a Partner Complains of Low Sexual Desire." *Medical Aspects of Human Sexuality* 20: 8–116, 1986.

Shaver, P. R., and C. Hazan. "A Biased Overview of the Study of Love." *Journal of Social and Personal Relationships* 5: 473–501, 1988.

Shaver, P.; C. Hazan; and D. Bradshaw. "Love as Attachment: The Integration of Three Behavioral Systems." In R. J. Sternberg and M. L. Barnes (eds.), *The Psychology of Love*. New Haven, Conn.: Yale University Press, 1988, pp. 68–99.

Simpson, J. A.; B. Campbell; and E. Berscheid. "The Association Between Romantic Love and Marriage: Kephart (1967) Twice Revisited." *Personality and Social Psychology Bulletin* 12: 363–372, 1986.

Spaulding, C. B. "The Romantic Love Complex in American culture." *Sociology and Social Research* 55: 82–100, 1971.

Sternberg, R. J. "A Triangular Theory of Love." *Psychological Review* 93: 119–135, 1986.

————. "Triangulating Love." In R. J. Sternberg and M. L. Barnes (eds.), *The Psychology of Love*. New Haven, Conn.: Yale University Press, 1988, pp. 119–138.

Sternberg, R. J., and M. L. Barnes (eds.). *The Psychology of Love*. New Haven, Conn.: Yale University Press, 1988, pp. 232–263.

Stuart, F. M.; D. C. Hammond; and M. A. Pett. "Inhibited Sexual Desire in Women." *Archives of Sexual Behavior* 16: 91–106, 1987.

Swensen, C. H. "Love: A Self-report Analysis with College Students." *Journal of Individual Psychology* 17: 167–171, 1961.

Swensen, C. H., and F. Gilner. "Factor Analysis of Self-report Statements of Love Relationships." *Journal of Individual Psychology* 19: 186–188, 1963.

Tennov, D. *Love and Limerence*. New York: Stein and Day, 1979.

Verhulst, J., and J. R. Heiman. "An Interactional Approach to Sexual Dysfunctions." *American Journal of Family Therapy* 7: 19–36, 1979.

Walster, E., and E. Berscheid. "Adrenaline Makes the Heart Grow Fonder." *Psychology Today* 5: 47–62, 1971.

5

Romantic Love and the Psychology of Sexual Behavior: Open and Closed Secrets

Duncan Cramer and Dennis Howitt

In this chapter, we ask some awkward questions about the relationship between romantic love and sexual behavior. First, is there such a thing as romantic love which people can readily distinguish from other types of love? This question is crucial in defining the psychological features of romantic love. Indeed there is evidence that love is a prerequisite for sexual behavior for some people. Second, how do romantic conceptions of love characterize sexual fantasy? Although sexual fantasy seems to be essential to much sexual behavior, the contents of this fantasy suggest that an underlying tension exists between the attitudinal or ideological aspects of romantic love and the imagery that accompanies sexual behavior. The two are not seamlessly linked. Despite the assumption in dominant ideology that romantic relationships lead to sexual liaisons characterized by romance, the underlying fantasy may be somewhat callous or brutal and nonexclusive.

Concepts such as romantic love and even sexual behavior can only be imprecisely defined psychologically. While the definition of sexual behavior may seem straightforward as sexual behavior has obvious physical and bodily expression, this clarity is somewhat illusory from a psychological point of view. Sexual behavior in humans involves complex cognitions such as attitudes, beliefs, thoughts and fantasies as well as even more intangible features associated with culture and lifestyle. So, in a very real sense, it is not possible to separate the physically sexual from the rest of a person's sexuality and other aspects of an individual's being. Furthermore, it is psychologically naive to assume that a restricted set of overt behaviors unproblematically defines and sets limits on what can be construed as sexual behavior.

For example, some psychologists have argued that crimes such as burglary are expressions of sexual motives even though no genital or attempted genital contact is involved (Revitch and Schlesinger 1988). Similarly, some feminist psychologists and others argue that rape is not an erotically motivated, sexual crime. Instead, they suggest, it should be regarded as yet another expression of male power and dominance motives that form the bedrock of sexual politics (Kelly 1988). This is clearly a psychological explanation of rape but one in which the erotic or the sexual component of genital contact is dismissed as unimportant compared to a macro-level analysis based on sexual politics far removed from the psychodynamics of an individual rapist. This feminist position likely has some validity, and this point of view is reinforced by evidence, for example, that rape is not sexually satisfying for at least a proportion of rapists (Groth and Hobson 1983). All of this is important since it reminds us that the parameters of human sexuality are not clearly defined or constrained within psychology and that for its understanding we must go far beyond an analysis of sex as merely a genital act.

Despite misgivings, we will arbitrarily restrict our consideration of sexual behavior to aspects manifestly related to its physical or bodily expressions. "Sexual behavior" is taken to refer to the attitudes, behavior, feelings, and cognitions that are concerned with sexual arousal and that lead to genital stimulation and, frequently, excitement. Of course, we cannot generalize with any precision about the nature of these attitudes, behaviors, feelings and cognitions since they vary widely between people. In short, our restricted and arbitrary definition essentially limits consideration of sexual behavior to the "erotic" which constitutes only a part of potential sexual behaviors. In this way we can establish a point of focus for our consideration of sexual behavior.

Inevitably, any definition of romantic love needs to differentiate it from the feelings involved in other forms of close attachments (such as that which may exist between parent and child or two close friends). It seems intuitively obvious that these different forms of "love" share many features in common. Features such as intensity, commitment, exclusivity and centrality seem more or less central to most forms of love and do not intuitively enable us to distinguish romantic love from other forms of love such as familial love. As a consequence of the complexity of the nexus of features that constitute the different forms of love, much of the research effort on love has been directed at attempts to identify ways of explicitly conceptualizing the essence of romantic love and distinguishing it from other forms of love.

CONCEPTUALIZING ROMANTIC LOVE AS AN ATTITUDE

When we speak of romantic love, we are using everyday language that may not readily translate into psychological processes. Romantic love is not just a feeling; for many it is also culturally an ideal and sought-after state. Thus, the concept carries with it not only implications of intense subjective and personal experiences, but also a great deal of ideological, attitudinal and belief baggage that may be to a degree independent of the subjective feelings. To answer questions about the nature of the psychological features of romantic love involves us trawling widely. A fundamental conceptual matter that follows from these considerations is that we should distinguish between two quite different, but possibly intercorrelated, concepts:

1. Attitudes toward and beliefs about the phenomenon.
2. Self-reported experiences or observations about the phenomenon.

This applies whether or not we are considering romantic love, sexual behavior or any other aspect of human experience. A newly married couple's beliefs about marriage—sharing, friendship, exclusivity, and so forth—may be radically different from how they experience marriage. Such a distinction between the "ideology of relationships" and the "subjective facts of relationships" has not always been clearly or consistently maintained by researchers in the assessment of romantic love (Cramer 1992). This is illustrated by attempts to measure the six theoretical lovestyles (Lee 1976) of Eros (physical attraction), Ludus (non-commitment), Storge (friendship), Mania (obsessiveness), Agape (altruism), and Pragma (practicality). The Love Attitude Scale (Hendrick and Hendrick 1987) mixed together items on (a) general attitudes about love (e.g.,"Love is really a deep friendship, not a mysterious, mystical emotion"), (b) characteristics of past relationships (e.g. "I can get over love affairs pretty easily and quickly"), and (c) behavior towards a current partner (e.g. "My lover and I really understand each other"). In other words, experiential love is treated as if it were just a small part of a bigger package which includes attitudinal and self-evaluative or descriptive components.

Researchers have also attempted to distinguish between romantic love as something idealized or sentimental and another type of love which might be described as realistic or conjugal. Typically, questionnaires for measuring romantic love include items implying that love overrides all other considerations concerning who to marry, that there are only very few people one can truly love and that love lasts forever. Among the first measures of romantic love was Gross's Romanticism Scale (1944). This was available in two similar but alternative versions, each of which consisted of romantic statements and realist statements.

A more recent measure is Sprecher and Metts's (1989) Romantic Beliefs Scale (1989).

The extent to which love can actually be conceptualized as either conjugal or romantic and whether individuals can effectively distinguish between the two are empirical matters. While in Western cultures the rhetoric surrounding love holds that there is a distinction between love as passion and love as something more comfortable and comforting, this needs to be confirmed by research. Munro and Adams (1978) obtained a number of questions that appear to measure either romantic or conjugal aspects of love. They found that empirically these items could be clustered or classified as involving (a) love as an ideal state, (b) conjugal-rational love, or (c) love as a powerful force. In other words, the findings were much in line with our Western expectations. They also correlated these three separate components of love with another three scales obtained by factor analyzing the Romanticism Scale (Knox and Sporakowski 1968). The factor analysis clusters together into groups the questionnaire items that are most closely related to each other: these factors or components can be described as representing "one true" love, "irrational" love and "love overcomes all" (Hinkle and Sporakowski 1975). As might be expected (if it is indeed possible to measure romantic love), it was found in a study of high-school-educated and college-educated residents of Calgary that Munro and Adams' romantic love items correlated moderately but significantly with the "one true love", "irrational love", and "love overcomes all" aspects of the Knox Romanticism Scale. One would expect that if conjugal-rational love is different from romantic love, that the measure of conjugal-rational love should coprrelate poorly with "one true love," "irrational love" and "love overcomes all" beliefs. So it was found since the Munro and Adams' measure of conjugal-rational love was not significantly correlated with any of these beliefs about love. Thus, at the attitudinal and ideological levels, the distinction between conjugal and romantic love is empirically supported.

How does this relate to sexual behavior? What limited evidence there is fails to show that sexual behavior is related to love as measured by any of the six common questionnaires measuring love attitudes (Dion and Dion 1973; Gross 1944; Hobart 1958; Knox and Sporakowski 1968; Munro and Adams 1978; Sprecher and Metts 1989). Munro and Adams (1978) included an item referring to sexual excitement ("Love is feeling warm, close and involved, but not necessarily sexually excited"). The evidence shows that conjugal love is correlated most highly with agreeing with this item and is not correlated with either of the two factors of romantic love. This would suggest that sexual excitement is independent of attitudes about romantic love. Romantic love may not coexist with sexual excitement. In contrast, conjugal love is seen as a state that stresses closeness and somewhat lacks a need for sexual excitement.

It should be obvious from this discussion that people seem to recognize a distinction between romantic or passionate love and conjugal or companionate love. At the same time, both seem to be construed positively, each with its own distinct virtues. Psychologists working on aspects of human sexuality other than love have given attention to measures of rather different aspects of sexuality. These contrast markedly with both the notions of romantic and conjugal love but may have some bearing on sexual behavior. The basic idea is that some people's sexualities (those of men, in particular) are dominated by sexually calloused attitudes which stress the unfeeling and exploitative attitudes of men towards women (Mosher and Anderson 1986). In the present context, this is important since the concept of sexual callousness stresses features of sexual attitudes that contrast markedly with the positive sentiments inherent in the concepts of conjugal and romantic love. A sense of the meaning of the concept of sexual callousness can be obtained from the following examples of items from the Sexual Callousness Scale:

A woman who is used to getting laid needs it as much as a man does.
You never know when you are going to meet a strange woman who will want to get laid.
You can fuck a bicycle if you have to.

As can be seen, the sexual callousness items reflect almost an antithesis to notions of both romantic and conjugal love. Sex is regarded as expedient and not dependent on the relationships inherent in romantic and conjugal forms of love. The interpretation of these items has been subject to a great deal of disagreement, if not controversy, since some researchers regard them as, in the main, reflecting licentious sexual attitudes, whereas other researchers regard them as manifesting overtly anti-women sentiments (Howitt and Cumberbatch 1990). The latter point of view is encouraged by the inclusion of items such as "You don't ask girls to screw, you tell them to screw," which perhaps indicates an element of sexual coercion in the measure. Of course, the choice of the description "sexual callousness" may or may not be apt. Some might suggest that the questionnaire reflects insensitive or hard attitudes only when judged from the ideologically founded perspectives of romantic and conjugal love.

EXPERIENTIAL ASSESSMENT OF ROMANTIC LOVE

Leaving these issues aside for the moment, we can turn to research and theory related to the experiential or phenomenological aspects of love. Probably the most widely used measure of experiential love is Rubin's (1970) Love Scale. Rubin suggests that this scale measures three major experiential components of love of another individual: (a) affiliative and dependent needs, (b) predispositions to help, and (c) exclusiveness and absorption. Dating partners score more highly on this scale than do same-sex close friends according to research on a sample of couples at the University of Michigan. One possible view of this is that the distinction between dating and same-sex close relationships is quantitative rather than qualitative. Each of the three components of romantic love measured by the scale is far from unknown in same-sex close relationships. On the other hand, it may merely reflect the idea that the Love Scale fails to identify the crucial qualitative differences between the two types of relationship. Experiential love as measured by the Love Scale also correlated moderately with agreement that they and their partner were "in love".

Given the commonly held view that passionate love declines with the length of a relationship, information on the relationship between degree of love and length of relationship may be of some significance in understanding what the Love Scale measures. Unfortunately, what little evidence there is on such temporal changes is inconsistent. In Rubin's study, women tended to love their partner more the longer they had been dating, although this relationship is best described as weak. In contrast, there was no significant relationship at all for men. Another study found that longer married couples showed less love (Cimbalo, Faling, and Mousaw 1976). Longitudinal studies on dating couples demonstrate that the relationships of those with lower Love Scale scores were more likely to break up later (Hill, Rubin, and Peplau 1976; Lund 1985).

Further evidence of the meaning of the Love Scale emerged from a study that compared a broad range of questions concerning love with ones from the Love Scale (Cramer 1992). Answers to items denoting physical and sexual attraction (e.g. "I am sexually attracted to ———" were largely unrelated to answers to questions from the Love Scale. This indicates that love can be distinguished from physical or sexual attraction. It is of interest, then, that the one item of the Love Scale that correlated with the physical attraction items was "When I am with ———, I spend a good deal of time just looking at ——— ". Perhaps this is further suggestive evidence of the independence of physical attraction from love. One might suggest that this precisely reflects aspects of the ideology of love common in Western cultures.

Several researchers have sought to distinguish the experiential aspects of romantic or passionate love from those of conjugal or companionate love. The Passionate Love Scale (Hatfield and Sprecher 1986) correlated highly and positively with Rubin's Love Scale in a sample of University of Wisconsin students. This would suggest that Rubin's scale of experiential aspects of love is measuring the romantic or passionate rather than the seemingly more comfortable conjugal or companionate love. Significantly, there was a positive relationship between the length of the relationship and the passion felt. However, none of the relationships studied was more than two years old. Among the Passionate Love Scale items at least two measured physical attraction ("11. I want—— physically, emotionally and mentally" and "29. I possess a powerful attraction for ——"). Furthermore, passionate love was moderately strongly associated with a desire to engage in sex with their partner. The Passionate Love Scale was unrelated to general sexual desire or libido independent of a specific partner (Beck, Bozman and Qualtrough 1991). The subjective experience of love as measured by Rubin's Love Scale is also moderately positively correlated with romantic beliefs (Sprecher and Metts 1989) and with romantic power (Munro and Adams 1978) and, in an high-school-educated sample, with a measure of romantic idealism.

In the absence of a scale for assessing experiential aspects of conjugal love and assuming that romantic and conjugal love are qualitatively distinct, lower scores on either the Love Scale or the Passionate Love Scale may indicate lower conjugal or companionate love. Earlier, Walster and Walster (1978) suggested that while Rubin's Love Scale may assess passionate love, his Liking Scale may measure companionate love, although later E. Walster stated that the Love Scale measured predominantly companionate love (Hatfield 1988) or a mixture of both (Hatfield and Sprecher 1986). As we have seen, the high correlation between Rubin's Love Scale and Hatfield and Sprecher's Passionate Love Scale shows that these questionnaires are measuring similar constructs. Nevertheless, there is no evidence to suggest that Rubin's Liking Scale assesses companionate love. Inspection of the content of the thirteen items indicate that eleven of them convey a favorable evaluation of the person rather than liking per se, and two of them reflect similarity.

Others have tried to identify and measure the crucial qualitative distinction between friendship and romantic love. For example, it has been suggested that trust is a feature of conjugal love which is lacking in romantic love (Driscoll, Davis and Lipetz 1972). On the other hand, Davis and Todd (1982) suggested that the three characteristics of fascination, exclusiveness, and sexual intimacy distinguish passion from friendship. These three characteristics as measured by the Relationship

Rating Form (Davis and Latty-Mann 1987) were found to discriminate most clearly between spouse/lover on the one hand and opposite-sex close friend, same-sex close friend, and best friend on the other (Davis and Todd 1982). Furthermore, it would appear that sexual intimacy is a relatively separate cluster of experiences from fascination and exclusiveness.[1]

The triangular theory of love (Sternberg 1986) distinguishes the two forms of love in other ways. It suggests that romantic love is characterized by high passion and intimacy but low commitment whereas companionate love is characterized by high intimacy and commitment but low passion. Both Hatfield and Sprecher's and Davis and Todd's passionate love scales correlate strongly with Sternberg's scale in unmarried students (Hendrick and Hendrick 1989), suggesting that the three scales are measuring the same quality. However, in a comparative study, Levy and Davis (1988) found only a moderate correlation between Sternberg's and Davis and Todd's scales.[2]

One theory regards types or styles of love as consisting of elements that may combine into distinctive compounds or mixtures (Lee 1976). The three primary elements are Eros (physical attraction), Ludus (noncommitment), and Storge (friendship). Three secondary compounds are Mania (Eros-Ludus), Agape (Eros-Storge), and Pragma (Ludus-Storge). Mania may be equated with obsessiveness, agape with altruism and pragma with practicality. Three secondary mixtures are ludic eros, storgic eros, and storgic ludus. In addition, three tertiary mixtures (consisting of a primary element and a secondary compound) are manic eros, manic ludus and manic storge. Eight of these twelve styles (omitting agape and the three tertiary mixtures) can be measured using either a short (Lee 1976) or a long (Lee 1975) questionnaire. The longer version also includes some items referring to sexual behavior. Factor analysis of this questionnaire based on data collected from students revealed a physical intimacy factor (Cramer 1987). This physical intimacy factor was positively related to eros (physical attraction) and negatively related to storge (friendship). In other words, sexual behavior was related to physical attraction but inversely related to friendship. This confirms the importance of sexual behavior in distinguishing between these two lovestyles.

Partly based on Lee's theory, Lasswell and Lasswell (1976) developed a questionnaire to assess the three primary and three secondary compound types. Later revised questionnaires seem better able to measure the six lovestyles (three primary and three secondary compound types) postulated by Lee (Hendrick and Hendrick 1986, 1989). Based on lists of questions established by previous research as the best measures of each of the six lovestyles, it proved impossible to differentiate empirically between the mania (obsessiveness) and agape (altruism) items (Cramer 1992). In this case, the sample was of British 16- to 17-year-old females. This offers the possibility that the structure of love is dependent on subcultural factors. The youthfulness of this sample might account for the association between obsessive love and altruism toward the loved one which might not apply in older, more experienced individuals.

Different facets of love have been postulated that are distinguishable from one another. These different styles of thinking about love and experiencing love have yet to be adequately differentiated. There seems to be fairly strong evidence that people experience passionate love, and this is what researchers have equated with romantic love. Whether this truly comes to grips with wider interpretations of romantic love, especially those of idealization and fantasy, is a moot point. Somewhat surprising is the failure to find evidence of conjugal love in research on experiential love, despite the evidence that people differentiate between the two effectively at the attitudinal level. This may be a result of research not addressing conjugal love anywhere as diligently as romantic love. In closely identifying romantic love with passion and passion with sexual behavior there is a risk of falling into the wide-open trap that faces all of those studying sexual behavior— the submersion of research in a sea of ideology. By this we mean that it is hard for a psychologist to escape the view that romantic love is good love and that sexual behavior is meaningful and satisfactory only in the context of romantic love. However, this is to ignore the emerging evidence that even in the context of romantic love the reality of our sexualities harbors deeper and superficially antagonistic secrets.

LOVE AND SEXUAL BEHAVIOR

In Western cultures, most people believe that sexual behavior should take place mainly within a loving or married relationship. In a nationally representative sample of 18- to 59-year-olds surveyed in the United States in 1992, about 66% of respondents said they would not have sex with someone unless they were in love with him or her (Laumann et al. 1994:514). In a similar survey carried out in the United Kingdom in 1990–1991, this kind of question was phrased in terms not of love but of having a regular relationship. About 80% of women and about 69% of men thought that having sexual relationships outside a regular relationship was always or mostly wrong (Johnson, Wadsworth et al. 1994:237). About 83% of the women and 58% of the men replied that having "one-night stands" was always or mostly wrong. Taken together, the answers to these two questions suggest that most people believe that sexual relationships should take place within a regular relationship. A nationally representative survey of 13-

to 19-year-olds undertaken in the United States in 1972 found that about 55% of the girls and 50% of the boys agreed with the statement that sex was immoral unless it is between two people who love each other (Sorensen 1973:412) while 38% of the girls and 40% of the boys believed that sex was immoral unless it was between two people who liked each other and had something in common (p. 414), implying that liking someone in many cases is sufficient reason for having sex. DeLamater and MacCorquodale (1979) surveyed a sample of 18- to 23-year-old students and non-students in Madison, asking them about the conditions under which it is acceptable to have sexual intercourse. The percentage of respondents who thought that sexual intercourse was acceptable if both wanted it but did not feel love or affection (p. 90) varied from 22 (in student women for females) to 46 (in non-student men for males).

A number of studies have found love to be related to various aspects of sexual behavior. One of the first studies to look at the relationship between love and sexual behavior was carried out by Burgess and Wallin (1953) on young couples married for three to five years and living in Chicago in the early 1940s. Love was assessed by five items that asked couples to rate the extent to which they were in love with their mate and their mate was in love with them, whether their mate had doubted their love and they their mate's love and whether their love had changed from before they were married (p. 497). Sexual satisfaction was measured by seventeen differentially weighted items (p. 673). Greater love was associated with greater sexual satisfaction. The relationship between the two variables was simply presented as a 3 x 3 contingency table (p. 691) but, calculated as a Pearson correlation, was .30 for both wives and husbands. Rettig and Bubolz (1983) found a moderately strong correlation between marital sexual relations and marital love and affection, both rated on a seven-point "Delighted-Terrible Scale," in both the wives and husbands of Michigan couples.

A study of wives and husbands in Toronto investigated what factors influenced the frequency of intercourse over a four-week period (Edwards and Booth 1976). Love was the strongest predictor of intercourse frequency for men and a weaker predictor for women. Although slightly lower, love remained significantly associated with intercourse frequency when the other variables were controlled for, indicating that this association was not due to the spurious effects of other variables such as age.

An investigation of various psychosocial correlates of premarital sexual behavior in 18- to 23-year-old students and non-students found that emotional intimacy in the current relationship was the variable most highly related to current sexual behavior in students (DeLamater and MacCorquodale 1979). Emotional intimacy was classified in six categories, varying from only one or two dates to being engaged. Current sexual behavior was measured through a nine-stage inventory that ranged according to physical intimacy from "necking" to fellatio on the male (with cunnilingus eighth and intercourse seventh on this scale). The point in emotional intimacy at which intercourse generally occurred was not reported. A number of other studies have found sexual behavior more likely to occur with greater affective commitment and in the later stages of premarital relationships (Bell and Blumberg 1959; Bell and Chaskes 1970; Burgess and Wallin 1953; Carns 1973; Christopher and Cate 1984; Kirkendall 1961; Lewis and Burr 1975; Miller and Simon 1974; Peplau, Rubin and Hill 1977; Reiss 1967; Schultz et al. 1977; Sherwin and Corbett 1985).

Although love has been found to be positively associated with sexual behavior, the causal nature of this relationship is unclear and has been little studied. Many people believe that sexual behavior should take place in a loving relationship and see sexual behavior such as intercourse as a romantic act (Hong et al. 1994; Hong and Faedda 1994). Consequently, they are more likely to engage in sexual behavior in such a relationship. It is more difficult to determine whether engaging in sexual behavior leads to love in a relationship characterized by affection or strong attraction and whether in a loving relationship such behavior helps to maintain or even increase love. Kanin and Davidson (1972) found that about 82% of female students and 80% of male students reported that their love for someone increased after their first experience of sexual intercourse with them and that this tendency was greater for those who were more strongly in love, suggesting that sexual behavior may intensify love. Longitudinal studies investigating the temporal relationship between love and sexual behavior within the same couple are needed to throw further light on this issue.

THE HIDDEN SECRET OF SEXUAL BEHAVIOR

So far, we have seen that romantic love is a salient concept for people and that the vast majority of people view loving relationships as a key element of sexual relationships. In other words, for most individuals love and romance are prerequisites of sexual activity, and the opportunistic sexual episodes characterized as sexual callousness are not considered the primary sites of sexual activity. However, increasingly research on sexual fantasy suggests that this "hidden" aspect of sexual activity reflects thoughts, acts, and relationships that are often directly antithetical to how people tell researchers they see their relationships and their sexual activity. Take, for example, the following written by "Phyllis":

When my husband fucks me, I often think of a former employer who gave me my first view of an erect penis when I was a virgin, then sixteen. It made such an impression on me that I have always remembered it, and like to picture the scene as it happened. He opened his trousers and took out his cock and I was amazed to see it standing up, so broad and stiff. He did not fuck me, but in my fantasies I see his big prick and try to imagine what it would have felt like if he had pushed it into me.

I always fantasize when I masturbate, which is usually when my husband is at work. I picture a scene at school when I was caned. The cane made me smart so much that I pissed in my knickers, which made me feel sexually excited afterwards. In my fantasies I can see the headmistress with her cane, and when I picture how she gave me those smart strokes, I soon reach a climax. (Friday 1976:196)

This is just one of many examples of women's sexual fantasies listed in a popular book on the subject. The rawness of the language should not lead us to ignore a number of important implications it seems to contain. In this example, Phyllis clearly relates her sexual fantasies to experiences of a sexual or parasexual nature. In other words, there is nothing in the fantasies that is fantastical since they reflect experiences rather than creations. Furthermore, there is an implication for this woman, at least, fantasy is a crucial component of masturbation. Her account does not make clear what role these fantasies play in sexual intercourse with her husband. Based on studies of sex offenders, it has been suggested that deviant sexual fantasies frequently reflect significant childhood experiences much as the fantasies Phyllis describes above do (Howitt 1995; Howitt and Cumberbatch, in press). Of course, fantasy can be reconstructed to a degree, and it is not unknown for offenders to reverse roles with their victims in their fantasy. For some offenders, offending does not seem to involve any immediate consumatory sexual release that offers the possibility that in some cases the primary function of offending is to provide experiences for further fantasy which may lead to orgasm through masturbation (Howitt 1995).

Although the research literature on sexual fantasy is relatively small, a number of trends are consistent enough to warrant consideration. We can organize the research around the following themes: (1) the extent of fantasy during sexual activity; and (2) the contents of this fantasy.

1. Research has demonstrated that from adolescence onward that fantasy commonly accompanies sexual activity, especially that potentially leading to orgasm. Relatively little sexual activity seems unaccompanied by fantasy. Sexual fantasy is common during adolescence. In a retrospective study in which young adults reported on fantasy during their adolescence (defined as onset of puberty to 21 years in this

study), it became clear that fantasy was strongly associated with masturbation (Kirkendall and McBride 1990). Nearly half of males (48%) reported that masturbation was *always* accompanied by fantasy, and none claimed it was *never* involved. The picture is not quite the same for girls since less than a third (29%) claimed that fantasy always accompanied masturbation and a fifth (20%) claimed that the masturbation was *never* accompanied by fantasy. The findings from a study of students who self-monitored their "sexual thoughts" over a period of time broadly confirm these trends (Jones and Barlow 1990). Sixty percent of males but only 12% of females reported *always* fantasizing when masturbating. Nearly half of females (49%) reported fantasizing but none of the males. Another study of students (Knafo and Jaffe 1984) found that over 90% of males had sexual fantasies during both masturbation and intercourse, figures that are matched by the female respondents. In terms of the percentages who *always or often* had sexual fantasies, it was shown that over 90% of men and over 75% of women did during masturbation. However, the figures were not so high for the frequency of reported sexual fantasies during intercourse—60% for men and 57% for women. The apparent differences in these studies between males and females were explained by the trends for more males *always* to use fantasy during sexual activities and for more females *never* to use fantasy. Some of the differences between studies can be accounted for by the differences in wording used in questions such as the difference between *always or often* and *always*.

2. The *contents* of sexual fantasy force us to question the idea that romance is a characteristic feature of sexual love. The clearest evidence for this can be found in adolescents. According to Kirkendall and McBride's (1990) study, most adolescents incorporate expressions of love into their fantasies. There was a more pronounced trend for this in girls (80%) than in boys (57%). Similarly, being seduced was very common in the fantasies of boys (71%) and girls (83%). Seducing another was less commonly reported by girls (27%) than boys (50%). Being forced into having sexual relations was more common for boys (36%) than for girls (23%), and forcing someone else to have sex relations was virtually exclusive to the boys (25%) and was rarely a characteristic of girls (3%). Fantasies that involved two or more other people were not uncommon (boys 56%, girls 27%).

When considering these findings, it is important to stress the age group involved. In particular, it is difficult to understand the similar and high figures for both sexes in terms of fantasies of being seduced. This clearly cannot be understood in terms of traditional concepts of gender socialization, although it may indicate that males of this age have anxieties about initiating sexual contact. These studies suggest that romantic conceptions of love are prevalent among girls and, to a lesser extent, among boys. Since normatively "deviant" fantasies, such as those involving force, are relatively uncommon, one can probably conclude that romantic imagery dominates in adolescent sexual fantasy although imagery of force was present in a substantial minority. This is not to suggest that their attitudes and beliefs about the opposite sex were correspondingly romantic, but merely that their sexual fantasies were predominantly so at this age. These adolescent fantasies seem essentially about seduction, which may be seen as part of the romantic conception of love and are not altogether comparable to adult fantasies that do not dwell on this theme. Furthermore, 53% of girls (but only 14% of boys) were triggered into fantasy by romance novels. As they progressed into adulthood, three-quarters experienced changes in their fantasies that began to concern people they were sexually involved with rather than fantasy people.

The outcome of this trend for fantasy to change with adulthood is most significantly revealed in studies of married couples. Research on married couples with children indicates that sexual fantasies involving one's spouse are not among the most common in a list of sexual fantasies (Hessellund 1976). Fifty percent of both women and men in the sample reported never having fantasies that included their spouse. For wives, the most common fantasy is sexual activity with someone other than their spouse (57%). Approximately 50% of men mentioned harem-like fantasies in which the man could choose from among a bevy of beautiful females which one he was to have intercourse with. Much the same pattern emerged for men in Gil's (1990) study of conservative Christians. For the wives in this study, the most frequent fantasy cited was "romantic," with sex implied but not explicitly mentioned. Almost as common in this sample of wives were fantasies of sexual intercourse with someone other than their spouse. Gil suggests that the fantasy themes emerging in this study were generally like the general population patterns found in earlier studies. Many of the participants in this research expressed guilt over the fantasies and 45% of the sample described their fantasies as "morally flawed or unacceptable."

University student samples probably have been the most common in studies of fantasy. Although their representativeness may be questionable, studies based on students are often among the most insightful. Hardin and Gold (1988–1989) compared the reported fantasies of male and female students. They report a significantly greater tendency for women to have romantic fantasies and for men to have group sex fantasies. However, their report fails to give details of the frequencies of different types of fantasy, making it impossible to assess the degree to which romantic fantasy dominated over other fantasy types for women in this sample. The study by Knafo and Jaffe (1984) of students suggested thematic differences between fantasy in intercourse and masturbation. For both men and women "Thoughts of an Imaginary Lover" were the most frequent type of fantasy during masturbation, but these were ranked 4 and 6, respectively, in terms of fantasy during intercourse. The prime fantasy for males during intercourse was "I pretend that I am another irresistible, sexy male" and that for females was "I imagine that I am being overpowered or forced to surrender." These were ranked 7 and 4 for masturbation for men and women, respectively.

Another study of female students assessed the frequency of different types of fantasies in various situations (Lentz and Zeiss 1984). Fantasy was classified as "romantic," "erotic" or "mixed." Most significant in the present context was the evidence that purely romantic fantasies were relatively uncommon during masturbation, which was dominated by erotic fantasy and mixed erotic/romantic fantasy. However, the position changed a little during foreplay and intercourse when the percentage of romantic fantasy practically doubled, whereas percentages of erotic fantasy declined by about a third. In this study, women students were asked to rate their arousal to three different types of story which they were given to read. Erotic and mixed stories produced by far the highest levels of arousal and the romantic stories were the least likely to arouse the reader. Interestingly, the women reported that it was easier to visualize (or fantasize) the erotic and mixed stories than the romantic stories. The only significant predictor of whether or not a woman was orgasmic during intercourse was her level of erotic fantasy during masturbation. Meuwissen and Over (1991) found that although women reported that sensuous fantasies such as those of cunnilingus were *subjectively* the most sexually arousing, this was not matched by data based on physiological measurements of sexual arousal. Objectively, it was the more forbidden activities that produced the greatest arousal in fantasy. These physiological, objective, measures showed that the greatest arousal in fantasy was produced by such culturally "forbidden" activities as having a partner watch the women masturbating or capturing a man and forcing him into sex. In other words, the most arousing themes were those furthest removed from even the widest definition of romantic fantasy. While it seems generally accepted that the sexual fantasies of women are more likely to be romantic than those of men (Leitenberg and Henning 1995), it seems equally true that romantic themes are far from characterizing female fantasy.

Despite the evidence that something akin to romantic conceptions of love is commonly regarded as a prerequisite for sexual activity between couples, fantasy tells a radically different story. Indeed, if one takes what we know about the contents of sexual fantasies in apparent normal adults and imaginatively regard the content of these fantasies as if they were reality, a picture emerges which stands ideas of sexual activity in the context of romantic love on their head. Indeed, by objective measurements, fantasies that could be best described as sexually callous, rather than those associated with romantic love, produce the most sexual arousal.

CONCLUSIONS

Generally, psychologists have equated romantic love with a passionate and intense form of love. This may have caused them to ignore the idealized, sentimental, and fanciful implications of the term. Of particular relevance, then, is the notion that romantic love has been distinguished from companionate love only at the attitudinal and ideological levels. While the experience of passionate love seems distinct enough, it is troubling that companionate love has not emerged as a clear component of the experience of love, given that it is recognized attitudinally. While this may be partly the consequence of a failure to explore the experience of companionate love fully, it may also reflect the idea that companionate love is experientially elusive. Since the purpose of this discussion is to explore the relationships between romantic love and sexual behavior, it is fascinating to note that once again, in terms of attitudes and ideology, clear relationships emerge between beliefs about sexual behavior and romantic and caring conceptions of relationships. At least during sexual acts, it is striking how this relationship breaks down. At the level of fantasy, romance plays a relatively minor role in stimulating erotic excitement. It might be suggested that romantic love and eroticism are distinct components of experience.

Aspects of the dilemma facing psychology can be illustrated by the paradoxes in what might be called the "ideology of rape" (Cumberbatch and Howitt 1989). Rape, with its implications of force, brutality, and uncaringness, might be regarded as antithetical to conceptions of romantic love. However, researchers investigating rape have found that rape may incorporate ideological components that are closer to romantic love than the sort of sexual callousness we discussed earlier:

> More commonly . . . the offender tries to see the situation in more generally acceptable terms. . . . Protestations of love are quite common. In one case, a woman of forty-four was asleep in her bedroom when attacked by a stranger fifteen years her junior: "During the struggle the assailant stated that he loved her. . . . All the time that he was trying this he kept saying that he loved her very much." (Clark and Lewis 1977:102)

Another example is that of the rapist who attacked a woman in a heavily wooded area and asked her if she loved him during the attack and even shouted goodbye as he ran away! Such examples further muddy our simplistic assumptions about the role of romantic love in sexual behavior.

NOTES

1. This point assumes that the order of items on the Passion Scale listed in Davis and Latty-Mann (1987) is the same as that used in Hendrick and Hendrick (1989).

2. See Lee's chapter "Ideologies of Lovestyle and Sexstyle" (Chapter 2) in this volume for a fuller description of these styles.

REFERENCES

Beck, J. Gayle; Alan W. Bozman; and Tina Qualtrough. "The Experience of Sexual Desire: Psychological Correlates in a College Sample." *Journal of Sex Research* 28:443–456, 1991.

Bell, Robert R., and Jay B. Chaskes, "Premarital Sexual Experience Among Coeds, 1958 and 1968." *Journal of Marriage and the Family* 32:81–84, 1970.

Bell, Robert R., and Leonard Blumberg. "Courtship, Intimacy and Religious Background." *Journal of Marriage and the Family* 21:356–360, 1959.

Burgess, Ernest W., and Paul Wallin. *Engagement and Marriage*. Chicago: Lippincott, 1953.

Carns, Donald. "Talking About Sex: Notes on First Coitus and the Double Sexual Standard." *Journal of Marriage and the Family* 35:677–688, 1973.

Christopher, F. Scott, and Rodney M. Cate. "Factors Involved in Premarital Sexual Decision-Making." *Journal of Sex Research* 20:363–376, 1984.

Cimbalo, Richard S.; Virginia Faling; and Patricia Mousaw. "The Course of Love: A Cross-Sectional Design." *Psychological Reports* 38:1292–1294, 1976.

Clark, Lorenne M. G., and Debra J. Lewis. *Rape: The Price of Coercive Sexuality*. Toronto: Women's Press, 1977.

Cramer, Duncan. "Dimensions of Romantic Love in British Female Adolescents." *Journal of Social Psychology* 133:411–413, 1993.

———."Lovestyles Revisited." *Social Behavior and Personality* 15:215–218, 1987.

———."Nature of Romantic Love in Female Adolescents." *Journal of Psychology* 126:679–682, 1992.

Cumberbatch, Guy, and Dennis Howitt. *A Measure of Uncertainty: The Effects of the Mass Media*. London: John Libbey, 1989.

Davis, Keith E., and Holly Latty-Mann. "Lovestyles and Relationship Quality: A Contribution to Validation." *Journal of Social and Personal Relationships* 4:409–428, 1987.

Davis, Keith E., and Michael J. Todd. "Friendship and Love Relationships." In Keith E. Davis, (ed.), *Advances in Descriptive Psychology*. Greenwich, Conn.: JAI Press, 1982, pp. 79–122.

DeLamater, John, and P. MacCorquodale. Premartial Sexuality: Attitudes, Relationships, Behavior. Madison, WI.:Wisconsin University Press, 1979.

Dion, Kenneth L., and Karen K. Dion. "Correlates of Romantic Love." *Journal of Consulting and Clinical Psychology* 41:51–56, 1973.

Driscoll, Richard; Keith E. Davis; and Milton E. Lipetz. "Parental Interference and Romantic Love: The Romeo and Juliet Effect." *Journal of Personality and Social Psychology* 24:1–10, 1972.

Edwards, John N., and Alan Booth. "Sexual Behavior In and Out of Marriage: An Assessment of Correlates." *Journal of Marriage and the Family* 38:73–81, 1976.

Friday, Nancy. *My Secret Garden: Women's Sexual Fantasies.* London: Quartet, 1976.

Gil, Vincent E. "Sexual Fantasy Experiences and Guilt Among Conservative Christians: An Exploratory Study." *Journal of Sex Research* 27:629–638, 1990.

Gross, Llewellyn. "A Belief Pattern Scale for Measuring Attitudes Toward Romanticism." *American Sociological Review* 9:463–472, 1944.

Groth, A. Nicholas, and William F. Hobson. "The Dynamics of Sexual Assault." In Louis B. Schlesinger and Eugene Revitch (eds.), *Sexual Dynamics of Anti-Social Behavior,* Springfield, Ill.: Charles C. Thomas, 1983, pp. 159–172.

Hardin, Kimeron N., and Steven R. Gold. "Relationship of Sex, Sex Guilt, and Experience to Written Sexual Fantasy." *Imagination, Cognition and Personality* 8:155–163, 1988–1989.

Hatfield, Elaine. "Passionate and Companionate Love." In Robert J. Sternberg, and Michael L. Barnes, (eds.), *The Psychology of Love,* New Haven, Conn.: Yale University Press, 1988. pp. 191–217.

Hatfield, Elaine, and Susan Sprecher. "Measuring Passionate Love In Intimate Relationships." *Journal of Adolescence* 9:383–410, 1986.

Hendrick, Clyde, and Susan S. Hendrick "A Theory and Method of Love." *Journal of Personality and Social Psychology* 50:392–402, 1986.

———."Research on Love: Does It Measure Up?" *Journal of Personality and Social Psychology* 56:784–794, 1989.

Hendrick, Clyde; Susan Hendrick; Franklin H. Foote; and Michelle J. Slapion-Foote. "Do Men and Women Love Differently?" *Journal of Social and Personal Relationships* 1:177–195, 1984.

Hendrick, Susan S.; Clyde Hendrick; and Nancy L. Adler. "Romantic Relationships: Love, Satisfaction, and Staying Together." *Journal of Personality and Social Psychology* 54:980–988, 1988.

Hendrick, Susan, and Clyde Hendrick, "Multidimensionality of Sexual Attitudes." *Journal of Sex Research* 23:502–526, 1987.

Hessellund, Hans. "Masturbation and Sexual Fantasies in Married Couples." *Archives of Sexual Behavior* 5:133–147, 1976.

Hill, Charles T.; Zick Rubin; and Letitia A. Peplau, "Breakups Before Marriage: The End of 103 Affairs." *Journal of Social Issues* 32:147–168, 1976.

Hinkle, Dennis E., and Michael J. Sporakowski. "Attitudes Toward Love: A Reexamination." *Journal of Marriage and the Family* 37:764–767, 1975.

Hobart, Charles W. "The Incidence of Romanticism During Courtship." *Social Forces* 36:362–367, 1958.

Hong, Sung-Mook; Malcolm Evans; Tracey Hall; and Patrick Sheehan. "Making Love: Australian Adults' Rating of Its Importance as a Romantic Act in a Relationship." *Psychological Reports* 75:47–50, 1994.

Howitt, Dennis. *Paedopophiles and Sexual Offences Against Children.* New York: John Wiley, 1995.

Howitt, Dennis, and Guy Cumberbatch. *Pornography: Impacts and Influences.* London: Home Office Research and Planning Unit, 1990.

———. *Criminogenic Fantasies and the Media.* London: Broadcasting Standards Council, in press.

Johnson, Anne M.; Jane Wadsworth; Kaye Wellings; and Julia Field. *Sexual Attitudes and Lifestyles.* Oxford: Blackwell Scientific Publications, 1994.

Jones, Jennifer C., and David H. Barlow. "Self-reported Frequency of Sexual Urges, Fantasies, and Masturbatory Fantasies in Heterosexual Males and Females." *Archives of Sexual Behavior* 19:269–279, 1990.

Kanin, Eugene J., and Karen R. Davidson. "Some Evidence Bearing on the Aim-Inhibition Hypothesis of Love." *Sociological Quarterly* 13:210–217, 1972.

Kelly, Liz. *Surviving Sexual Violence.* Cambridge, England: Polity Press, 1988.

Kirkendall, Lester A. *Premarital Intercourse and Interpersonal Relationships.* New York: Gramercy, 1961.

Kirkendall, Lester A., and Leslie G. McBride. "Preadolescent and Adolescent Imagery and Sexual Fantasies: Beliefs and Experiences." In M. E. Perry (ed.), *Handbook of Sexology, Vol. 7: Childhood and Adolescent Sexology.* Amsterdam: Elsevier, 1990, pp. 263–287.

Knafo, Danielle, and Yoram Jaffe. "Sexual Fantasizing in Males and Females." *Journal of Research in Personality* 18:451–462, 1984.

Knox, David, H., Jr., and Michael J. Sporakowski. "Attitudes of College Students Toward Love." *Journal of Marriage and the Family* 30:638–642, 1968.

Lasswell, Thomas E., and Marcia E. Lasswell. "I Love You But I'm Not in Love with You." *Journal of Marriage and Family Counseling* 38:211–224, 1976.

Laumann, Edward O.; John H. Gagnon; Robert T. Michael; and Stuart Michaels. *The Social Organization of Sexuality: Sexual Practices in the United States.* Chicago: University of Chicago Press, 1994.

Lee, John A. "Styles of Loving." *Psychology Today,* UK ed. 1:20–27, 1975.

———. *Lovestyles.* Rev. ed. London: Dent, 1976.

Leitenberg, Harold, and Kris Henning. "Sexual Fantasy." *Psychological Bulletin* 117:469–496, 1995.

Lentz, Sharon L., and Antonette M. Zeiss. "Fantasy and Sexual Arousal in College Women: An Empirical Investigation." *Imagination, Cognition and Personality* 3:185–202, 1984.

Levy, Marc B., and Keith E. Davis. "Lovestyles and Attachment Styles Compared: Their Relations to Each Other and to Various Relationship Characteristics." *Journal of Social and Personal Relationships* 5:439–471, 1988.

Lewis, Robert A., and Wesley R. Burr. "Premarital Coitus and Commitment Among College Students." *Archives of Sexual Behavior* 4:73–79, 1975.

Lund, Mary. "The Development of Investment and Commitment Scales for Predicting Continuity of Personal Relationships." *Journal of Social and Personal Relationships* 2:3–23, 1985.

Meuwissen, Ingrid, and Ray Over. "Multidimensionality of the Content of Female Sexual Fantasy." *Behavior Research and Therapy* 29:179–189, 1991.

Miller, Patricia Y., and William Simon. "Adolescent Sexual Behavior: Context and Change." *Social Problems* 22:58–75, 1974.

Mosher, D. L., and R. D. Anderson. "Macho Personality, Sexual Aggression, and Reactions to Guided Imagery of Realistic Rape." *Journal of Research in Personality* 20:77–94, 1986.

Munro, Brenda, and Gerald R. Adams. "Love American Style: A Test of Role Structure Theory on Changes in Attitudes Toward Love." *Human Relations* 31:215–228, 1978.

Peplau, Letitia Anne; Zick Rubin; and Charles T. Hill. "Sexual Intimacy in Dating Relationships." *Journal of Social Issues* 33:86–109, 1977.

Reiss, Ira L. *The Social Context of Premarital Sexual Permissiveness.* New York: Holt, Rinehart and Winston,1967.

Rettig, Kathryn D., and Margaret M. Bubolz. "Interpersonal Resource Exchanges as Indicators of Quality of Marriage." *Journal of Marriage and the Family* 45:497–509, 1983.

Revitch, Eugene, and Louis B. Schlesinger. "Clinical Reflections on Sexual Aggresssion." *Human Sexual Aggression: Current Perspectives* 528, August 12:59–61, 1988.

Rosenman, Martin F. "Liking, Loving, and Styles of Loving." *Psychological Reports* 42:1243–1246, 1978.

Rubin, Zick. "Measurement of Romantic Love." *Journal of Personality and Social Psychology* 16:265–273, 1970.

Schulz, Barbara; George W. Bohrnstedt; Edgar F. Borgatta; and Robert R. Evans. "Explaining Premarital Sexual Intercourse Among College Students: A Causal Model." *Social Forces* 56:148–165, 1977.

Sherwin, Robert, and Sherry Corbett. "Campus Sexual Norms and Dating Relationships: A Trend Analysis." *Journal of Sex Research* 21:258–274, 1985.

Sorensen, Robert C. *Adolescent Sexuality in Contemporary America: Personal Values and Sexual Behavior Ages Thirteen to Nineteen.* New York: World, 1973.

Sprecher, Susan, and Sandra Metts. "Development of the 'Romantic Beliefs Scale' and Examination of the Effects of Gender and Gender-role Orientation." *Journal of Social and Personal Relationships* 6:387–411, 1989.

Sternberg, Robert J. "A Triangular Theory of Love." *Psychological Review* 93:119–135, 1986.

Walster, Elaine, and G. William Walster. *A New Look at Love.* Reading, Mass.: Addison-Wesley, 1978.

SECTION III

EVOLUTIONARY AND INVESTMENT MODELS

6

Divorce as a Consequence of Spousal Infidelity

Todd K. Shackelford

Infidelity may have no rival in disrupting a marriage. Cross-culturally, a sexual infidelity by a woman, either actual or suspected, is the leading cause of wife battering and wife homicide (Daly and Wilson 1988; Wilson and Daly 1992). Anguish, depression, anger, and humiliation are among the emotional experiences of the partner of someone who has been unfaithful (Buunk and van Driel 1989; Lawson 1988). Of the 43 causes of divorce compiled by Betzig (1989) in her ethnographic study of 160 cultures, a spouse's infidelity was the most frequently cited cause, across cultures. Fully 79% of the cultures explicitly note infidelity as a cause of divorce.

Studies of divorce in Western countries suggest that between 25% and 50% of divorcees cite a spouse's infidelity as the primary cause of the divorce (Hunt 1974; Kelly and Conley 1987; Levinger 1976). Estimates of marital infidelity range from 26% to 70% for women and from 33% to 75% for men (Buss 1994; Fisher 1992; Hite 1987; Kinsey, Pomeroy, and Martin 1948; Kinsey et al. 1979). The discrepancy between the ranges of estimates of divorce due to infidelity and estimates of infidelity suggests that, although some marriages continue following a discovered infidelity, some marriages do not (Buunk 1987; Levinger 1976).

The divorce process often debilitates the psychological, emotional, and physiological health of the parting spouses (Kitson and Sussman 1982; Levinger 1976). Despite the tremendous costs involved, many couples divorce following detection of infidelity. That so many couples *do* divorce following the revelation or discovery of infidelity attests to the perceived costs that accompany infidelity.

Given the prevalence of and costs associated with infidelity and with divorce, an important empirical issue is what differentiates couples who divorce from those who stay together following infidelity. In addition, infidelity and dissolution as a consequence of infidelity are important issues from several theoretical perspectives. From an evolutionary psychological perspective (Buss 1995; Wilson and Daly 1992), infidelity signals the diversion of important reproductive resources. From an equity theoretical perspective (Messick and Cook 1983; Walster, Walster, and Berscheid 1978), infidelity may signal serious inequities in a relationship. From an investment model perspective (Rusbult 1980, 1983), infidelity signals lack of commitment to a relationship.

It could be argued from each of these perspectives that the decision to divorce as a consequence of infidelity involves a cost-benefit analysis by the betrayed partner in which the perceived costs and benefits of remaining married are weighed against those of divorce. The more costly a marriage is perceived to be, the less incentive the betrayed partner has to remain married to an adulterous spouse. David Buss and I (Shackelford and Buss 1997) tested this general proposal using a sample of recently married couples.

To assess the salience of infidelity as a potential cause of divorce, we developed an instrument in which each spouse estimates the probability that he or she would seek divorce if their partner engaged in the following activities: flirting with someone else, passionately kissing someone else, romantically dating someone else, having a one-night stand, a brief affair, and a serious affair. Following Buunk (1987), we assume that these types of infidelity reflect different degrees of spousal cost-infliction. A one-night stand, for example, almost certainly inflicts greater costs on the betrayed spouse than does an illicit, passionate kiss. A one-night stand, among other things, places the betrayed partner at risk of contracting a sexually transmitted disease carried by a spouse's lover.

Anticipations of seeking divorce as a consequence of spousal infidelity are clearly not assessments of actual divorces filed in response to spousal infidelity. Some individuals who anticipate seeking divorce as a consequence of spousal infidelity may refrain from doing so, and some who do not anticipate divorcing an adulterous spouse may do so. We have no reason to suspect, however, that estimates of the likelihood of divorcing an unfaithful spouse will consistently underestimate or overestimate actual divorce in response to spousal infidelity. Participants making these estimations may strive to appear intolerant of a spouse's philanderings rather than appear to be someone whom the spouse can "walk all over." At the same time, they may strive to appear forgiving, compassionate, and kind, the hallmarks of a desirable mate (Buss 1989a). Several longitudinal studies of marriage (Devine and Forehand 1996; Gottman and Levenson 1992) have documented that anticipated dissolution reliably predicts actual dissolution. These studies support the use of anticipated dissolution as a proxy for actual dissolution as a consequence of spousal infidelity.

The use of newlywed couples to study anticipated dissolution as a consequence of infidelity has several advantages. Divorce is most likely to occur in the first few years of marriage for a variety of reasons, including infidelity (Betzig 1989; Buss 1994; Fisher 1992). In addition, the early years of marriage are marked by a time of relationship negotiation, wherein each partner seeks to establish what is acceptable and unacceptable behavior (Veroff and Feld 1970). As spouses successfully negotiate their marital expectations, conflict generated by the negotiation process diminishes, as does the likelihood of dissolution as a consequence of such conflict. Therefore, recently married couples provide a more appropriate context than longer-married couples for investigating marital dissolution.

We examined several sources of spousal and relationship costs that might facilitate increased estimates of seeking divorce as a consequence of spousal infidelity, including discrepancies in the attractiveness and mate value of the spouses, spousal sources of upset and irritation, and marital dissatisfaction. Later we present our specific predictions about the relationships between these sources of costs and anticipations of divorcing an unfaithful spouse.

Relative mate value refers to the relative desirability of the two partners on the "mating market" (Buss 1994; Symons 1987). In our study, two interviewers independently assessed each spouse's mate value and attractiveness. Where a discrepancy existed, we expected that the partner higher in relative value would provide higher likelihood estimates of seeking divorce as a consequence of spousal infidelity. The rationale for this prediction was that in marrying, the more valuable partner incurs greater costs than the less valuable partner. These greater costs include opportunity costs associated with foregone marriage to a more valuable partner (see Buss 1994; Rusbult and Buunk 1993).

Spousal sources of upset and irritation provide relatively direct assessments of the costs inflicted by a spouse (Buss 1989b). According to Buss's (1989b) strategic interference model, the degree of upset felt in response to a particular spousal behavior tracks the perceived severity of the costs inflicted by that behavior. We expected, therefore, that spousal sources of upset would positively correlate with anticipations of divorcing an unfaithful spouse.

Marital satisfaction and dissatisfaction may track the costs and benefits associated with a particular marriage (Shackelford and Buss 1996a). It could be argued from several theoretical perspectives (see above) that anticipations of divorcing an unfaithful spouse involve assessments of the costs and benefits of the current marriage, weighed against the costs and benefits of divorce. Greater perceived costs and fewer perceived benefits, on these accounts, should facilitate increased anticipations of divorcing an adulterous spouse. We therefore expected that men and women who were less satisfied with their marriage would anticipate greater likelihoods of divorcing an unfaithful spouse.

In addition to general marital satisfaction, assessments of sexual and emotional satisfaction were secured. These two facets may be crucial, because of the known links between a woman's emotional dissatisfaction and her likelihood of ending the relationship and a man's sexual dissatisfaction and his likelihood of ending the relationship (Betzig 1989; Glass and Wright 1977, 1985, 1992). A man may be especially likely to anticipate divorcing an unfaithful partner if he is sexually dissatisfied with the marriage. A woman, in contrast, may be especially likely to anticipate divorcing an unfaithful partner if she is emotionally dissatisfied with the marriage.

METHOD

Participants

Participants were 214 individuals, 107 men and 107 women, who had been married less than one year. Participants were obtained from the public records of marriage licenses issued within a large Midwestern county. All couples married within a six-month time period were contacted by letter and invited to participate in this study. The majority of participants were white. The mean age of the wives was 25.52 (SD = 4.06; range = 18 to 36). The mean age of husbands was 26.79 (SD = 3.75; range = 17 to 41). This was the first marriage for 96% of the sample. Ninety-six percent of couples had no children. Couples had been romantically involved for an average of 44 months (SD = 24.64; range = one month to eight years). Two-thirds of couples had cohabited prior to marriage for an average of 1.26 years (SD = 1.8 years). Thirty-two percent of the sample reported that they were Protestant, 22% Catholic, about 4% Jewish, and 11% "Other." Thirty-one percent of respondents reported no religious affiliation. The annual income of husbands ranged from $0 (unemployed) to $87,000, averaging $21,000 ($SD$ = $12,000). The annual income of wives ranged from $0 (unemployed) to $68,000, averaging $16,400

(SD = \$10,500). Husbands had completed an average of 16.47 years of education (SD = 2.71; range = 11 to 23 years). Wives had completed an average of 15.99 years of education (SD = 2.94; range = 7 to 25 years).

Procedure

Participants participated in three separate waves of assessment. First, they received through the mail a battery of instruments to be completed at home in their spare time. Second, participants came to a laboratory testing session approximately one week after receiving the battery of self-report instruments. During this session, spouses were separated to preserve independence and to prevent contamination due to discussion. During this session, participants completed the instrument in which they provided the probabilities that they would end their marriage following each of the six forms of spousal infidelity. Participants also completed a marital satisfaction instrument and an index of spousal sources of upset and irritation.

Third, couples were interviewed toward the end of the testing session by one male and one female interviewer drawn from a rotating staff of ten interviewers to secure independent information about each spouse's mate value and attractiveness. Participants were asked a standard set of questions about how they met, the nature of their relationship, sources of attraction, sources of conflict, and their similarities and differences. Immediately following the interview, the interviewers completed a standard instrument in which they recorded their perceptions of the mate value and attractiveness of each participant. The confidentiality of all responses was assured. Not even the participant's spouse could obtain responses without written permission from the relevant partner.

Materials

Marital Satisfaction. The Marital Satisfaction Survey (Shackelford and Buss 1996a) consisted of thirty-one questions assessing the respondent's satisfaction with various aspects of their marriage and their spouse. Three items were employed in this study. *General marital satisfaction* was assessed by the item: "Thinking about things all together, how would you say you feel about your marriage?" *Sexual satisfaction* was assessed by the item "How do you feel about your sexual relationship?" *Emotional satisfaction* was assessed by the item "How do you feel about your spouse as a source of encouragement and reassurance?" All three items were rated on a 7-point Likert scale with 1 = unsatisfied and 7 = extremely satisfied. A

composite marital satisfaction index was created by summing with
unit weighting scores on the general, sexual, and emotional satisfaction items (alpha = .72).

Mate Value and Attractiveness Discrepancies. Two interviewers drawn from a ten-member team provided independent assessments of the husband's and wife's "overall attractiveness as a
potential mate (mate value to opposite sex)" on a scale where 1 = extremely low and 7 = extremely high. A mate value discrepancy variable was created by subtracting husband's from wife's interviewer-
rated mate value. The two interviewer-assessments of mate value
correlated r = .53 (p < .001) and were averaged to create a more reliable measure of mate value discrepancy. Interviewers also provided
assessments of overall physical attractiveness for each spouse. Overall attractiveness was assessed on a 7-point scale anchored by 1 =
overall unattractive and 7 = overall attractive. The two interviewer-
assessments of overall attractiveness correlated r = .64 (ps < .001).
An overall physical attractiveness discrepancy variable was created
using the same strategy employed to create the mate value discrepancy variable.

Spousal Sources of Upset. During the laboratory testing session
when the husband and wife were physically separated, participants
completed an instrument entitled "Sources of Irritation and Upset."
This instrument contained the following instructions: "Below is a list
of things that spouses sometimes do that irritate, annoy, anger, or
upset each other. Please place an 'X' next to those acts your husband
[wife] has performed *within the past year* that have irritated, an-
noyed, angered, or upset you." Following these instructions were 147
acts or events, previously nominated by a separate panel (see Buss
1989b).

Factor analysis (Buss 1989b) revealed fifteen factors (sample acts
in parentheses): *Condescending* (S/he treated me like I was stupid or
inferior), *Jealous* (S/he acted jealous), *Neglecting* (S/he would not
spend enough time with me), *Abusive* (S/he hit me; S/he verbally
abused me), *Unfaithful* (S/he had sex with another person), *Inconsiderate* (S/he did not help to clean up), *Physically Self-Absorbed* (S/he
fussed too much with her/his appearance), *Moody* (S/he acted moody),
Sexually Withholding (S/he refused to have sex with me), *Sexualizing
of Others* (S/he talked about how good-looking another person was),
Abusive of Alcohol/Emotionally Constricted (S/he drank too much
alcohol; S/he hid emotions to act tough), *Disheveled* (S/he did not take
care of her/his appearance), *Insulting of Partner's Appearance* (S/he
told me I was ugly), *Sexually Aggressive* (S/he tried to force sex acts
on me), and *Self-Centered* (S/he was self-centered).

Anticipated Dissolution Following Infidelity. During the testing session in which the spouses were separated from each other, each completed an instrument entitled "Events with Others" (Buss and Shackelford 1997). In addition to providing a series of other ratings, participants estimated the likelihood that they would end the marriage as a consequence of each of six types of spousal infidelity: flirting, passionately kissing, going on a romantic date, having a one-night stand, having a brief affair, and having a serious affair. Participants provided estimates on separate 11-point scales for each type of infidelity. The low end of the scale indicated 0%, and the high end indicated 100%, with the scale marked off in 10% increments.

RESULTS

Anticipated Dissolution Following Infidelity

Table 6.1 shows the means and standard deviations for the reported probabilities of ending the marriage in response to the six types of spousal infidelity. The probabilities increased as a function of the seriousness of the extramarital involvement. For example, husbands' estimates that they would end the marriage if their wife flirted with another man averaged about 4%, engaged in passionate kisses with another man 21%, went out on a romantic date 36%, had a one-night stand 49%, had a brief affair 55%, and had a serious affair 67%.

To determine whether the sexes differed in their estimates of anticipated dissolution following the various spousal infidelities, correlated-means t-tests were conducted for each of the variables. No significant sex differences were found (all $ps > .05$, two-tailed). For each of the six extramarital activities, men and women anticipated equal probabilities that they would end the relationship in response to spousal infidelity.

Mate Value and Attractiveness Discrepancies

None of the correlations between men's anticipations of divorcing an unfaithful spouse and attractiveness discrepancy reached statistical significance (all $ps > .05$, one-tailed). A single significant correlation was obtained between men's anticipations of divorcing an unfaithful spouse and mate value discrepancy. Men judged to be higher in relative mate value provided higher likelihood estimates of seeking divorce if their wife flirted with another man ($r = -.21$, $p < .05$, one-tailed).

Table 6.1
Anticipated Dissolution Following Spousal Infidelity

Type of Spousal Infidelity

	Flirt		Passionate Kiss		Romantic Date		One-night Stand		Brief Affair		Serious Affair	
	Mean	(SD)	Mean	(SD)	Mean	(SD)	Mean	(SD)	Mean	(SD)	Mean	(SD)
Husband's anticipation of divorcing wife as a consequence of her infidelity	3.78	(9.75)	20.49	(29.89)	35.62	(35.25)	48.93	(38.91)	55.30	(39.09)	66.56	(37.46)
Wife's anticipation of divorcing husband as a consequence of his infidelity	2.50	(7.58)	21.60	(27.50)	37.32	(34.61)	49.20	(37.53)	57.75	(37.78)	69.03	(35.27)

Note: N (Men) = 107, N (Women) = 107. Means are average estimates of the probability of seeking divorce as a consequence of spousal infidelity. Estimates were provided on 11-point scales anchored by 0% and 100%, presented in 10% increments (i.e., 0%, 10%, 20%).

In contrast, women's anticipations of divorcing an adulterous husband consistently covaried with interviewer-rated mate value and attractiveness discrepancies. Women judged to be higher in relative mate value provided higher likelihood estimates of seeking divorce if their husband went on a date with another woman ($r = -.21$), had a one-night stand ($r = -.19$), or a brief affair ($r = -.18$; all $ps < .05$, one-tailed). Women judged to be more attractive than their husband provided higher likelihood estimates of seeking divorce if he went on a date with another woman ($r = -.26$, $p < .01$), had a one-night stand ($r = -.24$, $p < .01$), a brief affair ($r = -.24$, $p < .01$), or a serious affair ($r = -.18$, $p < .05$; all ps one-tailed).

Spousal Sources of Upset

Eight of the fifteen spousal sources of upset were significantly and negatively related to men's or women's anticipations of divorcing an unfaithful spouse. Table 6.2 displays these correlations.

The upper panel of Table 6.2 shows that men's anticipations of divorcing an unfaithful spouse were most consistently related to their complaints that their wife has previously been unfaithful. These correlations were significant for the four more serious types of infidelity: romantically dating, having a one-night stand, a brief affair, and a serious affair. Men who complained that their wife sexualized others reported higher probabilities that they would divorce her if she flirted with another man or had a one-night stand. Men who complained that their wife was inconsiderate also reported higher probabilities of divorcing a wife if she had a one-night stand. Men who complained that their wife abused alcohol and was emotionally constricted, and men who complained that their wife was condescending, respectively, reported higher probabilities that they would divorce their wife if she flirted with another man or had a brief affair.

The lower panel of Table 6.2 shows that women who complained that their husband is inconsiderate, and women who complained that their husband abused alcohol and was emotionally constricted, reported greater likelihoods that they would seek divorce if he flirted with another woman, passionately kissed another woman, went on a romantic date, had a one-night stand, a brief affair, or a serious affair. Women who complained that their husband was jealous, sexually withholding, and sexualized others reported greater likelihoods of seeking divorce if he flirted with another woman. Finally, women who complained that their husband was condescending, and women who complained that their husband was jealous, respectively, reported higher probabilities that they would divorce their husband if he had a one-night stand or went on a romantic date with another woman.

Table 6.2
Correlations of Anticipated Dissolution Following Spousal Infidelity with Spousal Sources of Upset

Husband's Estimate That He Would End Marriage If Wife:

Spousal Source of Upset	Flirts	Kisses	Dates	One-Night Stand	Brief Affair	Serious Affair
Condescending	-.07	-.10	-.10	-.09	-.17*	-.11
Jealous	-.02	-.05	.07	.12	.06	.06
Unfaithful	.02	.16	.20*	.28**	.22**	.25**
Inconsiderate	.09	.04	.05	.17*	.10	.10
Moody	.15	-.05	-.06	-.01	-.07	.00
Sexually Withholding	.06	.05	.07	.07	.02	.07
Sexualizing of Others	.31**	.11	.14	.23**	.14	.15
Abusive of alcohol/ Emotionally Constricted	.19*	.01	-.05	-.01	-.05	.04

Wife's Estimate That She Would End Marriage If Husband:

Spousal Source of Upset	Flirts	Kisses	Dates	One-Night Stand	Brief Affair	Serious Affair
Condescending	.17	.09	.02	.16*	.15	.16
Jealous	.47***	.14	.16*	.13	.11	.14
Unfaithful	-.14	-.13	-.10	.01	.00	-.02
Inconsiderate	.26**	.21*	.25**	.24**	.19*	.23**
Moody	.21*	.01	-.01	-.07	.10	.13
Sexually Withholding	.24**	.03	.02	.02	.03	.00
Sexualizing of Others	.07	-.09	.02	.01	.00	.03
Abusive of Alcohol/ Emotionally Constricted	.21*	.20*	.19*	.29***	.30***	.28**

Note: N (Men) = 107, N (Women) = 107.
*p ≤ .05, **p ≤ .01, ***p ≤ .001 (one-tailed).

Table 6.3

Correlations of Husband's Anticipated Dissolution Following Wife's Infidelity with Husband's Marital Satisfaction

	H's estimate that he would end marriage if W:					
H's Marital Satisfaction	Flirts	Kisses	Dates	One-night stand	Brief affair	Serious affair
General	-.20*	-.16*	-.16*	-.13	-.03	-.06
Sexual	-.15	-.17*	-.09	-.11	-.09	-.16
Emotional	-.11	-.20*	-.25**	-.19*	-.12	-.13
Composite [a]	-.14	-.20*	-.25**	-.20*	-.10	-.13

[a] Mean of general, sexual, and emotional satisfaction.
Note: H = Husband, W = Wife; N (Men) = 107.
$*p \leq .05$, $**p \leq .01$ (one-tailed).

Marital Satisfaction

None of the correlations between women's general, sexual, emotional, or composite marital satisfaction and women's estimates that they would divorce an unfaithful husband achieved statistical significance (all $ps > .05$, one-tailed). Men's marital satisfaction, in contrast, displayed consistent relationships to their anticipated dissolution following spousal infidelity. Table 6.3 shows the latter correlations.

Men who reported lower general marital satisfaction reported higher probabilities that they would divorce their wife if she flirted with another man, kissed another man, or had a one-night stand. Men who reported lower emotional satisfaction, and men with lower composite marital satisfaction scores, reported higher probabilities that they would divorce their wife if she kissed another man, went on a romantic date with another man, or had a one-night stand. Finally, men reporting lower sexual satisfaction reported higher probabilities that they would divorce their wife if she passionately kissed another man.

DISCUSSION

The general hypothesis tested in this study was that anticipations of divorcing an unfaithful spouse entail a cost-benefit analysis by the betrayed person in which the perceived costs and benefits of the marriage are weighed against the perceived costs and benefits of divorce. Greater perceived costs and fewer perceived benefits were expected to facilitate heightened likelihood estimates of divorcing a spouse as a consequence of his or her infidelity.

We examined several sources of spousal and relationship costs that might facilitate increased estimates of dissolution as a consequence of adultery. This discussion highlights the most important findings of the study and locates these findings within an evolutionary psychological perspective.

Mate Value and Attractiveness Discrepancies

From an evolutionary psychological perspective, women of higher mate value and attractiveness than their husband may be squandering their reproductive capacity on men who provide them with fewer financial resources or lower quality genes than these women might have received from alternative mating arrangements (Buss 1994; Gangestad 1993). Accordingly, we predicted that relatively more valuable wives would report higher probabilities of divorcing an adulterous husband. This prediction was supported for the more serious types of husband infidelity, including having a one-night stand and a brief affair.

In contrast, men married to relatively less valuable and attractive women did not provide consistently higher estimates that they would divorce their wife if she were unfaithful. The use of interviewer assessments of women's mate value and attractiveness may have been inappropriate. Men married to women rated as relatively less attractive by the interviewers might perceive their wives to be equally or more attractive than the men perceive themselves to be. It may have been more appropriate to assess *husband's* perceptions of their wife's relative attractiveness and mate value rather than rely as we did on independent assessments of these variables. This speculation does not address, however, why men's, but not women's, perceptions of their spouse's mate value and attractiveness might deviate from independent parallel assessments. Future research should first test the replicability of the sex-linked findings. If these findings are replicated, future research could test the speculation that men's, but not women's, perceptions of their spouse's mate value and attractiveness deviate from independent parallel assessments. If this speculation is supported, additional research could profitably investigate the origin of the sex-linked discrepancies between spousal and independent assessments of mate value and attractiveness.

Spousal Sources of Upset

According to Buss's (1989b) strategic interference model of conflict between men and women, spousal sources of upset represent relatively direct assessments of spousal cost-infliction. Greater upset signals greater cost-infliction. If the perceived costs of marriage to the current spouse figure into the betrayed person's considerations of whether to divorce or remain married to an adulterous spouse, then spousal sources of upset should predict estimates of the likelihood of divorce as a consequence of spousal infidelity.

More than half of the spousal sources of upset reported by men and women in this sample negatively covaried, as predicted, with likelihood estimates of divorcing an unfaithful spouse. The most consistent predictor of higher likelihood estimates of divorcing an adulterous wife was a man's complaint that his wife had previously been unfaithful to him. Men who complained that their wife had previously been unfaithful anticipated higher likelihoods of divorcing her if she went on a romantic date with another man, had a one night stand, a brief affair, or a serious affair within the next year. The predictive importance of men's complaints about wifely infidelity can be placed squarely within an evolutionary psychological perspective.

From an evolutionary psychological perspective, one of the most serious transgressions of a presumably monogamous marriage is a partner's infidelity. A spouse's unfaithfulness is likely to have imposed serious reproductive costs on ancestral men and women alike (Buss et al. 1992; Buss and Schmitt 1993; Daly, Wilson, and Weghorst 1982; Shackelford and Buss 1996b). Because of the asymmetry in certainty of genetic parentage, however, a wife's infidelity is potentially much more costly to her husband than is a husband's infidelity to his wife. The wife of a philandering man stands to lose some portion of her husband's investment to another woman. Even if she loses the bulk of his investment, however, any children she bears are unquestionably her genetic progeny. The husband of an unfaithful wife stands to lose the entire reproductive capacity of his spouse, for at least one child-bearing cycle. In addition, the unsuspecting cuckold risks investing years, even decades, of precious tangible and intangible resources in a rival's offspring.

The results suggest that men married to an unfaithful wife may have issued an ultimatum to their partner upon discovery of her extramarital activities: If you ever cheat on me again, I will divorce you. Given the potentially tremendous costs of wifely infidelity, an important question is why some men offer their adulterous partner a second chance to demonstrate fidelity. These apparently more forgiving men might receive benefits from their wife, such as more frequent sexual access, that equal or outweigh the potentially huge costs of a wife's infidelity (see Baker and Bellis 1995).

Marital Satisfaction

If anticipations of seeking divorce as a consequence of a spouse's infidelity involve taking stock of the benefits and costs of remaining married to and divorcing an adulterous partner, and if marital satisfaction negatively covaries with spousal cost-infliction, then lower marital satisfaction should predict higher likelihood estimates of divorcing an unfaithful spouse. We found support for this prediction for men's, but not women's, likelihood estimates of divorcing an unfaithful spouse. Men's general marital dissatisfaction predicted higher likelihood estimates of divorcing a wife if she flirted with another man, passionately kissed another man, or romantically dated another man.

Previous research indicates that men are more likely to end a relationship when they are sexually dissatisfied with the relationship, whereas women are more likely to end a relationship when they are emotionally dissatisfied with the relationship. In our sample, however, sexual and emotional dissatisfaction are unrelated to women's

reports that they would divorce an unfaithful husband. Furthermore, our research suggests that men's emotional dissatisfaction is
more consistently predictive of anticipations of divorcing an unfaithful wife than is their sexual dissatisfaction. Failure to find the predicted sex differences in anticipated dissolution due to sexual versus
emotional dissatisfaction with the marriage might be due to the use
of single-item measures of unknown reliability to assess sexual and
emotional dissatisfaction.

We created a composite measure of dissatisfaction using all three
single-item indexes of dissatisfaction (general, sexual, and emotional). The results indicate that men's (but not women's) composite
marital dissatisfaction consistently and positively covaries with their
likelihood estimates of divorcing an unfaithful spouse. Men reporting
greater composite marital dissatisfaction provide higher likelihood
estimates of divorcing a wife if she passionately kissed another man,
romantically dated another man, or had a one-night stand.

An important question for future research is why men's, but not
women's, marital dissatisfaction predicts anticipations of divorcing
an unfaithful spouse. From an evolutionary psychological perspective, we might have expected results opposite to those obtained. Because a spouse's infidelity is potentially much more reproductively
costly for a man than for a woman, it might have been predicted that
men's, relative to women's, anticipations of divorcing an unfaithful
spouse would be less predictable from feelings of marital dissatisfaction. The reproductive costs of cuckoldry are as certain and as devastating for the maritally satisfied man as they are for the maritally
dissatisfied man. A man's reproductive resources, in contrast, can be
partitioned between his wife and an extramarital lover. His wife's
marital satisfaction might in part track the portion of his investment
that she continues to receive. A woman's anticipation of divorcing an
unfaithful husband, on this account, might vary with her marital satisfaction. Women married to unfaithful men might nevertheless express marital satisfaction, proportionate to the portion of her husb-
and's investment she continues to receive. In light of the relative
clarity of evolutionary psychological predictions regarding the sex-
linked association between marital satisfaction and anticipated dissolution following spousal infidelity, future work should investigate the
replicability of the findings of our study.

Limitations and Conclusions

This study contained some notable limitations. First, we assessed
expectations of dissolution as a consequence of spousal infidelity,
rather than actual divorces filed as a consequence of spousal infidel-

ity. Not all people who predict that they would divorce an unfaithful spouse actually do. Similarly, not all people who predict that they would remain married to an adulterous spouse actually do. Developmental changes across the marital life span, such as the birth of children, may have important and unanticipated effects on the betrayed person's deliberations about whether to seek divorce as a consequence of spousal infidelity.

We have no reason to suspect, however, that likelihood estimates of divorcing an unfaithful spouse will consistently underestimate or overestimate actual divorce as a consequence of spousal infidelity. Several results of our study, such as the linkages between men's marital dissatisfaction and increased anticipation of dissolution following infidelity, mirror Buunk's (1987) findings regarding the conditions that promote *actual* dissolution as a consequence of *admitted* infidelity. Furthermore, previous research has documented significant positive covariance between anticipated and actual dissolution, more generally. In sum, anticipated dissolution as a consequence of spousal infidelity appears to be a reasonable proxy for actual dissolution as a consequence of spousal infidelity.

A second limitation pertains to the sample of couples, all of whom had married within the previous year. The nature of the sample may have occasioned reduced variance in anticipations of dissolution in response to infidelity, since the first year of marriage may be a time when individuals are least concerned not only with future infidelities, but also with the possibility of divorce, whether due primarily to infidelity or to some other cause. This range restriction would have made it more difficult to detect the predicted relationships. Restricting the range of responses on two variables forces the responses to cover a smaller range and, consequently, forces the variables to have less variance. Correlations represent an attempt to account for the variance shared by two variables. A correlation coefficient describes the linear relationship between two variables that maximally accounts for the variance shared by the variables. The less variance there is to work with, the smaller the detectable relationship will become. To the extent that the variables we assessed were range-restricted, the magnitudes of the results may be lower-bound estimates of the actual relationships between anticipated dissolution as a consequence of infidelity and the sources of spousal and relationship costs examined in this study.

We have greatly simplified the complexity of events and processes that accompany marital dissolution. In addition, we recognize that infidelity is not the only cause of divorce. Other frequently cited reasons for divorce include infertility, physical abuse, and failure to provide expected financial resources (Betzig 1989; Gottman 1994; Kelly and Conley 1987). The present study was specifically concerned, however, with the predictability of anticipations of marital dissolution as a consequence of spousal infidelity. A single study cannot offer the final word on marital dissolution, on marital dissolution following infidelity, or even on anticipations of dissolution following infidelity. This study represents one step toward gaining a better understanding of the conditions and contexts under which infidelity might lead to marital dissolution.

The results of this study are consistent with the hypothesis that anticipations of divorcing an unfaithful spouse involve a cost-benefit analysis by the betrayed partner in which the costs and benefits of remaining married are weighed against those of divorce. This study highlights the importance of mate value and attractiveness discrepancies, spousal sources of upset, and relationship dissatisfaction in creating conditions conducive to dissolution upon discovering a spouse's infidelity.

An evolutionary psychological perspective provides a profitable interpretational framework for the results of this study. We note, however, that many of these results are consistent with other perspectives, including equity theory and Rusbult's Investment Model of close relationships. Regardless of theoretical orientation, however, a critical direction for future research is determining whether the sources of spousal and relationship costs we have identified as important predictors of anticipations of divorcing an unfaithful spouse are similarly predictive of actual divorce filed as a consequence of a discovered infidelity.

ACKNOWLEDGMENT

The research reported in this chapter was conducted in collaboration with David M. Buss, who also provided many helpful suggestions on a draft of this chapter.

REFERENCES

Baker, Robin R., and Mark A. Bellis. *Human Sperm Competition*. London: Chapman and Hall, 1995.

Betzig, Laura. "Causes of Conjugal Dissolution: A Cross-cultural Study." *Current Anthropology* 30:654–676, 1989.

Buss, David M. "Sex Differences in Human Mate Preferences: Evolutionary Hypotheses Tested in 37 Cultures." *Behavioral and Brain Sciences* 12:1–49, 1989a.

———. "Conflict Between the Sexes: Strategic Interference and the Evocation of Anger and Upset." *Journal of Personality and Social Psychology* 56:735–747, 1989b.

————. *The Evolution of Desire*. New York: Basic Books, 1994.

————. "Evolutionary Psychology: A New Paradigm for Psychological Science." *Psychological Inquiry* 6:1–49, 1995.

Buss, David M., and David P. Schmitt. "Sexual Strategies Theory: An Evolutionary Perspective on Human Mating." *Psychological Review* 100:204–232, 1993.

Buss, David M., and Todd K. Shackelford. "Susceptibility to Infidelity in the First Year of Marriage." *Journal of Research in Personality* 31:193–221, 1997.

Buss, David M.; Randy J. Larsen; Drew Westen; and Jennifer Semmelroth. "Sex Differences in Jealousy: Evolution, Physiology, and Psychology." *Psychological Science* 3:251–255, 1992.

Buunk, Bram P. "Conditions That Promote Break-ups as a Consequence of Extradyadic Involvements." *Journal of Social and Clinical Psychology* 5:271–284, 1987.

Buunk, Bram P., and Barry van Driel. *Variant Lifestyles and Relationships*. London: Sage, 1989.

Daly, Martin, and Margo Wilson. *Homicide*. Hawthorne, N.Y.: Aldine de Gruyter, 1988.

Daly, Martin; Margo Wilson; and Suzanne J. Weghorst. "Male Sexual Jealousy." *Ethology and Sociobiology* 3:11–27, 1982.

Devine, Danielle, and Rex Forehand. "Cascading Toward Divorce: The Roles of Marital and Child Factors." *Journal of Consulting and Clinical Psychology* 64:424–427, 1996.

Fisher, Helen E. *Anatomy of Love*. New York: W. W. Norton, 1992.

Gangestad, Steven W. "Sexual Selection and Physical Attractiveness: Implications for Mating Dynamics." *Human Nature* 4:205–235, 1993.

Glass, Shirley P., and Thomas L. Wright. "The Relationship of Extramarital Sex, Length of Marriage, and Sex Differences on Marital Satisfaction and Romanticism: Athanasiou's Data Reanalyzed." *Journal of Marriage and the Family* 39:691–703, 1977.

————. "Sex Differences in Type of Extramarital Involvement and Marital Satisfaction." *Sex Roles* 12:1101–1119, 1985.

————. "Justifications for Extramarital Relationships: The Association Between Attitudes, Behaviors, and Gender." *Journal of Sex Research* 29:361–387, 1992.

Gottman, John M. *What Predicts Divorce?* Mahwah, N.J.: Lawrence Erlbaum Associates, 1994.

Gottman, John M., and Robert W. Levenson. "Marital Processes Predictive of Later Dissolution: Behavior, Physiology, and Health." *Journal of Personality and Social Psychology* 63:221–233, 1992.

Hite, Shere. *Women and Love*. New York: Alfred A. Knopf, 1987

Hunt, Morton. *Sexual Behavior in the 1970's*. Chicago: Playboy Press, 1974.

Kelly, E. L., and J. J. Conley. Personality and Compatibility: A Prospective Analysis of Martial Stability and Marital Satisfaction. *Journal of Personality and Social Psychology* 52:27–40, 1987.

Kinsey, Alfred C.; Wardell B. Pomeroy; and Clyde E. Martin. *Sexual Behavior in the Human Male*. Philadelphia: W. B. Saunders, 1948.

Kinsey, Alfred C.; Wardell B. Pomeroy; Clyde E. Martin; and Paul H. Gebhard. *Sexual Behavior in the Human Female*. Philadelphia: W. B. Saunders, 1953.

Kitson, Gay C., and Marvin B. Sussman. "Marital Complaints, Demographic Characteristics, and Symptoms of Mental Distress in Divorce." *Journal of Marriage and the Family* 44:87–101, 1982.

Lawson, Annette. *Adultery*. New York: Basic Books, 1988.

Levinger, George. "A Social Psychological Perspective on Marital Dissolution." *Journal of Social Issues* 32:21–47, 1976.

Messick, David M., and Karen S. Cook (eds.). *Equity Theory*. New York: Praeger, 1983.

Nunnally, Jum. C., and Ira H. Bernstein. *Psychometric Theory,* 3rd ed. New York: McGraw-Hill, 1994.

Rusbult, Caryl. E. "Commitment and Satisfaction in Romantic Associations: A Test of the Investment Model." *Journal of Experimental Social Psychology* 16:172–186, 1980.

———. "A Longitudinal Test of the Investment Model: The Development (and Deterioration) of Satisfaction and Commitment in Heterosexual Involvement." *Journal of Personality and Social Psychology* 45:101–117, 1983.

Rusbult, Caryl. E., and Bram P. Buunk. "Commitment Processes in Close Relationships: An Interdependence Analysis." *Journal of Social and Personal Relationships* 10:175–204, 1993.

Shackelford, Todd K., and David M. Buss. "Marital Satisfaction Tracks Spousal Cost-infliction: Personality, Infidelity, and Other Sources of Upset." Manuscript under review, 1996a.

———. "Betrayal in Mateships, Friendships, and Coalitions." *Personality and Social Psychology Bulletin* 22:1151–1164, 1996b.

———. "Anticipation of Marital Dissolution as a Consequence of Spousal Infidelity." *Journal of Social and Personal Relationships* 14:793–808, 1997.

Symons, Donald. *The Evolution of Human Sexuality*. New York: Oxford University Press, 1979.

———. "If We're All Darwinians, What's the Fuss About?" In Charles Crawford; Martin Smith; and Dennis Krebs (eds.), *Sociobiology and Psychology*. Hillsdale, N.J.: Lawrence Erlbaum Associates, 1987, pp. 121–146.

Veroff, Joseph, and Sheila Feld. *Marriage and Work in America*. New York: Van Nostrand Reinhold, 1970.

Walster, Elaine; G. William Walster; and Ellen Berscheid. *Equity*. Boston: Allyn and Bacon, 1978.

Wilson, Margo, and Martin Daly. "The Man Who Mistook His Wife for Chattel." In Jerome Barkow, Leda Cosmides, and John Tooby (eds.), *The Adapted Mind*. New York: Oxford University Press, 1992, pp. 289–322.

7

Race, Gender, and Romantic Commitment

Michael J. Strube and Larry E. Davis

Research on romantic commitment—the intention to continue with a romantic relationship—holds promise for revealing much about a topic of considerable public interest but also a topic with widespread social implications. Some of the most staggering statistics about human social life reflect the general lack of commitment in relationships or the breakdown of relationships that were once committed. Indeed, as is well known, approximately half of all marriages end in divorce. The societal fallout includes disruptions in child-rearing, educational difficulties, and work-related problems. Once viewed as a noble goal and the norm for serious relationships, commitment now seems to be viewed by many as a quaint anachronism, sometimes referred to pejoratively as the "C" word.

Overall divorce rates underscore the general magnitude of the problem, but they also obscure a more complex pattern. As we will point out, there are good reasons to expect race and gender differences in romantic commitment. Understanding the determinants of those differences may provide important insights into relationship dynamics and their broader consequences. In this chapter, we will first briefly review social statistics suggesting race and gender differences in romantic commitment. Then we will describe a theoretical model that we believe provides a useful vehicle for studying the psychological concomitants of those demographic differences. Some empirical work that we have conducted will then be described, followed by a discussion of future research directions.

RACE, GENDER, AND RELATIONSHIP OUTCOMES

The importance of considering race and gender differences in romantic commitment is apparent when we consider the substantial racial differences in rates of marriage, divorce, and remarriage.[1] Marriage rates for all Americans have decreased over the past two decades (U.S. Bureau of the Census 1994), but in comparison to other ethnic groups, blacks are particularly unlikely to marry (Bennett, Bloom, and Craig 1989; South 1993). Approximately two-thirds of all blacks are single in comparison to one-third of all whites. Moreover, approximately half of all white marriages end in divorce, whereas the figure for blacks is approximately two-thirds (Cherlin 1992). And the majority of whites who divorce will remarry, whereas the majority of blacks will remain single. Even once married blacks have a higher probability of divorce than do their white counterparts—approximately 66% compared to 50% (Martin and Bumpass 1989). The end result of these differences is that blacks in comparison to whites are less likely to marry, more likely to divorce, less likely to remarry once they are divorced, and more likely to divorce again following remarriage.

One possible factor in these dramatically different marriage and divorce rates is the gender imbalance between black males and black females, a problem that scholars for some time now have noted with concern (Bennett, Bloom, and Craig 1989; Guttentag and Secord 1983; Jackson 1975; Wilson 1987). Indeed, as Guttentag and Secord (1983:199) point out, "aside from postwar shortages of men in various countries, American blacks present us with the most persistent and severest shortage of men in a coherent subcultural group that we have been able to discover during the era of modern censuses." This shortage in the numbers of black men relative to black women is largely a function of the high infant mortality and homicide rates of black men. Add to that the high rates of drug addiction, incarceration, and unemployment, and it is little surprise that a serious marriage squeeze (Glick, Heer, and Beresford 1963) exists in the black community (Guttentag and Secord 1983; Scanzoni 1977; Wilson 1987). It is conjectured that because of this low ratio of black men to black women that as many as 25% of black women will never marry (Cherlin 1992). Based on existing demographic data, such predictions seem neither unwarranted nor exaggerated.

The social consequences of a significant gender imbalance are described well by Guttentag and Secord (1983:20):

Women in such societies would have a subjective sense of powerlessness and would feel personally devalued by the society. They would be more likely to be valued as mere sex objects. Unlike the high sex ratio situation, women would find it difficult to achieve economic mobility through marriage. More men and women would remain single or, if married, would be more apt to get divorced. Illegitimate births would rise sharply. The divorce rate would be high, but the remarriage rate would be high for men only. The number of single-parent families headed by women would increase markedly. . . . The outstanding characteristic of times when women were in oversupply would be that men would not remain committed to the same woman throughout her childbearing years. The culture would not emphasize love and commitment, and lower value would be placed on marriage and family. Instead, transient relationships between men and women would become important.

This description clearly predicts less commitment to romantic relationships for the gender in the shortest supply largely as a function of available alternatives. Missing in these demographic accounts of romantic commitment, of course, is a compelling conceptual model that ties gender imbalances to perceptions about relationship alternatives. Furthermore, racial differences in romantic commitment may arise from more than mere differences in the availability of partners. Fortunately, contemporary models of relationship dynamics provide promising conceptual models for exploring these differences in greater detail.

THE INVESTMENT MODEL

Most of the psychological research on romantic commitment has relied on some variation of equity theory and social exchange theory (e.g., Adams 1965; Blau 1964; Homans 1961; La Gaipa 1977; Thibaut and Kelley 1959). Rusbult's Investment Model (Rusbult 1980, 1983; Rusbult and Buunk 1993; Rusbult, Johnson, and Morrow 1986a, 1986b; Sprecher 1988) is an excellent example of this conceptual approach and the one we have used in our own work. According to the Investment Model, relationship commitment is a function of three factors: (a) satisfaction with the relationship, (b) investments in the relationship, and (c) alternatives to the relationship. Satisfaction with the relationship reflects the rewards relative to the costs of the current relationship in comparison to expectations. Satisfying relationships are more rewarding and less costly than the typical or expected relationship one might have. Not surprisingly, the Investment Model predicts a positive relationship between satisfaction and commitment. Investments in the relationship are those resources put into the relationship and the benefits one would lose if the relationship were to end. These include the time, money, effort, and emotional resources that are expended to make the relationship work. Included as well are the mutual friends, shared material possessions, and shared memories that would be lost if the relationship were to end. According to the Investment Model, commitment increases with increasing investments because it becomes psychologically more difficult to walk away from a relationship on which one has spent considerable resources. To do so is to admit having wasted those resources. Finally, the attractiveness of alternatives to the relationship exert a negative influence on commitment. The attractiveness of relationship alternatives is essentially the satisfaction one would expect to get from the best available alternative to the current relationship. The model can thus be summarized as follows: Commitment = Satisfaction + Investments – Alternatives. The weighting of the components is an empirical question.

One appealing feature of the Investment Model is that it helps account for relationships that are dissatisfying but in which the partners remain committed. This can occur, for example, when investments are high but alternatives are low. In these cases, partners may be "trapped" in their relationships (Strube 1988, 1991; see also Rusbult and Martz 1995) and engage in the emotional and romantic equivalent of "throwing good money after bad." The Investment Model also allows for different pathways to commitment, a feature that we found appealing for the investigation of race and gender differences. The model essentially allows similar levels of commitment to arise for fundamentally different reasons. Generally, the support for the Investment Model has been impressive. It has been found to predict commitment in heterosexual as well as homosexual relationships (Duffy and Rusbult 1985–1986), to account for responses to relationship difficulties (e.g., Rusbult, Zembrodt, and Gunn 1982; Rusbult, Zembrodt, and Iwaniszek 1986; see also Johnson and Rusbult 1989), and to extend to non-romantic relationships such as those that exist in the work arena (Farrell and Rusbult 1981; Rusbult and Farrell 1983; Rusbult et al. 1988). The model thus appears to have general applicability and substantial empirical backing.

Research has also found that the influence of particular model components may vary. Most typically, satisfaction and alternatives, but not investments, have been found to be reliable predictors of commitment (e.g., Rusbult, Johnson and Morrow 1986b; Sprecher 1988). Relatively little attention, however, has been given to possible racial differences. Of course, we anticipated just these kinds of differences. Specifically, if one major difference between black couples and white couples is their different gender ratios, then these groups may differ in the importance of available alternatives as a determinant of romantic commitment: alternatives may be a stronger predictor of commitment for blacks than for whites. Gender differences within racial groups might also be expected. For example, black men and black women may differ in the role that alternatives play in predicting commitment given that they are presumed to have differential access to alternatives. By comparison, the number of alternatives is roughly equivalent for white men and white women so that differential predictability may not be expected. Investments also might play differential roles for black men and black women. Black women may place greater importance on investments if having fewer alternatives to their current relationships means they must devote more resources to making the current relationship function well, particularly if they know their partners have more numerous alternatives. We explored these possibilities in two recent studies.

EMPIRICAL EVIDENCE

Study 1

Our first attempt to study the Investment Model examined both race and sex differences in intact dating couples (Davis and Strube 1993). The sample included 20 white couples and 20 black couples ($N = 80$) with an average age of 22 years. The couples were recruited from a small, private Midwestern university with a predominantly middle-class to upper-middle-class student population.

The members of each couple independently completed questionnaires that assessed the Investment Model components.[2]   Participants completed the questionnaire in a quiet room at the university and were supervised by one of two graduate student assistants (one black, one white). Equal numbers of black couples and white couples were supervised by each graduate assistant to reduce bias. Commitment was measured using four questions (e.g., How committed are you to your partner?). Satisfaction was measured with two questions (e.g., If you decided to end your relationship, to what extent would you be giving up a very satisfying relationship?). Investments were assessed by a single question: To what extent would you lose important investments associated with your partner (e.g., time, mutual friends, material goods, activities, memories, emotions)? Alternatives were also assessed by a single question: How attractive would the alternatives be as compared to your relationship? Alternatives may be to begin a relationship, begin seeing several other people, or spend time alone. When possible, multiple items were combined to produce more reliable composite measures of the model components.

Initial analyses indicated that the only difference in mean ratings was that men, regardless of race, rated their alternatives as more attractive than did women. Apparently, *both* the black males and the white males believed that they had better alternatives than their female partners.

Table 7.1
Commitment as a Function of Investment Model Components,
Sample 1

	Women		Men	
Predictor	β	t	β	t
Satisfaction	0.46	3.42*	0.26	1.69
Investments	0.10	0.72	0.10	0.61
Alternatives	-0.37	0.20*	-0.46	3.17*

Note: Standardized regression coefficients are from the final, simultaneous solution.
* p < .05.

Multiple regression analyses were then conducted, predicting commitment from satisfaction, investments, and alternatives. The analyses were conducted separately for men and women, with race differences investigated both as main effects and as interactions with the Investment Model components. The results produced three major findings: (a) generally strong support for the Investment Model, (b) virtually no evidence for race differences, and (c) gender differences in the particular components that were related to commitment. Overall, the Investment Model components were significant predictors of commitment for both men and women (p < .005), accounting for 33% and 48% of the variance respectively, with all components in the predicted direction. As Table 7.1 shows, however, the magnitude and significance of the individual predictors were a bit different for men and women. The only significant predictor for men was alternatives to the relationship, whereas for women alternatives and satisfaction were significant predictors. The investment component was not a significant predictor for either men or women. Interestingly, race did not interact with alternatives or investments for either men or women. These components influenced commitment similarly for blacks and whites and Table 7.1 shows no differential predictiveness for men and women. The investigation of race differences revealed only one effect: Satisfaction with the relationship was a stronger predictor of commitment for white men than for black men.

This first study demonstrated that (a) the Investment Model provides a useful account of the predictors of commitment, (b) the predictors are similar for blacks and whites and (c), investments did not play an important role in predicting commitment in this sample. The generally strong support for the Investment Model is crucial because it makes the lack of race differences somewhat easier to explain. That is, the general lack of race differences is unlikely to be due to an inappropriate conceptual model or to completely insensitive measures. The only racial difference that did emerge was an unanticipated interaction between race and satisfaction. This interaction indicated that satisfaction was positively related to commitment for white men but not for black men. Any interpretation is admittedly post hoc, but elsewhere (Davis and Strube 1993) we have suggested that this interaction may reflect the knowledge on the part of black males that alternatives are readily available to them so that even if they are satisfied in their current relationship, they can imagine being still more satisfied in a different relationship (even though one might not currently be a viable alternative). Consequently, current satisfaction may play a less important role for black men as an indirect outcome of differentially available alternatives. As we will see, however, the relatively uninfluential role of relationship satisfaction may be particular to college men and not true of black men in the broader community.

In retrospect, the lack of race differences may have been a product of our sample selection. Most participants were students at a small, private Midwestern university, and most students possessed the economic status, social status, and aspirations expected of such a select group. Although the gender ratios in this sample, both black and white, mimic those in the general population, it is also likely that this student group is shielded from many of the pressures that confront couples in the broader community. In particular, this sample probably experiences little difficulty finding romantic partners, given the relatively close and frequent contact of students on small college campuses. Differential access to alternatives for black men and black women may thus be less salient than in the general population. In addition, college dating is generally short term and unstable so that it may not be surprising that investments played little role in predicting commitment. Finally, the measurement of Investment Model components, though similar to much past research, was rather limited, particularly for investments and alternatives (one-item scales). Accordingly, we conducted a second study that attempted to remedy these problems.

Study 2

In a second study that we recently completed, we attempted to measure the Investment Model components more completely. In addition, we focused exclusively on a group of black professionals in order to explore in more detail the dynamics of commitment in the context of more realistic concerns about alternatives and investments. The sample for the second study consisted of forty single black men and fifty-nine single black women, all attendees at a national black professional conference. This sample, of course, obviates the study of differences between black and whites, but it did present itself as a unique opportunity to examine gender differences within black relationships in more detail. Besides, the first study suggested that the Investment Model components operate similarly for blacks and whites, so we felt that greater attention to the dynamics of black relationships was a more pressing concern.

Each participant agreed to complete a questionnaire as part of a workshop on black male-female relationships conducted by the second author (a black male). All participants were college graduates with 80% of the men and 71% of the women holding graduate degrees. Seventy-five percent of the men and 68% of the women reported incomes exceeding $40,000 a year. The mean age for men was 34 years, and for women it was 32 years. Seventy-five percent of both men and women reported that they had never been married. The mean length of time they had been dating their current partners was 1.57 years for men and 1.87 years for women. Eighty-five percent of men and 98% of women reported that they hoped to marry, with the vast majority hoping to do so within five years. Thus, commitment was a clear concern for this group, and they had been in their relationships long enough to invest considerable resources. Furthermore, this sample was expected to be more susceptible to the forces of differential alternatives than was true for the college sample. If differential access to romantic partners is a clear concern in black romantic relationships, then this sample would be expected to provide a reasonably sensitive vehicle for detecting those concerns.

The questionnaire included items designed to assess the Investment Model components much more completely than in the first study. Commitment was measured by a total of nine questions (e.g., For how much longer do you want your relationship to last? Do you feel committed to maintaining your relationship with your partner? How likely is it that your relationship will end in the near future?). Satisfaction was measured with twelve questions (e.g., all things considered, to what degree do you feel satisfied with your relationship? Taking into account all of the qualities that are most important to you, how does your relationship compare to that of other peoples'? All things considered, how does your relationship compare to your ideal?). Investments in the relationship were assessed by twelve questions (e.g., have you put things into your relationship that you would in some sense lose if the relationship were to end [e.g., time spent together, secrets disclosed to one another]? Are there things that are now "tied" to your relationship that you would in some sense lose if the relationship were to end [e.g., material possessions, housing]? Are there special activities associated with your relationship that you would in some sense lose [or they'd be more difficult] if the relationship were to end [e.g., shared friends, child rearing, recreational activities, job]?). Finally, alternatives to the relationship were assessed with twelve questions (e.g., All things considered, how attractive are the people other than your partner with whom you could become involved? If you weren't dating your current partner, would you do okay—would you find another appealing person to date? How do your alternatives [dating another, spending time alone, etc.] compare to your relationship with your partner?) Individual items measuring commitment, satisfaction, investments, and alternatives were combined into more reliable composites.

Comparison of mean scores on the Investment Model components indicated that males rated their alternatives as significantly more attractive than did women ($p < .05$), a result that replicates the first study and that lends support to the notion that differential alternatives may be a salient feature of black relationships. Other model components did not differ significantly between men and women. Separate regression analyses for men and women again revealed strong overall support for the Investment Model ($p < .001$), with 72% and 54% of the variance in commitment accounted for by the model predictors for men and women respectively. As Table 7.2 indicates, the magnitude and significance of individual predictors were different for men and women. The results for women were remarkably similar to the first sample; that is, satisfaction and alternatives were significant predictors of commitment but the investment component was not. The results for men, however, were quite different. Among this sample of black professional men, all model components were significant predictors of commitment.

The results for the second study indicate two key differences compared to the college sample, both regarding the determinants of romantic commitment for males. First, unlike black males in college, professional black males report a strong and positive relation between satisfaction with the current relationship and commitment to that relationship. This, of course, is precisely what is expected by the Investment Model. The difference in findings between the two samples may simply reflect better measurement in the second study, or, it may reflect a real shift in the perceived importance of relationship rewards and costs for black male professionals. The latter would not be surprising given that this sample had been in their current relationships for a fair amount of time and generally expressed a strong desire for marriage within the next five years. Given the long-term outlook of this group, it is sensible that they would be concerned about the rewards and costs of their current relationships.

Table 7.2
Commitment as a Function of Investment Model Components,
Sample 2

	Women		Men	
Predictor	β	t	β	t
Satisfaction	0.59	4.97*	0.59	5.27*
Investments	0.14	1.20	0.25	2.22
Alternatives	-0.18	1.87*	-0.24	2.62*

Note: Standardized regression coefficients are from the final, simultaneous solution.
* $p < .05$, one-tailed.

The second notable difference in the second study was the emergence of investments in the relationship as a significant predictor of commitment for males. Investments have historically been the most difficult to find as important predictors of commitment and, indeed, investments were not significant predictors in the first study, nor for females in the second study. Why then do investments emerge as important to professional black males, contrary to our initial speculations? One reason may be that economic resources are relatively plentiful for this group but may also be perceived to be particularly special or fragile. Black males as a group have not risen to high-salaried positions in great numbers so this group of males may view themselves as quite privileged and see the resources they have acquired to be quite precious. Spending those resources on relationships may thus carry more important psychological implications. These speculations will require additional research to verify. Nonetheless, the shift in predictors of commitment for black males in college compared to professional black males is quite dramatic, both in the nature of the predictors and in the overall amount of commitment variance accounted for by the predictors (33% vs. 72%). By comparison, the predictors of commitment for black women are remarkably stable in their nature and in the overall commitment variance for which they account (48% vs. 54%). These differences certainly deserve additional and careful study.

Taken together, the two studies provide additional overall support for the Investment Model and provide an important extension of this model to black romantic relationships. Both studies suggest that black males have perceptions of their alternatives that track the documented gender imbalance. The relation of alternatives to commitment is similar for black men and black women, however. The gender differences in the role of investments will require additional study, but is particularly noteworthy given past difficulty in finding much impact for the investment component. Despite these empirical puzzles, these studies provide a useful first step in the systematic understanding of black romantic relationships. To date, the factors affecting the commitment of black males and black females have received relatively little attention. Work such as that presented here is a step toward bringing those relationships under a common conceptual umbrella that may lend greater understanding to the dynamics that produce the relationship instability so prevalent in this group.

GENERAL IMPLICATIONS

We began this chapter by discussing marriage and divorce disparities between blacks and whites. We believe the broader implications of studying relationship commitment lie ultimately in addressing issues such as this, particularly the consequences for black relationships. Since the 1960s, considerable attention has been given to the plight of black families (Coner-Edwards and Spurlock 1988). However, little attention has been given to the careful study of factors affecting the single individuals who engage in the formation of those families (Taylor et al. 1990). In particular, little research has focused on the premarital relationships of black men and black women (Jackson 1975; Staples 1981). This is surprising because the study of romantic and close relationships has increased over the years (Ashmore and Del Boca 1986; Brehm 1985; Clark and Reis 1988; Derlega et al. 1991). As a consequence, there currently exists a particularly deficient understanding of those factors that guide relationship commitment in black romantic relationships. Conceptually guided work, such as that using the Investment Model, will help remedy this problem.

As the percentage of single and divorced individuals continues to increase in our society, factors that affect romantic commitment will likely receive greater attention. Indeed, the decision to stay together, or to go their separate ways, is a question that virtually all couples address at some point in their relationships. One of the most important avenues for future research in this area, then, will be the study of relationships in transition. Undoubtedly, macro-level factors (e.g., poverty) are responsible for much of the instability that is witnessed among black couples (Tucker and Mitchell-Kernan 1995; Wilson 1987). But here too we believe that attention to psychological factors has the potential to shed considerable light on this problem.

The Investment Model in particular provides some useful guidance. Past work has shown that the components of the Investment Model have clear implications for the direction that relationships are likely to go when they experience difficulties (e.g., Rusbult, Johnson, and Morrow 1986a; Rusbult, Zembrodt, and Gunn 1982). Four typical responses to relationship turmoil have been identified: Exit, voice, loyalty, and neglect. Exit and voice represent active responses to relationship difficulties but differ in their implications for relationship stability. Exit, of course, is the dissolution of the relationship, whereas voice is the active attempt to solve the problems in the relationship. By comparison, loyalty and neglect are passive responses to relationship turmoil. Loyalty represents a hopeful "waiting for improvement," whereas neglect represents a passive and pessimistic "waiting for the end."

Past work indicates that the approach taken to relationship difficulties depends on satisfaction, investments, and alternatives (e.g., Rusbult, Zembrodt, and Gunn 1982). Exit, for example, is most likely to occur when satisfaction is low, investments are few, and alternatives are attractive. Under these conditions, there is little to hold a person in a relationship and there are good reasons to leave. Voice, on the other hand, occurs when satisfaction is high and investments are high. Under these conditions, individuals are motivated to save the relationship because it has been very satisfying and much has been put into making the relationship work. The presence of attractive alternatives may further instigate active and positive attempts to resolve relationship difficulties because having alternatives provides a source of power for effecting change. Loyalty occurs when satisfaction is high, and investments are high, but alternatives to the relationship are unattractive. There is nowhere else to go, and so there is no real leverage through which to take an active stance toward relationship improvement (e.g., voice). The only viable option is to remain in the relationship and make the best of it. Neglect, also a passive response, occurs when satisfaction is low, investments are low, and alternatives are poor. To date, no attempt has been made to examine closely these responses in black couples experiencing relationship difficulties. This kind of work may provide additional insight into the problems produced by gender ratio imbalances. Given different alternatives, one might expect differential reliance by black men and black women on active and passive responses to relationship difficulties.

It will also be important in future research to investigate specifically the role played by sexual dynamics. For example, it is undoubtedly true that sexual satisfaction and frustration are part of the rewards and costs that produce the overall satisfaction with the relationship. But just how crucial are sexual rewards and costs? Do men and women, blacks and whites, place different importance on sexual relations? Are the sexual expectations for the relationship (the benchmark against which the current relationship is compared) different for these groups? How important are sexual opportunities in the perception of alternatives to the relationship? Is a monogamous sexual relationship considered an important investment in the relationship? Are sexual experiences an important source of relationship turmoil, and do they influence the responses to that turmoil? These questions are crucial to address because sexual experiences and decisions involving sex may not have quite the same rational character as is typically implied by the Investment Model.

As work on romantic commitment progresses, it will become increasingly important to broaden careful investigation to include more than white college samples, to study the development and decline of relationships over time, and to broaden investigation to include the sexual dynamics that are central to many relationships. The practical consequences are clear in the different rates of marriage and divorce across racial groups. But the potential conceptual gains should not be ignored either. Comprehensive and compelling conceptual accounts will only emerge from "boundary tests" that map the full range of relationship experiences and include all types of relationships.

NOTES

1. As will be apparent, race and gender effects are bound together and will be discussed together.

2. Other measures were included in the questionnaire (e.g., self-esteem, self-rated attractiveness, perceived attractiveness of partner); these are described in greater detail in Davis and Strube (1993). Generally, we have found that variables other than the Investment Model components sometimes predict relationship commitment but do so independently.

REFERENCES

Adams, J. S. "Inequity in Social Exchange." In L. Berkowitz (ed.), *Advances in Experimental Social Psychology*, Vol. 2. New York: Academic Press, 1965, pp. 267–297.

Ashmore, R. D., and F. K. Del Boca (eds.). *The Social Psychology of Male-Female Relationships: A Critical Analysis of Central Concepts.* New York: Academic Press, 1986.

Bennett, N. B.; D. E. Bloom; and P. H. Craig. "The Divergence of Black and White Marriage Patterns." *American Journal of Sociology* 95:692–722, 1989.

Blau, P. N. *Exchange and Power in Social Life.* New York: John Wiley, 1964.

Brehm, S. *Intimate Relationships.* New York: McGraw-Hill, 1985.

Cherlin, A. J. *Marriage, Divorce, Remarriage.* Cambridge, Mass.: Harvard University Press, 1992.

Clark, M., and H. Reis. "Interpersonal Processes in Close Relationships." *Annual Review of Psychology* 39:609–672, 1988.

Coner-Edwards, A. F., and J. Spurlock. *Black Families in Crisis: The Middle Class.* New York: Bruner/Mazel, 1988.

Davis, L. E., and M. J. Strube. "An Assessment of Romantic Commitment Among Black and White Dating Couples." *Journal of Applied Social Psychology* 23:212–225, 1993.

Derlega, V. J.; S. S. Hendrick; B. A. Winstead; and J. H. Berg. *Psychotherapy as a Personal Relationship.* Chicago: Nelson-Hall, 1991.

Duffy, S. M., and C. Rusbult. "Satisfaction and Commitment in Homosexual and Heterosexual Relationships." *Journal of Homosexuality* 12:1–23, 1985–1986.

Farrell, D., and C. Rusbult. "Exchange Variables as Predictors of Job Satisfaction, Job Commitment, and Turnover: The Impact of Rewards, Costs, Alternatives, and Investments." *Organizational Behavior and Human Performance* 28:78–95, 1981.

Glick, P. C.; D. M. Heer; and J. C. Beresford. "Family Formation and Family Composition: Trends and Prospects." In M. B. Sussman (ed.), *Sourcebook in Marriage and the Family,* 2nd ed. Boston: Houghton Mifflin, 1963, pp. 30–40.

Guttentag, M., and P. Secord. *Too Many Women? The Sex Ratio Question.* Beverly Hills, Calif.: Sage, 1983.

Homans, G. *Social Behavior: Its Elementary Forms.* London: Routledge and Kegan Paul, 1961.

Jackson, J. "The Attitudes of Black Females Toward Upper and Lower Class Males." *Journal of Black Studies* 1:107–128, 1975.

Johnson, D. J., and C. Rusbult. "Resisting Temptation: Devaluation of Alternative Partners as a Means of Maintaining Commitment in Close Relationships." *Journal of Personality and Social Psychology* 57:967–980, 1989.

La Gaipa, J. J. "Interpersonal Attraction and Social Exchange." In S. Duck (ed.), *Theory and Practice in Interpersonal Attraction.* New York: Academic Press, 1977, pp. 129–161.

Martin, T., and T. Bumpass. "Recent Trends in Marital Disruption." *Demography* 26:37–51, 1989.

Rusbult, C. "Commitment and Satisfaction in Romantic Associations: A Test of the Investment Model." *Journal of Experimental Social Psychology* 16:172–186, 1980.

———. "A Longitudinal Test of the Investment Model: The Development (and Deterioration) of Satisfaction and Commitment in Heterosexual Involvements." *Journal of Personality and Social Psychology* 45:101–117, 1983.

Rusbult, C., and B. P. Buunk. "Commitment Processes in Close Relationships: An Interdependence Analysis. Special Issue: Relational Maintenance." *Journal of Social and Personal Relationships* 10:175–204, 1993.

Rusbult, C., and D. Farrell. "A Longitudinal Test of the Investment Model: The Impact on Job Satisfaction, Job Commitment, and Turnover of Variations in Rewards, Costs, Alternatives, and Investments." *Journal of Applied Psychology* 68:429–438, 1983.

Rusbult, C., and J. M. Martz. "Remaining in an Abusive Relationship: An Investment Model Analysis of Non-voluntary Dependence." *Personality and Social Psychology Bulletin* 21:558–571, 1995.

Rusbult, C.; D. Farrell; G. Rogers; and A. Mainous. "Impact of Exchange Variables on Exit, Voice, Loyalty, and Neglect: An Integrative Model of Responses to Declining Job Satisfaction." *Academy of Management Journal* 31:599–627, 1988.

Rusbult, C.; D. Johnson; and G. Morrow. "Determinants and Consequences of Exit, Voice, Loyalty, and Neglect: Responses to Dissatisfaction in Adult Romantic Involvements." *Human Relations* 39:45–63, 1986a.

————. "Predicting Satisfaction and Commitment in Adult Romantic Involvements: An Assessment of the Generalizability of the Investment Model." *Social Psychology Quarterly* 49:81–89, 1986b.

Rusbult, C.; I. M. Zembrodt; and L. K. Gunn. "Exit, Voice, Loyalty, and Neglect: Responses to Dissatisfaction in Romantic Involvements." *Journal of Personality and Social Psychology* 43:1230–1242, 1982.

Rusbult, C.; I. M. Zembrodt; and J. Iwaniszek. "The Impact of Gender and Sex-Role Orientation on Responses to Dissatisfaction in Close Relationships." *Sex Roles* 15:1–20, 1986.

Scanzoni, J. *The Black Family in Modern Society: Patterns of Stability and Security.* Chicago: University of Chicago Press, 1977.

South, S. J. "Racial and Ethnic Differences in the Desire to Marry." *Journal of Marriage and the Family* 55:357–370, 1993.

Sprecher, S. "Investment Model, Equity and Social Support Determinants of Relationship Commitment." *Social Psychology Quarterly* 51:318–328, 1988.

Staples, R. *The World of Black Singles: Changing Patterns of Black Male/Female Relations.* Westport, Conn.: Greenwood Press, 1981.

Strube, M. J. "The Decision to Leave an Abusive Relationship: Empirical Evidence and Theoretical Issues." *Psychological Bulletin* 104:236–250, 1988.

————. "A Rational Decision Making Approach to Abusive Relationships." *Revista Intercontinental de Psicologia y Educacion* 4:105–120, 1991.

Taylor, R. J.; L. M. Chatters; M. B. Tucker; and E. Lewis. "Developments in Research on Black Families: A Decade Review." *Journal of Marriage and the Family* 52:101–111, 1990.

Thibaut, J. W., and H. H. Kelley. *The Social Psychology of Groups.* New York: Wiley, 1959.

Tucker, M. B., and C. Mitchell-Kernan (eds.). *The Decline in Marriage Among African-Americans: Causes, Consequences, and Policy Implications.* New York: Russell Sage Foundation, 1995.

U.S. Bureau of the Census. *Statistical Abstract of the United States.* Washington, D.C.: U.S. Government Printing Office, 1994.

Wilson, W. J. *The Truly Disadvantaged: The Inner City, the Underclass, and Public Policy.* Chicago: University of Chicago Press, 1987.

8

Romantic Ideals as Comparison Levels: Implications for Satisfaction and Commitment in Romantic Involvements

Gregory D. Morrow and Chris O'Sullivan

The proposal that romantic idealism might be injurious to romantic relationships was first emphasized in the writings of Burgess (1927) and de Rougement (1940, 1948). Schulman (1974:139) notes that "the *problem* of romanticism and idealization in our society has been a recurrent theme of family sociologists and marriage educators" [italics added]. The "problem" concerns the negative impact that unrealistic expectations arising from the romantic ideal may have on an individual's romantic involvement. That is, individuals often enter relationships imbued with fantasies and unrealistic expectations concerning their partners and their relationships. With the passage of time, and often following marriage, these individuals come to realize that their expectations are not being met. This realization often results in disillusionment and dissatisfaction; in essence, "the honeymoon is over." "This process of idealization and disillusionment is seen as a threat to the institution of marriage and the family insofar as it is held responsible for high divorce rates and one-parent families" (Schulman 1974:139). This concern, in various but similar forms, has been echoed by a number of authors (e.g., Crosby 1985; Dean 1962; Ellis 1985; Hobart 1958) and seems to be widely accepted by today's society. However, data to support these assertions are rare.

In this chapter, we report the results of a study in which we sought to examine the association between individuals' romantic ideals and both satisfaction and commitment. The theoretical context of this investigation is provided by Rusbult's (1980a, 1983) Investment Model. This model proposes that individuals evaluate their relationships in relation to their overall expectations for such involvements. If a relationship meets or exceeds expectations, then the individual should be satisfied. If a relationship fails to meet those expectations, it should be viewed as unsatisfactory. This hypothesis has not been addressed by previous research on the Investment Model. Thus, the present study examines two questions: (1) are individuals' romantic ideals associated with satisfaction in romantic relationships? (2) Are those ideals related to the commitment to maintain such relationships?

Prior to exploring these questions in depth, however, several issues merit further examination. Given that the Investment Model provides the theoretical framework for this study, we will examine that model (the comparison level construct in particular) in greater detail. We will also review earlier research on romanticism which first led us to address these questions, and discuss three studies that have looked at the role of the comparison level in the individual's judgments of satisfaction.

THE INVESTMENT MODEL

The Investment Model (Rusbult 1980a, 1983) views individuals' behavior in relationships in simple economic terms. Individuals are assumed to act in ways that give them the greatest profit in terms of maximizing rewards and minimizing costs.

Satisfaction

The Investment Model views satisfaction with and attraction to a relationship as determined by the difference between the outcome value of the relationship and the individual's comparison level (CL), which is broadly defined as what the individual expects from a relationship (Thibaut and Kelley 1959). Outcome value is defined as the difference between the rewards (positively valued attributes) and costs (negatively valued attributes) associated with the relationship. Satisfaction (SAT) then is defined as the discrepancy between the outcome value and the comparison level, and may be expressed mathematically as:

$$SAT = (REW) - (CST) - CL \quad [1]$$

An individual's satisfaction with a relationship is viewed as a function of the rewards and costs of the relationship and his or her expectations regarding that type of relationship. To the extent that an individual receives high rewards, encounters few costs, and expects little from an involvement, satisfaction with that relationship should be high.

Commitment

The Investment Model defines commitment as the individual's feelings of attachment to a relationship and his or her intentions to remain in that relationship. As might be expected, greater satisfaction with a relationship is often associated with greater commitment to that relationship. However, some people do remain highly committed to unsatisfying involvements or, conversely, show little or no commitment to relationships that are sources of great satisfaction. Such counter-intuitive outcomes are a result of two other variables that influence individuals' commitment levels—investments in a relationship and potential alternatives to a current involvement.

Investments refer to any resources connected with a relationship that would be lost should the relationship end (i.e., money, time, emotional effort, material possessions, mutual friends, etc.). Investments tend to increase commitment by increasing the costs of ending a relationship. In essence, an individual may become trapped in a relationship because he or she would lose too much should that involvement end.

The final determinant of commitment is the individual's perceived alternatives to his or her current relationship. The attractiveness of a given alternative is a function of the rewards and costs of the alternative and the individual's comparison level. Thus, an alternative should be more attractive to the extent that it provides many rewards, few costs, and exceeds the individual's comparison level. An individual's possible alternatives to a current relationship are not limited to establishing another involvement, but also include such options as spending time alone or spending additional time in established relationships (e.g., with friends or family). In any case, the possession of an attractive alternative weakens commitment to the current relationship, while the lack of viable alternatives strengthens that commitment.

In summary, the Investment Model views commitment as a multiply-determined phenomenon. Commitment to maintain a relationship is a function of the individual's satisfaction with the relationship, the investments put into the relationship, and the possible alternatives to that relationship. Mathematically, this formulation can be expressed as:

$$COM=SAT+INV-ALT \quad [2]$$

To date, research has been highly supportive of the predictions set forth by the Investment Model. Rusbult and her colleagues (Farrell and Rusbult 1981; Rusbult 1980a, 1980b, 1983; Rusbult and Farrell 1983; Rusbult, Johnson, and Morrow 1986) have found that the model constructs predict both satisfaction with and commitment to romantic relationships and friendships, as well as job satisfaction, job commitment, and turnover.

There is one aspect of the investment model, however, that previous research has virtually ignored, in spite of its theoretical importance. Rusbult and her colleagues have consistently neglected the comparison level because of difficulties in dealing with this construct, which is more abstract than the other model variables. In examining the ability of the investment model to predict satisfaction and commitment in romantic involvements, Rusbult (1980a) notes that "no attempt was made to measure CL in these experiments because of the intimate connection of respondents' reports of reward and cost values with their general expectations (most people cannot separate what exists objectively from what they expect in general)" (p. 176 n.1). Insofar as the Investment Model provided the theoretical context for the present study, the comparison level construct deserves further examination.

The Comparison Level

According to both interdependence theory and the Investment Model, the basic function of the comparison level is to provide some value against which the individual can subjectively evaluate both the level of satisfaction attained in his or her relationship and the potential for alternative relationships to provide satisfaction. Thibaut and Kelley (1959:81) note that the comparison level may be defined "as being some modal or average value of all the outcomes known to the person (by virtue of personal or vicarious experience), each outcome weighted by its salience (or the degree to which it is instigated for the person at the moment)." Similarly, the Investment Model defines the comparison level as representing "the average relationship outcome value that the individual has come to expect . . . determined by the quality of past experience with relationships and comparison to associations of similar others" (Rusbult 1980a:173).

In part, the comparison level is based on the outcomes experienced directly by the individual: specifically, the outcome values of past involvements. In addition, the individual's comparison level is influenced by experience with others' relationships. The outcome values observed in relationships involving parents, friends, peers, relatives, and acquaintances may all play roles in forming the individual's comparison level. Thibaut and Kelley (1959) suggest that idealized and/or fantasized relationships affect the comparison level. They also state that the salience of the various outcomes that comprise the individual's experiences plays an important role in determining the comparison level: "A person's CL depends not only on the outcomes he has experienced or seen others experiencing but also upon which of these are actively stimulating to him—are obtruded on him, are vivid and perhaps implicitly rehearsed as he makes an evaluation of his circumstances" (Thibault and Kelly 1959:81–82).

The salience of each particular outcome is partially dependent on whether it was incorporated into the comparison level through personal or vicarious experience. Personally experienced outcomes are assumed to be more salient and, therefore, to exert a greater impact on the comparison level. For vicariously experienced outcomes, greater weight (salience) is given to those outcomes where individuals perceive greater similarity between themselves and those whose experience they observe. For example, an individual's comparison level should be influenced more strongly by his or her parent's relationship than by a neighbor's relationship.

The present study examined the comparison level construct within the context of subjects' expectations for the ideal romantic relationship. These ideal expectations comprise one component of the comparison level. Thus, any discrepancy between the individual's real relationship and his or her conceptualizations of the ideal romantic involvement should affect satisfaction with that relationship in accordance with Investment Model predictions. We, however, are not the first investigators to suggest that romanticism might be injurious to romantic relationships.

ROMANTICISM

What exactly is romantic love? Averill and Boothroyd (1977:235) state: "Love is a passion: One does not enter into love quietly and with deliberation; rather, one is 'gripped,' 'seized,' and 'overcome' by love. That, at least, is the romantic stereotype or ideal." This description of romantic love is similar in many respects to that used by other researchers. Romantic love is often characterized as involving a sudden onset or love at first sight (Averill and Boothroyd 1977; Knox and Sporokowski 1968), intense emotional reactions (Averill and Boothroyd 1977), excitement and daydreaming (Knox and Sporokowski 1968), physiological arousal and complete absorption with the loved one (Berscheid and Walster 1972; Knox and Sporokowski 1968), expectations of future involvement—particularly marriage (Averill and Boothroyd 1977; Crosby 1985), and belief in statements such as "love conquers all" and "true love only comes once" (Knox and Sporokowski 1968). Specific behaviors such as watching a sunset together, kissing goodbye, and hearing "I love you" are also commonly considered to be part of traditional romantic love (Prentice, Briggs, and Bradley 1983).

Strauss (1946) found that about 80% of his sample of engaged or recently married individuals had an image of an ideal mate and most of his subjects used this image in evaluating potential marriage partners. On the other hand, Udry (1965) compared subjects' ideal mate characteristics with the characteristics of the actual mate and concluded that the idealized image had little impact on actual mate selection. Kemper and Blough (1980) re-examined Udry's study and stated that his conclusion was "based on a misinterpretation of the statistics he calculated to test the several hypotheses" (p. 35). In their re-analysis of Udry's data, Kemper and Blough report a strong relationship between the ideal and real partner. Simpson, Campbell, and Berscheid (1986) report that romantic love, defined as "the emotional experiences that the state of romantic love popularly implies" (p. 365), is currently viewed by both male and female college students as crucial to the selection of a marital partner as well as the maintenance of the marital relationship.

Schulman (1974) proposed that idealization should result in perceptual distortion. For example, an individual would view his or her relationship as running smoothly when, in reality, disagreement within the relationship was high. He found that idealists were significantly less likely to recognize high levels of disagreement than more realistic couples. An attempt to assess the impact of idealization on relationship happiness proved untenable, because subjects in the study rated their relationships uniformly high in happiness. The obtained happiness ratings are not surprising, for Shulman's sample consisted entirely of engaged couples.

Spanier (1972) examined the relationship between romanticism and marital adjustment. He defined romanticism as, "a general disposition an individual has toward love, marriage, the family, and with relationships involving male-female interaction in which the affective component is regarded as primary and all other considerations are excluded from conscious reflection" (pp. 481–482). Two hundred and eighty married subjects (140 couples) completed the Locke-Wallace Marital Adjustment Scale and the Dean Romanticism Scale. A non-significant correlation ($r = .104$) was obtained between subjects' scores on the two measures. Based on this finding, Spanier concludes that there is no evidence to support the thesis that romanticism exerts a negative impact on marital adjustment.

In summary, we have some evidence of the importance of romantic ideals in the mate selection process and some indication that disillusionment may occur as relationships progress. The widely held assumption that endorsement of romantic ideals is detrimental to individuals' real relationships remains, however, virtually unexamined and to date, unsupported.

RESEARCH ON THE COMPARISON LEVEL

An extensive review of the literature located only three studies that gave specific attention to the comparison level construct. Pittman and McKenry (1983) examined respondents' comparison level for their marriage and six other variables (i.e., sex, self-esteem, religiosity, spousal hostility, extra-familial involvements, and self-disclosure anxiety) as predictors of marital cohesion. The comparison level for the marriage was measured by a single item that asked subjects to assess their marriage in comparison to the marriages of other couples with whom they were familiar. They report that the respondents' comparison level was the best single predictor of marital cohesion. The more favorably the respondents viewed their own marriage in comparison to others, the higher their marital cohesion. Since marital cohesion was defined as attraction between members of the marital dyad, this finding supports the Investment Model prediction that satisfaction should increase to the extent that the relationship exceeds the individual's comparison level.

Sternberg and Barnes (1985) conceptualized the comparison level as a realistic ideal "defined for subjects in terms of what might be realistic in their lives rather than in terms of some impossible standard that could never be met" (p. 1588). Twenty-four graduate and undergraduate student couples completed the Rubin (1970) Love and Liking scales and the Levinger, Rands, and Talaber (1977) Scale of Inter-personal Involvement under four different sets of instructions. Each subject was asked to complete the scale according to "(a) how they feel about the other, (b) how they believe the other feels about them, (c) how they would wish to feel about an ideal other, and (d) how they would wish an ideal other to feel about them" (p. 1588). The differences between partners' perceptions were then assessed with respect to the impact of those discrepancies on satisfaction. The results indicate that both the absolute outcomes from the relationship and subjects' obtained outcomes relative to their ideals were predictive of relationship satisfaction.

In an application of the comparison level concept to consumer satisfaction, LaTour and Peat (1980) examined the effects of prior experience with a product (glass cleaner) on subjects' satisfaction with a new glass cleaner product. After experimentally manipulating the goodness of subjects' prior experience, it was found that subjects with poor prior experience (low comparison level) were more satisfied with the new product than were those with more favorable prior experience (high comparison level). LaTour and Peat clearly demonstrated the impact of the comparison level (as determined by prior experience) on subjects' judgments of satisfaction.

Although there is little empirical research on the comparison level construct, the available evidence clearly supports predictions that the comparison level plays a role in individuals' judgments of satisfaction. The results of these three studies offer support for the idea that individuals' judgments of satisfaction in interpersonal relationships are influenced by their expectations for those involvements. Specifically, individuals tend to be satisfied when their outcomes meet or exceed their expectations, while outcomes that fail to meet those expectations often lead to dissatisfaction.

Two points are of major importance with respect to the study presented here. First, a primary reason that the comparison level construct has not received greater attention from researchers is that it has been defined in abstract terms by its original proponents (e.g., Rusbult 1980a, 1983; Thibaut and Kelley 1959). Thus, one goal of this study is to examine a single specific component of the comparison level, namely, individuals' romantic ideals. Second, research on the comparison level and relationship expectations in general has focused almost entirely on the role these factors play in determining relationship satisfaction. The present study expands that focus by examining the role of the comparison level within the context of the Investment Model. In addition to exploring the impact of the comparison level on satisfaction, this study also examined the relationships between the comparison level and other Investment Model variables, namely, commitment, rewards, costs, investments, and alternatives.

METHODS

Participants

Two hundred and seventy-six University of Kentucky students (145 males, 131 females) participated in the study. Only those subjects involved in a romantic relationship of at least one month's duration participated. This relationship could be of any degree of seriousness, from casual dating to marriage. Data obtained from 36 subjects (25 males, 11 females) were not included in subsequent analyses because these individuals were either not romantically involved at the time of their participation in the study or returned incomplete questionnaires. Thus, analyses were carried out on data from 120 male and 120 female subjects.

The respondents ranged in age from 17 to 45 with a median age of 18. The sample was 93.7% white and 3.8% black, with the remaining 2.5% falling into some other category (i.e., Hispanic, Asian, or other). Relationship duration ranged from a minimum of three weeks to a maximum of fifteen years, with a median of one year.

Procedure and Questionnaire

Subjects in same-sex groups of 15 to 30 individuals completed a questionnaire designed to assess respondents' feelings and beliefs about both the ideal romantic relationship and his or her current relationship. The questionnaire contained measures of Rusbult's (1983) Investment Model variables (i.e., rewards, costs, satisfaction, investments, alternatives, and commitment). Rewards and costs were each assessed by two questions: How rewarding is your relationship? And, how costly is your relationship? The remaining variables were measured using the following four questions: (1) satisfaction: "To what extent are you satisfied with your current relationship?"; (2) investments: "How much have you invested in your relationship with your partner (e.g., time, energy, self-disclosure, shared experiences, emotional investments)?"; (3) alternatives: "How appealing are your alternatives (e.g., a different relationship or spending time without a serious romantic relationship)?"; and (4) commitment: "How committed are you to maintaining your relationship?" Reliability coefficients (*alphas*) calculated for each of the four-item scales were as follows: satisfaction (0.78), investments (0.77), alternatives (0.79), and commitment (0.88). The fact that the reward and cost scales consisted of only two items each precluded the calculation of *alpha* coefficients. Interitem correlations for rewards (r = .70) and costs (r = .68), however, indicated a strong association between the individual measures of each variable.

The remainder of the questionnaire consisted of three sets of questions designed to assess respondents' feelings and beliefs about the ideal romantic relationship and how closely their current involvement approximated that ideal. A total of sixty-one items were used. Forty-one items were taken from the Levinger et al. (1977) Scale of Interpersonal Involvement, developed for the purpose of measuring rewards and costs associated with interpersonal relationships. The remaining 20 items consisted of descriptions of behaviors taken from a study of attitudes toward romantic behaviors by Prentice, Briggs, and Bradley (1983). In a factor analysis of 195 relationship behaviors, these twenty behaviors were found to be rated as highly romantic by most individuals. The behaviors can be grouped into two clusters: traditional romantic behavior (e.g., hearing "I love you," watching a sunset together) and sexual behavior (e.g., being undressed by the partner, engaging in sexual foreplay). These items were included in the present study due to their romantic nature and were utilized to better assess respondents' romantic ideals.

Respondents were asked to rate each of the sixty-one items three times on a nine point scale in which 1 = not at all important; 5 = moderately important, and 9 = extremely important. First they were asked to evaluate the degree to which the behaviors and feelings described occurred in their present relationship; second, to evaluate the degree to which each item would occur in the ideal romantic relationship; and third, to rate the items according to how important they felt each was in a romantic relationship.

RESULTS

Comparison Level

According to the Investment Model and interdependence theory, the comparison level represents the individual's overall expectations for his or her relationship. Within this context, outcomes that fail to meet the comparison level are sources of dissatisfaction, while outcomes that meet or exceed the comparison level contribute to satisfaction with the relationship. In contrast, romantic ideals represent the outcome levels for partner/relationship attributes that are ideal. Thus, in the present study it was assumed that any outcome level discrepant from the ideal, regardless of whether that outcome fell short of the ideal or exceeded it, would contribute to dissatisfaction in the relationship.

As a preliminary examination of the relationship between the comparison level construct and the Investment Model variables, two sets of zero-order correlations were calculated. One series of correlations was calculated between the Investment Model variables (rewards, costs, satisfaction, investments, alternatives, commitment) and unweighted current outcome—ideal outcome discrepancy (CID) scores for each of the 61 relationship attribute items noted previously. These CID scores were obtained by calculating the absolute value of the discrepancy between the respondent's ideal outcome (IO) score and the corresponding current relationship outcome level (CO) score for each item. A second series of correlations was calculated between the Investment Model variables and 61 weighted CID scores. The weighted CID scores were obtained by multiplying each of the unweighted CID scores by their corresponding importance ratings obtained from respondents. Examination of the obtained correlation coefficients indicated that the unweighted CID scores were more strongly associated with the Investment Model variables than were the weighted CID scores. Accordingly, subsequent analyses utilized the 61 unweighted CID scores.

Principal Components Analysis

As an exploratory measure, a series of principal components analyses utilizing varimax rotation was carried out on the 61 unweighted CID scores described above. Examination of a scree plot indicated the presence of four distinct factors. The four factors (Table 8.1) included 34 of the original 61 CID scores. Each of these factors is described below.

Factor 1 consisted of fifteen scores focusing on CIDs related to emotional intimacy and support—for example, helping the other grow personally, growing personally through the relationship, and sharing deeply personal ideas and feelings. Factor two consisted of six scores focusing on CIDs in sexual behavior, e.g., having sexual intercourse, undressing each other, engaging in sexual foreplay. Factor 3 included eight CID scores relevant to traditional romantic behavior such as walking on the beach, lying in front of a fire, and being together out in nature. Finally, factor 4 was made up of five scores measuring CIDs in feelings of security and trust, for example, feeling secure in your future together, making a binding commitment for the future, having no secrets from each other. One CID score (learning about the other's daily activities) was dropped from factor 4. This item had a factor loading of only .290 and did not fit well with the other items making up the factor. Reliability coefficients (coefficient $alpha$) were calculated for each of the four CID score factors. The reliability coefficients obtained for the factors emotional intimacy ($alpha$ = .91), sexual behavior ($alpha$ = .88), romantic behavior ($alpha$ = .84), and security/trust ($alpha$ = .83) all exceeded levels recommended by Nunnally (1978). Single scores were therefore computed by averaging the unweighted CID scores across the items comprising each factor. The average CID scores for each of the four factors were then employed in all subsequent analyses. CO scores and IO scores were also calculated for emotional intimacy, sexual behavior, romantic behavior, and security/trust by averaging subjects' current or ideal outcome scores, respectively, across the items comprising each of the four factors. These variables were included in the analyses as an exploratory measure.

Zero-Order Correlations

It was predicted that the respondents would be more satisfied with relationships in which their current outcome levels approximated their romantic ideals. As a preliminary test of this hypothesis, a series of zero-order correlations was used to assess the relationships among the Investment Model variables (rewards, costs, satisfaction, investments, alternatives, commitment) and the four CID factors (emotional intimacy, sexual behavior, romantic behavior, security/trust). Respondents' CO and IO scores for each of the four factors were also included in the correlational analyses. The results of these analyses are presented in Table 8.2.

Table 8.1
Principal Components Analysis of Current Outcome—Ideal Outcome Discrepancy Scores

	Factor Loadings			
Items	Emotional Intimacy	Sexual Behavior	Romantic Behavior	Security/ Trust
Help other grow	.749	.135	.049	-.057
Grow personally	.735	.012	.117	.093
Offer emotional support	.658	.140	.088	.178
Share personal ideas/feelings	.645	.081	.058	.208
Listen to other's confidences	.644	.055	.098	-.027
Give help	.635	.222	.108	.083
Make other feel needed	.609	.110	.019	.159
Receive emotional support	.585	.109	.179	.229
Share hopes & dreams	.561	.156	.178	.342
Say I love you	.545	.270	.217	.533
Feel needed	.531	.118	.118	.400
Understand the other well	.525	.003	.065	.339
Share ideas & information	.510	.033	.072	.193
Receive help from other	.482	.187	.017	.238
Accept other's limitations	.407	-.086	.163	.138
Have sexual intercourse	.119	.809	.126	.109
Have spontaneous sex	.111	.782	.207	.113
Undress each other	.175	.763	.139	-.011
Be undressed by the other	.151	.760	.077	.069
Engage in sexual foreplay	.083	.718	.044	.093
Climax at the same time	.022	.632	.374	.115
Share a jacuzzi/hot tub	.060	.208	.761	.184
Walk on the beach	.082	.141	.750	.132
Lie in front of a fire	.080	.137	.726	.087
Shower together	.126	.342	.628	.163
Walk in the moonlight	.243	-.005	.586	.020
Vacation together	.101	.017	.533	.095
Be together in nature	.176	.088	.508	.009
Find love notes	.295	.265	.406	.219
Feel secure in the future	.268	.099	.188	.750
Make a binding commitment	.177	.114	.238	.745
Feel secure in the relationship	.345	.065	.178	.548
Hear I love you	.468	.290	.195	.530
Have no secrets	.194	.138	.011	.479
Eigenvalue (after rotation)	15.76	3.74	3.20	2.17

Note: Items are presented here in abbreviated form.

Satisfaction. As predicted, satisfaction was negatively correlated with increased CID scores for all four factors (emotional intimacy, sexual behavior, romantic behavior, and security/trust). Greater satisfaction was also associated with greater CO levels and higher IO levels for each of the four factors. In addition, higher levels of satisfaction were positively associated with rewards ($r = .78$, $p < .01$) and negatively associated with costs ($r = -.47$, $p < .01$). Finally, greater satisfaction was positively correlated with greater investments ($r = .61$, $p < .01$) and negatively correlated with the possession of better alternatives to the current relationship ($r = -.60$, $p < .01$).

Commitment. Higher levels of commitment were consistently and negatively associated with greater CID scores for emotional intimacy, sexual behavior, traditional romantic behavior, and security/trust. Increased commitment was positively correlated with respondents' CO levels for each of those four factors. In addition, higher levels of commitment were associated with higher IOs for emotional intimacy, romantic behavior, and security/trust. Greater commitment was positively correlated with higher levels of rewards ($r = .65$, $p < .01$), satisfaction ($r = .74$, $p < .01$), and investments ($r = .59$, $p < .01$) and negatively correlated with increased costs ($r = -.38$, $p < .01$) and the possession of better alternatives ($r = -.65$, $p < .01$).

Summary of Zero-Order Correlations. The correlational analyses supported the predicted relationship between CIDs and individuals' relationship satisfaction. That is, decreased satisfaction was associated with increased discrepancies between individuals' actual relationship outcomes and their romantic ideals. Higher levels of commitment were also correlated with lower CIDs. These correlations support previous research on the investment model. Levels of both satisfaction and commitment were positively correlated with respondents' CO levels for emotional intimacy, sexual contact, romantic behavior, and security/trust, and with their IOs for these factors (excepting ideals for sexual behavior). With the exception of sexual behavior, individuals' CO scores were more strongly associated with satisfaction and commitment than were their CID scores. This finding was explored further in the following regression analyses.

Multiple Regression Analyses

In order to assess the simultaneous effects of the model variables on satisfaction and commitment, a series of stepwise regression analyses was carried out. The results of these analyses are examined below.

According to the Investment Model, relationship satisfaction is a function of the rewards and costs associated with the relationship and the individual's comparison level (refer to Eq. 1). In order to test these

Table 8.2
Zero-Order Correlations Between Investment Model Variables and
Current Outcome—Ideal Outcome Discrepancy Scores, Current
Outcome Level Scores, and Ideal Outcome Level Scores

	Rew	Cst	Sat	Inv	Alt	Com
EI–CID	-.62**	.40**	-.65**	-.49**	.42**	-.60**
SB–CID	-.32**	.16**	-.34**	-.28**	.16**	-.28**
RB–CID	-.14*	.15**	-.20**	-.17**	.07	-.18**
ST–CID	-.51**	.42**	-.58**	-.45**	.40**	-.56**
EI–CO	.72**	-.39**	.75*	.58**	-.52**	.70**
SB–CO	.29**	.00	.26**	.30**	-.08+	.26**
RB–CO	.34**	-.16**	.36**	.34**	-.11*	.34**
ST–CO	.67**	-.44**	.71**	.57**	-.51**	.72**
EI–IO	.44**	-.14*	.41**	.36**	-.34**	.38**
SB–IO	.03	.15**	-.04	.05	.11*	-.03
RB–IO	.19**	-.01	.16**	.16**	-.02	.13*
ST–IO	.33**	-.08+	.28**	.27**	-.26**	.32**

Note: Rew = Rewards, Cst = Costs, Sat = Satisfaction, Inv = Investment Size, Alt =
Alternative Quality, Com = Commitment, EI = Emotional Intimacy, SB = Sexual
Behavior, RB = Romantic Behavior, ST = Security/trust, CID = Current–Ideal
Discrepancy, CO = Current Outcome Level, IO = Ideal Outcome Level. Thus, for example
ST–IO = Ideal Outcome Level for Security/trust.
* $p < .05$, + $p < .10$ (marginal),** $p < .01$.

predictions, measures of rewards, costs, and the four CID factors
(emotional intimacy, sexual behavior, romantic behavior, and
security/trust) were regressed onto satisfaction. The results of these
analyses are presented in Table 8.3. A three-factor model emerged
which included rewards ($t[3, 234] = 12.22$, $p < .01$) the CID score for
security/trust ($t[3, 234] = -.2.8$, $p < .01$) and the CID score for emotional
intimacy ($t[2, 234] = -2.78$, $p < .01$). None of the remaining variables

(costs, CIDs for sexual behavior or romantic behavior) was significantly related to satisfaction levels. The three-factor model was able to account for 66% of the variance in satisfaction and offers good support for the investment model predictions.

Further analyses were carried out in order to assess the impact of the model variables on respondents' commitment to their current relationships. Specifically, satisfaction, investments, alternatives (refer to Eq. 2), and the four CID factors were regressed onto commitment. A four-factor model (Table 8.4) emerged, which included satisfaction ($t[4, 231] = 6.25$, $p < .01$), alternatives ($t[4, 231] = -5.89$, $p < .01$), the CID score for security/trust ($t[4, 231] = -3.26$, $p < .01$), and investments ($t[4, 231] = 3.03$, $p < .01$). This model was able to account for sixty four percent of the variance in commitment.

The results of the correlational analyses reported earlier indicated that individuals' CO scores were more strongly associated with satisfaction and commitment than were their CID scores. Sternberg and Barnes (1985) also reported individuals' actual relationship outcomes

Table 8.3
Stepwise Analysis: Rewards, Costs, and Current Outcome—Ideal
Outcome Discrepancy Factors as Predictors of Satisfaction

	Beta	t	R	R^2	df	F
Model 1			.78	.60	1/236	354.88**
Rewards	.77	18.84**				
Model 2			.80	.65	2/235	215.08**
Rewards	.65	14.45**				
ST–CID	-.25	-5.54**				
Model 3			.81	.66	3/234	150.05**
Rewards	.59	12.22**				
ST–CID	-.16	-2.80**				
EI–CID	-.17	-2.78**				

Note: ST–CID = Current Outcome–Ideal Outcome Discrepancy for Security/trust,
EI–CID = Current Outcome–Ideal Outcome Discrepancy for Emotional Intimacy.
** $p < .01$.

Table 8.4
Stepwise Analysis: Satisfaction, Investments, Alternatives, and Current Outcome—Ideal Outcome Discrepancy Factors as Predictors of Commitment

	Beta	t	R	R²	df	F
Model 1			.73	.54	1/234	269.89**
Sat	.73	16.43**				
Model 2			.78	.60	2/233	178.10**
Sat	.54	10.55**				
Alt	-.32	-6.37**				
Model 3			.79	.62	3/232	129.42**
Sat	.44	7.91**				
Alt	-.31	-6.25**				
ST–CID	-.18	-3.64**				
Model 4			.80	.64	4/231	102.80**
Sat	.37	6.25**				
Alt	-.29	-5.89**				
ST–CID	-.16	-3.26**				
Inv	.15	3.03**				

Note: Sat = Satisfaction, Alt = Alternative Quality, ST–CID = Current Outcome–Ideal Outcome Discrepancy for Security/trust, Inv = Investment Size.
** $p < .01$.

to be superior to several comparison level factors as predictors of relationship satisfaction. To explore the possibility that respondents' CO scores might be better predictors of satisfaction and commitment than their CID scores, a second set of regression analyses was carried out. Specifically, the two previous analyses were repeated, with the four CO factors replacing the CID factors. The results of these analyses (Tables 8.5 and 8.6) indicated that the CO factors were, in fact, somewhat better predictors of both satisfaction and commitment.

Table 8.5
Stepwise Analysis: Rewards, Costs, Current Outcome—Ideal Outcome Discrepancy, Current Outcome Level, and Ideal Outcome Level Factors as Predictors of Satisfaction

	Beta	t	R	R^2	df	F
Model 1			.77	.60	1/236	354.88**
Rewards	.77	18.84**				
Model 2			.82	.68	2/235	244.92**
Rewards	.50	9.35**				
EI–CO	.39	7.38**				
Model 3			.83	.69	3/234	172.06**
Rewards	.46	8.68**				
EI–CO	.26	3.83**				
ST–CO	.19	3.04**				

Note: EI–CO = Current Outcome Level for Emotional Intimacy, ST–CO = Current Outcome Level for Security/trust.
** $p < .01$.

Table 8.6
Stepwise Analysis: Satisfaction, Investments, Alternatives, Current
Outcome—Ideal Outcome Discrepancy, Current Outcome Level, and
Ideal Outcome Level Factors as Predictors of Commitment

	Beta	t	R	R^2	df	F
Model			.73	.54	1/234	269.89**
Sat	.73	16.43**				
Model 2			.79	.62	2/233	188.76**
Sat	.44	7.79**				
ST–CO	.41	7.11**				
Model 3			.82	.67	3/232	155.71**
Sat	.31	5.39**				
ST–CO	.36	6.67**				
Alt	-.36	-5.90**				
Model 4			.82	.67	4/231	119.72**
Sat.	.27	4.57**				
ST–CO	.33	6.01**				
Alt	-.22	-5.67**				
Inv	.10	2.14*				

Note: Sat = Satisfaction, ST–CO = Current Outcome Level for Security/trust, Alt =
Alternative Quality, Inv = Investment Size.
* $p < .05$, ** $p < .01$.

Gender Effects

As an exploratory measure, a one-way multivariate analysis of
variance (males, females) was carried out on all Investment Model
variables (rewards, costs, satisfaction, investments, alternatives,
commitment) and the four CID factors (emotional intimacy, sexual

behavior, romantic behavior, security/trust). The results of these analyses indicated that subject sex had a significant impact on only three variables: investments, alternatives, and commitment. Examination of the cell means indicated that women reported investing more in their relationships ($M = 26.69$) than did men ($M = 25.01$), $F(1, 234) = 4.76$, $p = .03$ and that women were more committed to their relationships ($M = 27.98$) than were men ($M = 25.39$), $F(1,234) = 5.75$, $p = .02$. In addition, men perceived themselves to have better alternatives ($M = 18.82$) than did women ($M = 16.88$), $F(1,234) = 5.26$, $p = .02$.

A second series of one-way multivariate analysis of variance was carried out in order to assess any sex differences in respondents' CO levels or IO levels for emotional intimacy, sexual behavior, romantic behavior, or security/trust. These analyses indicated that only respondents' romantic ideals differed according to subject sex. Women ideally desired greater emotional intimacy in their relationships ($M = 123.12$) than did men ($M = 119.63$), $F(1,237) = 5.12$, $p = .02$. These data also indicate that for men, the ideal relationship involved more sexual contact ($M = 41.27$) than was the case for women's ideal involvements ($M = 38.21$), $F(1,237) = 3.82$, $p = .05$.

Differences in High Versus Low Satisfaction Relationships

Based on the relationship between the comparison level and satisfaction set forth by the Investment Model, it could be proposed that high comparison levels might be linked to reduced satisfaction in relationships. That is, individuals who expect a great deal from their relationships may find it more difficult to satisfy those expectations in comparison to individuals who expect relatively little from their interpersonal involvements. In order to explore this proposition further, a median split was used to separate subjects into high and low satisfaction groups. A series of one-way multivariate analysis of variance was then carried out on respondents' IO, CO, and CID scores for emotional intimacy, sexual behavior, romantic behavior, and security/trust. The results of these analyses (refer to Table 8.7) indicated that individuals involved in more satisfying relationships had higher romantic ideals (with the exception of the ideal level of sexual contact), higher current relationship outcomes, and fewer discrepancies between their current relationship outcomes and their ideal relationship outcomes when compared to those individuals involved in less satisfying relationships. Thus, the possession of higher romantic ideals seems to be linked to higher rather than lower levels of relationship satisfaction.

Table 8.7
Mean Comparison Level, Current Outcome Level, and Ideal Outcome
Level Scores for Emotional Intimacy, Sexual Behavior, Romantic
Behavior, and Security/Trust: High versus Low Satisfaction
Relationships

	Low Satisfaction (N = 108)	High Satisfaction (N = 115)
EI–CID	1.93	0.74 **
SB–CID	2.79	1.66 **
RB–CID	3.45	2.96 *
ST–CID	3.13	1.18 **
EI–CO	6.20	7.96 **
SB–CO	4.43	5.61 **
RB–CO	2.83	3.90 **
ST–CO	4.70	7.36 **
EI–IO	7.82	8.41 **
SB–IO	6.72	6.58
RB–IO	6.10	6.67 **
ST–IO	7.51	8.02 **

Note: EI = Emotional Intimacy, SB = Sexual Behavior, RB = Romantic Behavior, ST =
Security/trust, CID = Current Outcome—Ideal Outcome Discrepancy, CO = Current
Outcome Level, IO = Ideal Outcome Level. All scores had a possible range of 1 to 9.
* $p < .05$,** $p < .01$.

DISCUSSION

We sought to address two questions: Are individuals' romantic ideals
associated with satisfaction in romantic relationships? Are those ideals
related to the commitment to maintain such relationships independent
of the effects of satisfaction, investments, and alternative quality?

Several important findings emerged from our study. The results of
the correlational analyses clearly support the notion that discrepancies between respondents' actual relationship outcomes and their romantic ideals are associated with lower levels of rewards, satisfaction,

investments, and commitment, and increases in costs and alternative quality. Not all of the romantic ideal factors examined appear to be equal with regard to their associations with the Investment Model variables, and several aspects of our findings deserve further attention. In particular, the emotional intimacy factor was consistently more strongly related to the Investment Model variables than were the other factors examined. The regression analyses indicated that emotional intimacy and security/trust were the only comparison level factors to emerge as significant predictors of satisfaction. The security/trust factor accounted for only 1% of the variance in satisfaction. Feeling emotionally close to one's partner appears to be more important to relationship satisfaction than are any of the other comparison level factors examined.[1]

Our findings are consistent with those of a number of authors who have stressed the importance of intimacy in determining individuals' satisfaction with their romantic involvements (Berscheid and Campbell 1981; Steck et al. 1982). In a literature review on ideal mate characteristics, Powers (1971:214) reported that "the surprising stability of preferred mate characteristics suggests a continued emphasis on interpersonal compatibility, the primacy of personal relations and the appreciation of mates as persons."

A related issue concerns sex differences in individuals' desire for intimacy in their relationships. In the present study, males were found to desire more sexual contact in their involvements, while females desired greater emotional intimacy in their ideal relationships. This is consistent with the findings of other researchers (e.g., Morais and Tan 1980; Wills, Weiss, and Patterson 1974). Some insight into this pattern is offered by Helgeson, Shaver, and Dyer (1987), who present evidence to suggest that males and females conceptualize intimacy in opposite-sex relationships somewhat differently. Both sexes considered intimacy to entail positive feelings for one's partner, the expression of such feelings, talking about personal issues, and shared activities. Males, however, reported physical closeness and sexual contact to be indicative of intimacy with their partners, while these factors were not part of females' concept of intimacy. Though both males and females may desire greater intimacy in their relationships, the means through which those desires are satisfied differ.

Also of interest is the finding that the security/trust factor emerged as a significant predictor of respondents' commitment to maintain their relationships. The CID score for security/trust accounted for approximately 2% of the variance in commitment, while the CO score for security/trust accounted for some 8% of the variance in respondents' commitment beyond that accounted for by satisfaction. Given that the Investment Model predicts that the comparison level should have a direct influence only on satisfaction, we felt that a closer examination of this variable was in order.

Studies by Rempel et al. (1985) and Larzelere and Huston (1980) have found increased trust to be associated with greater love for one's partner. In his triangular theory of love, Sternberg (1988) proposes a cognitive component of love relationships; decision/commitment. In the short term, this includes the decision that one is in love, and in the long term, the commitment to maintain the relationship. Our findings would seem to indicate that individual decisions to make a commitment to a romantic relationship may depend, in part, on whether they trust their partner and feel secure in the future of that relationship, independent of how satisfying the relationship might be. Thus, individuals may make a commitment to a relatively unsatisfying but "safe" involvement or, conversely, decide not to commit to a satisfying relationship because they do not trust in the security of the relationship with that partner, for example, the relationship falls short of the comparison level for security/trust).[2]

Given the widespread speculation regarding the potentially damaging impact of unrealistic romantic expectations on relationship satisfaction, we were somewhat surprised to note that the romantic behavior factor exhibited only relatively weak associations with the Investment Model variables. Previous investigators have examined the impact of various behaviors on relationship satisfaction. Such studies, however, have focused on such factors as instrumental versus affectionate behavior (Wills, Weiss, and Patterson 1974) and positive (e.g., warmth, positive outlook) versus negative (e.g., possessiveness, untrustworthiness) behaviors that bear little resemblance to the traditional romantic behaviors examined in this study. In the present study, the romantic behaviors subscale consisted of eight specific behaviors consistent with the notion of romantic idealism. These items do not, however, represent the more idealistic notions often associated with such idealism (i.e., love conquers all, true love never dies) and to date there is little pertinent data to indicate what role, if any, these more specific behaviors play in individuals' romantic involvements. Our data would seem to indicate, though, that such romantic behaviors are less important to relationship satisfaction than such factors as intimacy and trust in one's partner.

We were also surprised to observe that the associations between sexual behavior and both satisfaction and commitment were relatively weak. A strong, positive association between sexual satisfaction and relationship satisfaction has been documented by numerous investigators (e.g., Gebhard 1966; Howard and Dawes 1976; Hunt 1974; Perlman and Abramson 1982; Thornton 1977). Most of these investigations, however, have focused principally on marital and other established relationships (e.g., cohabitation). Thus, for this sample (composed primarily of college freshman and sophomores) sexual behavior may not yet have become an integral part of romantic involvements. In addition, many of the studies noted above have focused on the association between relationship satisfaction and various measures of overall sexual satisfaction. As was noted previously, however, the items making up the sexual behavior subscale in this study focused on the degree to which respondent's relationships allowed them to engage in a specific set of sexual behaviors (i.e., have sexual intercourse, engage in spontaneous sex, engage in sexual foreplay, climax together). If individuals tend to conceptualize sexual satisfaction in global terms, more specific behavioral measures may not be strongly associated with overall relationship satisfaction. Few studies, however, have examined the importance of specific sexual behaviors in romantic involvements; this is clearly an area where greater empirical attention is warranted.

Only in the case of sexual behavior was the CID score more strongly correlated with the Investment Model variables than was the CO score. In particular, the CID scores on the sexual behavior sub-scale were more strongly related to costs ($r = .16$, $p < .01$), satisfaction ($r = -.34$, $p < .01$), and alternatives ($r = .16$, $p < .01$) than were the CO scores for sexual behavior ($r = 0.00$, ns, $r = .26$, $p < .01$, $r = .08$, $p < .10$, respectively). While this trend must be considered with caution, it may be indicative that, at least within a college population, individuals may be more acutely aware of those instances when their sexual outcomes fall short of their expectations than is the case for other aspects of relationship behaviors.

A final issue deserving of attention is the fact that individuals' COs tended to be more strongly associated with the Investment Model variables than were CIDs. Any attempt to explain why individuals' COs were superior to the CID factors in their ability to predict satisfaction and commitment must take into account the nature of the romantic ideal as a comparison level. Specifically, what contributions do individuals' romantic ideals make to their overall comparison level? Both interdependence theory and the Investment Model propose that individuals' past experience in relationships and the vicarious experiencing of others' relationships are more influential in determining the comparison level than are their romantic ideals. Thus, it may be that individuals' romantic ideals are simply less relevant to judgments of relationship satisfaction than are other components of the comparison level.

This proposition is supported by the results of two previous studies of the comparison level construct. Sternberg and Barnes (1985) found the absolute relationship outcomes obtained by their subjects to be better predictors of satisfaction than several comparison level factors. These authors did find, however, that subjects' comparison levels for outcomes they felt were realistically obtainable had an effect on satisfaction independent of the effects of the absolute relationship outcomes. In a related study, Pittman and McKenry (1983) presented evidence that the relationships of similar others may also function as comparison levels. The data from this study indicated that couples who ranked high in marital cohesion tended to view their own marriages more favorably in comparison to other marriages with which they were familiar. Thus, comparisons with more realistically obtainable outcomes may be more important in determining relationship satisfaction than comparisons with more unrealistic standards such as individuals' romantic ideals.

Walster et al. (1966) propose that the choice of a romantic partner is similar in many respects to the choice of other goals. To the extent that this supposition is valid, some additional insight into the role of the romantic ideal as a comparison level can be inferred from some basic tenets of Level-of-Aspiration Theory. Early researchers in this area (Lewin et al. 1944) distinguished between ideal goals and more realistic goals. According to Lewin et al., ideal goals are based almost entirely on the desirability of the goal, with little consideration given to the possibility of goal attainment. Realistic goals, however, are based to a large extent on the probability of goal attainment. Realistic goals, then, are likely to be viewed as attainable but usually do not represent the individual's most desired outcomes. This distinction between ideal and real goals or aspiration levels has been maintained by numerous authors (e.g., Campbell 1982; Forward and Zander 1971; Stras-Romanowska 1979; Zander 1980).

This ideal–real aspiration level distinction has been developed in greater detail and applied to bargaining and negotiation settings by Tietz and his colleagues (Tietz and Weber 1978; Werner and Tietz 1982). Tietz proposes that several different aspiration levels may exist and that different levels may become more or less relevant throughout the course of negotiations. Werner and Tietz (1982:67) present the following aspiration levels that may applied throughout the negotiation process: (1) the planned goal, (2) the agreement that is seen as attainable, (3) the lowest acceptable agreement, (4) the planned threat to break off negotiations, and (5) the planned breakoff of negotiations. The authors propose that as one moves from the planned breakoff point toward the planned goal, the desirability of the aspiration level increases while the probability of attainment decreases. Application of this structure to romantic relationships results in five comparison levels: (1) the ideal relationship, (2) the realistically attainable relationship, (3) the lowest acceptable relationship, (4) the point at which the individual plans to threaten to end the relationship, and (5) the point at which the individual plans to end the relationship. Thus, the romantic ideal may be the most desired goal, but it is also the least likely to be attained. If individuals in fact perceive the ideal to be unattainable, this would help explain why individuals' CIDs did not predict relationship satisfaction when their current outcomes were taken into account. This would also account for the findings of the studies noted above in which more realistic comparison levels were found to influence relationship satisfaction and marital cohesion. In any event, future research would likely profit by examining the different comparison level factors that may influence individuals' perceptions of their relationships.

SUMMARY AND CONCLUSIONS

In light of past research into the importance of intimacy and trust in romantic involvements, it is not surprising that subjects' CO levels for these two factors emerged as significant predictors of satisfaction and commitment. The Investment Model proposes that individuals' satisfaction with romantic involvements is, in part, dependent on the outcome levels for various relationship attributes. The results of this study have indicated two such attributes that may be particularly relevant to such judgments. Future research might benefit from the examination of other variables (e.g., physical attractiveness, attitudinal similarity, partner interaction) that have been shown to be important in determining attraction and satisfaction in romantic involvements. These data clearly indicate the importance of emotional intimacy and security/trust as determinants of satisfaction and commitment in romantic involvements. Future research should also be directed toward further clarification of the role of more realistic aspects of comparison levels (e.g., personal experience, vicarious experience) in individuals' evaluations of their relationships. In addition, these data provide some interesting clues as to the mechanisms through which individuals' expectations might serve to influence evaluations of romantic and other interpersonal interactions. A greater understanding of individuals' expectations for interpersonal involvements, the sources of those expectations, and the means by which they influence perceptions of satisfaction and commitment can only enhance our understanding of the dynamics of romantic relationships.

NOTES

1. These findings may also be the result of differences in the items comprising the different factors. Specifically, the emotional intimacy and

security/trust subscales contain a number of items regarding more general aspects of the respondent's relationship (i.e., helping the other grow, receive emotional support, feel secure in the future, make a binding commitment), whereas the items comprising the sexual behavior and romantic behavior factors tend to be more specific in nature (i.e., have sexual intercourse, undress each other, walk on the beach, lie in front of a fire). Perhaps the subscales made up of more general items provide a more accurate picture of respondents' involvements than do those consisting of more specific behavioral measures.

2. In the present study, the questionnaire item with the second highest factor loading on the Security/Trust factor (refer to Table 8.1) assessed the degree to which respondents felt that they and their partner had made a binding commitment for the future. Thus, individuals' scores on the security/trust outcome measure may simply provide an assessment of their commitment to maintain their relationships. Given this possibility, our speculation as to the relationship between these variables should be considered with some caution.

REFERENCES

Averill, J. R., and P. Boothroyd. "On Falling in Love in Conformance with the Romantic Ideal." *Motivation and Emotion* 1:235–247, 1977.

Berscheid, E., and B. Campbell. "The Changing Longevity of Heterosexual Close Relationships." In M. J. Lerner (ed.), *The Justice Motive in Social Behavior*. New York: Dover, 1981, pp. 209–234.

Berscheid, E., and E. Walster. "Beauty and the Best." *Psychology Today* 5:42–46, 74, 1972.

Burgess, E. W. "The Romantic Impulse and Family Disorganization." *Survey* 57:290–294, 1927.

Campbell, D. J. "Determinants of Choice of Goal Difficulty Level: A Review of Situational and Personality Influences." *Journal of Occupational Psychology* 55:79–95, 1982.

Crosby, J. F. *Illusion and Disillusion: The Self in Love and Marriage*, 3rd ed. Belmont, Calif.: Wadsworth, 1985.

de Rougement, D. *Love in the Western World*. New York: Pantheon Books, 1940.
———. "The Romantic Route to Divorce." *The Saturday Review of Literature* 31:9–10, 59, 1948.

Dean, E. S. "Psychotherapy and Romantic Love." *American Journal of Psychotherapy* 16:441–451, 1962.

Ellis, A. "Romantic Love." In J. F. Crosby (ed.), *Reply to Myth: Perspectives on Intimacy*. New York: John Wiley, 1985, pp. 307–321.

Farrell, D., and C. E. Rusbult. "Exchange Variables as Predictors of Job Satisfaction, Job Commitment, and Turnover: The Impact of Rewards, Costs, Alternatives, and Investments." *Organizational Behavior and Human Performance* 27:78–95, 1981.

Forward, J., and A. Zander. "Choice of Unattainable Group Goals and Effects on Performance." *Organizational Behavior and Human Performance* 6:184–199, 1971.

Gebhard, P. H. "Factors in Marital Orgasm." *Journal of Social Issues* 22:88–95, 1966.

Helgeson, V. S.; P. Shaver; and M. Dyer. "Prototypes of Intimacy and Distance in Same-Sex and Opposite-Sex Relationships." *Journal of Social and Personal Relationships* 4:195–233, 1987.

Hobart, C. W. "Disillusionment in Marriage, and Romanticism." *Marriage and Family Living* 20:156–162, 1958.

Howard, J. W., and R. M. Dawes. "Linear Prediction of Marital Happiness." *Personality and Social Psychology Bulletin* 2:478–480, 1976.

Hunt, M. *Sexual Behavior in the 1970s.* New York: Dell, 1974.

Kelley, H. H., and Thibaut, J. W. *Interpersonal Relations: A Theory of Interdependence.* New York: Wiley, 1978.

Kemper, T. D., and R. W. Blough. "The Ideal Love Object: Structural and Family Sources." *Journal of Youth and Adolescence* 9, 33–48:1980.

Knox, D. H., and J. Sporokowski. "Attitudes of College Students Toward Love." *Journal of Marriage and the Family* 30:638–642, 1968.

Larzelere, R. E., and T. L. Huston. "The Dyadic Trust Scale: Toward Understanding Interpersonal Trust in Close Relationships." *Journal of Marriage and the Family* 42:595–604, 1980.

LaTour, S. A., and N. C. Peat. "The Role of Situationally-Produced Expectations, Others' Experiences, and Prior Experience in Determining Consumer Satisfaction." *Advances in Consumer Research* 7:588–592, 1980.

Levinger, G.; M. Rands; and R. Talaber. *"The Assessment of Involvement and Rewardingness in Close and Casual Pair Relationships."* National Science Foundation Technical Report. Amherst: University of Massachusetts, 1977.

Lewin, K.; T. Dembo; L. Festinger; and P. Sears. "Level of Aspiration." In J. McV. Hunt (ed.), *Handbook of Personality and the Behavior Disorders.* New York: Ronald Press, 1944, pp. 333–378.

Morais, R. J., and A. L. Tan. "Male-Female Differences in Conceptions of Romantic Love Relationships." *Psychological Reports* 47:1221–1222, 1980.

Nunnally, J. C. *Psychometric Theory.* St. Louis: McGraw-Hill, 1978.

Perlman, S. D., and P. R. Abramson, "Sexual Satisfaction Among Married and Cohabiting Individuals." *Journal of Consulting and Clinical Psychology* 50:458–460, 1982.

Pittman, J. F., and P. C. McKenry. "Marital Cohesion: A Path Model." *Journal of Marriage and the Family* 45:521–531, 1983.

Powers, E. A. "Thirty Years of Research on Ideal Mate Characteristics: What Do We Know?" *International Journal of Sociology of the Family* 1:207–215, 1971.

Prentice, D. S.; N. E. Briggs; and D. W. Bradley. "Romantic Attitudes of American University Students." *Psychological Reports* 53:815–822, 1983.

Rempel, J. K.; J. G. Holmes; and M. P. Zanna, "Trust in Close Relationships." *Journal of Personality and Social Psychology* 49:95–112, 1985.

Rubin, Z. "Measurement of Romantic Love." *Journal of Personality and Social Psychology* 16:265–273, 1970.

Rusbult, C. E. "Commitment and Satisfaction in Romantic Associations: A Test of the Investment Model." *Journal of Experimental Social Psychology* 16:172–186, 1980a.

———. "Satisfaction and Commitment in Friendships." *Representative Research in Social Psychology* 11:96–105, 1980b.

————. "A Longitudinal Test of the Investment Model: The Development (and Deterioration) of Satisfaction and Commitment in Heterosexual Involvements." *Journal of Personality and Social Psychology* 45:101–117, 1983.

Rusbult, C. E., and D. Farrell. "A Longitudinal Test of the Investment Model: The Impact on Job satisfaction, Job Commitment, and Turnover of Variations in Rewards, Costs, Alternatives, and Investments." *Journal of Applied Psychology* 68:429–438, 1983.

Rusbult, C. E.; D. J. Johnson; and G. D. Morrow. "Predicting Satisfaction and Commitment in Adult Romantic Involvements: An Assessment of the Generalizability of the Investment Model." *Social Psychology Quarterly* 49:81–89, 1986.

Schulman, M. L. "Idealization in Engaged Couples." *Journal of Marriage and the Family* 36:139–147, 1974.

Simpson, J. A.; B. Campbell; and E. Berscheid. "The Association Between Romantic Love and Marriage: Kephart (1967) Twice Revisited." *Personality and Social Psychology Bulletin* 12:363–372, 1986.

Spanier, G. B. "Romanticism and Marital Adjustment." *Journal of Marriage and the Family* 34:481–487, 1972.

Steck, L.; D. Levitan; D. McLane; and H. H. Kelley. "Care, Need, and Conceptions of Love." *Journal of Personality and Social Psychology* 43:481–491, 1982.

Sternberg, R. J. "Triangulating Love." In R. J. Sternberg and M. L. Barnes (eds.), *The Psychology of Love.* New Haven, Conn.: Yale University Press, 1988, pp. 119–138.

Sternberg, R. J., and M. L. Barnes. "Real and Ideal Others in Romantic Relationships: Is Four a Crowd?" *Journal of Personality and Social Psychology* 49:1586–1608, 1985.

Stras-Romanowska, M. "Theoretical and Empirical Meaning of the Concept 'Level of Aspiration.'" *Polish Psychology Bulletin* 10:67–77, 1979.

Strauss, A. "The Ideal and Chosen Mate." *American Journal of Sociology* 52:204–208, 1946.

Thibaut, J. W., and H. H. Kelley. *The Social Psychology of Groups.* New York: John Wiley, 1959.

Thornton, B. "Toward a Linear Prediction Model of Marital Happiness." *Personality and Social Psychology Bulletin* 3:674–767, 1977.

Tietz, R., and H. J. Weber. "Decision Behavior in Multivariable Negotiations." In H. Sauermann (ed.), *Bargaining Behavior.* Tubingen: J. C. B. Mohr (Paul Siebeck), 1978, pp. 60–87.

Udry, J. R. "The Influence of the Ideal Mate Image on Mate Selection and Mate Perception." *Journal of Marriage and the Family* 27:477–482, 1965.

Walster, E.; D. Aronson; D. Abrahams; and L. Rottmann. "Importance of Physical Attractiveness in Dating Behavior." *Journal of Personality and Social Psychology* 7:211–215, 1966.

Werner, T., and R. Tietz. "The Search Process in Bilateral Negotiations." In R. Tietz (ed.), *Aspiration Levels in Bargaining and Economic Decision Making: Proceedings, Winzenhohl, Germany 1982.* New York: Springer-Verlag, 1982, pp. 67–79.

Wills, T. A.; R. L. Weiss; and G. R. Patterson. "A Behavioral Analysis of the Determinants of Marital Satisfaction." *Journal of Consulting and Clinical Psychology* 42:802–811, 1974.

Zander, A. "The Origins and Consequences of Group Goals." In L. Festinger (ed.), *Retrospections on Social Psychology*. New York: Oxford University Press, 1980, pp. 206–235.

SECTION IV

AIDS AND CULTURAL NARRATIVES

9

Narratives of Love and the Risk of Safer Sex

Elisa J. Sobo

INTRODUCTION

This chapter describes the links between low levels of condom use and inner-city women's experiences and understandings of heterosexual love in the context of conjugal partnership. (For efficiency's sake, I use "conjugal" to refer to both legal and common-law unions.) Specifically, I examine the causes, contexts, and mechanisms of HIV/AIDS-risk denial, the maintenance of which enables and necessitates unsafe (condomless) sex.[1] The findings come from a study conducted in 1991–1993 with clients of the Maternal and Infant Health Care Program (M&I) in Cleveland, Ohio (Sobo 1995a).

The study grew out of a recognition that black[2] women, who comprised the majority of M&I clients, are about fourteen times more likely than white women to be diagnosed with AIDS (Campbell 1990). This is not because black women practice risky sex more frequently than other Americans; they do not (Fullilove et al. 1990; Kline, Kline, and Oken 1992; Seidman, Mosher, and Aral 1992; Worth 1990; Wyatt and Dunn 1991; Wyatt, Peters, and Guthrie 1988). For poor black women, substandard health care, the frequency of intravenous drug use and untreated venereal infection (Ward 1993), the negative effects of racial and economic oppression on men's approach to heterosexual intercourse (Anderson 1990; Liebow 1967; Oliver 1989; Pittman et al. 1992), and the high prevalence of HIV in inner-city environments increase the chances that unprotected sex among poor urban blacks will involve HIV transmission.

In light of the high-level AIDS awareness, why do women have unsafe sex at all? After demonstrating that materialist models linking unsafe sex among women with financial need are superficial at best and racist at worst, I contend that the main reasons women engage in unsafe recreational sex can be traced to cultural models of conjugal love. These models are evident in the narratives through which the women in this study both justify condomless sex and, because the narratives are internalized, motivate themselves to engage in it. The narratives I identify include the Wisdom Narrative and the Monogamy Narrative. Data on women's social networks contained within their discourse suggest the possibility that the perceived necessity of actualizing the Monogamy Narrative is inversely related to the size of a woman's extraconjugal support system, a possibility that I explore in the last section of the chapter.

The cultural models of conjugal love used by black women in the Wisdom and Monogamy Narratives share key components with those used by other American women (i.e., whites). Gender and related power structures and expectations—not ethnicity per se—are the main determinants of women's unsafe sex choices. I conducted the research on which I base these conclusions in a social welfare center that served the population serviced by the M&I program and in the M&I clinic setting. The research involved focus groups, questionnaires, and interviews. (Methods are described in detail elsewhere, e.g., Sobo 1995a). Over 150 women participated. The typical participant was about 28 years old, black, had completed the eleventh grade, and had two children. While all of the women lived impoverished inner-city lives, the majority had some sort of regular income: over one-third were employed in the paid labor force (usually at menial part-time jobs) and about half received welfare assistance. Some participants made money by doing hair or nails for other women or by babysitting or cleaning houses; some reported receiving financial assistance from their male partners. About three-quarters of the women were in serious relationships. Most had plans to better their lives, whether by attending nurse's aide certification classes or by saving money so that they and their children could move to a better apartment or duplex.

BACKGROUND: PREVIOUS RESEARCH

Black Sexuality: Accepted Models Versus Excepted Findings

Much of the literature dealing with heterosexually transmitted HIV/AIDS among women describes a model in which impoverished minority women engage in unprotected sex for material gain or because of financial coercion and their lack of a developed sense of power or agency (cf. Carovano 1991; Kline, Kline, and Oken 1992; e.g., Ward 1993; Worth 1989; see also Jones 1991). But certain economic data indicate that the notion that women are dependent on men for financial survival may be in error (Sobo 1995b). As is widely noted, a disproportionate number of black males are unemployed, underemployed, or imprisoned.[3] This limits the material benefits that women receive from heterosexual partners. Indeed, some black women, knowing that the supply of marriageable or employed men is small, choose to build families and network connections without the perceived burden of a husband or boyfriend (Wilson 1986). Having responsibilities to a child is often a prerequisite for membership in resource-sharing female support networks (Ward 1990; see also Stack 1974:121).

A stereotypic "image of black females as independent baby-makers" (Pittman et al. 1992:340) has emerged partly as a result of these facts. Ample evidence suggests that black women are socialized to be economically independent (Pittman et al. 1992). As Kline et al. report, "Rather than occupying financially dependent roles in relationships with men, [poor urban] women [are] often forced to assume economic control" (Kline, Kline, and Oken 1992:450). Growing up, black girls often learn early to assume adult responsibilities, and they experience a more egalitarian family structure and have less traditional sex-role expectations than do whites (Wingood and DiClemente 1992). And black women often provide male lovers with money rather than the other way around (Weinberg and Williams 1988; see also Stack 1974:110).

But the literature on black women's heterosexuality generally ignores economic self-sufficiency when the discussion centers on behavior that is deemed puzzling, deviant, or immoral, such as unsafe, premarital, or non-monogamous sex. Scholars seem to prefer to ascribe such conduct to simple financial necessity (for an exception, see Kline, Kline, and Oken 1992). Through a focus on immediate neediness, scholars provide women engaged in such behavior with "rational" motivations, and they can adopt an ostensibly non-judgmental stance: profit-seeking makes sense according to capitalist logic (which itself helps create needy underclasses), and hunger excuses or at least explains moral breeches.

I do not deny the force of financial need in certain cases. Poverty does play a key role in enabling HIV transmission, and political and economic conditions linked to gender do circumscribe the range of sexual options that are open to poor urban women. However, the women in this study explained their preference for condomless sex with reference to love, not money. Sexual decisions, therefore, are based largely in cultural ideals for heterosexual relations and gender roles that leave most women emotionally and socially dependent on relationships with men, and affect their perceptions of risk such that unsafe sex seems a safe bet (Sobo 1993; see also Kline, Kline, and Oken 1992).

Cultural ideals for heterosexual relations and gender roles, and the social and emotional needs these ideals entail, have as much to do with political and economic conditions as more tangible financial needs do (Rapp 1987; Sacks 1974; Stack 1974; Thorne 1987; cf. Bott 1971/1957; and Rubin 1976). After briefly discussing these conditions and the cultural ideals for love related to them (for an in-depth treatment, see Sobo 1997), I describe what participants in this study had to say about applying their love ideals in real life. Generally, the actualization of these ideals meant that safer sex was out of the question.

Some Political and Economic Aspects of Conjugal Partnership

Sacks (1974) and Thorne (1987) suggest that in stratified or class societies, women's affinal kin role in relation to men as privatized (legal or common-law) wives far overshadows women's blood kin roles, such as sisters. This is related to women's subordination to men (see also Stack 1974:113–114, 124–125). The emphasis on the wife role culturally reinforces the structural subordination of women. Women are seen as beings whose completion lies in their articulation with men. This idea holds for many urban black women as well as for mainstream whites. While many blacks favor marrying later than whites do and many condone single parenthood (Pittman et al. 1992), both groups hold the same basic ideals for conjugal relations (e.g., Anderson 1990; Cochran 1989; Liebow 1967; Oliver 1989:21 & 60; Stack 1974; see also Pivnick 1993).

Patriarchal social organization underlies the fact that black women draw self-esteem from their relationships with men (as do most mainstream U.S. women). So do industrial capitalism and the family romance that this political and economic system has fostered. The cultural idealization of monogamy and of the type of loving, loyal family relations entail exist in "symbolic opposition to work and business, in other words, to the market relations of capitalism." They exist in opposition to "the market, where we sell our labor and negotiate contract relations of business, that we associate with competitive, temporary, contingent relations" (Collier, Rosaldo, and Yanagisako 1987:34).

As participants in the capitalist economy, we think of the family in terms of expressive relations and love rather than instrumental relations and money, which we associate with "the market" (Rapp 1987).[4] We seek to organize our households according to our notions of family, and these notions "absorb the conflicts, contradictions, and tensions actually generated by those material, class-structured relations that households hold to resources in advanced capitalism" (Rapp 1987:171; see also Collier, Rosaldo, and Yanagisako 1987).

Women who participate in households as wives and in keeping with family ideals do a disproportionate share of the labor by which the workforce is maintained and reproduced. Rapp explains that they are paid off in a "coin called love" (Rapp 1987:184), both by men who may participate in these households, and by other household members, as all attempt to actualize the ideas associated with family. For those who would participate in the political and economic context described, doing so is essential to status, esteem, and self-concept.

But households formed in relation to family ideals cannot always withstand the pressures of the political-economic environment in which they are built (Rapp 1987:174).[5] In a now-classic study, Stack shows that among urban impoverished blacks, economic oppression and related resource shortages discourage stable household formation to begin with (1974, e.g., p. 91).[6] Male responses to unemployment and underemployment further undermine household stability. It is widely argued that poor urban men denied access to jobs or decent wages also are denied access to self-fulfillment through the classic male act of supporting a spouse and children.

Besides alcohol use or domestic violence (Rapp 1987; Rubin 1976:44), partial or complete desertion is a common response to the inability to contribute to one's partner's and children's welfare. Inner-city men often figure desertion not as a sign of failure but as one of the ultimate signs of manliness (Liebow 1967:214). As an alternate to desertion, men can express ascendancy in the context of conjugal relations by acting with the power vested in them as family head or patriarch to control their female partners. This can involve a man's exerting control over his main conjugal partner's movements and the extent of her extraconjugal relationships, which can intensify her social and emotional dependence on him and so her need for unsafe sex (more of which later).

The cultural expectation that men will have multiple sex partners (cf. Fullilove et al. 1990; Liebow 1967) and the aforementioned high rates of homicide, unemployment, and incarceration for inner-city males cause a scarcity of "good" men to begin with. Despite the fact that racist and other social and cultural conditions that contradict the monogamy imperative make most women's achieving it nearly impossible, belief in what Elijah Anderson calls "the dream" of faithful monogamy does persist. It is promoted through television soap operas, popular songs, and women's magazines (1990:113–117). Accordingly, attaining "the dream" or even a close approximation brings prestige (cf. Mays and Cochran 1988). Conversely, most black women look upon other women who accept male infidelity with pity and scorn (Fullilove et al. 1990).

According to a widely shared American model for conjugal love—a model that I call the conjugal ideal—a healthy relationship involves a healthy, disease-free partner—a partner who need not bother with condoms: a partner who, because he is monogamous, carries no germs. Without such loyal male partners, women can be subject to shortages of emotional and social resources. Manlessness can leave women feeling unloved or lonely; it can lower their status and self-esteem.[7]

Women actively use unsafe sex as part of a psycho-social strategy for building and preserving an image of themselves as having attracted a good partner and having achieved the conjugal ideal. It often is noted that, in addition to indicating social distance (cf. Patton 1990:100; Sibthorpe 1992), using condoms announces that partners are not sexually exclusive and signals a lack of mutual trust. Accordingly, condom use denotes failure in a relationship.[8] Conversely, because of the trust and closeness that it connotes, unsafe sex signals the perfect union (Sobo 1993).

This research shows that women can build status and self-esteem by presenting themselves to others as having attracted loyal, upstanding partners and as having attained perfect, intact unions. Women commonly pattern stories about their relationships with men on either or both of two narrative forms: "The Monogamy Narrative" and "The Wisdom Narrative." The latter involves claims of having used wisdom in making partner choices; the former involves claims of having an excellent and monogamous relationship (Sobo 1993). I discuss these narratives of the conjugal ideal after briefly describing the basic findings on condom use per se.

RESEARCH FINDINGS

Condom-Use Patterns

Participant condom-use rates were quite like those reported elsewhere for similar populations.[9] Eighty-nine of the ninety questionnaire respondents indicated their condom-use patterns on a Likert-type scale. Forty (44.9%) of the eighty-nine used condoms "never" or "rarely"; twenty-nine (32.6%) used them "sometimes" or "often"; and twenty (22.5%) used them "very often" or "always."

Of the ninety questionnaires completed, thirty were pilot and sixty were final-form versions. One of the few differences between the two forms was that, to eliminate extended recall bias, the final version of the questionnaire asks only sexually active women for information about condom use during their last sexual encounters. Eleven (22.4%) of the forty-nine final-form questionnaire respondents who were sexually active said that they used condoms the last time that they had sex; thirty-eight (77.6%) claimed not to have.[10] Similarly, of the twenty-five clinic interviewees, all of whom were involved in relationships, seven (28%) said that they had and eighteen (72%) said that they had not used condoms during their last sexual encounters.

No significant differences in age, education, number of children, or even age-range of children emerged. (However, and as would be expected, non-users were more likely than users to be in the clinic for pregnancy-related care.) However, women who used condoms during their last sexual encounters (hereafter called "users") were less likely than those who did not ("non-users") to be involved in steady conjugal relationships. Furthermore, involved non-users had been with their partners much longer than involved users had and were three times as likely to live with their partners.[11]

Despite expectations that male partners might be financially supporting (or coercing) their non-condom using girlfriends or wives, the data on condom-use patterns did not support the materialist hypothesis. Non-use of condoms was not related to female unemployment. Moreover, most of the women reported being on their own financially. Fifty-four of the ninety questionnaire respondents (60%) were household heads, and seventy-five (83.3%) drew resources regularly in their own names. The explicit financial data collected[12] suggest that women contribute far more to their household budgets than theories focusing on the instrumental patron-client dimension of heterosexual relations imply. Money is not at the root of unsafe sex; rather, love is.

Loving Sex

For most M&I clinic clients, as for other urban black women (e.g., Mays and Cochran 1988), cultural ideals regarding heterosexual relations make committed unions with men essential for achieving status and attaining happiness. Sex is an integral aspect of conjugal relations. Indeed, for most women in this study, including women who had experienced a negative incident(s), sex was a good thing involving much pleasure and little pressure.

Twenty-four-year-old Falasha, a pregnant mother of an 8-year-old boy, said that sex with her boyfriend is "sort of like we have a conversation, like a 'Do you like this?' kind of thing. So there will be sort of things like we would have a conversation and carry [them] out." Donna said that her partner will say "'So, how does it feel?' He asks me that stuff." Bernice's partner, who was older, asked her to carry out a few non-traditional sexual actions but, she said, "I didn't feel comfortable 'cause I never did it before. It didn't cause any confusion. He didn't get angry. He was like, 'Whatever [you] feel comfortable with, that's what you are to do.'" Bernice continued, saying, "Sometimes I didn't [think

I satisfied him sexually] but he always said he was." Sexual encounters with steady partners were, for the most part then, reported to be enjoyable.

Shelly told me how she and her boyfriend first came to have sex:

Two months after we was together we was talking and, you know, I kissed him and he kissed me. We just felt—all of a sudden we were hooked up and we [realized we] were gonna go too fast. . . . He waited about two weeks afterward and then I said, "Oh well, lets go to the hotel." And he was like, "For real?" And I was like, "Sure." He was like, "Do you really—it's only if you really willing and ready to do it; I mean I'm not gonna push you or anything." And I was like, "OK. I want to go," and I did—I wanted to go. So we went and we made love and everything went just fine.

Sex can be just plain lustful but as Janet, a single mother of seven children aged 2 through 17 and a community college student who hoped to be a teacher, explained, women often have sex to "feel loved, needed, wanted." Janet also pointed out that with unsafe sex there is "nothing in between you both physically and emotionally. You are the closest to him that you can be." The emotional aspect of condom use is paramount for Janet and for many women who do not like the way that condoms feel.

"I guess it just feels like a lot of rubber in between us," said Rose, who had lived with her boyfriend for five years. When asked if she meant that the physical feeling of the rubber bothered her or if she meant something else, Rose replied, "Well, mental thing. It was more of a mental thing." Similarly, Falasha said that her dislike of condoms was "a mental thing but I can't get it to feel good."

With the mental or emotional component of condom use in mind, the following statement by a focus-group participant about how good sex with condoms can feel physically and her addendum about her preference to forgo them makes perfect sense: "First, I want to say they do have these really good condoms. No, really, these condoms are so good, I'm telling you. . . .You will not know—I couldn't tell that he had one on. But secondly, I would prefer not to use them."

In response to an open-ended question about the advantages of not using condoms, almost half of the women interviewed in the first phase of the research brought up the issue of trust. Condomlessness was directly described as "a sign of trust" and of "honesty" and "commitment." It was seen as "more romantic . . . special." One woman said, "It makes me feel like the relationship is strong and healthy and trustworthy and faithful"; another reported, "We feel closer to each other without condoms." Condomlessness serves to index the attainment of high-quality conjugal love.

Trust Talk

The frequency of spontaneous talk of trust among first-phase interviewees when discussing the benefits of condomlessness was surprisingly high in light of the noted question's tone and placement in the interview schedule (after a question about how condoms work), indicating the importance of the trust-related aspect of condom symbolism. Other data from the study suggest that the frequency of what I call "trust-talk" among the first-phase interviewees would have been much greater—perhaps 100%—had a question about trust been posed directly. So second-phase (clinic) interviewees were asked specifically about the qualities that they desired in men as well as about how they felt about condoms.

Shelly, who had only recently been released from prison, declared, "If I can't trust my man then who can I trust? You know what I'm saying?" If a woman wants to be able to justify being with a particular man, she must feel able to say that he is trustworthy. Bernice, who at 24 had a 5-year-old daughter, explained, "If you question a person a lot that means that you don't trust them and that's bad. [If you] can't trust each other, you ain't got no relationship, 'cause [relationships are] based on trust." Twenty-one-year-old Sarah had the same opinion: "Trust is the whole thing in a relationship, trust and honesty. If there is no trust, there is no honesty; there's no relationship."

Trust also came up in the context of condom use itself. Betsy, who was having troubles with her partner, told of an incident in which her man came to her for sex while having an affair: "I didn't trust him so I asked him to use a condom. He didn't want to, because he told me to trust him." Non-use of condoms demonstrates that trust has been established, as Peg's testimony shows: "When I first met [my partner] I used them 'til I really felt secure that he wasn't having sex with other people, and I didn't push the issue that much, but sometimes I would. I'd say, 'Better get your friend out of the drawer right there.'"

According to the women, using condoms announces that partners are not sexually exclusive and signals a lack of mutual trust. This is made clear in the following interchange reported by a clinic focus-group participant:

"I went to my physical and everything and they told me that it was best that I started using rubbers. . . . So I went and told my old man. I said, "Look, we have to start using rubbers" over the phone, and he said, "Well, I haven't done anything with anyone but you since we've been together."

Her "old man" responded as if in asking him to use condoms the woman had accused him of infidelity. The strength of the association between condoms and extraconjugal sex means that condom use denotes failure in a relationship.

Josephine, a first-phase focus-group participant with one young son had been with her partner for over five years. Despite the fact that he infected her with gonorrhea three years prior to the project, Josephine's belief in her partner's current faithfulness was high, and she saw no need for condoms: "I know my man ain't, you know, doing this and that [i.e., cheating]." Clinic interviewee Linda, who had been married five years, said, "I don't worry about [condoms] because my husband, as far as I know, has been faithful to me, and I believe he is, so I don't worry about it."

The Divisiveness of Condoms

Because of condoms' connotations, even simply having them on hand can cause problems. Interviewee Mary said, "If you're honest to him, what do you need them for?" Later, in defining honesty, Mary equated it with the word "monogamy." Like Mary, Peg felt that she did not need condoms. Still, she had "a drawer full of them. He counts [them] some days to see if I have other lovers." Clarissa was the suspicious one in her relationship: "I found one in the glove compartment and he [suggested that] maybe I put it in there, and I'm like, 'Oh, right.' I ripped it right open and [punched a hole in it as he looked on. And I said] 'I don't appreciate you accusing me.'" She asked him rhetorically, "What is this for? You know, I'm going in your pocket when I wash your clothes and finding them." The implication that her partner has extraconjugal sex was clear to her.

Nicole told a story about her boyfriend "trying to wear a condom to really piss me off, because we had been together for so long." This statement's intelligibility to the listener depends on his or her having knowledge of the connotations condoms carry, which Nicole made explicit as she went on. She and her partner had broken up, and one day he paid her a visit:

We was kissing and doing our love, and I had no clothes on and he had no clothes on and he was like, "Wait a minute" [while he got a condom]. He was really pissing me off, but I hid it 'cause I was just like "Oh, OK," you know. He's just trying to make me think like he was with somebody, 'cause we was totally away from each other. . . . It's games. He like to play mind games.

Marvelle tells a similar story, speaking from the opposite position: "Sometimes [I] want to aggravate him, so I'll get him and say, 'Here, you gotta use this [condom] cause I don't know where you've been,' and there's an argument you know, [him saying] 'What do you mean, I have been good, what [are] you thinking?'" In telling this story, Marvelle made the assertion that implying that one's partner is untrustworthy (unfaithful) is a cunning way to annoy him. Importantly, she was not saying that her partner actually did cheat. In fact, just seconds prior to telling the story, Marvelle said, "I'll only believe that he doesn't [cheat]."

Women generally prefer to ignore their men's shortcomings when they can because without partners women are subject to shortages of emotional and social resources. Manlessness can leave women feeling unloved or lonely, and it can lower their self-esteem and status. So women actively use unsafe sex to demonstrate to themselves that their men do not cheat. They do so as part of a psycho-social strategy for building and preserving an image of themselves as having achieved the conjugal ideal.

Women can build status and self-esteem by presenting themselves to others as having attracted loyal, honorable partners and as having attained perfect, intact unions. They commonly pattern stories about their relationships with men on either or both of two narrative forms, "The Monogamy Narrative" and "The Wisdom Narrative." The latter involves claims of having used wisdom in making partner choices; the former involves claims of having an excellent and monogamous relationship.

The narratives I will describe were identified after a content analysis of interview transcripts in which special attention was paid to the patterned use of metaphors, key words, and scenarios. They were by far the most prominent narratives culled from the stories the interviewees told. Each reflects a different, but related, cultural script or idealized sequence of actions that serve as steps to attaining the conjugal ideal. Each focuses on or models a slightly different aspect of the relationship between romantic love and sexual interaction. Like any narrative, each provides a skeleton structure on which to hang or with which to interpret individual experience.

In conforming to the Wisdom and Monogamy Narrative structures, the individual stories women told were the culturally influenced result of, or expression of, belief in the conjugal ideal (or at least of a desire to convince an audience of this belief). Women's actions also hinged on this ideal. In many cases, they were motivated by a commitment to it or a deep belief in it; in others, they were interpreted as such when they were recounted, whether for me, verbally, or for the individual in question, in other settings, in her own mind. The existence of these narratives demonstrates the high degree to which the conjugal ideal has been embraced or internalized, and adherence to these narratives constitutes condomless sex as not only acceptable but also highly symbolic of the achievement of the conjugal ideal.

Unsafe Sex and "The Wisdom Narrative"

The main reason why women engage in unsafe sex has less to do with economics than with condom symbolism and women's social and affective needs, which include the needs for status and esteem. In fact, an active distaste for instrumentally motivated sex informs condom-use decisions: a woman who uses condoms is likened to (or is) a prostitute. Prostitutes or sex workers are said to use condoms with each customer. Their sexuality appears to be unrelated to any desire to establish or maintain long-term relationships. But even prostitutes tend to practice unsafe sex with boyfriends and husbands because, even to prostitutes, condoms imply a social distance and a profit motive that is inappropriate in the context of an existing—or a potentially existing—intimate relationship (Miller, Turner, and Moses 1990:260–261; see also Sibthorpe 1992).

Most women want to establish long-term relationships that meet the standards entailed in heterosexual relationship ideals. Women know that, in light of these ideals, to achieve and maintain self-respect and the respect of others, they must first of all be able to determine the past sexual (and IV drug) histories and the present intentions of men. Then, they must act accordingly. Talk and action that supports a belief in one's own ability to identify "clean" (disease-free) and "conscious" (honorable) men or that advertises this ability to one's peers conforms to or actualizes what I call "The Wisdom Narrative."

Unsafe sex is an essential element in the Wisdom Narrative. An unattached woman engaging in casual sex maintains the belief that her ability to judge men is well developed and that her standards for partners are high by not using condoms, for to use them would be—except in certain contexts soon discussed—to label herself as a careless, unintelligent person unable to discriminate a "good" man from a "bad" one. A woman's insistence on condoms casts her partner as diseased and so of poor quality—certainly not steady boyfriend or husband material. One focus-group participant described a scenario in which a high school student tossed the condoms ("safeties") passed out to her and the other students in her health class to a friend, teasing, "You need these more than me. You're messing with Joe, and you don't know *what* he has."

Condom use implies that a man cannot be trusted, despite his claim to be "clean," and despite his claims to respect and love whichever woman he may go home with that night. Even a casual liaison with such a man is not esteemed, for while a man may have sex with a woman purely for gratification, and despite her ultimate "badness" or "goodness," a double standard is held whereby women are expected to seek stable relationships and so should only have sex with men fit to be involved with conjugally. A woman's ability to spot and deal wisely with (i.e., avoid) men who are sweet-talking "[game] players"—and so potential HIV carriers—is essential.

According to participants, men say anything to have condomless sex (regarding men and sex procurement-related lies, see Cochran 1989). Many women reported that men will say that they do not enjoy sex with condoms when such is not the case simply so that they do not have to bother with the condoms. In addition to the typical coercive laments regarding "feeling," men tell women that they are "clean" and not involved with any other women. But as clinic focus-group women said, "They're going to lie. They don't want to tell a woman what they done did," and "They lie, 'cause that's a man."

In an extended statement on male lying, made in relation to men in general but also with her ex-long-term partner and children's father in mind, Adrienne explained: "Well, men say they don't have no other woman or lady friends, and a man is a liar about staying with his family, taking care of his family, where he'll go out in the streets and take care of another family. He lies about sexual things. The man will give you a disease and tell a lie and beat you up and say you gave him the disease. A man is just a liar, he's a born liar." Earlier, in regard to the ex-partner, I had asked her, "Did you love him?" Adrienne replied, "Yeah, very much. I still do." The force of love, which sometimes blossoms inappropriately (e.g., for an unworthy man), can outweigh the wisdom imperative.

As far as condoms go, men may tell women that they use them with all the others so there is no need to worry, or that they just got out of prison and have not had sex for many years (with a woman, that is; but this remains unsaid). The sincerity of some such promises notwithstanding, it is very painful for women to admit that the men they are intimate with may lie and possibly even use them as sex objects. "Other" men may lie but acknowledging a particular, chosen partner's duplicity by using condoms could force a woman to experience her decision to undertake intercourse as stupid or unwise and so as humiliating.

So, despite male tale-telling, women often assume that the men they themselves would have sex with are truthful—and true (cf. Kinsey 1994). In response to a fellow focus-group participant's request for condom users to raise their hands, and perhaps because she knew that the project's aim was condom-use promotion, one woman asked, "How many of us sit here and take the risk? We got educated. You [a staff member] educated us. We sat here and [you] gave out the rubbers. Who used them? The same as we talk to a crowd of friends, and say 'Girl, you better use some rubbers'—." The woman was cut off by another participant, who declared, "You haven't used none with the three guys you've been with." Following some good-natured banter about the number of men implicated (a failed ploy to change the subject), the woman responded, "No, I did not use them; I did not raise my hand."

Women may "take the risk" of condomless sex because condom use would undermine their claims to having chosen partners wisely. That is, unsafe sex can be preferable to ruining one's self-esteem and perceived social standing. One's AIDS risks can be denied through the very acting out of Wisdom Narratives through unsafe sex (as through the telling of these narratives, to oneself and to others). In addition to its role in demonstrating one's wisdom, unsafe sex with a date or a not-yet-permanent partner demonstrates one's desire to establish that partner's permanency (cf. Pivnick 1993). He has been deemed worthy, and a committed, stable, monogamous conjugal relationship—a relationship true to the model that this culture recommends—is shown to be the goal.[13]

Long-Term Relationships and "The Monogamy Narrative"

The Wisdom Narratives of women who define themselves as involved in long-term relationships (rather than as single or dating) are contained within a larger narrative form which I call "The Monogamy Narrative." This narrative describes an idealized, monogamous, heterosexual union—the kind of union that participants feel brings the most status and esteem (see Worth 1990; also see Wilson 1987 regarding choosing not to attempt such unions, in which case, perhaps, Wisdom Narratives suffice). Both male manipulations, like making promises not intended for keeping, and the popular heterosexist discourse on coupling communicated by the media and by female peers fuel belief in this American dream (see Anderson 1990:113–117).

Research participants (and visiting males in the first-phase focus groups) often stated that "men are dogs" who eagerly cheat on their main conjugal partners. Findings from the literature lend support to the contention that men cheat. At least one in three unmarried but cohabiting urban American men who participated in a study by Blumstein and Schwartz had extraconjugal sex (cited in Turner, Miller, and Moses 1989:111). Nearly 40% of unmarried black men between the ages of 18 and 45 have multiple partners (Bower 1991).[14] Because admitting that one's partner has sex with other women damages "self-pride" and social position, women in unions deny infidelity by telling Monogamy Narratives, proclaiming that their men, and so their relationships, are ideal. Like the Wisdom Narrative it subsumes, the Monogamy Narrative involves implicit, self-congratulatory comparisons to other women's rocky conjugal relations; it is infused with Neil Weinstein's "optimistic bias" (Weinstein 1989).

Optimistic bias is implicit in statements from clinic focus-group women responding to a fellow participant's above-mentioned request for a show of hands by those who did use condoms. As if speaking for the group, one woman said, "I don't use nothing with [my baby's father] 'cause we're not cheating." Another woman told the others that she did not need condoms with her partner because he "hasn't done anything with anyone but me." Someone asked her, "How long have you been together?"

"About a year and a half, but when I met him he was a celibate."
"He told you he was celibate?"
"Yeah, he was celibate; he didn't mess around."
"Well I don't know and you don't know, but if he says so, fine."

The put-down in the last statement was partly provoked by the first woman's unspoken claim that her partner is cut from better or at least different cloth than most men. While the ability to see optimistic biases in one's own statements and actions (e.g., condomless sex with a self-proclaimed "celibate") is rare, women often can see them in others'. This was implicit in the aforementioned assertion that "the same as we talk to a crowd of friends, and say 'Girl, you better use some rubbers' [we don't use them]."

Clarissa, the woman who at one point in her interview at the clinic told me that she found condoms in the glove compartment and in her partner's pocket, said optimistically at a later point that she did not think he was seeking sex from an outside source. "Uh-uh," she said; "No. But if he does—I don't think so, cause he loves me. He wouldn't." However, other women should use condoms "like they wear underwear. You wear underwear everyday, and you use [a condom] every time."

Similarly, non-user Dee, who was 36, said of condoms:

I recommend everyone use them now. [When] I have friends that are going out with somebody, I give them three or four and make sure they put them in their purses. I have nothing against them at all. I'm one-hundred percent behind them. . . . I say, "Well, it's better to be uncomfortable for a few minutes than have AIDS for the rest of your life." ["But in your relationship you don't?"] No, I don't use them.

I said to Dee, "You don't think they're necessary?" and she said, "As far as I believe in my relationship, I don't think so. But as far as anyone else just starting up with someone, yeah." Like Clarissa and Dee, Linda explained that she did not use condoms because her partner was faithful. She then went on to say, "I don't worry about [condom use] for myself, but I see all these people out here [i.e., at the clinic] and they don't realize how close it is. They think it can't happen to them and it really can. That's what my friend, who is married to this man that is cheating on the side—it bothers me." Linda had previously explained,

[Her husband] had like about five venereal diseases in the last five months and he hasn't gave her any but still, I told her, "As quick as he can give you those, he can give you AIDS. I think that you love somebody who is just throwing your life away as well as theirs, you know, and who's gonna be there to raise your child?"

Linda also said, "I have a lot of friends who are married and it's like, I wouldn't want to be married to their spouses, not at all. They're cheating or they not spending any time, or they want to do what they want to do and my husband is not like that. I have to give him a lot of credit."

To maintain Monogamy Narratives—to provide themselves with behavioral evidence of or support for them—women engage in unsafe sex; safer-sex would signal infidelity (regarding IV drug-using women in particular, see Pivnick 1993 and Sibthorpe 1992). Gloria, a focus-group participant, said, "If my husband came to me and handed me some condoms, I think I'd shoot him because I'd know then that he's out there doing something that he ain't got no business doing." Similarly, women who introduce condoms themselves can imply that they have been unfaithful: as one focus-group participant said, "If she just comes out of the blue with something like that, he might think *she's* messing around."[15] Another, in the clinic group, patiently explained this to the researcher present: "Well, they think that you're going to have sex with some other man, honey, like you got some kind of infections." Someone added, "When they first see them, they're mad." The negative connotations of condoms regarding a woman's sex life also were invoked through interviewee Nicole's self-saluting claim, "They're not necessary, 'cause I'm just with one man."

In any case, few women said that they would ask their partners to use condoms. Because women have faith in the conjugal ideal and because their status is based partly on the loyalty and other qualities of their mates, a double standard exists by which all men except one's own are bound to "mess around." As in the simpler Wisdom Narratives, generic men and one's own man are held in mind separately so that cognitive processes do not bring them into contact and expose their similar tendencies. The same woman who declares, "A man is going to be a man" and advises other women to be sure to use condoms will boast, "I got a *good* man," using claims about her relationship to impress her family and friends. As focus-group participants said, "They want to believe the best," and "They want to *trust* that person—to feel that they can *trust* them."

A clinic focus-group participant recognized the dangers of such wishful thinking and warned that "In every walk of life there's a man out there screwing around, and that's what we as women have to look at. Don't think 'cause my man is in this category here, he doesn't mess around." That is, he does. But as a woman in the same group explained, "If you are married or whatever and you have been with a person for twelve years or whatever, you automatically assume you've been faithful to one another and then if the issue comes up, then 'What do we need a condom for? I ain't been with nobody'." In many cases, this reasoning is based on truth, but quite often, it is not.

As one focus-group participant explained, even when evidence is to the contrary, "You kind of overlook things, you know. You find excuses to not believe." Participants described the female tendency to deny the reality of adultery much as Anderson describes female partner idealization and male manipulation in a hypothetical poor, young, urban pair:

The girl's faith in the dream clouds her view of the situation. . . . Until she completely loses confidence in him, she may find herself strongly defending the young man to friends and family who question her choice. . . . Aware of many abandoned young mothers, many a girl fervently hopes that her man is the one who will be different. (1990:115–116)

Many women believe that they will be able to tell if their partners are indeed cheating. In the context of a focus-group discussion of condoms and male cheating, one woman said, "I don't use them at all with my man, I think he'd tell me if—I'd notice when he had—" Another participant cut her off: "You can't risk that." In other words, "you might not know or guess that he was cheating and you should not take that chance." But women do take such chances, because, as the first speaker said, "Well, I think I [would] know." Clues include shifts in partners' sexual preferences, changes in their visiting patterns, and changes in the frequency with which they want to have sex. As interviewee Dee said, "I probably know just about how often he like to have sex, and if [it changes] then I know, see."

Even so, women do not always know—or believe—that they are being cheated on. As a staff member who popped in on the clinic focus-group explained to the participants,

A lot of young ladies come in who have STDs and they come back and they say, "He says he don't have it." I say, "Have you been unfaithful to him?" and they say "No, I haven't been unfaithful." I says, "You sit here telling me that you know you haven't been outside the relationship but you know that that man is telling you you've got this out of thin air?" And they will take that in, but they say "But I love him."

Love transcends; its existence allows the client to create in her mind, if temporarily, a monogamous situation in which one does not exist, and she appeals to love to justify not conforming to the recommended narrative when this can no longer be hidden. In other cases, ignorance fills the gap between the real (polygyny) and the ideal (monogamy). Interviewee Mary explained that often it was not out of "thin air" that one got such diseases: "You get infections from wearing tampons; you get infections from wearing panties."

Women's appeal to love when seeking to mystify reality also was evident in a focus-group discussion of education tactics. Many participants suggested that educators should use "scary-ass" pictures or films that show the physical devastation that AIDS involves. But they abandoned the idea because, as one participant said, most women would claim, "Hell, my baby won't look like that. My baby has a good daddy. And this daddy doesn't mess around—he only messes with *me*." In other words, the participants thought that women would assume that their partners' love for them would keep them faithful. The same participant's own response to this anticipated claim was, "Well, honey, that's what *you* think. I just saw him over at Gloria's house, and it was more than a social call he was making."

When monogamy is the ideal, being cheated on brings hurt feelings: "You kind of know [about his extraconjugal affairs], and you don't want to face it because you know it's going to hurt your heart," said focus-group participant Ernestine, who had been cheated on by her current partner. Partners' affairs also bring shame, especially to women who publicly boast of their men's faithfulness. Disinclined to experience pain or lose status, a woman will deny the possibility of adultery in their relationships. Not using condoms signals her belief in his fidelity.

Women know that suggesting condom use can hurt their partners' feelings because of the connotations associated with condoms. Thus, some women threaten to punish cheating with forced condom use, increasing the negative symbolic load that condoms carry (cf. Fullilove et al. 1990). Punishment, if enacted, lasts only a few days: the time it takes for the man to cleanse his body of the sexual fluids and essence left behind by the other woman (or man). While empowering for women, the emphasis on punishment and hygiene masks the long-term possibilities of disease transmission and so is self-defeating.[16]

Refusing to acknowledge the possibility that one's mate has sex with other women (or men) supports the Monogamy Narrative. Unsafe sex also supports it: unsafe sex deflects attention from adultery and deceit and focuses it instead on the trust and honesty. It helps women maintain the belief that theirs are monogamous, caring, satisfying unions that leave neither partner desirous of sex or love from outside sources, as is prescribed by the popular U.S. conjugal ideal.

SOCIAL NETWORK FACTORS

Jealous Men

While participants talked about their desires for conjugal closeness and many described how these were accommodated or met through unsafe sex, many also reported keeping to themselves and maintaining few friends. Some reported that their male partners preferred that they limit exraconjugal contacts. Women with smaller extraconjugal support networks might depend more on their conjugal partners to meet their emotional and social needs and so might experience a more intense need to idealize and justify their relationships and to deny the possibility of conjugal problems, as through unsafe sex. Similar patterns, albeit with outcome measures other than unsafe sex, have been documented for other groups of people (e.g., Bott 1971, 1957; Browner 1983).

Social network data and data on conjugal style were gathered from clinic interviewees. Only one of the six interviewees who used condoms during their last sexual encounters with their primary partners[17] considered her partner to be among her two closest social companions, while exactly half of the eighteen non-users did so. Users' lists of their two closest social companions contained slightly more relatives than the lists of non-users, and they also contained slightly more women. Furthermore, while only one of the six users (16.7%) talked about having a jealous partner, twelve (66.6%) non-users said they had jealous partners. (A total of thirteen women or 52% deemed their partners jealous men.)

The small size of the sample notwithstanding, interviewee testimony suggests that there may be significant differences in the ways that users and non-users relate to their conjugal partners, and in the quality as well as the quantity of their extraconjugal social relations. It could be that women with jealous partners are more dependent on their men for emotional and social resources and that their social circles are kept small by and for their men. This may lead them to be more likely to list their partners as close social companions.

Roberta explained that her partner is jealous, saying he's "nosy, yes, [like] 'Who's that on the phone?'. . . If a guy calls me up, he just sits there right in my face while I'm talking to the guy on the phone, trying to figure out what the guy is saying." Rose had a similar problem:

"I would let the phone ring and just let him pick it up so he won't think it was [a man], you know. I even went as far as buying a phone where he can hear our conversations. I just do that 'cause when I be talking, I'll just be saying 'yeah, yeah, OK, uh-huh,' and he'll be thinking I'm talking to a [man]. So I bought a speaker phone where he could hear the conversations. Then it got so bad—every time I'm not at home and the phone would ring he would say, 'Is your boyfriend calling here and hanging up?' So I bought an answering machine so he could screen the calls."

Male–female interaction is assumed, at least by some jealous men, to be based on a sexual agenda. It follows for these men that, in keeping with the monogamy ideal, women already in relationships should not talk with other men. Clarissa, who keeps very few friends, describes her situation: "All my friends were male and so I had to leave them all alone, and then the one [female] friend that I had, he can't stand her 'cause she's not married." Some jealous partners who do not trust their women around men also will not like them to socialize with single girlfriends. As Marvelle explains, "He figures they have an influence on me." Betsy said the same thing: "He thinks that they're going to introduce me to a guy."

Minutes earlier in the interview, Betsy, who likes to spend time by herself playing solitaire, watching television, or reading books had said, "He's jealous. He wants me to stay in all the time. Don't even want me to see my mom. If I'm over to my mom's house, he's always thinks that me and my sisters have a guy over there for—everywhere I go he thinks that it's because a guy is there for me or I'm gonna have an affair. . . ."

Sarah also focused on her partner's suspicions when discussing his jealousy. She explained, "When the relationship first started off, I had a lot of man friends. [My partner] thought it was more of a sexual thing [with them]. I told him it wasn't like that: they was just friends." But Sarah had to leave them behind in order to keep her partner happy. Besides men, her partner also does not like Sarah to spend time with people he does not know. When asked why, she said, "I asked him that, and he said 'Cause I don't know [them and] ain't no telling what you all be up to.'"

Male control over female social circles is not only driven by men's fears that their women will contravene the conjugal ideal by committing adultery or leaving them. Men's desires to spend time with their partners in accord with romantic ideals can lead them to act jealously. Since many couples do not live together, time alone can be a rarity. "Sometimes he has a fit, like this Friday," said Dee, explaining that her partner told her 'You're going to just stay here with just me, that's just it.' He's possessive, she said, because he "just wants that private night." Moreover, as Nicole explained, concerns for male reputation also play a role: "[To socialize with] my mother, then that's OK. But like if I was to stay here [and socialize with] my friend Tom, [my partner] would be like 'No.' No, men are out; that's just totally no way. It's not because—I don't think [my partner gets] scared. It's just that he's the kind of guy that worries about what people think of him, so if somebody was to see me and Tom, you know, and come and tell [my partner], 'Well I've seen [Nicole] with Tom,' you know, it's 'Oh God!'"

Men's jealousy limits women's social circles, forcing women who decide to stay in relationships with jealous men to be more emotionally and socially dependent on their primary partners. Furthermore, as a few of the interviews revealed, men's jealousy can sometimes find expression in more extreme forms of controlling behavior, like verbal and physical abuse. Some women who have controlling partners see that control as beneficial (cf. Pivnick 1993). Winsome, for instance, said of her boyfriend's insistence on guarding her, "In a way I like it 'cause he takes care of me." He fulfills a conjugal obligation toward her in this way.

Well-meaning or not, jealous men who, in Peg's words, "put their control" seek to suppress women's independence. Clinic focus-group participant Betty explained why some men do this: "If [a woman has] got a lot of friends and a lot of family to talk to and stuff, she's not so dependent on that man. [Women get dependent on a man if] he don't want her to have outside friends; or family here—he don't want no family participating. If the family tells her the sky blue, he say it's green. The sky blue, but [what he says is what she] goes by. He don't want her to listen to her family and friends." Contradicting the monogamy ideal and undermining the Monogamy Narrative is extremely threatening in this kind of situation, so women with jealous or controlling partners are perhaps the most likely to be non-users of condoms. Indeed, as noted, only one (16.7%, N = 6) condom-using interviewee portrayed her partner as jealous, while twelve (66.6%, N = 18) non-using interviewees did so.

Women and Friendship

Isolation is not solely due to men's wishes. Many interviewees expressed little interest of their own in socializing. Typical of many interviewees were Michelle's declarations, "I don't keep a lot of friends," "I'm just quiet," and "I'm more like a private person"; Betsy's statement, "I can be social but I don't like to, not too much"; Sarah's pronouncement, "I don't have too many women friends; I don't have too many friends, period"; and Donna's blunt statement, "I don't have any friends."

Mary said, "I used to have friends but I didn't understand life, the value of life. No, I don't have any friends [now.]" Friends keep people from taking the righteous, sober path, she said, adding, "I'm being honest, honey. I don't know how anybody else sees it, but I'm telling you exactly how I feel."

Peg pointed to the responsibilities that motherhood brings rather than focusing on the trouble that friends can involve, explaining, "I don't hang out or anything. I'm at home. I'm playing with my kids and I ain't got no more time for nothing else. Kids keep you busy, you know." A few minutes later, she said, "I don't have people coming in and out of my doors. [My partner] loves it 'cause it's secluded like that. It's basically just me and him." Rose, who similarly said, "My main way is to be homebound," stated simply, "My partner is my best friend." While the meaning of friendship would have to be investigated if we were to be sure, Rose's and Peg's discourse suggests that they subscribe to a companionate idea for conjugality, one in which love is expressed through (among other things) communication, sharing, and emotional closeness.

Five of the twenty-five clinic interviewees (20%) counted their partners as their best friends; five more (20%) counted them as their second closest companions. Mary instructed me, "You don't need people [i.e., friends]. The only person you need is that man for you and that's enough. If you can understand him and yourself, you don't need to be around other people." "He's my best friend. I can say that, 'cause I can tell him anything, you know," said Sarah.

The discontinuity between condom use and considering lovers as close friends was made clear in a focus-group discussion in which one participant called the group's attention to the optimistic bias, asking, "How many of us in here are using condoms with our man?" Someone quickly declared in response (and in defense), "Our mates are our friends." Friendship, at least for these women, is a component of conjugal love.

Twelve clinic interviewees (48%) found keeping female friends particularly dangerous. This was not only because their partners did not like them to do so, but also because, as the women explained, so-called friends often do not have one's best interests in mind. As Mary said, "People can get you in a lot of trouble." So the narrowness of some women's social circles seems to be related not only to partner jealousy or to companionate models of conjugal love but also to their own selective preference for solitude.

Sometimes, women fear that their so-called friends will advertise their secrets to the world; other times, they fear that their so-called friends will try to steal their partners away. (In this section, I use "friends" only in reference to females, or girlfriends, as did the interviewees.) As Roberta explained, "Friends could take your boyfriend or husband away from you. They can slander your name, you know—things you tell them in confidence they can tell someone else." Just as concern for esteem motivates women to seek loving partners, so too does it motivate them to limit their extraconjugal social ties. For if conjugal ideals are to be fulfilled they cannot afford to lose their partners, jealous or otherwise.

THE CONDOM CONUNDRUM

In addition to suggesting that many women are active players in sexual decisions and that financial coercion plays only a minor role in driving unsafe sex, the study findings suggest that there is a positive correlation between unsafe sex and emotional and social dependence on men. Impoverished inner-city women idealize loving monogamy and hope for loyal conjugal partners. Much of their relationship-related talk describes a dream of fidelity, puts forth a claim of having achieved it, or supports a belief in its reality. Because condoms are associated with infidelity and deceptive behavior, using them implies that partners do not truly love one another. Admitting to this in regard to one's own relationship is emotionally painful and shaming. Condom use undermines the Monogamy (and Wisdom) Narratives that women are encouraged to and need to tell; therefore, women avoid it.

Women who are less dependent on men for self-esteem and support—women who have strong extraconjugal networks that they feel good about—may be less likely to forgo condoms. Women with few or weak extraconjugal ties may tend to focus on their conjugal relationships more than other women do and so may tend to engage in more of the wishful thinking about monogamy that leads to unsafe sex. The less women rely on friends and relatives for companionship and social support, the more likely they may be to have unsafe sex—the more likely they may be to engage in wishful thinking and deny the possibility of non-monogamy during the emotionally charged period of lovemaking.

Women who agree with and aspire to fulfill mainstream relationship ideals put themselves in danger by practicing unsafe sex. Supporting one's denial of the possibility of a partner's infidelity by having unsafe sex is an adaptive, psychosocially beneficial practice in the short run. But this strategy can have deadly long-term costs—especially when invoked in the context of poverty and sexism. Unfortunately, it will continue to be invoked: HIV/AIDS education may even increase risk behavior because, in endorsing the belief that condoms are for those who have failed to achieve the conjugal ideal, in suggesting that condomlessness can index true love, education messages may actually raise the love-related symbolic value and desirability of condomless sex.

Results from the study suggest that unsafe sex occurs most frequently among socially isolated women who derive self-esteem and status mainly from having conjugal partnerships with men. But the study does have its limitations. It did not measure levels of social status and self-esteem thought to correlate with Monogamy and Wisdom Narrative tale telling. It did not collect data from men, whose narratives may differ greatly from those described. Furthermore, because this project used small convenience samples, generalizations about black women or about women of other ethnicities, poor and urban or otherwise, are out of the question.

Findings from general health-risk perception and HIV/AIDS-risk perception research carried out with ethnically mixed groups show correspondences between the marriage and gender-related aspirations of women of color and those of white U.S. women (e.g., Kline, Kline, and Oken 1992; Prohaska, Albrecht, and Levy 1990; Sibthorpe 1992; Weinstein 1987, 1989; see also Carovano 1991). These correspondences, as well as my own exploratory comparative work, support my belief that the condom-use and other HIV/AIDS-related patterns and processes that I describe can also be found among white and perhaps other U.S. women as well. Gender-linked love ideals and the narratives that express and reinforce them may well be more important than ethnicity and geography, and often even direct material needs, in engendering personal AIDS-risk denial.

ACKNOWLEDGMENT

A majority of the analysis was completed while the author was with New Mexico State University, and much has been adapted from the project book, *Choosing Unsafe Sex: AIDS-Risk Denial among Disadvantaged Women* (University of Pennsylvania Press 1995). Grants from Cleveland's Community AIDS Partnership Project and the Spring Foundation for Research on Women in Contemporary Society supported the research. Sara Colegrove, Donna Dayse, Richard Glaze, Barbara Hood, Jill Korbin, Michelle Nawrocki, Margaret Ruble, Philip Toltzis, Deborah Washington, Gregory Zimet, Robert Carlson, and the members of the Case Western Reserve University Center for Adolescent Health's subcommittee on sexuality have all contributed to the study's development.

NOTES

1. All condomless sex is unsafe sex, even when one's partner swears that s/he is monogamous, because as participants said, "You never know."
2. I use the term "black," as did most participants in the research to be described.
3. Women's risk for HIV infection rises with male incarceration rates, because homosexual relations are common in prison. Furthermore, heterosexually coupled men often cheat bisexually (Muir 1991:91; Turner et al. 1989:152). Covert bisexuality is probably more common among black men than whites

because of the ways the African-American identity is constructed (Dalton 1989; Mays and Cochran 1990).

4. As Thorne (1987) notes, the two realms of home or family and market interpenetrate, and expressive and instrumental relations are not mutually exclusive.

5. For instance, when money is in short supply and rent goes unpaid, eviction and the dispersal of household members can follow. Substance use, itself tied to the tensions generated by political economic conditions, also can lead to a household's disintegration, sometimes in tandem with state intervention. Regarding the link between unemployment and alcoholism, see Singer et al. 1992.

6. Moreover, kin networks often discourage single members from forming conjugal unions, because this would mean the few resources that those individuals would otherwise contribute to the group would be siphoned off to spouses (Stack 1974:113–115,124–125).

7. Some people, including some lesbians and gays, do not accept this. The research does not deal with populations that reject mainstream conjugal ideals.

8. Condom use also signals instrumental rather than expressive motivations for sexual congress: a woman who uses condoms is likened to (or is) a prostitute, for her sexuality appears unrelated to a desire to establish or maintain a long-term relationship. In reality, prostitutes do tend to use condoms with clients; however, they tend to practice unsafe sex with boyfriends because condoms imply a distance and a profit motive that are inappropriate in the context of a personal relationship (Miller et al. 1990:260–261; see also Sibthorpe 1992).

9. Comparing reported condom-use rates is a treacherous undertaking, for different studies use different methods to elicit this information and women's feelings about the studies, and so their honesty will vary. But it seems that an average of about 20 to 25 % of poor urban minority women claim always to use condoms. The lower end of the range is seen in Catania et al. (1993), who report that 14% use condoms always, 26% use them sometimes, and 60% never use them; the higher end is a "trichotomy" in which approximately one-third of the sample used condoms consistently, one-third sometimes, and one-third never.

10. Among the pilot questionnaire respondents, twelve (40%) used condoms during their last sexual encounters; seventeen (56.7%) did not (information was missing for one woman).

11. Data from the final questionnaire indicated that significantly more non-users (58.5%, N = 34) than users (9.1%, N = 11) lived with partners.

12. Thirty-eight women (42.2%) brought in paychecks; 36 (40%) received only public assistance; one (1.1%) reported both having a job and receiving public assistance. (Had we asked directly about food stamps and other non-liquid state or federal assistance, rather than asking about aid in general, the frequency of aid reported would probably have been higher.) The final questionnaire was revised with the need for specific financial data in mind. The 44 sexually active women who provided such information brought, on average, $300.00 to $400.00 into their households each month from wages, financial assistance checks, and money earned through entrepreneurial activity (e.g. babysitting, sewing, doing nails or hair for neighbors). Both users and non-users received an average of about $145.00 each month in financial aid. Despite the guarantee of anonymity,

many women may have kept some of their wage and other income secret for fear of being reported to financial assistance or other state authorities. This would lead to a conservative average monthly income figure.

13. Both "The Wisdom Narrative" and "The Monogamy Narrative" hold strong sway over the ways in which sexuality and condom use are (and are not) actualized. However, there are exceptions to the rules. Some women do practice safer sex despite the cultural pressures against it. While safer sex implies that one needs to protect oneself from one's partner and so suggests that one's partner is not of high quality, an alternative interpretation exists. In certain circumstances, and if one represents one's choice to use condoms very carefully both to oneself and to others, practicing safer sex can be considered very wise indeed. For instance, if a woman in a long-term relationship decides to have extraconjugal sex, condom use is considered judicious. Sarah proclaimed, "If you cheat, wear a condom."

14. Blacks were underrepresented (by about half) in Blumstein and Schwartz (1983, as cited in Turner et al. 1989:110–11), education levels were higher than is average for our participants, and because of sampling methods, that study is not generalizable. But it is the only study to my knowledge that explores extraconjugal affairs among unmarried, cohabiting couples as well as married ones.

15. Participants say that women often cheat, too, but are more likely than men to deny it. According to Blumstein and Schwartz, 21% of married and 30% of cohabiting women have extraconjugal sex. However, because Blumstein and Schwartz's sample was only 5% African-American, and because African-American women appear to have more conservative sexual repertoires and fewer partners than white women (e.g., Worth 1990; Wyatt 1988, as cited in Turner et al. 1989:112), a downward adjustment is needed. At any rate, participants say that women who cheat are even more worried and in deeper denial about their partners' infidelities, because they project their own desires and behaviors onto their men.

16. The link between women's self-empowerment and insistence on condom use seen here fits with Ward's finding that family planning programs work only when contraceptive practice is perceived as empowering (1991).

17. A seventh interviewee had used a condom during her last sexual encounter, but as this was with an outside partner she is excluded from the analyses in this section.

REFERENCES

Anderson, E. *Streetwise: Race, Class, and Change in an Urban Neighborhood.* Chicago: University of Chicago Press,1990.

Bott, E. *Family and Social Network: Roles, Norms, and External Relationships in Ordinary Urban Families.* New York: Free Press, 1971.

Bower, B. "Risky Sex and AIDS." *Science News* 140(9):141, 1991.

Browner, C. H. " Male Pregnancy Symptoms in Urban Colombia." *American Ethnologist* 10(3):494–511, 1983.

Campbell, C. "Women and AIDS." *Social Science and Medicine* 30(4):407–415, 1990.

Carovano, K. "More Than Mothers and Whores: Redefining the AIDS Prevention Needs of Women." *International Journal of Health Services* 21(1):131–142, 1991.

Catania, J.; T. Coates; J. Peterson; M. Dolcini; S. Kegeles; D. Siegel; E. Golden; and M. Fullilove. "Changes in Condom Use Among Black, Hispanic, and White Heterosexuals in San Francisco: The AMEN Dohort Survey." *Journal of Sex Research* 30:121–128, 1993.

Cochran, S. "Women and HIV Infection: Issues in Prevention and Behavioral Change." In V. Mays, G. Albee, and S. Schneider (eds.), *Primary Prevention of AIDS: Psychological Approaches.* Newbury Park, Calif.: Sage Publications, 1989, pp. 309–327.

Collier, J.; M. Rosaldo; and S. Yanagisako. "Is There a Family? New Anthropological Views." In B. Thorne and M. Yalom (eds.), *Rethinking the Family.* Boston: Northeastern University Press, 1987, pp. 25–39.

Dalton, H. "AIDS in Blackface." *Daedalus* 118(3):205–227, 1989.

Fullilove, M. T.; R. E. Fullilove III; K. Haynes; and S. Gross. "Black Women and AIDS Prevention: A View Towards Understanding the Gender Rules." *Journal of Sex Research* 27(1):47–64, 1990.

Jones, R. "The Political and Economic Dynamics of STDs." Paper presented at the 90th Annual Meeting of the American Anthropological Association, 1991.

Kinsey, K. "'But I Know My Man': HIV/AIDS Risk Appraisals and Heuristical Reasoning Patterns Among Childbearing Women." *Holistic Nurse Practitioner* 8(2):79–88, 1994.

Kline, A.; E. Kline; and E. Oken. "Minority Women and Sexual Choice in the Age of AIDS." *Social Science and Medicine* 34(4):447–457, 1992.

Liebow, E. *Tally's Corner: A Study of Negro Streetcorner Men.* Boston: Little Brown, 1967.

Mays, V., and S. Cochran. "Issues in the Perception of AIDS Risk and Risk Reduction Activities by Black and Hispanic/Latina Women." *American Psychologist* 43(11):949–957, 1988.

————. "Methodological Issues in the Assessment and Prediliction of AIDS Risk-related Sexual Behaviors Among Black Americans." In B. Voeller, J. Reinisch, and M. Gottlieb (eds.), *AIDS and Sex.* New York: Oxford University Press, 1990, pp. 97–120.

Miller, H.; C. Turner; and L. Moses. *AIDS: The Second Decade.* Washington, D.C.: National Academy Press, 1990.

Muir, M. *The Environmental Context of AIDS.* New York: Praeger Publishers, 1991.

Oliver, W. "Sexual Conquest and Patterns of Black-on-Black Violence: A Structural-Cultural Perspective." *Violence and Victims* 4(4):257–273, 1989.

Patton, C. *Inventing AIDS.* New York: Routledge, 1990.

Pittman, K.; P. Wilson; S. Adams-Taylor; and S. Randolph. "Making Sexuality Education and Prevention Programs Relevant for African-American Youth." *Journal of School Health* 62(7):339–344, 1992.

Pivnick, A. "HIV Infection and the Meaning of Condoms." *Culture, Medicine, and Psychiatry* 17(4):431–453, 1993.

Prohaska, T.; G. Albrecht; and J. Levy. "Determinants of Self-perceived Risk for AIDS." *Journal of Health and Social Behavior* 31:384–394, 1990.

Rubin, L. *Worlds of Pain: Life in the Working-class Family.* New York: Basic Books, 1976.

Sacks, K. "Engels Revisited: Women, the Organization of Production, and Private Property." In M. Rosaldo and L. Lamphere (eds.), *Woman, Culture, and Society.* Stanford, Calif.: Stanford University Press, 1974, pp. 207–222.

Seidman, S.; W. Mosher; and S. Aral. "Women with Multiple Sexual Partners: United States, 1988." *American Journal of Public Health* 82(10):1388–1394, 1992.

Sibthorpe, B. "The Social Construction of Sexual Relationships as a Determinant of HIV Risk Perception and Condom Use among Injection Drug Users." *Medical Anthropology Quarterly* 6(3):255–270, 1992.

Sobo, E. J. "Inner-city Women and AIDS: The Psycho-Social Benefits of Unsafe Sex." *Culture, Medicine, and Psychiatry* 17(4):455–485, 1993.

———. *Choosing Unsafe Sex: AIDS-Risk Denial Among Disadvantaged Women.* Philadelphia: University of Pennsylvania Press, 1995a.

———. "Finance, Romance, Social Support, and Condom Use Among Impoverished Inner-city Women." *Human Organization* 54:115–128, 1995b.

———. "Love, Jealousy, and Unsafe Sex Among Impoverished Inner-city Women: Social and Psychocultural Mediators of Political Economy's Impact on AIDS Risk Perception." In M. Singer (ed.), *The Political Economy of AIDS.* Amityville, N.Y.: Baywood, 1997.

Stack, C. *All Our Kin: Strategies for Survival in a Black Community.* New York: Harper, 1974.

Thorne, B. "Feminist Rethinking of the Family: An Overview." In B. Thorne and M. Yalom (eds.), *Rethinking the Family.* Boston: Northeastern University Press, 1987, pp. 1–24.

Turner, C.; H. Miller; and L. Moses. *AIDS: Sexual Behavior and Intravenous Drug Use.* Washington D.C.: National Academy Press, 1989.

Ward, Martha. "Cupid's Touch: The Lessons of the Family Planning Movement for the AIDS Epidemic." *Journal of Sex Research* 28(2):289–346, 1991.

———. "A Different Disease: AIDS and Health Care for Women in Poverty." *Culture, Medicine, and Psychiatry* 17(4):413–430, 1993.

———. "The Politics of Adolescent Pregnancy: Turf and Teens in Louisiana." In W. P. Handwerker (ed.), *Births and Power: Social Change and the Politics of Reproduction.* San Francisco: Westview Press, 1990, pp. 147–164.

Weinberg, M., and C. Williams. "Black Sexuality: A Test of Two Theories." Journal of Sex Research 25(2):197–218, 1988.

Weinstein, N. "Unrealistic Optimism About Susceptibility to Health Problems: Conclusions from a Community-wide Sample." *Journal of Behavioral Medicine* 10(5):481–500, 1987.

———. "Perceptions of Personal Susceptibility to Harm." In V. Mays, G. Albee, and S. Schneider (eds.), *Primary Prevention of AIDS: Psychological Approaches.* Newbury Park, Calif.: Sage Publications, 1989, pp. 142–167.

Wilson, P. "Black Culture and Sexuality." *Journal of Social Work and Human Sexuality* 4(3):29–46, 1986.

Wilson, W. *The Truly Disadvantaged.* Chicago: University of Chicago Press, 1987.

Wingood, G., and R. DiClemente. "Cultural, Gender, and Psychosocial Influences on HIV-related Behavior of African-American Female Adolescents:

Implications for the Development of Tailored Prevention Programs." *Ethnicity and Disease* 2(4):381–388, 1992.

Worth, D. "Sexual Decision-making and AIDS: Why Condom Promotion Among Vulnerable Women Is Likely to Fail." *Studies in Family Planning* 20(6):297–307, 1989.

————. "Minority Women and AIDS: Culture, Race, and Gender." In D. Feldman (ed.), *Cultural Aspects of AIDS*. New York: Praeger Publishers, 1990, pp. 111–136.

Wyatt, G., and K. Dunn. "Examining Predictors of Sex Guilt in Multiethnic Samples of Women." *Archives of Sexual Behavior* 20:471–485, 1991.

Wyatt, G.; S. Peters; and D. Guthrie. "Kinsey Revisited, Part II: Comparisons of the Sexual Socialization and Sexual Behavior of Black Women over 33 Years." *Archives of Sexual Behavior* 17(4):289–332, 1988.

10

Contemporary Youths' Negotiations of Romance, Love, Sex, and Sexual Disease

Susan M. Moore and Doreen A. Rosenthal

What do the words "romantic love" mean to you?

That means to me, I think, losing a grip on reality, changing your perception of something, and all the world is wonderful, and you are blind to the other person's faults. It is like you acknowledge them (the faults) but they don't exist.

I would say that is someone who really really cares for somebody, you actually love somebody and you sleep with them because you are really close. It is different to a sexual partner.

I don't think there is much of that around. It is sort of like the thing your parents have. I guess it is possible in this day and age, but it has changed so much. I think romantic love is left to the older people these days.

Roses, chocolates, just sort of trying to be nice and considerate. Going out of your way to please the other person.

Romance is all right I suppose, but fuck the love.

The above quotes express some of the views about romance offered by 16-year-olds (Buzwell, Rosenthal, and Moore 1992; Moore and Rosenthal 1993a). These themes, varying from cynicism to idealization, illustrate the complex range of ideas that young people have about this confusing topic. This chapter presents an analysis of the views of young people on romance and its relationships with love, sex, and disease protection, in particular HIV/AIDS protection. The conflicts and ambiguities in youths' conceptions of these issues will be investigated, as will gender differences and their potential for leading to mis-communication. The role of romance in negotiating safe or unsafe sex will be discussed.

It is recognized that people possess many different conceptions of love and hold different models of what is appropriate to expect from their love relationships. Many classifications of love have been suggested by theorists, all including the idea of romance or romantic love, though not necessarily using the terminology. Hendrick and Hendrick (1986), for example, describe six varieties of love, including passionate love, game-playing love, friendship love, logical love, possessive love, and selfless love. Romance plays a different role in each variety, ranging from a central place in passionate love to a much less important part in friendship love. Attitudes toward love have been described as varying on the dimension of need for romance, with cross-cultural differences on this dimension being quite marked (e.g., Sprecher et al. 1992). Some theorists use the terms "love" and "romantic love" interchangeably (e.g., Hatfield and Rapson 1995). In this chapter we will consider romance as a potential, but not necessary, feature of love relationships and explore whether young people perceive love, romance, and sexual relationships as separate or essentially overlapping categories.

ROMANCE, LOVE, AND INTIMACY AMONG ADOLESCENTS AND YOUTH

Erikson (1959, 1968) wrote that the development of the capacity for intimacy, as well as its culmination in the formation of a life partnership, was a vital psychological task for young adults. He was referring to emotional as well as physical intimacy—the ability to share feelings with another, to self-disclose and to listen, to set mutual goals and to compromise individual desires in order to work toward "couple" goals—as well as to share one's body in harmonious and mutually satisfying sexuality. Intimacy and falling in love are closely associated. Intimate relationships, or expectations about their development, are often initiated in the charged emotional climate of falling in love.

Youth and falling in love seem to go hand in hand, but the outcome is not always intimacy. One common developmental path begins with the hero worship and crushes of the early teenage years. Price-Adams and Greene (1990) argue that crushes on celebrity figures can form an important part of the process of self-concept development. The adolescent projects an ego ideal onto the object of the crush. Crushes can be explored through fantasy in ways that do not involve high risk to self-esteem (see also Person 1991). Eventually, fantasy objects (in the sense that they are unattainable) are replaced by a "real" love object, in which partners share a romantic vision of their relationship.

Erikson argues that adolescent falling in love is part of the quest for identity or self-definition, whereby the young person sees an idealized version of him- or herself reflected through the eyes of another. The process is conceptualized as something akin to looking in a very flattering mirror: "To a considerable extent, adolescent love is an attempt to arrive at a definition of one's identity by projecting one's diffused self-image on another and by seeing it thus reflected and gradually clarified. That is why so much young love is conversation" (Erikson 1968:132).

Falling in love is part of the process of growing up and discovering oneself and one's sexuality. It may happen several times before a relationship develops into one characterized by the mutuality and sharing of intimacy—a "mature"relationship in Erikson's terms. (Of course, there is no guarantee that such relationships will ever develop, depending as they do on the psychosocial maturity of both partners, the social climate, and ultimately, good luck.) The role of romance may be seen as facilitating falling in love, as contributing to the courting process and thus the establishment of a relationship.

No doubt, ideas of love and romance are popular with young people, and the more open and explicit sexual expression of today's youth is, for many, set in a context of beliefs about true love and commitment. Loving, caring, and affection were the primary motivations for having sex among the majority of the middle-class samples of adolescents we have interviewed (Moore and Rosenthal 1993b). Most approved of and idealized romance as part of love and incorporated sexual feelings within this whole concept. The cynical ones were cynical about love in general, conceptualizing love and romance as different from sex rather than different from each other.

A common relationship pattern for young people is "serial monogamy" (Sorensen 1973), characterized by a succession of relatively committed relationships in which the partners fall in love at the beginning of the relationship and out of love again at the end. These relationships may last as long as a few years to as short a time as a couple of weeks or months. Thus, many adolescents and young adults experience multiple partnering (although they are unlikely to define this as promiscuity), the result being heightened risk of sexually transmitted disease (STD). In the following sections we discuss rates of STDs and their possible links with young people's conceptions of love and romance.

SEX AND DISEASE

The seriousness of the HIV/AIDS epidemic makes it important to understand the ways that sexual encounters are understood differentially in terms of love and romance, and the implications of these understandings for safe sex practice. By safe sex, we mean consistent condom use for penetrative sex, unless the individual is in a relationship that is genuinely long term, monogamous, and with a partner who is unambiguously known to be uninfected.

HIV/AIDS and other STD infection rates among adolescents and youth are of relevance here. Teenagers currently represent only a small proportion of the total number of AIDS cases reported in the United States, Europe, and Australia (Bury 1991; DiClemente 1992; National Centre in HIV Epidemiology and Clinical Research 1994). Nevertheless, worldwide, most deaths from AIDS occur in the 20 to 40 age group. AIDS is the sixth leading cause of death for persons aged between 15 and 24 years in the United States, and the number of teenagers infected with HIV increased by 70% in the two years between 1990 and 1992 (Haffner 1992). In addition, youth is itself a clear "risk factor" for transmission of STDs, most of which can be prevented through consistent condom use. Stevenson et al. (1992) report data showing that the highest rates of gonorrhoea and chlamydia in the United States occur among 15- to 19-year-olds. STDs are among the major causes of mortality and morbidity for adolescents, with approximately 86% of all STDs occurring among young people between the ages of 15 and 29 years (Ellickson et al. 1993). Infection rates for chlamydia were as high as 37% of adolescents among some populations reported in Ellickson's review. In addition, national U.S. data showed that in 1989 teenagers between the ages of 10 and 19 accounted for 30% of new gonorrhea cases. Ellickson's report concludes that, overall, approximately one in five adolescents will have acquired a sexually transmitted disease by the time he or she is 21 years of age. Thus, sexually transmitted diseases are a major concern for young people and one that could be eradicated through consistent condom use.

Although there has been considerable increase in young people's acceptance of condoms during the past decade, studies of condom use show that many young people use them inconsistently or not at all. Hingson and Strunin (1992) surveyed adolescent HIV/AIDS knowledge, attitudes, beliefs, and behaviors in Massachusetts in 1986, 1988, and 1990. They used statewide random digit-dial telephone surveys, yielding 16- to 19-year-old samples of 826, 1,762, and 1,152, respectively. While the number of young people who adopted condom use specifically because of the AIDS epidemic rose markedly over the five years of the study, by 1990 still only 37% of sexually active young people were using condoms consistently. Furthermore, the proportion of the age group who were sexually active had increased by 10% from 55% in 1986 to 65% in 1990. Consequently, the percentage of the later cohorts having unprotected intercourse was not much lower than the percentage in 1986, despite increases in knowledge, educational campaigns, and wide publicity. Paralleling this, across seven British studies published between 1987 and 1992, reviewed by Breakwell and Fife-Schaw (1992), the number of non-virgins using a condom in their most recent sexual encounter varied between 15 and 66%, a variation due largely to the different age subgroups studied within the 16- to 25-year range. Most of the more obvious barriers to condom use, such as lack of knowledge, negative attitudes, and problems with access, have eroded, yet clearly other barriers, of a more subtle nature remain, affecting the use of prophylactics among young people. We now discuss those barriers related to adolescents' conceptions of love and romance.

ROMANCE, TRUST, AND SAFE SEX

One conflict that surfaces in the AIDS and love literatures is that between the romantic notions of "sexual magic" and true love, and the practicalities of safe sex. Disquiet about destroying romance features strongly among young people as a rationale for not using condoms for HIV protection.

Galligan and Terry (1993) indicated from their self-report questionnaire study of 18- to 29-year-old university students that non-use of condoms is determined to a large extent by emotional concerns. Typically, these concerns are not taken into account when formulating intentions about condom use. Thus "good intentions" may not be carried out because of emotional issues of the moment. Worry about jeopardizing romance was one of these issues. Those who did not use condoms with new or casual partners were far more likely to believe that their use "would make sex seem like a business contract rather than a spontaneous affectionate act," and "would partly destroy the sense of trust and intimacy in the relationship," and "would destroy the magic of freely relating to another." Clearly, a romantic view of these casual encounters was being entertained. Conflict was inherent in perceiving sex as disconnected from love or from love's potential development through a romantic encounter.

Concerns about romance were much more likely to relate to non-use of condoms in the case of young women. This needs to be seen in the light of findings suggesting that young women's interpretation of what constitutes a casual relationship may be different from that of young men. A study by Rosenthal, Moore, and Brumen (1990) of approximately 750 non-virgin Anglo-Australian university students aged 17 to 20 years illustrates this point. This research indicated that young men were more likely than young women to be taking sexual risks with partners they described as "casual", but the reverse was true for partners defined as "regular" or "steady." For example, while percentages of females admitting unprotected vaginal inter-course or withdrawal with a casual partner were quite low (23 and 19% respectively, compared with males, 42 and 34%), they were higher than the corresponding male rates when the activity was per-ceived to have occurred with a steady partner (females: 66 and 53%; males: 62 and 44%). Despite these differences, it was noteworthy that both sexes were quite similar in their patterns of partnering over the previous six months, most having had zero, one, or two sex-ual partners. It is possible that young women are "romancing" some encounters through defining them as regular and steady, while their male partners view them as casual, with lower levels of commitment attached. For both sexes, the perception of a relationship as steady appears to impart permission for unsafe practices to occur, the ten-dency being stronger for young women.

Interestingly, in Galligan and Terry's study, young men who actu-ally used condoms in regular partnerships thought they "were more likely to ruin the special atmosphere of a sexual encounter and make it seem matter-of-fact," and that condoms "would partly destroy my feeling that my partner was of special significance to me." Galligan and Terry surmised that these young males who identified a loss of romance with condom use with regular partners would apply strong pressure for their partners to change to a less intrusive contraceptive method.

Another aspect of this perceived relationship between ro-mance/love and *not* using condoms comes from the idea that it is less necessary to use protection when your partner is someone you know well, love, and trust. This is not so much the idea that condom use destroys romance, but that caring for someone means you have noth-ing to fear from them—a generally adaptive notion that does not hold up quite so well when it comes to the spread of sexually transmitted disease. Such an idea works for monogamous long-term relation-ships with uninfected partners, but it is a flawed strategy for disease protection when multiple unprotected partnering occurs, as is more likely to be the case for adolescents. For this age group, partnerships rarely last "until death do us part." In addition, although within these serial relationships faithfulness is often an idealized norm, it is not consistently upheld. Young people, beginning their sexual lives earlier than their parents, and marrying later, are therefore likely to have more partners in a lifetime than was the norm in previous generations (Johnson et al. 1994; Moore, Rosenthal, and Mitchell 1996).

It would not be surprising if young women were more inclined toward this "trusting to love" justification for not using condoms, given the social forces that shape women's perceptions of their sexuality and its links with love and romance. While some researchers argue that the "double standard" of sexual behavior no longer has a strong influence on adolescents (McCabe and Collins 1990; Reiss 1971; Steinberg 1985), other research indicates that young women are still far more concerned about their reputation than young men and fear the disapproval associated with casual sex (Lees 1993). As a result, young women are likely to re-interpret their casual encounters as something more meaningful and long-term, and so judge them to be low risk. For example, many young Australian women believe they can control their vulnerability to HIV/AIDS (and presumably other STDs) by limiting their sexual activity to regular partners (Abbott 1988).

The "trusting to love" justification has been noted among adult women as well as teenagers. Sobo's (1993) qualitative research on poor black U.S. women describes a similar justification underlying non-condom use. She calls it "The Monogamy Narrative." This narrative represents a recognition that many men cheat on their partners, but the idealized heterosexual union is one of faithfulness and trust. Believing that one's partner could be unfaithful damages feelings of pride and social position. It also damages the emotional comfort and security the relationship brings because it breaks the idealized fantasy of "true love." To not use condoms is one way of keeping this romantic fantasy alive.

Use of love and trust as justification for not using condoms is less likely to occur for gay men than for heterosexuals, according to Altman (1992). He argues that there is a far higher acceptance of multiple partnering among gay men and that "fidelity" in the sense of love and trust within homosexual relationships does not carry the same expectation that these relationships will be sexually exclusive. This makes it easier to develop safe sex practices, for couples can admit to themselves that there may be risk of infection from other partners without jeopardizing their central relationship. Discussions about how disease may be avoided are possible within this context, while for heterosexual couples they may be perceived to imply low levels of commitment. For heterosexuals, "negotiated safety" tends to revolve around pregnancy protection. Once this is ensured, the couple may believe there is no socially acceptable avenue left for them to discuss disease protection without calling the nature of the relationship into question.

COMMITTED AND RECREATIONAL SEX: DIFFERENT IMPLICATIONS FOR SAFETY

The research discussed above shows us that a schism has developed between perceptions of sex as part of love and sex as related to hedonistic pleasure and need reduction, that is, romantic versus pragmatic views of sex. This schism can act as a barrier to safe sex practice. It arises in part because of the conflicting social presentations of sex, which is idealized when linked with love and commitment. Sex is also idealized in a different way, especially for males, when viewed as healthy recreation. Here the emphasis is on "scoring" as many partners as possible. Safe sex campaigns often only target the "sex as recreation" theme and so enable those who view their sexual relationships in terms of commitment and fidelity (that is, a majority of teenagers) to ignore the safety messages. For example, a safe sex television campaign in Australia posed the question, "Who are you sleeping with tonight?," focusing on one young couple in bed. The camera then panned out to show hundreds of such couples. The point to be made was that although each member of the couple in the original shot was currently having sex with only one other person, they had each had several other partners, who had in turn had several partners, multiplying greatly the possibilities of spreading sexual disease. This is a message many young couples, in the throes of love and romance, would prefer to ignore. Similarly, catchy slogans aimed at encouraging young women to take the initiative in safe sex ("Tell him if it's not on, it's not on"), may miss their mark because they appear to treat sex too casually.

The reality of youthful sexual relationships (and those of adults as well) seldom fits with their ideal. Relationships break up and new ones begin, often within relatively short periods of time, and faithfulness is not always maintained even when it may be promised. Our studies suggest that almost all adolescents expect their sexual partners to be faithful. However, while most girls had similar expectations for their own behavior, the boys were less willing to commit themselves to one partner at a time. In one study of Anglo-, Greek-, Italian-, and Chinese-Australian youth, on average, only 75% of young men said they would try to be monogamous in a steady relationship. There were clear cultural differences however. For example, only 50% of the Greek-Australian males expected they would be faithful to their partners (Rosenthal et al. 1990). Another element of relationships in which practice falls short of ideals is the maintenance of honesty about other partners. According to Mays and Cochran (1993), "dishonesty is an intimate feature of dating life." Their study indicated that 47% of male and 42% of female college students would not admit to a new partner the number of partners they had in the past. Furthermore, over one-third of both sexes would not admit to their partner if they had been unfaithful, bringing further into question the wisdom of "trusting to love" strategies for STD protection.

Indeed, to an outsider teenage sex may look more like casual than committed sex, but young people themselves eschew this view. They express disapproval of one-night stands and casual sexual encounters (or admit to them as "mistakes" rather than examples of planned action). The following examples are from 15- to 18-year-old girls and boys from an interview study conducted by the authors (Moore and Rosenthal 1993a).

What do you think of one-night stands?

They're not on. Myself, I have had one-night stands and they don't make you feel too good. I believe in sex if you love someone and that's the main thing. (boy)

I think they are pretty bad, I wouldn't have one. It is a pretty slutty thing to do and it is dangerous. (girl)

Depends on whether you are drunk or not. If I was drunk I might sometimes. (girl)

In this study, while most respondents (77%) approved of sex before marriage, far fewer were comfortable with the idea of one-night stands (27%). The minority view is expressed in this quote from a 16-year-old boy:

I think they are healthy as long as there is an understanding between the two people, and that is all it is.

On the whole, adolescents and youth disapproved of casual encounters. If girls engage in these behaviors, they secure an extra dimension of disapproval among a substantial proportion of teenagers. Asked about their views of girls and boys who "sleep around," 41% maintained that such behavior is acceptable or only mildly disapproved of for boys, but anathema for girls (Moore and Rosenthal 1993a). The views of this 15-year-old boy illustrate this framework of double standards:

What do you think about girls who sleep around?

Probably think that they are sluts. . . . If I was in a girl's position I would never do that, I don't like them.

What about boys?

Here it changes because he is classified as a stud, pretty lucky. I would think he knows how to pick up, how to control everything, you would probably say that he is cool. . . . Boys are the stronger species—it is like if I had a daughter I wouldn't let her do such things. I would give a boy more freedom.

Even among the 59% majority who wished to express the importance of equal sexual rules for males and females, there was recognition that this did not always occur in the real world, as in the following quote from a female, asked what she thought of boys who sleep around:

I don't think much of them. I wouldn't be part of it. I don't see that it is any different from a girl, they are both the same as each other. But it really annoys me if a girl sleeps around she gets the reputation of a slut, but if a guy does it, it's like, "oh good one mate, stud," that type of thing.

Probably as a result of differing standards of behavior for the sexes, young women are especially prone to conceptualize their casual encounters as if they are romantic and hold the potential for long-term commitment, as discussed previously. Unfortunately, interpreting a relationship as committed can encourage the justification that condom use is not necessary, as the "trust" in the relationship is perceived as providing de facto safe status. Another example of the potential distortions arising from a romantic view of events comes from a study by Muram et al. (1992). These researchers showed that teenage girls who had been pregnant were more likely than never-pregnant teenagers to judge soap operas and romance novels as epitomizing real life. The ability of young women to fool themselves about a relationship's likely status is encouraged by the social pressure on women to have sex only within such a context. In the next section we will further discuss this "double standard" in beliefs about how sex and love/romance should be linked.

MALE AND FEMALE CONSTRUCTIONS OF LOVE/ROMANCE/SEX RELATIONSHIPS

How different are male and female interpretations of the meaning of sex in terms of its relationship with love and romance? Leigh (1989) studied the reasons for having sex among an adult sample of about 1,000 men and women, using a mail-back survey sent to a systematic random sample of 4,000 households. Men attached significantly more importance to pleasure, pleasing a partner, conquest, and relief of tension than did women, who were significantly more likely to rate emotional closeness as an important reason for having sex.

Consider the very pragmatic views of sex presented by three 20- to 24-year-old single males recruited from discos and singles bars for an interview study about love and sex (Rosenthal, Moore, and Fernbach 1997):

What does the word "sex" mean to you?

Sex is like a need I suppose, it's sort of like water, and, er, oxygen, no air and water I suppose. I mean it's sort of, er, physiological need, you know, if you like. Um, sort of you need water to survive, you need food, but you don't really need sex to survive do you? You're not going to die if you don't get it, but if you did well it's one of those things in life where, well, everyone I suppose wants to have sex sometime in their life. I mean it's natural to, it's not everything, I'd say it's not everything, it's just a part, it's not everything.

What do you think of sex?

All right, it's kind of, er [pause], well like you don't sort of, er, your body wants sex, and it's sort of like wanting a glass of water, you try and get it, if you can't well what I think of it, yeah it's all right. It's kind of just like a relief, like going to the toilet [laughter].

Why do you have sex?

Because my spermatozoa accumulate in my testicles and it swells up, and I have to ejaculate my load because it gets me horny after about two or three weeks.

In comparison, four females from the same age group and recruited in the same manner had more emotional, relationship-oriented views:

What does the word "sex" mean to you?

Some type of bonding, I suppose or coming together as one.

Why do you have sex?

Um, because I want to show affection to the person that I actually am in love with them.

Um, I guess to express those emotions of caring for someone, and that.

What do you expect of sex?

Er [pause] a nice cozy feeling. Yeah. I mean if I don't reach orgasm or anything then that's fine, you know, I mean that's great if I do, if I don't well, I
still cuddle up afterwards.

These thematic trends of males stressing the physical and females
the emotional side of sex were reflected across the whole sample of
ninety-one respondents in this study (forty-eight males, forty-three
females). In answer to the question "Why do you have sex?," a large
proportion gave responses combining physical and emotional reasons
(44% of males and 40% of females). Of the remainder, however, the
gender split was marked. Fifty percent of the men as opposed to 23%
of the women said they had sex because of reasons having to do with
physical satisfaction and release, and 6% of the men compared with
37% of the women mentioned love and intimacy-related reasons as
their major motives for sex.

Nielsen (1991), arguing on the basis of studies such as those by
Bell (1988), and Juhasz and Schneider (1987), believes that young
men and women see sex differently and that little change has taken
place in this phenomenon over the last generation. She states that
"boys are more likely to see intercourse as a way of establishing their
maturity and of achieving social status, whereas most girls see intercourse as a way of expressing their love and of achieving greater intimacy. As a consequence, boys are more apt to have sex with someone
who is a relative stranger, to have more sexual partners, and to dis-
associate sex from love. Even in their sexual fantasies boys are more
likely to imagine sexual adventures detached from love and emotional intimacy" (Nielsen 1991:370).

Hollway (1984), in her analysis of the social constructions of sexuality, suggests that three separate systems of understanding or discourses represent male-female interactions in Western society. Sex
and relationships, says Hollway, are interpreted in terms of the Male
Sex Drive discourse, the Have/Hold discourse, or the Permissive discourse. The first of these arises out of the idea that men have strong
biological sex drives that are a pervasive force in their relationships
with women. Men can be "excused" for sexual adventuring, unfaithfulness, and multiple partnering because of this biological imperative, but women have no such excuse. Certainly, many of the young
men in the studies we have reviewed were expressing elements of
this discourse in their views about sexual release, motivation for sex,
and fidelity. The role of romance within such a discourse may be as a
tool to achieve male conquest, or as an idealization of male "suffering" through lack of release. Condoms may be eschewed within such

a framework because they are viewed as detracting from male pleasure.

The central propositions of the Have/Hold discourse are those encapsulated by the ideals of marriage, such as sexual commitment, emotional bonding, monogamy, and long-term relationships. These ideals are expressed by young people of both sexes, but young women appear to be more heavily influenced by them. Romance within this discourse may serve to heighten emotionality and so strengthen bonding and, ultimately, trust. The role of romance as counterproductive to condom use within this framework has been a major theme of this chapter.

Finally, the Permissive discourse reflects the idea that there should be sexual freedom for both sexes "so long as no-one gets hurt," and that the expression of sex drive is "legitimate" for both men and women. Such a view is perhaps less romantic than that presented by the other discourses, but it may be one that is more amenable to the pragmatics of sexual health precautions. It is a view that has been expressed by the young people we have interviewed in several studies, in the sense that they approve of sex before marriage (within committed serial relationships) and (by a small majority only) disapprove of the sexual double standard. Yet there is no doubt that elements of the other discourses also characterize the sexual attitudes and behaviors of these young people. These discourses can be mutually conflicting in their implications of behavior, and the conflicts are reflected in inconsistencies between young people's reasonable knowledge about STDs, relatively positive attitudes to precautions, but inconsistent condom use.

In summary, young people's views about love and romance can act as "excuses" for not taking sexual health precautions. In addition, considerable differences still exist between young men and women in their conceptions of sex and love. Young women value romantic love more (Cimbalo and Novell 1993) and incorporate it into their interpretations of the meaning of sex. They develop "feeling norms" about romance at an early age—for example, beliefs about the importance of monogamy—which will not always be shared by the boys they have sex with (Simon, Eder, and Evans 1992). The romanticizing of sex by young people, especially young women, has an idealistic and touching quality and may serve a purpose in the development of both self-perception and intimacy. However, in an era of high rates of sexually transmitted disease, including the deadly AIDS, romantic views of the world can well interfere with rational decision making in the safe sex arena. Romantic love can indeed be blind.

REFERENCES

Abbott, S. "AIDS and Young Women." *The Bulletin of the National Clearing-house for Youth Studies* 7:38–41, 1988.

Altman, D. "AIDS and Discourses of Sexuality." In R. W. Connell and G. W. Dowsett (eds.), *Rethinking Sex: Social Theory and Sexuality Research.* Melbourne: Melbourne University Press, 1992.

Bell, R. *Changing Bodies, Changing Lives: A Book for Teens on Sex and Relationships.* New York: Random House, 1988.

Breakwell, G. M., and C. Fife-Schaw. "Sexual Activities and Preferences in a United Kingdom Sample of 16-20 Year Olds." *Archives of Sexual Behaviour* 21:271–293, 1992.

Bury, J. K. "Teenage Sexual Behaviour and the Impact of AIDS." *Health Education Journal* 50:43–9, 1991.

Buzwell, S.; D. A. Rosenthal; and S. M. Moore. "Idealising the Sexual Experience." *Youth Studies Australia-HIV/AIDS Education* 1:3–10, 1992.

Cimbalo, R. S., and D. O. Novell. "Sex Differences in Romantic Love Attitudes Among College Students." *Psychological Reports* 73:15–18, 1993.

DiClemente, R. J. "Epidemiology of AIDS, HIV Prevalence and HIV Incidence Among Adolescents." *Journal of School Health* 62:325–330, 1992.

Ellickson, P. L.; M. E. Lara; C. D. Sherbourne; and B. Zima. *Forgotten Ages, Forgotten Problems.* Santa Monica, Calif.: Rand, 1993.

Erikson, E. "Identity and the Life Cycle." *Psychological Issues* 1:1–71, 1959.

———. *Identity, Youth and Crisis.* New York: Norton, 1968.

Galligan, R., and D. Terry. "Romantic Ideals, Fear of Negative Implications, and the Practice of Safe Sex." *Journal of Applied Social Psychology* 23:1685–1711, 1993.

Haffner, D. "Youth Still at Risk, Yet Barriers to Education Remain: SIECUS Testimony for the National AIDS Commission." *SIECUS Report* November/December, 1992.

Hatfield, E., and R. L. Rapson. *A World of Passion: Cross Cultural Perspectives on Love and Sex.* New York: Allyn and Bacon, 1995.

Hendrick, C., and S. S. Hendrick. "A Theory and Method of Love. *Journal of Personality and Social Psychology* 50:392–402, 1986.

Hingson, R., and L. Strunin. "Monitoring Adolescents' Responses to the AIDS Epidemic: Changes in Knowledge, Attitudes, Beliefs, and Be-haviours." In R. J. DiClemente (ed.), *Adolescents and AIDS: A Generation in Jeopardy.* Newbury Park, Calif.: Sage, 1992.

Hollway, W. "Women's Power in Heterosexual Sex." *Women's Studies International Forum* 7:66–68, 1984.

Johnson, A. M.; J. Wadsworth; K. Wellings; and J. Field. *Sexual Attitudes and Lifestyles.* Oxford: Blackwell Scientific Publications, 1994.

Juhasz, A., and M. Schneider. "Adolescent Sexuality: Values, Morality and Decision Making." *Adolescence* 22:580–590, 1987.

Lees, S. *Sugar and Spice: Sexuality and Adolescent Girls.* London: Penguin Books, 1993.

Leigh, B. C. "Reasons for Having Sex: Gender, Sexual Orientation, and Relationship to Sexual Behavior." *Journal of Sex Research* 26:199–209, 1989.

Mays, V. M., and S. D. Cochran, "Ethnic and Gender Differences in Beliefs About Sex Partner Questioning to Reduce HIV Risk." *Journal of Adolescent Research* 8:77–88, 1993.

McCabe, M., and J. Collins. *Dating, Relating and Sex.* Sydney: Horowitz Grahame, 1990.

Moore, S. M., and D. A. Rosenthal, "The Social Context of Adolescent Sexuality: Safe Sex Implications." *Journal of Adolescence* 5:415–435, 1993a.

———. *Sexuality in Adolescence.* London: Routledge, 1993b.

Moore, S. M.; D. A. Rosenthal; and A. Mitchell. *Youth, AIDS, and Sexually Transmitted Diseases.* London: Routledge, 1996.

Muram, D.; D. Rosenthal; E. A. Tolley; and M. M. Peeler., "Teenage Pregnancy: Dating and Sexual Attitudes." *Journal of Sex Education and Therapy* 18:264–276, 1992.

National Centre in HIV Epidemiology and Clinical Research. *Australian HIV Surveillance Report* 10:1–36,1994.

Nielsen, L. *Adolescence: A Contemporary View.* Fort Worth, Tex.: Holt, Rinehart and Winston, 1991.

Person, E. "Romantic Love: At the Intersection of the Psyche and the Cultural Unconscious." *Journal of the American Psychoanalytic Association* 39 (Suppl):383–411, 1991.

Price-Adams, C., and A. L. Greene. "Secondary Attachments and Adolescent Self-concept." *Sex Roles* 22:187–98, 1990.

Reiss, I. L. "How and Why American Sex Standards Are Changing." In H. D. Thornbury (ed.), *Contemporary Adolescence: Readings.* Belmont, Calif.: Brooks Cole, 1971.

Rosenthal, D. A.; S. M. Moore; and I. Brumen. "Ethnic Group Differences in Adolescents' Responses to AIDS." *Australian Journal of Social Issues* 25:220–239, 1990.

Rosenthal, D. A.; S. M. Moore; and M. Fernbach. "The Singles Scene: Safe Sex Practices and Attitudes Among At-risk Heterosexual Adults." *Psychology and Health,* 12:171–182, 1997.

Simon, R. W.; D. Eder; and C. Evans. "The Development of Feeling Norms Underlying Romantic Love Among Adolescent Females." *Social Psychology Quarterly* 55: 29–46, 1992.

Sobo, E. J. "Inner City Women and AIDS: The Psycho-social Benefits of Unsafe Sex." *Culture, Medicine and Psychiatry* 17:455–485, 1993.

Sorensen, R. E. *Adolescent Sexuality in Contemporary America.* New York: World Publishers, 1973.

Sprecher, S.; A. Aron; E. Hatfield; A. Cortese; E. Potapova; and A. Levitskaya. "Love: American Style, Russian Style, and Japanese Style." Paper presented at Sixth International Conference on Personal Relationships; Orono, Maine, July, 1992.

Steinberg, L. *Adolescence.* New York: Alfred A. Knopf, 1985.

Stevenson, E.; D. Gertig; N. Crofts; J. Sherrard; J. Forsyth; and A. Breschkin. "Three Potential Spectres of Youth: Chlamydia, Gonorrhoea and HIV in Victorian Youth, January 1991 to June 1992." Paper given at the Australian Scientific Congress on Sexually Transmissible Diseases, Sydney, November, 1992.

SECTION V

CROSS-CULTURAL STUDIES OF LOVE AND SEX

11

Love and Limerence with Chinese Characteristics: Student Romance in the PRC

Robert L. Moore

That the mere glimpse of a plain coat
Could stab my heart with grief!
Enough! Take me to your home.

That a mere glimpse of plain leggings
Could tie my heart in tangles!
Enough! Let us two be one.

—From *Shi Qing* (*The Book of Songs*), ca. 600 B.C.

INTRODUCTION

In a scene from the *Heart of the Dragon*, a documentary on marriage, a young peasant woman is asked by an interviewer why she chose to accept a marriage proposal from the man who had been courting her. As the question is asked, she smiles shyly and starts to list her fiance's winning qualities. "He's very clever," she says, and then, after a long pause she adds, "very clever." At this point, her self-consciousness seems to grow as she stares at her hands and gropes for more things to say. Then, her face broadens into a confused, self-conscious smile, until, completely overwhelmed with embarrassment, she buries her face in the crook of her arm. Finally, as though mustering the self-possession to face an overwhelmingly embarrassing fact, she looks up at the camera and adds, "He works hard and he's very warm-hearted."

The difficulty this young peasant woman had in handling what would seem to Westerners to be a fairly innocent question is an index of the continuing reluctance by many Chinese to expose their romantic feelings to public scrutiny. As a person of rural background in the early 1980s, this young woman exemplified the continuing shyness over questions of love that has long been presumed by Chinese to be the basis of good character, particularly for females.

A less sensitive response to lovers' shyness can be seen in the following description by a young woman from Guangzhou of a key ritual at her 1989 wedding feast. Her family and friends had gathered for a wedding banquet in a rented hall. Eventually, the couple's friends began demanding that the bride and groom step into the center of the room and validate their affection with a loving kiss. The demand was accompanied by a cacophony of clapping, whistling, and shouting that made clear this was not to be a genuinely tender moment, but one whose sole purpose was to tease and embarrass the couple. The embarrassment was prolonged by repeated protestations that someone's camera had failed to capture the magic moment, and that bride and groom must therefore press lips together yet again. The teasing of the bride and groom during a Chinese wedding is actually a long-established tradition; what is new in the case described here is doing so by insisting on a public kiss.

These two incidents mark points on a scale that measures the acceptability of physical or romantic attraction as a valid subject for public scrutiny or discussion. At a still more conservative point on the scale would be the traditional Chinese ideal that said all respectable marriages should be arranged by the parents, the bride and groom themselves would not even have the option of seeing each other, much less evaluating each other's attractiveness, until the wedding day.

Clearly, as the two incidents described above illustrate, Chinese who express romantic affection publicly are vulnerable to embarrassment in a way that most Americans are not. And while shyness in expressing romantic feelings is common in China today, shyness in matters of sexual behavior is even more pronounced.

Yet the puritanical injunctions against romance and sexuality that constrained young Chinese during the Cultural Revolution of the 1960s and 1970s have long been dismantled. If there are no legal or political barriers preventing Chinese from "leaping into Love River" with abandon, what kinds of forces are at work that result in an approach to love that Westerners would describe as shy and constrained?

The shyness concerning matters of the heart and the embarrassment over physical expressions of affection are not totally unfamiliar to Europeans and North Americans. Westerners share enough of an understanding with Chinese to see where a person of a certain temperament, or perhaps of no special temperament but with a certain kind of upbringing, might feel embarrassed when attention is drawn to his or her romantic sentiments. In other words, in matters of romantic love and sexuality, China and the West are both similar to and different from each other. There are fundamental similarities bestowed on us by our genetic heritage which define us as human beings, while our differences are shaped largely by cultural and idiosyncratic experiences. Here I will attempt to outline the fundamental similarities and the cultural differences in the experience of romantic and sexual relationships among Chinese university students and their American counterparts. These differences can, I believe, be accounted for mainly in terms of cultural differences in understanding the nature of the individual, the family, and the parent-child relationship. The model most suited to comparing the cultural construction of romance and sexuality is one which sees culture as acquired in "chunks" or, to use a more technical term, schemas, rather than bit by granular bit. These chunks or schemas are internalized by the individual in hierarchical complexes so that some serve as high-level programs that contain, nested within, lower-level schemas. These internalized schemas guide both the behavior of the individual and his or her interpretations of the behavior of others. This study is aimed at providing a rough outline of the hierarchy of schemas that shape the romantic and sexual behavior of university students in the People's Republic of China.

DATA

My data for this study come from interviews undertaken in the United States with recent graduates of several major Chinese universities from such diverse cities as Beijing, Chengdu, Jinan, and Guangzhou, to name a few. In addition, I spent a year (1993–1994) as a foreign expert on the faculty of Qingdao University in Shandong Province in the People's Republic of China. During this year, I interviewed forty different students, many of them two or three times. These interviews ranged over a number of topics, but topics receiving the most attention were romantic love and other aspects of the emotional lives of young urban Chinese. Other interviews and conversations with faculty members and other Chinese citizens also provided information. Furthermore, I asked my students if they would be willing to allow me to use their class essays (anonymously) as a source of data in my study of Chinese culture. All of them were kind enough to give their permission.

On four different university campuses (Qingdao University, Qinghua University, Beijing Aerospace University, and Luoyang Teachers' College) I distributed questionnaires to students (totaling 231) with relating mainly to parent-adolescent, friendship, and romantic relationships. For data relating to contemporary American patterns, I have collected information on the vocabularies and customs of dating and courtship from American college and university students. I also distributed a set of 181 questionnaires on parent-adolescent relationships to American college and university students in central Florida.

CHINA AND THE UNITED STATES: SIMILARITIES AND DIFFERENCES

William Jankowiak describes a world of courtship, romance, and seduction for the Chinese of Huhhot that, he argues, is fundamentally similar to what one might find in any Western city. For example, he cites the following passages from his field notes which record the unhappy love affair of a female college graduate:

4-3-83: I met a man named Chen from my hometown. He was very nice and we talked for sometime. . . .

4-9-83: . . . When I went home my first impression of him is that he is clever, honest, and a tremendous talker. When I asked my parents if I could continue seeing him, they said, "of course."

4-14-83: We don't know each other very well so we have to write more letters in order to improve our feelings. . . .

5-2-83: I received a letter today from my mother. She told me about Chen and said that I'm old enough to marry. . . . I've only known him for less than a month. . . . We will have to talk about a lot of things. If not, we must part immediately.

6-17-83: Chen hasn't written to me. I think he has found someone else. . . .

6-30-83: Chen still hasn't written. . . . I can't bear life. All my interests in life have disappeared. I find I am so poor, so sad. I know I shouldn't have such thoughts and I should study harder. But I think the future is dark. (1995:177–179)

After quoting these words, Jankowiak writes: "What may be most significant about this diary is its lack of cultural specificity. If one was not told otherwise, one could easily imagine its author as American or European" (1995a:179).

Actually, a close reading of the young woman's story does reveal some features that would be surprising were they to come from the story of an American or European. The first is that this woman, a college graduate, checked with her parents for permission to establish a relationship with a man. Then there is the emphasis on getting to know him thoroughly (rather than, for example, merely going out with him for the sake of a good time) and the insistence that they must "part immediately" if they cannot find a way "to talk about a lot of things."

Jankowiak correctly states that the girl describes her pain in exactly the language an American might use who was suffering unrequited love. But it is what she attends to as the affair develops that distinguishes her experience as culturally constructed. A broken heart is the same traumatic experience in China as it would be in Poland or in Puerto Rico, but the manner in which the individual puts herself at risk for a broken heart is distinct from culture to culture.

With regard to the Chinese approach to romance, Hershatter, writing in the mid-1980s, noted that, "from grammar school on, powerful cultural factors constrain male-female interaction" (1984:238). What was true when Hershatter wrote continues to be true in the 1990s, but to a somewhat lesser degree. By the early 1990s, most Chinese universities accepted the idea that romantic love had arrived on campus for good and hence made no official efforts to discourage their students from courting. However, as the following accounts from Qingdao and other university campuses demonstrate, even university students act with restraint and caution where romance and sexuality are concerned.

STUDENT LOVE AFFAIRS IN CHINA

For most Chinese university students, life is a mixture of academic studies and the relative boredom of free time. Qingdao students, for example, rarely have enough money to sustain a fun-filled recreational life and consequently spend a good deal of their spare time playing card games (in which the only stakes are pride) or simply talking. Once in a while an opportunity to attend a dance or a party, to go to a movie, or to have a meal in a local restaurant may arise, but such occasions are rare. The lack of opportunities for entertainment is one factor offered to me as a reason for the widespread interest in romantic affairs.

Boyfriend–girlfriend relationships are widely viewed as desirable, and, in fact, a good deal of gossip and much of the teasing that goes on among students are focused on secret love affairs or romantic longings that classmates are alleged to harbor. But since love affairs are conducted with so great a degree of caution, the talking and teasing seem to amount to a lot deal of smoke generated by relatively little fire.

Love affairs are initiated by males, since it is considered improper for a female to approach a boy with the overt intention of developing a romantic relationship. Some students remarked that it is not unknown for a female student to have an interest in a male classmate and to make an effort to show up at places where she expects him to be. In order to avoid damage to her reputation by being perceived as *qingfu* (frivolous—a term to be discussed later in this chapter), a female's efforts along these lines must be carried out with a subtlety that conceals her motive.

A potential affair typically begins when a male student signals his interest to a female student either through a campus mail note inviting her to meet him, or by approaching her and beginning a conversation with her when she is alone. A relationship so begun may gradually develop until it becomes a full-fledged boyfriend–girlfriend affair.

A student who had recently graduated from a university in Chengdu described his love affair with the classmate who eventually became his wife as beginning when he asked her if she would be interested in "being his friend." This occurred after a period of several weeks during which he had helped her with her computer programming assignments. In fact, he posed the question to her—and she responded positively—while they were working together at a computer terminal.

Students of rural background say that marriages in the country are still commonly semi-arranged in that young people are often matched up on the basis of arrangements made through networks of parents and other senior kinsmen. In such cases, the young people involved typically have the right to break off the arranged relationship. It is my impression that rural students with university degrees would not be likely to follow this pattern, unless they were males pursuing careers in the military (which many do since they lack the necessary connections to get good city jobs). In such a case, a young man might find it difficult to meet eligible spouses and so would turn to his kinship network for introductions.

Semi-arranged matchups of college graduates are also not unknown. One of my friends in China was a very bright and ambitious Shandong University graduate who met his future wife while he was still a student. He was asked by a friend if he would be interested in meeting a female student who seemed to match him in personality and accomplishments. He agreed to the meeting, he and the young lady took to each other, and eventually their love affair culminated in marriage.

Student affairs end abruptly early on if any important negative indicators appear—laziness or lack of seriousness on the part of either partner, for example, or merely the failure of either to develop feelings of affection for the other. The greater sensitivity to the pragmatic aspects of an affair or potential affair (i.e., the question of whether or not a possible romantic mate would make a good spouse) is one way in which Chinese student affairs are more conservative than those of their

American counterparts. The notion of a love that sweeps all before it—social condemnation, parental disapproval, economic concerns, flawed reputation of the beloved—is not typical for these young Chinese, nor is it glorified.

Students often keep their developing affairs secret, but in a case where a boy is being attentive to a girl within a context where they are surrounded by classmates, it becomes very difficult for the couple to conceal their mutual interest. Nevertheless, when they begin to meet each other privately for conversation and romantic walks, they often will not let their friends know. Thus, the depth of their relationship may remain a secret for weeks.

Couples go out alone together only if they have a potential or real romantic interest in each other. This interest should be long term given the fear students have of being labeled *qingfu*. Some student lovers plan to marry after graduation, but most do not. Couples not destined for marriage ordinarily stay together for a year or two or perhaps longer, although some only last a matter of months. To break up with one lover and find another makes one vulnerable to criticism.

All of the students I spoke to agreed that it is considered bad form to have two dating relationships at the same time. And a series of love affairs in fairly rapid succession was also frowned on by most students, both rural and urban. A person who was known to have had three girl-friends or boyfriends within the course of a single year would be considered *qingfu* by most of his or her classmates.

Those love affairs viewed as not likely to lead to marriage (that is, the majority) are sometimes labeled as cases of "playing around" (*wanwan*). Students who entered into these long-term but nonmarriage-oriented affairs did so with the same caution as those whose courtship was expected to lead to marriage.

The "playing around" love affair presents some danger in that such affairs are uncomfortably close to *qingfu* behavior. The compromise situation that has arisen is one in which the lovers maintain long-term affairs, rather than going quickly from one short fling to another, avoid sexual relations outside of long-term love affairs, and practice secrecy and caution in developing and maintaining love affairs. This allows for the fun and emotional satisfaction of the girlfriend–boyfriend relationship, but recognizes the limits placed on the affairs by the temporary and somewhat artificial arena of university life. The "playing around" affair falls between marriage-oriented courtship and the free and loose relationships, often short-term and sexualized, that are common among American university students.

Falling in love, and all the acting out of emotions this entails, requires a setting wherein potential lovers can get to know each other. In the West this is the dating scene. Some argue that in contemporary

China there is still no dating culture (e.g., Whyte and Parish 1984:119; Xu and Whyte 1990:716). This is not true unless one defines dating culture very narrowly to include only the popular dating-for-recreation system typical of young Westerners. The Western dating culture involves nighttime activities in a variety of contexts often with a succession of different partners to whom few long-term obligations are felt.

The Chinese system of dating, compared to its Western counterpart, is restricted in terms of the number of sites where it can take place, the number of partners with whom one can date without damage to one's reputation and the degree of publicity that one typically accepts concerning one's dating behavior. When urban Chinese go on dates, they usually go to one or another of a few appropriate settings. They often use techniques (such as carrying an open umbrella to conceal their identities or sitting in obscure areas of a park where they will be hidden by bushes) designed to prevent kin and acquaintances from knowing what they are up to.

Another quality that characterizes Chinese student romance is subtlety (hanxu). One young native of Ningpo went so far as to say that if a guy asked a girl directly whether she had a boyfriend, she would most likely reject him out of hand for his lack of subtlety. As a couple privately develops their affair, they reveal their affection for each other in carefully calibrated increments. As a rule, actions are more significant than words in indicating to the other the extent of one's romantic interest. This, as will be discussed further below, is related to the reluctance to express feelings verbally or to give weight to expressed feelings in the absence of actions that validate them. I was told by a number of Chinese, for example, that lovers do not ordinarily say "I love you" to each other. If such a phrase is used, it will ordinarily be in a letter and then in many cases only through the distancing medium of English rather than Chinese.

The dating and courtship behavior of university students is not necessarily exactly like that found in other sectors of Chinese society. Prostitution and extramarital affairs, for example, are not particularly rare in China. It may be that university students are more influenced by their parents than are Chinese of more advanced years. Furthermore, both the close-knit nature of university student life and the general lack of resources available to students may have constraining effects on their behavior.

TYPICAL COURTSHIPS AND DATING EXPERIENCES

A courtship that took place among students studying in Beijing in 1986 is typical of those I elicited in interviews. Most of the information for this courtship came from the male principal in the affair, with a little supplemental material from a friend of the female. This affair took place between two natives of Guangzhou who were undergraduates at a prestigious Beijing university. They were introduced by mutual friends who clearly had no intention of "matching them up" (the young woman had a boyfriend at the time), but who thought they should meet simply because they were natives of the same city.

After several months of socializing as a group, in typical college student fashion, it happened that the woman (let's call her Qiu Lin) broke up with her boyfriend, and the man (Huang Zhiwen) continued, by happenstance (he said), to run into her and have occasional private conversations with her. Then, back in Guangzhou for the winter holidays, they met again at the house of a third friend, and that evening Huang Zhiwen offered to walk Qiu Lin home. This offer was what told Qiu Lin that they were becoming something more than ordinary friends. Eventually, they did spend long hours together back in Beijing, and, after several months, it became obvious to their fellow students that they were boyfriend and girlfriend. Within a year of that they were married.

Some of the typical features of this courtship are the secrecy that the principals managed to maintain for several months, even though they were often out in the company of a group of friends; the limited sites wherein the private courtship could be pursued—mainly via walks in the park, movie dates, and secret meetings in one or the other's dorm room when their roommates were elsewhere; and, finally, the subtlety with which the affair advanced from friendship to romantically interested friendship to engagement and, ultimately, to marriage.

The following incident illustrates the weight given to parental opinion in romantic affairs. A senior in one of my classes at Qingdao described a loving relationship she had had as a high school student with a man who was a few years her senior. Her mother objected strenuously to the relationship and demanded that she give the man up. She did so, in accordance with her mother's wishes, and was quite sad over the loss. At this point, her mother had a quiet heart-to-heart talk with her and told her that if she really loved the man, she would be allowed to continue seeing him. The student decided that her mother's initial vehement objections to this man had been mainly a test to see how much the affair meant to her. Once her mother gave her permission to start the affair up again, the student declined to do so, thinking that perhaps her mother was correct in the first place in telling her she was too young to have a boyfriend so much older than she. On a trip to Beijing a few years after the breakup, the student met her former boyfriend and his new wife. She got the feeling that the man, though married, was still truly in love with her. Her feelings toward him were warm but by no means full of the passion she had felt a few years before.

The relationship this story illustrates, between this young lady and her mother, is typical of many that I noted among the students I interviewed. For one thing, the student deferred to her mother's wishes even though it was painful to do so. Second, the mother obviously felt a great deal of sympathy for her daughter and was willing to discuss and even to compromise on this issue of the heart. And finally, the student accepted her mother's viewpoint partly because she believed her mother's experience endowed her with wisdom that she herself lacked.

Some parents are not inclined to be flexible. A young woman at a university in Guangzhou fell in love with a classmate and he with her. Although they spent a great deal of time with each other and decided to get married, the girl's father objected. He told her the career choice she had made would require a great deal of international travel and that she must marry a man in her field or her marriage would fail. She begged him to relent, but he adamantly refused to allow her to marry the student she loved. Eventually, she followed her father's orders and said goodbye to him and within a few years married a man who met her father's criteria. The rejected boyfriend, according to the story told me by a friend of the woman, lost his will to live as a result of the breakup, dropped out of the university, and fell into a debilitating illness.

WORDS OF LOVE AND LICENTIOUSNESS: *QINGFU, TIAOQING, CHI*

Qingfu is a Mandarin term describing people who lack self-discipline and a sense of propriety, particularly in romantic and sexual affairs. The powerfully negative force of the label *qingfu* both prevents students from engaging in short-term affairs and compels those involved in long-term affairs to behave cautiously.

Qingfu literally means "light and floating," and is one of several Chinese metaphors wherein things deemed lacking in weight or purposeful direction symbolize weakness of character. Another term in this realm which stands in direct opposition to *qingfu* is *wenzhong*, or "steady and weighty." This term describes people of good and serious character (Hu 1944:). Also in this metaphorical universe is the term *liumang*, which literally means "drifting mob," but is commonly used to refer to gangsters (Stafford 1995:63). The pervasiveness of the metaphorical opposition between things that are light, floating, drifting and unworthy on the one hand and heavy and serious on the other is a measure of the importance with which seriousness of purpose is taken in Chinese culture.

Qingfu is often translated as "frivolous," but it is much more derogatory than this English word. It is generally applied only to young people, and it almost always refers to romantic and sexual behavior that is not strict and conservative. One of my students said that a young employee who is negligent about his work responsibilities or is not properly deferential toward his boss could be described as *qingfu*, but, though some other respondents were willing to accept this as a kind of *qingfu* behavior, the term is not commonly used in this context. The fact that *qingfu* is rarely used except to refer to romantic and sexual behavior implies that for Chinese students these are the arenas wherein the virtue of discipline is best gauged.

Examples offered to me of individuals whose behavior would be labeled *qingfu* include the following: a girl who talks loudly on a public bus and makes eye contact with people she doesn't know; a young woman who speaks flirtatiously to a young man, particularly to one she doesn't know well; a young man who calls out to or attempts to talk to a woman he doesn't know; a boy or girl who goes through a series of love affairs in relatively short order; a woman who is too ready to begin a sexual relationship; or a man who is a sexual predator. In general, females are more vulnerable to the damning label of *qingfu* than are males. Thus, the prototypical *qingfu* individual is a female who does not show discipline in matters of sex and romance. In the cognitive terminology to be discussed below, the image of the *qingfu* person is a negative goal-schema that has a dampening effect on the romantic and sexual behavior of Chinese students. It is an image of what not to be and how not to behave.

There are contexts in urban China that are disreputable by virtue of their association with prostitution and with those females whose employment status is widely thought to include prostitute-like behavior. Some of the female employees in certain hotels were thought by my students to be "easy" or, as my students said, *qingfu* in their sexual relationships with wealthy patrons.

A kind of *qingfu* image associated with males is that of the *huahua gongzi*, a term that is usually translated as "playboy." The *huahua gongzi* is a sexual predator who seduces women indiscriminately often by pretending to be interested in a long-term relationship. The behavior of the *huahua gongzi* was discussed by both male and female students in terms that clearly expressed contempt.

The *qingfu* concept is useful in explaining the conservatism of Chinese students in part because it so often comes up in discussions about different kinds of romantic and sexual behavior. In fact, if we were to accept at face value Chinese student explanations for their own behavior, we would be compelled to characterize this behavior as conservative largely because of the fear of being labeled *qingfu*.

Flirtatious behavior is regarded by Chinese students as *qingfu*. The Mandarin word meaning "to flirt" is *tiaoqing*. This word is closely associated with the behavior of prostitutes in their attempts to lure men into liaisons. It can also be used to refer to the behavior of a couple who are involved in or planning an illicit affair, for example an adulterous one. *Tiaoqing* is a strongly negative term and cannot be used in a morally neutral context. I could find no morally neutral word used by my students to refer to flirtation, nor could I elicit descriptions of flirtatious behavior that Qingdao students considered acceptable.

The English word "infatuation" typically describes an attraction felt toward another, often toward someone who is known only superficially. Infatuation is commonly regarded as a sentiment that is similar to love but distinguished by virtue of its transitory nature. In other words, it refers to a sentiment that Chinese students would regard as *qingfu*. There is, in fact, no Chinese word corresponding to "infatuation." Although a Chinese student may be drawn to another from afar or on the basis of a superficial acquaintance, such a sentiment is not institutionalized in student discourse to the point where a label for it has emerged.

The Chinese word *chi* is sometimes misleadingly glossed as infatuation. *Chi* suggests a passionate love that renders one foolish and to which one clings with a kind of stubbornness that appears supernaturally inspired. In China's earliest modern romantic fiction (ca. 1912–1930), both male and female characters were typically described as possessed by *chi*. However, this condition was due to their supersensitive, even spiritually charged natures, not their susceptibility to what American students would call "crushes." Their *chi* was a timeless passion that suggested a connection preordained by fate (*yuanfen*), not a fleeting fancy (Link 1981).

In contemporary China *chi* refers to a love that is one-sided and unrequited. It may also describe the feelings of the abandoned party when his or her beloved has ended an affair. The fleeting or trivial quality connoted by the English word "infatuation" is absent from the Chinese word *chi*. In other words, the very quality that the English word "infatuation" emphasizes—superficiality—is absent from the Mandarin word commonly used to translate it.

Young Chinese often refer to the concept of fate, or *yuanfen*, to explain the forces that seem to draw people together. My Qingdao students were convinced of its importance in bringing together not only lovers but also lifelong friends. *Yuanfen* is related to *chi* in that it is by virtue of fate that *chi* is usually thought to overtake an individual. *Chi* is an enduring link stemming from the very order of the cosmos, not a flighty, passing emotion.

CONSERVATISM: CHINESE VERSUS AMERICAN

In some ways, the conservatism of Chinese university students is reminiscent of the conservatism of young Americans before the sexual revolution of the 1960s. But contemporary Chinese conservatism is distinct in two significant ways: first, it refers not only to sexual but also to non-sexual romantic behavior. For example, a young American female in the 1950s could have had dating relationships with two or more different people at the same time or might have gone through two or more boyfriends within a year without being labeled a woman of questionable virtue. A female Chinese student who did such things would have her reputation tainted. Such behavior would also cause some damage to a male student's reputation.

The second feature of Chinese conservatism that distinguishes it from 1950s American conservatism is the relative lack of emphasis on virginity as a symbol of moral purity. For contemporary Chinese students, virginity seems much less important than the general principles of caution and restraint. In other words, if a sexual relationship existed, it would not ruin the reputation of a Qingdao University student were she involved in a long-term relationship with her partner. The emphasis in the Chinese students' moral code on sexuality emphasizes the issues of discipline, modesty, and restraint but does not focus on an abstract essence of female "purity" that the traditional Western concept of virginity represented. The relaxed attitude toward virginity among contemporary Chinese university students marks a change from China's traditional patriarchal past when virginity was even more crucial for a bride than it was in pre-1960s America.

If we interpret Chinese conservatism in love and sexuality as a matter of keeping romance in its place and not allowing it to dominate the individual's life, there is another dimension along which this conservatism can be identified: this is the value given to romantic love in justifying a marriage decision. The Chinese students and graduates with whom I spoke differ from their American counterparts in their matter-of-fact acceptance of marriages secured for reasons other than love. A variety of factors were offered to me as valid justifications for marriage, including an interest in monetary or status gains, a desire for an opportunity to live overseas, reciprocation for a favor owed, or an interest in not being single when a certain age was reached

There are Chinese students (I am tempted to characterize them as the more "Westernized" types) who argue that a marriage made for reasons other than love is a bad marriage. However, the most widespread attitude among the students I interviewed is that love is the best or most desirable, but not the only valid motivation for getting married.

Of course, Americans pay attention to the same pragmatic variables the Chinese attend to. But American attitudes are such that most people would be embarrassed to acknowledge marrying for any reason other than love. The American view of marriage, widely if not universally held, has it that marriages based on anything other than love are to be looked on with pity or even moral condemnation. Hendrick (1988) sees the ideal that one should marry for love as a vital component of romantic love, and Sprecher and Metts (1989) included the imperative that one choose a partner for love rather than more practical reasons as a principal component of their American-based "romanticism scale."

In a sense, the Chinese view of marriage (as opposed to love) can be considered more "liberal" than the Western in that it offers a greater range of respectable rationales for marriage. Compared to the Chinese, Americans might be seen as living in the grips of a romantic tyranny that demands a love affair for every marriage. And of course, given that many marriages in America do take place for reasons other than love, the reduced emphasis of the Chinese on romantic love can be seen as merely realistic compared to the Western viewpoint.

UNIVERSAL ATTRIBUTES OF ROMANCE AND SEXUALITY

If we accept the notion that young, educated Chinese pursue romantic love and sexual experiences in a style that is more conservative than that followed by their American counterparts, we must also account for the core of common experience that Jankowiak has shown to underlie the layers of difference in Chinese and American romance. In fact, a number of researchers in the fields of anthropology, biology, and psychology have produced data in support of the universality of this core of commonality and its biological basis (Buss 1994; Fisher 1992; Jankowiak 1995a; Jankowiak and Fischer 1992; Liebowitz 1983).

Clearly, sexual and romantic longing are universal human qualities. No matter how much they may vary by virtue of the negotiations and contestations that, in various social settings, surround them with requirements of ritual, sacrifice, or restraint, they still powerfully influence human behavior everywhere and do so in broadly predictable ways.

Psychologist Dorothy Tennov has coined the term "limerence" to refer to an emotional complex that is useful in the delineation of universal versus culture-specific aspects of love and sexuality. Limerence is the anxious, giddy, and obsessive response of those who are "hopelessly in love" or "lovesick." It consists of a complex of feelings and behaviors that commonly co-occur and that, though covering some aspects of what we call "love," is more specific and focused in meaning than love.

Tennov developed this concept after soliciting descriptions of love affairs from several hundred American respondents. The list of traits that she attributes to limerence can be summarized as follows:

intrusive thinking [about the beloved, or limerent object, abbreviated as LO in her terminology] . . . acute longing for reciprocation dependency of mood on LO's actions . . . inability to react *limerently* to more than one person at a time . . . fleeting and transient relief from unrequited limerent passion through vivid imagination . . . fear of rejection . . . intensification through adversity . . . acute sensitivity to any act or thought or condition that can be interpreted favorably . . . an aching of the "heart" . . . buoyancy (a feeling of walking on air) when reciprocation seems evident . . . a general intensity of feeling that leaves other concerns in the background [and] . . . a remarkable ability to emphasize what is truly admirable in LO and to avoid dwelling on the negative. . . . (Tennov 1979: 23–24)

According to Tennov, the LO is always a potential sexual partner. However, the essence of limerence is not sexual longing but rather the longing for the reciprocation of affection. Tennov writes that "[s]ex is neither essential, nor in itself, adequate to satisfy the limerent need. But sex is never entirely excluded in the limerent passion, either" (1979:20). A person experiencing limerence, for example, will often indulge in fantasies about his or her LO, but the limerent fantasy has as its climax "not sexual union but emotional commitment" by the LO (1979:39).

Limerence, then, includes two emotional processes, the first and most prominent of which is the designation of a specific other as a unique and ideal individual whose attention and affection are desperately sought. The other process, somewhat less prominent, is the longing for sexual union with this specific other.

There is no reason to believe that all people have identical sexual urges or that all people are naturally inclined to seek heterosexual unions both within and outside the context of love. Tennov makes clear that some people seem disinclined ever to experience limerence (1979:110–118). Furthermore, doubtlessly there are complicating factors behind individual human inclinations and behaviors that are influenced by temperament, cultural learning, and specific situational factors (Holland 1992).

Tennov is not the only theorist to view sexual longing and the craving for emotional reciprocation as distinct but intertwined processes. Attachment theory also draws attention to the overlapping interests of these two complexes. Shaver et al. (1988), for example, divides romantic love into three behavioral systems: attachment, caregiving and sexuality. If we (somewhat cynically) leave aside the care-giving system for the purposes of our present discussion, the systems that remain, according to attachment theory, closely match the two systems that Tennov sees as underlying limerence. That is, the "attachment" of the attachment theorists is very similar to the emotional reciprocation longed for in Tennov's limerence, and each is linked to sexuality.

There are more data that is helpful in elucidating the relationship between romantic love and sexual longing. Anthropologists and psychologists who look at human mating in an evolutionary context (e.g., Buss 1994; Fisher 1992), tend to depict our species as seeking sexual encounters in two distinct contexts: that of a long-term pairbond, and that of short-term encounters. Evidence from other pair-bonding species, various species of birds, for example, supports this evolutionary portrayal of what I call a "dual mating strategy" for humans (Fisher 1992).

It is an oversimplification to describe humans as seeking sexual encounters only in two distinct contexts, the long-term pair bond and the "one-night stand," as it were. There are sexual relationships lying on a continuum between these two which include, for example, the romantic affair that ends after a matter of weeks or months, the off-and-on affair, the affair that may continue a lifetime but is only activated occasionally, as when the principals happen to be in the same city, and so on. By a "dual mating strategy" I mean a pattern of sexuality that includes as its extreme manifestations (1) sex within the context of a long-term love and (2) sex for its own sake in the absence of any expectation of a continuing romantic or sexual affair. Obviously, for any given individual, countless variations may occur between these two extremes.

LOVE, SEX, AND LIMERENCE AS "SCHEMAS" OR CULTURAL MODELS

Both the "seeking sexual union with one's beloved" and "the seeking of a short-term sexual partner" are best viewed as enactments of schemas. According to D'Andrade, a schema is "a distinct and strongly interconnected pattern of interpretive elements [that] can be activated by minimal inputs" (1992:29). A schema is an internal model according to which an individual's experience is interpreted and his or her behavior is shaped.

D'Andrade does not speculate about the possibility that a high-level schema like "romantic love" might be a function of genetic programming, but he does argue that emotions are a kind of informational system, sharing some of the same functions as ordinary perception and cognition. Also, there is a growing consensus concerning the limited number of basic emotions that characterize the human condition, and this consensus points to genetic shaping (D'Andrade 1995:218–229).

It is the genetic basis for seeking sexualized attachments that, I maintain, is responsible for the fundamental similarities in romantic love and sexuality across cultures. It is this genetic basis that makes the experience of the sixth-century lover of China's *Book of Songs* resemble that of her modern counterpart, described by Jankowiak, who yearns for the love of her friend Chen. And it is the basis of "limerence" as described by Tennov's American respondents.

Most schemas, of course, are internalized during an individual's socialization within a given culture; that is to say, they are learned. Furthermore, they are internalized in hierarchical order. That is, some broad, high-level schemas include as sub-components, lower-level modules. Starting from a very low level (the "finding a seat" schema), D'Andrade illustrates the hierarchical structure of schemas as follows: "One recognizes some chair as part of the 'finding a seat' schema, which is part of the 'attending a lecture' schema, which is part of the 'finding out what's going on' schema, which may be for some people part of the 'doing anthropology' schema, or perhaps a 'meeting friends' schema, or whatever (1995:30).

In D'Andrade's terminology, falling in love can be viewed as a high-level schema or a master motive:

At the top of the interpretive system are those which function as a person's most general goals. These might be called master motives—for things like love and work, which instigate action with no more ultimate goal in sight. Further down the hierarchy are schemas for things like marriage, my job, surfing, etc., . . . Near the bottom of the hierarchy would be schemas for things like memos, birthdays, and water glasses. (1995:30–31)

A schema that instigates action is a goal-schema (D'Andrade 1992:28–29). Goal-schema hierarchies help us to identify particular situations, at the individual level, within which some motives are activated and others are left dormant. People are not machines, and the mere learning of a goal-schema does not compel an individual to follow a line of behavior that corresponds to it. But it is according to a complex of hierarchically related schemas that individuals act. For example, an American student may have internalized goal-schemas both for rebellious, fun-loving, partying behavior, and for proper, parentally approved behavior. His actual behavior will depend on the goal-schema he selects to enact.

At the cultural level, a model of widely shared, hierarchically structured goal-schemas helps us understand how a cultural tradition like China's, which includes well-regarded erotic fiction and Daoist sexual manuals as well as an elegant courtesan culture, could generate schemas for extreme shyness in matters of sex among its modern adolescents and young adults (Egerton 1962; Hershatter 1997; Li 1990; Ruan 1991).

Obviously, lower-level schemas are much more likely to be culture-specific than the master motives within which they are hierarchically nested. An intriguing feature of limerence is that it includes a number of relatively low-level schemas which nevertheless appear to be genetically driven: intrusive thinking about the LO, for example, or dramatic surges of buoyancy or despair contingent on interpretations of trivial behaviors of the LO. It would appear from these that where a behavioral complex of such importance as mate-seeking is concerned, nature is willing to interfere even in microbehavior to see that the task at hand gets accomplished.

Of course, people employ certain small-scale behaviors in order to initiate a love affair or sexual encounter, which are typically shaped and encouraged or discouraged in various cultural contexts. Such behaviors might include making eye contact, smiling, and seeking opportunities to touch, for example. These small-scale behaviors can be seen as nesting within a larger behavioral schema, one that we might call "seeking a sexual encounter." The "seeking a sexual encounter" schema itself is often nested within a higher, more inclusive schema, for example, the "seeking an attachment bond with a specific other" schema.

In accordance with the model of "dual mating strategies" outlined above, an individual's "seeking a sexual encounter" schema can be activated for its own sake, with no reference whatsoever to the attachment schema. I would also grant that a desexualized version of the "seeking an intense attachment with a specific other" can be activated. This, I suspect, only occurs in cultural settings wherein sexual unions or certain kinds of sexual relationships are denigrated as immoral or unworthy, and sexual longings are somehow deleted or repressed from the individual's consciousness. Lindholm's descriptions of the attachment that cult followers exhibit vis-`a-vis charismatic leaders represent such intense, yet desexualized, adult attachments (Lindholm 1995).

Desexualized adult attachments were also the basis of the "mandarin duck and butterfly" romances of early twentieth-century China. The cultural context for these stories was a newly modernizing urban environment, influenced by Western notions of individualistic romance, but not yet comfortable with sexualized romance. The heroes and heroines of these stories were drawn to each other by virtue of *chi* (described above), a spiritual force emanating from fate, which doomed them to a romantic affair (lacking a sexual component) with an inevitably tragic end (Link 1981).

LOVE AND SEX: AN AMERICAN MODEL

The similarities and differences in Chinese and American student romance can best be understood in light of contrasting models of hierarchically nested schemas. Again, the assumption is that some high-level schemas, those that represent human universals, are likely to be genetically based or at least to have a genetically based core. Other high-level schemas may merely reflect important, widely applicable cultural values.

For comparative purposes, here I will review some of the features typical of American university student romance. In doing so, the reader should keep in mind the extremely wide range of standards typifying American students compared with the relatively narrower range of standards typical of Chinese students. That is, some Americans are just as conservative as the most conservative of Chinese students, while others are casual in their approaches to love and sex in ways that no Chinese students that I encountered could ever be (Moffatt 1989).

Most American university students pursue one or more of various kinds of romantic/sexual affairs, the simplest of which is the one-night stand or brief sexual encounter. A more involved relationship is that of casual dating, which may include a sexual component and may also include a significant romantic attachment on the part of one or both members of a couple. Such a relationship sometimes entails the presumption of jealousy toward a partner who expresses romantic or sexual feelings toward a third party. Finally, there is the exclusive commitment envisioned as long term and in some cases marriage-oriented. Each of these possible relationship types can be shaped by one or more of the following master motives, or higher-level goal schemas:

1. Love: A fulfilling love affair that includes emotional reciprocation and sexual intimacy or the expectation of sexual intimacy, and that may or may not culminate in marriage.
2. Sex: Sexual intimacy in the absence of romantic love (Moffatt 1989).
3. Companionship: A partner with whom to enjoy such leisure activities as attending a party or going to the movies.
4. Prestige: Increased prestige through being seen by one's peers as the object of affectionate attention from a high-prestige companion of the opposite sex (Holland and Eisenhart 1990; Holland and Skinner 1987; cf. Waller [1937] for some 1930s American ideas on dating and prestige).

A hierarchical model describing an American student's schemas for the seeking of love might look something like this: at the top of the system would be the longing for emotional reciprocation with a specific other, a powerful master motive that controls various lower-level goals.

Within this master motive are nested secondary schemas such as (A) the seeking out of locations where a potential partner might be encountered, (B) the maintenance of a highly alert state of mind sensitive to the presence of cues indicating a given other might be a potential long-term mate, and (C) the presenting of oneself as an ideal partner for a long-term relationship.

If we pursue the "maintenance of an alert state of mind" secondary schema (B), this might subsume such tertiary nested schemas as the evaluation of prospective mates in terms of (1) physical features, (2) economic status, (3) character traits, (4) reciprocated interest, and so forth.

An analysis of the "attention to reciprocated interest" tertiary schema (4), might reveal such low-level schemas as noticing the way a prospective partner (a) looks at you, (b) controls voice intonation, (c) offers kindnesses, (d) says things to impress you, (e) touches you, and so on.

An American student whose behavior at a given time is driven not by a search for a long-term love, but merely for the desire for a good time, companionship, sex, or an opportunity to show off his or her mate-getting powers, would enact a different set of schemas, though most likely not an entirely different set.

Some of the various love-seeking procedures outlined above also pertain to the behavior of Chinese love and courtship behavior. But there are culturally determined differences in the way the secondary and lower-level schemas are implemented. For example, where an American might visit a singles bar in the hopes of introducing herself to a stranger who could turn out to be the love of her life, both singles bars and the idea that approaching an anonymous stranger in order to find a lifelong mate are alien to Chinese university students.

Chinese student courtship can be described as shaped largely by the following master motives or high-level goal schemas: a long-term love; the fun and diversion provided by a long-term boyfriend–girlfriend relationship; and avoidance of behavior that one's peers might label frivolous (qingfu).

Most importantly, Chinese student courtship is typically shaped by a master motive of "familism." This master motive includes as components an image of parent–child relations marked by a recognition of parental wisdom and authority and the understanding that an individual's worthiness will be judged by others largely in terms of behavior toward his or her parents. Furthermore, the family is envisioned as a source of emotional sustenance within which affectionate intimacy flourishes. Obviously, not every Chinese family

matches these goal schemas, but the existence of the schemas as idealized goals influences virtually every student's approach to romantic love. Other aspects of parent–child relationships will be discussed later in this chapter.

Companionship and prestige do not motivate Chinese students in the ways that they do Americans. Love affairs can, of course, provide a degree of companionship for young Chinese, but most students rely on their friends and roommates for company, since most students are not part of a couple. To go out with a member of the opposite sex to a movie or other event just for companionship with the possibility of light (or heavy) sexual play is not done.

Chinese students have some interest in prestige-seeking as they pursue their love affairs, but it differs from the American prestige-seeking described by Holland and her colleagues (Holland and Eisenhart 1990 and Holland and Skinner 1987). For these Americans, to be seen dating or enjoying the attentions of a high-status partner is a source of prestige. For the Chinese, status calculations are made mainly (though not entirely) in terms of the qualities offered by a potential spouse. For a Chinese student it is a minor source of prestige to have a beautiful girlfriend; but to be engaged to a girlfriend whose father is a high-level party official is much more prestige-enhancing.

The ways in which a Chinese student's life is involved with his family are crucial and multifaceted. In D'Andradian terms, it can be said that a number of high- and mid-level family-related schemas intervene in a Chinese student's approach to seeking a long-term mate. I am not arguing that Americans and other Westerners don't care about their families. Rather, I would say that when it comes to seeking romantic and sexual partners, American students are likely to regard their families as only tangentially relevant to this aspect of their lives, whereas for Chinese the family is immanent.

NICKNAMES AND FAMILY INTIMACY

One symbol system that can serve as a marker of Chinese versus American understandings of the family in courtship is that of nicknames. Nicknames in urban China are used to create boundaries around different kinds of informal contexts. The common nickname, for example, known in Mandarin as *waihao*, or "outside name," is employed among middle school students, university students, and workers to mark contexts of playful informality. But in addition to the *waihao* or playful nickname, there is the family nickname or *xiaoming*. This nickname is usually bestowed on an infant or young child by his or her parents. Traditionally, the *xiaoming* (or, as it was sometimes known, the *ruming*) was seen as protecting a child from being taken by

malevolent spirits, but today its use is associated with the warm, affectionate intimacy of the family. So where the *waihao* always carries connotations of humor and teasing, the *xiaoming* calls forth a sense of affection. Not only are these two kinds of nicknames distinct in Chinese culture, but also they are never allowed to cross over into each other's territory. The *xiaoming* of family intimacy is not used by one's peers (except in rare cases where it undergoes an appropriate transformation in tone), and the playful, teasing *waihao* is absolutely inappropriate in the context of family intimacy (Moore 1993).

Teasing is not absent within the Chinese family. Stafford (1995), for example, describes a pattern of child-teasing in Taiwanese peasant households, but this teasing is different from the egalitarian free-for-all found in some school contexts in that it is distinctly hierarchical and is seen by those resorting to it as having a specific didactic function.

The affectionate intimacy expressed in the use of the *xiaoming* is related to what Stafford describes as *ke'ai*, or "loveableness," a quality viewed as inherent in children and many young people. Certainly, one of the first things outsiders notice when they spend time in China, Taiwan, or Hong Kong is the great deal of affectionate attention bestowed on children in these societies. This generalized affection for children is a broad feature centered on the prototype of affection that parents, particularly mothers, bestow on their own children. If the establishment of a warm, loving intimacy between a mother and her children is seen as a widespread, high-level Chinese schema, then use of the *xiaoming* in the family context is one of its more visible subschemas.

Lovers in China (as elsewhere) commonly use pet names for each other. But Chinese lovers' names, which in tone resemble family nicknames, mark the relationship between lovers as something distinct from the playful, teasing friendship typical of adolescents and young adults. A sense of support, intimacy, and cooperation between serious lovers replaces the competitive play typical of roommates and ordinary classmates.

A graduate of the Beijing Art Institute said that by the time he and his girlfriend had reached the point where they intended to marry, he had stopped calling her by her formal name and had begun using the family nickname her parents had given her as a child. At the same, time she began to use a nickname for him, "Huhu," which was not his family nickname, but similar to a *xiaoming* in that it was a token of affectionate intimacy that had no suggestion of the teasing repartee that characterizes *waihao*. Nobody but his fiancee (who eventually did become his wife) ever used this name.

The duplicative structure of the meaningless name "Huhu" is reminiscent of typical family nicknames that are often similarly

structured. The names "Guaiguai" and "Maomao," for example, are commonly used as family nicknames. Huhu also calls to mind the sweet, affectionate tone of the names typically given to pandas, for example, Lingling and Xingxing.

It is not unusual for lovers to have pet names for each other in many cultural settings besides China. The distinctly Chinese aspect of nickname usage is that lovers' or spouses' pet names are sometimes family nicknames (*xiaoming*) newly used between equals rather in their original hierarchical context. Furthermore, the family nickname, as it is used, creates and identifies an air of affectionate intimacy for family members and at the same time emphasizes the boundaries between this family intimacy and the more rough-and-tumble intimacy of young friendship.

PARENT–CHILD RELATIONSHIPS AND ATTACHMENT THEORY

Attachment theory, which has already been invoked to help distinguish sexuality from emotional attachment, is also relevant to the Chinese family on another level. As noted earlier, attachment theory maintains that romantic love consists of a complex of behavior patterns that include attachment, caregiving, and sexuality. Furthermore, adult romantic relationships are shaped by the prototypical relationship of emotional attachment, that between a young child and his or her primary caregiver, usually the mother (Shaver et al. 1988:70).

According to Shaver et al., the effects of infant attachment patterns become evident later in life since "infants and children construct mental models of themselves and their major social interaction partners, and . . . these models regulate a person's social behaviors and feelings throughout life" (1988:72). People who feel securely attached to their parents as children tend to have stable, rewarding romantic love affairs. Those reporting their attachment patterns with their parents as insecure tend to have love affairs that are neither as long-lasting nor as satisfying as those of the "securely attached" respondents (1988:80). Similarly, Owens et al. found evidence that "attachment models formed in childhood serve as important prototypes for subsequent conceptualizations of romantic relationships" (1995:223).

The viewing of the infant–caregiver attachment process as a "prototype" is significant here inasmuch as cognitive theorists emphasize the importance of the prototype in the construction of cognitive schemas (D'Andrade 1992; Rosch and Mervis 1975). Ordinarily, a schema or concept emerges for an individual on the basis of an already established concept; the new concept represents an elaboration or modification of the original or prototypical one. Seen in this light, the bond between a young child and her primary caregiver becomes a prototypical schema in terms of which other bonds will be established later in life.

In evolutionary terms, this attachment model suggests that the evolution of the long-term pair bond typical of modern humans emerged on the basis of the already established mammalian prototype attachment between a mother and her offspring. A relatively slight shift in DNA arrangements could have replicated in mate-seeking adults some of the genetically controlled behaviors already established for mothers and their young.

It is typical for infants to show anxiety when their tie to their primary caregiver is threatened and to be relatively relaxed and interested in exploring their surroundings when they feel their tie to the caregiver is secure. There is an obvious parallel here between the anxious infant and the anxious lover who senses the possibility of the loss of his or her beloved. Conversely, there is a parallel between the child who, feeling secure in the mother's presence, has the confidence to explore her surroundings and the lover, sure of her beloved's feelings, who consequently feels confident enough to turn her attention toward others in her environment.

Attachment theorists are not the only ones to find a causal connection between childhood relationships and adult romantic and sexual attachments. In a recent analysis of a massive body of marriage statistics in Taiwan, Arthur Wolf has demonstrated a negative correlation between husbands and wives who were raised together in the same household and the strength of the sexual and emotional bonds between them in adulthood (1995). Wolf's study does not focus on parent–child attachment, but is interesting and relevant nevertheless in that it demonstrates a robust statistical correlation between early childhood experience and adult romantic and sexual tendencies.

Although attachment theorists have focused mainly on individual attachments in Western contexts, they have also paid some attention to cross-cultural variation in patterns of attachment, (Harwood et al. 1995; Waters et al. 1995). Some of the differences between Chinese and American romantic lovestyles are rooted in different, culturally prescribed parenting styles that establish different prototypical attachment patterns in childhood. Chinese parent–child relations, which emphasize emotional closeness between mothers and their children and which do not encourage demonstrations of independence in children, help create the secure bonds between parents and children that attachment theorists correlate with secure, long-lasting adult romantic relationships.

Culturally prescribed relations between parents and adolescents are also significant in shaping youthful romantic behavior. Chinese adolescents, who tend to have more open and less combative relationships with their parents than do their American counterparts, enjoy a continuing sense of security that no doubt decreases the emotional cravings typical of adolescents who are not so close to their parents.

The best work in English on Chinese child-rearing focuses on Taiwan rather than mainland China. However, the values underlying the family and parent–child relations in Taiwan are similar to those of the mainland. According to Stafford (1995), the moralizing texts found in Taiwanese primary and middle schools include a great deal of material on the ideal relationship between a child, particularly a son, and his mother. The morality preached in these texts, and supplemented by lessons learned outside the school, highlights the devotion a mother shows to her children and the sacrifices she makes on their behalf. So great are these motherly virtues, it is impossible that the children will ever be able to repay them. The lesson, according to Stafford, is that "mothers contribute to the health, well-being and education of their children. They do so by providing food and clothing, but also by engaging in an emotional relationship, involving anxiety, suffering, consideration, encouragement and instruction. The second, related, theme in the text is the sense of (unrepayable) obligation which a mother's contribution instills in her child" (1995:72).

Stafford's description of the emotional links between mothers and children is in some ways a reiteration of the argument made by Margery Wolf that the "uterine family," including a woman and her children, is of central importance in the lives of rural Chinese in Taiwan. This uterine family is distinct from and in some ways opposed to the patriline prescribed by traditional Confucianism. In terms of sentiment, it is this family which Wolf sees as evoking the strongest feelings in a child: "The uterine family has no ideology, no formal structure, and no public existence. It is built out of sentiments and loyalties that die with its members" (1972:37).

Stories of filial devotion, in which sons, daughters or even daughters-in-law make sacrifices for the sake of their parents' health—sometimes literally of parts of their own bodies—are both legion and longstanding in traditional China. Writing of the Song Dynasty (A.D. 960–1279) for example, Ebrey cites the popular story of Princess Miao-shan who "gouged out her eyes and cut off her arms in order that they might be used to cure [her father]" (1981:78). Francis Hsu cites several biographies in which a son or daughter was described as having used parts of his own flesh as part of a medical prescription for a parent (1981:82–83).

Contemporary Chinese would probably not resort to mutilation to express their attachment to their parents. In fact, it is likely that such tales from the past were largely apocryphal. Nevertheless, they represent a conceptualization of the parent–child tie as vital in a unique and unparalleled way. The relationship between children and their parents, particularly between children and their mothers, is laden with ties of affection, devotion, and an acute sense of obligation.

In the eyes of my Qingdao students, respect and devotion toward parents is a key feature that distinguishes Chinese culture from Western. In the eyes of attachment theorists, the close emotional bonds encouraged in China between children and their parents, particularly their mothers, would be expected to result in adult romantic relationships that are stable and enduring rather than meteoric, tumultuous, and fleeting. These secure parent–child attachments allow for more control by the individual who is either in the process of, or exposed to the possibility of, falling in love. Furthermore, we would expect people who can exercise this control to proceed slowly and cautiously in matters of love, allowing an affair to advance gradually as part of a deliberate learning process. Such deliberation would be especially crucial in a social setting where impulsive behavior could result in not only a broken heart but also a damaged reputation.

POWER, WISDOM, AND DISCIPLINE IN PARENT–CHILD RELATIONS

There are other ways in which Chinese parent–child relations shape student romantic and sexual behavior. Several of my students mentioned parental power as something to be respected, and at some level of consciousness many young Chinese no doubt make calculations concerning the power of their parents to help them with advice and connections. On a number of occasions I noted that where Chinese adolescents deferred to parental wisdom in situations where an American would probably have made up his or her own mind. Many students choose a university in accordance with parental advice, for example. Some students pursue a course of study that one or another of their parents has insisted on but that they would not choose on their own. After graduation, most students seek employment with the assistance of their parents, especially their fathers. Often it is only the father's connections (*guanxi*) that make it possible for a graduate to obtain a desirable position. A number of my students stated outright that they deferred to a parent's wishes in terms of studies or in job-seeking efforts because of their parent's superior experience and wisdom.

Another goal-schema typical of Chinese culture that reinforces the "go-slow" approach in romance is discipline. Here again parent–child relationships are crucial in that discipline is ordinarily taught within the context of the family. Children in China and other Confucian cultures grow up within a kind of "iron triangle" comprising maternal attention, the drive for an education, and the inculcation of discipline. Mothers whose heroic sacrifices call forth dedication and sacrifice from their children are legendary in the Confucian cultures of East Asia. In China, Japan, Korea, and Vietnam adolescents are typically encouraged to consume every waking hour in diligent memorization of materials provided by the schools. An observer might be excused for suspecting that this emphasis on endless hours of rote memorization is designed mainly to inculcate discipline, secondarily to stifle romantic impulses, and only tertiarily to teach useful information.

The emphasis on discipline in Chinese culture also has an effect on the general expression of emotion. A number of authors have noted that in China the significance of emotions (except for the emotions tying children to their parents) is commonly downplayed. In a number of situations where Westerners might be expected to focus attention on an individual's emotions, the Chinese response is often based on disregard for individual feelings. Hsu, one of the first to make note of this difference, described the Chinese as having a "tendency . . . to underplay all matters of the heart," a feature that he explicitly contrasts with American "emotionality" (1981:12).

Kleinman reached similar conclusions based on his therapeutic work with urban Taiwanese. Deeply felt emotions, he reported, were revealed only under special circumstances and only with the most intimate of friends. Talking about deeply held feelings was seen as "embarrassing" or "shameful" (1980:136). Kleinman argues that the Chinese are inclined to slight emotion-centered or "experiential" descriptions in favor of the "concrete situational context of personal problems" (1980:136).

Potter and Potter, on the basis of their work in Guangdong, argue that rural Chinese believe that "a person's significant characteristics are products of the social context, rather than derived from within" (1990:183). They assert that it isn't that Chinese peasants are reluctant to express emotion; rather they consider emotions all but irrelevant to the social order. One informant, when asked how he felt about raising a quota of chickens for the state, responded by saying, "How I feel doesn't matter." Another informant, asked to describe her feelings when, during her childhood, her father had impoverished the family through compulsive gambling, declined to answer directly but instead diverted attention to her survival strategy by saying, "I got a job carrying double shoulder loads of paper" (Potter and Potter 1990:187).

According to Potter and Potter this rural community handles love somewhat differently from other emotions. Whereas other emotions are expressed when felt but simply considered unimportant, love is seen as powerful and dangerous, and expressions of love are thought best avoided. "Love itself," they write, "remains infinitely private" (ibid:192).

This downplaying and dampening of emotions results in an approach to romantic love that subordinates romantic behavior to the demands of discipline. Discipline has already been highlighted inasmuch as it stands in direct opposition to the negative quality of *qingfu*. It is encouraged first and foremost by the student's parents and is seen as ensuring that he or she will behave in ways that promote economic success and responsibility. Obviously, parents benefit when their children develop a habit of resisting impulsive behavior in favor of behavior that enhances status and economic well-being—the payoffs of discipline.

The deferring by young Chinese to the interests of their parents calls to mind the Confucian virtue of *xiao*, or filial devotion. However, this classical Confucian word might lead to misinterpretations in that it calls forth traditional stereotypes about parent–child relationships and misses the specific aspects of attachment and family-centeredness in matters of romance that I wish to emphasize here. It is best to view the parent–child tie as operating on an internal and not quite conscious level where the prototypical schema of emotional attachment is concerned, and on an external level where young adults consciously recognize the cultural values that support familism.

A Chinese student's decision to initiate a romance with a classmate might be motivated by the joys and pleasures that such an affair ideally entails—given our genetic endowment which makes such joys and pleasures possible. But the motivation to seek such pleasures is shaped—and made a bit less desperate than might otherwise be the case—by the intensely important relationship enjoyed with his or her parents. This relationship helps dampen the appeal of the quick and casual love affair both by virtue of providing a prototype for lasting, stable, and secure affectionate liaisons and by providing ongoing emotional security for Chinese adolescents and young adults. Furthermore, the habit of emotional restraint developed in the family context, the discipline that this restraint implies, and the recognition of parental power, experience, and wisdom in China contrast with an American viewpoint that expects emotional exuberance and even rebelliousness from its youth. Consequently, where American student romances enact master motives of love, sexuality, companionship, and prestige, Chinese courtship is shaped by love, sexuality (within a long-term relationship), discipline, and familism.

CONCLUSION

Yet another high-level schema, almost a "meta-schema," is relevant to Chinese student romance: the concept of China itself as an ancient, mighty, and morally worthy entity. Barbara Ward once wrote that "Anyone who has ever asked unsophisticated Chinese informants why they follow such and such a custom knows the maddeningly reiterated answer: 'Because we are Chinese'" (Ward 1965:113). I agree with Ward on this point, but I would add that equally common, among both the sophisticated and unsophisticated, is the phrase "Chinese culture has deep roots." The implication is that Chinese culture, like China itself, is so ancient, its roots being so deep, that it changes only very slowly and often not at all. The great age of China's cultural roots are thought to imbue Chinese ways with a wisdom that is lacking in other cultural traditions.

China looms large in the minds of Chinese university students as a cultural/linguistic/historic entity consisting of a set of features that define its uniqueness and its greatness. These features include China's unparalleled antiquity, commonly referred to as extending back 5,000 years; the Chinese language, especially in its written form; China's literary tradition, including in particular traditional poetry and pithy sayings; Confucian philosophy, including especially an emphasis on family harmony and respect and devotion toward parents and elders; Chinese food and traditional medical practices; and an innate Chinese glory expressed in terms of the military and cultural pre-eminence of the Han and Tang dynasties and in such technological innovations as gunpowder, the compass, and the printing press. Many Chinese students expect China's pre-eminence to reemerge in the twenty-first century and in so emerging to vindicate the unnatural and brutal treatment China suffered in the late Qing Dynasty and early twentieth century at the hands of Westerners and Japanese.

The glorification of Chinese ways is not always without ambivalence. Western influences, which are themselves complex and self-contradictory, have been rendered more problematic by official por-trayals of some of them as sources of "spiritual pollution" (jingsheng wuran). University students, a kind of avant-garde segment of Chinese society, hold attitudes toward the West that are an especially com-plicated mixture of historical resentment, admiration, moral condemnation, and desire to emulate. The tendencies to admire and emulate the West will certainly bring about some changes in Chinese courtship behavior in the coming decades. However, the moral pre-judices against the West will ensure that the Chinese style will never precisely match that of the West.

There is a sense among many Chinese, students and others, that Chinese ways, given their durability, have something to offer that the rest of the world, to its sorrow, lacks. Images of the West as a realm of moral inadequacy are sometimes used by those who seek to uphold China's cultural conservatism. Michael Moser cites an incident in Taiwan, for example, where a female Chinese judge admonished a wife who was petitioning for a divorce. The judge:

Divorce will not solve these problems, but only create more troubles. You have a duty to your children, and to their grandmother, to care for them—isn't this the glory of being a mother and a daughter-in-law? You cannot let every little trouble provide you with an excuse to run off. That is selfish. You have special responsibilities in your husband's family. The good wife knows how to cultivate forebearance—this is why the Chinese family system has endured for thousands of years. Westerners don't care about things like this and that is why today their families are dying. (Moser 1982, cited in Wilson 1993)

That the family in the West is not dying is less significant here than the fact that the judge portrayed it as such and used this "dying family" image from the West to highlight China's cultural/moral superiority. Some of these ideas concerning China's morality, with its ancient roots, are highlighted in the following quotations taken from classroom essays by my students on the topic of filial devotion (*xiao* or *xiaoshun*):

In ancient China, *Xiaoshun* was regarded as a virtue and it was highly advocated by many famous people, among whom the most important was Confucius, whose thoughts controlled people's minds for more than 2,000 years. Today *xiaoshun* is still considered a virtue based on tradition handed down from our ancestors and our natural affection for our parents. So for most people, they may seldom talk about *xiaoshun*, but it is deeply rooted in their minds and it shows itself in daily life in a very natural way. [senior, female]

For some Chinese people, the idea of family in Western society can't be understood. If one says he loves his parents, how can he leave his old parents to live alone without the happiness of a family? [senior, female]

The idea of *xiao* will continue to be a prevalent Chinese social morality and retain its core no matter what outer change happens to it. [senior, male]

For my students, respect for "Chinese tradition," has a conservative effect in that this tradition is cast as worthy by virtue both of its antiquity and its requirement that the individual sacrifice personal interests for the sake of the family. In the realm of romance and sexuality, this means avoiding fleeting infatuations, casual sexual encounters, and a dating context within which light sexual play is permitted and family concerns are forgotten.

This is to say that young Chinese do fall deeply in love and experience the same joys and sorrows of romance as young Westerners do. But they do so according to standards that require caution, slow pacing, and limited experiences. This conservatism, which uses "Chinese tradition" as an evaluative mirror, reinforces the constraint demanded by the bonds that emerge with quiet but insistent force in the embrace of the parent–child relationship.

ACKNOWLEDGMENTS

Many thanks to Victor de Munck, William Jankowiak, and Zhang Wenxian for their helpful comments on earlier versions of this chapter. I would also like to express my appreciation for funds provided by Rollins College, including a grant sponsored by the Christian A. Johnson Endeavor Foundation.

REFERENCES

Banton, Michael (ed.). *The Relevance of Models for Social Anthropology, ASA Monograph 1*. London: Tavistock, 1965.

The Book of Songs (Shi Qing). Trans. Arthur Waley. New York: Grove Press, 1937.

Buss, David M. *The Evolution of Desire: Strategies of Human Mating*. New York: HarperCollins, 1994.

D'Andrade, Roy. "Schemas and Motivation." In R. D'Andrade and C. Strauss (eds.), *Human Motives and Cultural Models*. New York: Cambridge University Press, 1992.

———. *The Development of Cognitive Anthropology*. New York: Cambridge University Press, 1995.

D'Andrade, Roy, and Claudia Strauss (eds.). *Human Motives and Cultural Models*. New York: Cambridge University Press, 1992.

Dittmer, Lowell, and Samuel Kim. *China's Quest for National Identity*. Ithaca, N.Y.: Cornell University Press, 1993.

Ebrey, Patricia Buckley. *The Inner Quarters: Marriage and the Lives of Chinese Women in the Sung Period*. Berkeley: University of California Press, 1981.

Egerton, Clement. *The Golden Lotus*. New York: Paragon Book Gallery, 1962.

Fisher, Helen E. *Anatomy of Love: The Natural History of Monogamy, Adultery and Divorce*. New York: W. W. Norton, 1992.

Harwood, Robin L.; Joan G. Miller; and Nydia Lucca Irizarry. *Culture and Attachment: Perceptions of the Child in Context*. New York: Guilford Press, 1995.

Heart of the Dragon. An Antelope-Sino-Hawkshead Films Co-production with the English Association Trust. Mischa Scorer, writer and director, 1984.

Hendrick, Clyde. "Roles and Gender in Relationships." In S. Duck (ed.), *Handbook of Personal Relationships: Theory, Research and Interventions*. New York: John Wiley, 1988.

Hershatter, Gail. "Making a Friend: Changing Patterns of Courtship in Urban China." *Pacific Affairs* 57(2):237–251, 1984.

———. "Sexing Modern China." In Gail Hershatter; Emily Honig; Jonathan N. Lipman; and Randall Stross (eds.), *Remapping China: Fissures in Historical Terrain*. Stanford, Calif.: Stanford University Press, 1996.

———. *Dangerous Pleasures; Prostitution and Modernity in Twentieth-Century Shanghai*. Berkeley: University of California Press, 1997.

Holland, Dorothy. "How Cultural Systems Become Desire." In R. D'Andrade and C. Strauss (eds.), *Human Motives and Cultural Models*. New York: Cambridge University Press, 1992.

Holland, Dorothy, and Margaret Eisenhart. *Educated in Romance: Women, Achievement and College Culture*. Chicago: University of Chicago Press, 1990.

Holland, Dorothy, and Naomi Quinn (eds.). *Cultural Models in Language and Thought*. New York: Cambridge University Press, 1987.

Holland, Dorothy, and Debra Skinner. "Prestige and Intimacy: The Cultural Models Behind Americans Talk about Gender Types." In N. Quinn and D. Holland (eds.), *Cultural Models in Language and Thought*. New York: Cambridge University Press, 1987.

Hsu, Francis L. K. *Americans and Chinese: Passage to Difference*. Honolulu: University of Hawaii Press, 1981.

Hu, Hsien-chin. "On the Chinese Concepts of Face." *American Anthropologist* 46(1):45–64, 1944.

Jankowiak, William. *Sex, Death and Hierarchy in a Chinese City*. New York: Columbia University Press, 1993.

———. (ed.). *Romantic Passion: A Universal Experience?* New York: Columbia University Press, 1995a.

———. "Romantic Passion in the People's Republic of China." In William Jankowiak (ed.), *Romantic Passion: A Universal Experience?* New York: Columbia University Press, 1995b.

Jankowiak, William, and Edward Fischer. "A Cross-cultural Perspective on Romantic Love." *Ethnology* 31(2):149–55, 1992.

Kleinman, Arthur. *Patients and Healers in the Context of Culture: An Exploration of the Borderland between Anthropology, Medicine and Psychiatry*. Berkeley: University of California Press, 1980.

Li, Yu. *The Carnal Prayer Mat* (Patrick Hanan, trans.). New York: Ballantine, 1990.

Liebowitz, Michael. *The Chemistry of Love*. Boston: Little, Brown, 1983.

Lindholm, Charles. "Love as an Experience of Transcendance." In W. Jankowiak (ed.), *Romantic Passion: A Universal Experience?* New York: Columbia University Press, 1995.

Link, Perry. *Mandarin Ducks and Butterflies: Popular Fiction in Early Twentieth Century Chinese Cities*. Berkeley: University of California Press, 1981.

Moffatt, Michael. *Coming of Age in New Jersey: College and American Culture*. New Brunswick, N.J.: Rutgers University Press, 1989.

Moore, Robert. "Nicknames in Urban China: A Two-Tiered Model." *Names* 41(2):67–86, 1993.

Moser, Michael J. *Law and Social Change in a Chinese Community: A Case Study from Rural Taiwan*. Dobbs Ferry, N.Y.: Oceana, 1982.

Owens, Gretchen; Judith A. Crowell; Helen Pan; Dominique Treboux; Elizabeth O'Connor; and Everett Waters. "The Prototype Hypothesis and the Origins of Attachment Working Models: Adult Relationships with Parents and Romantic Partners." In Everett Waters et al. (eds.), *Caregiving, Cultural and Cognitive Perspectives on Secure-base Behavior and Working Models*. Chicago: University of Chicago Press, 1995.

Potter, Sulamith, and Jack Potter. *China's Peasants: The Anthropology of a Revolution*. New York: Cambridge University Press, 1990.

Rosch, Eleanor, and Carolyn Mervis. "Family Resemblances: Studies in the Internal Structure of Categories." *Cognitive Psychology* 7(4):573–605, 1975.

Ruan, Fang Fu. *Sex in China: Studies in Sexology in Chinese Culture.* New York: Plenum, 1991.

Shaver, Phillip; Cindy Hazan; and Donna Bradshaw. "Love as Attachment." In Robert J. Sternberg and Michael L. Barnes (eds.), *The Psychology of Love.* New Haven, Conn.: Yale University Press, 1988.

Sprecher, Susan, and Sandra Metts. "Development of the 'Romantic Beliefs Scale' and Examination of the Effects of Gender and Gender-role Orientation." *Journal of Social and Personal Relationships* 6:387–411, 1989.

Stafford, Charles. *The Roads of Chinese Childhood: Learning and Identification in Angang.* Cambridge: Cambridge University Press, 1995.

Sternberg, Robert J., and Michael L. Barnes (eds.). *The Psychology of Love.* New Haven, Conn.: Yale University Press, 1988.

Tennov, Dorothy. *Love and Limerence: The Experience of Being in Love.* Chelsea, Mich.: Scarborough House, 1979.

Waller, Willard. "The Rating and Dating Complex." *American Sociological Review* 2:727–734, 1937.

Ward, Barbara E. "Varieties of the Conscious Model: The Fishermen of South China." In Michael Banton (ed.), *The Relevance of Models for Social Anthropology, ASA Monograph 1.* London: Tavistock, 1965.

Waters, Everett; Brian E. Vaughn; German Posada; and Kiyomi Kondo-Ikemura (eds.). *Caregiving, Cultural and Cognitive Perspectives on Secure-base Behavior and Working Models: New Growing Points of Attachment Theory and Research. Monographs of the Society for Research in Child Development.* Serial No. 244, Vol. 60, Nos. 2–3. Chicago: University of Chicago Press, 1995.

Whyte, Martin, and William Parish. *Urban Life in Contemporary China.* Chicago: University of Chicago Press, 1984.

Wilson, Richard W. "Change and Continuity in Chinese Cultural Identity: The Filial Ideal and the Transformation of an Ethic." In Lowell Dittmer and Samuel S. Kim (eds.), *China's Quest for National Identity.* Ithaca, N.Y.: Cornell University Press, 1993.

Wolf, Arthur. *Sexual Attraction and Childhood Association: A Chinese Brief for Edward Westermarck.* Stanford, Calif.: Stanford University Press, 1995.

Wolf, Margery. *Women and the Family in Rural Taiwan.* Stanford, Calif.: Stanford University Press, 1972.

Xu, Xiaohe, and Martin Whyte. "Love Matches and Arranged Marriages: A Chinese Replication." *Journal of Marriage and the Family* 52:709–722, 1990.

12

Lust, Love, and Arranged Marriages in Sri Lanka

Victor C. de Munck

The conventional wisdom regarding societies where arranged marriages are the norm is that love is unimportant in the process of selecting a mate. According to this wisdom, held by most anthropologists and the general public, love marriages are typical of the modern, Western world. In the West and Westernized world, we believe that single men and women have the freedom, some would say license, to select their own mates solely on the basis of romantic, passionate love. "We love and therefore we marry," goes the cultural equation. In the West, mate selection is an individual choice, unconstrained by parental input or by considerations of "the business of raising a family." In contrast, arranged marriages are presumed to be based solely on a social economic calculus determined by parents. The prospective newlyweds are strangers to each other. Children of marriageable age have no input into with whom they are expected to live, mate and raise a family.

This chapter is intended to debunk this dichotomous and ethnocentric conception of arranged versus love marriage practices and the correlative notion that this distinction reflects a larger dichotomy between collectivist and individualist types of societies (e.g., Dion and Dion 1993, 1996). "Close-to-nature" societies (Gatewood 1985) do rely on collectivist ideologies to recruit labor and to respond to crises that affect the entire community such as war, epidemics, and drought. Modernization and Westernization do emphasize love marriages and individualism over the collectivity, but this emphasis does not imply the absence of individualist motives and love prior to modernization and Westernization. Processes of modernization shift culturally universal emotions, such as passionate love, and ideologies, such as individualism, from the background to the foreground of cultural practice and, in the process, cultural conceptions of love and individualism are modified so that they can adapt with other, perhaps new, social forms. Registering and attending to these processual shifts leads researchers and, often, natives, to think that romantic love and individualism are new cultural phenomena. But they are not. Rather, their locus and modes of expression have undergone major shiftings as a result of cultural change. The notion of typologizing societies and presuming that cultures are homogeneous agentive entities that shape people into "fax models" of that culture is overly simplified at best, and an ethnocentric distortion at worst (Strauss 1992:9). In this chapter, I first show that romantic love is an important background criterion for arranged mate selection in the Sri Lankan Muslim village of Kutali. The background is not less important than the foreground, but it is invisible from public view. Second, I explain how villagers "harmonize" romantic love and sexual desire with the social structures and economic processes that experts use to justify and explain arranged marriage practices (Trawick 1990:127). Third, I describe how villagers' definitions of romantic love are similar to Tennov's (1979) definition of limerence (see also Chapters 4 and 11 in this volume). For villagers, sexual desire is a core attribute of romantic love, and the latter emotion is not possible without the former motivation. I begin with a discussion on arranged marriage systems and their social functions. This is followed by a brief description of Kutali Village. I will then discuss how social practices shape love to fit village kinship structure and economic processes. In shaping the course of love, Kutali provides an example of a village with an arranged marriage system that allows for and even encourages passionate love between the prospective bride and groom. I would argue that this local model is applicable to most of rural South Asia as Trawick (1990) also indicates.

THINKING ETHNOCENTRICALLY ABOUT ARRANGED MARRIAGES

Popular articles on arranged marriages, such as van Willigen and Channa's (1991) article on the high rate of dowry death through "accidental" kitchen burnings in India only underscore our belief in the ethical wrongness of arranged marriages. China has instituted laws that ban arranged marriages. Television shows such as "60 Minutes," "20/20," and "Oprah Winfrey" have documented the failings and often brutal consequences of arranged marriages. The message being conveyed is that despite all the problems of Western-style love marriages, it is still a better system than one that diminishes the couple themselves to economic and political pawns.

The subtext that underwrites these cultural messages is rooted in our Western and perhaps panhuman tendency to perceive and categorize people, ideas, and things into dichotomies—the self and others, us and them, the modern and the primitive, societies and cultures that allow and reward individuality and those that subordinate the individual to group interests (e.g., Dion and Dion 1993, 1996; Doherty et al. 1994). Love marriages symbolize democracy, freedom of choice, and individuality, whereas arranged marriages symbolize parental authority, calculation, and subjugation to the group. Love and arranged marriages are thus part of a larger, more inclusive system of categorization that distinguishes between cultures like our own and those that are different.

Consequently, studies on love marriages in India and Sri Lanka have linked an increase in love marriages to processes of modernization, Westernization, or individualization (Bambawale and Ramanamma 1981; Caldwell et al. 1989, Ghosh 1971; Gupta 1976; Kurian 1979; Sørensen 1997). Modernization leads to social differentiation and individual autonomy (Lee and Stone 1980) that bring in its wake autonomous mate selection because the economic welfare of individuals is no longer tied up in the family. In contrast, arranged marriage systems are adaptations to and persist when economic resources are family owned, produced, and consumed. Arranged marriage systems ensure that property is not lost through mate selection based on "blind" love.

MARRIAGE AS AN ECONOMIC TRANSACTION

Arranged marriages evoke a turgid sensibility of life, where land and cattle are what matter. Women are commodities, sex an act of reproduction, the family a unit of social reproduction. The family becomes a socio-economic entity where intimacy, desire, and longing have no place. If we reckon love to be central to our own, Western sense of self-fulfillment, then cultures that extinguish the flame of love are perceived as nasty and brutish. What wonder is aroused in us is our amazement at the flatness and uniformity of their lives. Love is reduced to sex, and women are likened to commodities used as currency in the formation of alliances between males.

Arranged marriages, as Schlegel and Eloul (1988) point out, are transactions between families and, in South Asia, are always linked to the dowry. Goody and Tambiah (1973) refer to the dowry as a form of pre-mortem inheritance, because family wealth is transferred at the time of marriage by the bride's family to the newlyweds. Dowries

usually consist of cash, a house, and agricultural lands. Dowry negotiations between the prospective bride's and bridegroom's families are
mediated either by a marriage broker or a religious functionary. In
these proceedings, both families are cognizant of the going rate for
dowries between families of comparable social and economic status.
The dowry is an economic transaction in which wealth is exchanged for
a groom who enhances the status of the bride's family (de Munck 1988,
1996; Yalman 1967). The prospective groom's family attempts to maximize the dowry value, while the prospective bride's family tries to
minimize that cost; both families seek to enhance their prestige by
marrying into a socially reputable family. The bride and groom accept
these negotiations because their parents have authority over them and
also because the dowry provides them with an economic base to begin
their life together. Marriage is a business.

But the business of arranging a marriage in Sri Lanka is more
complicated than this. The wealth and prestige of the two families are
not all that matter. Authority does not compel obedience. The bride's
family is not going to hand over their lands and other kinds of wealth
to a groom who is going to mismanage the property and dissipate the
wealth. In Sri Lanka, as elsewhere in South Asia, there is a preference
for cross-cousin marriage. A first cross-cousin is anyone who is the
offspring of a parent's cross-sex siblings (i.e., mother's brothers, father's
sisters). The term for cross-cousin (*machan* for males and *mathini* for
females) covers not only first cross-cousins but any extension off this
basic principle. Parallel cousins refer to anyone who is the offspring of
a parent's same-sex siblings (e.g., mother's sisters, father's brothers).
Thus, nearly all generational cohorts in a community are likely to be
classified as cross-cousins or siblings.

The term for niece and daughter-in-law is *marumagal*; the term for
nephew and son-in-law is *marumagan*. Only one kinship term is used
to designate father-in-law and uncle (*maama*) and mother-in-law and
aunt (*maami*). Consequently, when a daughter marries her cross-
cousin, her parents are providing a dowry for their daughter and their
nephew. The relationship between a nephew and his aunt and uncle is
characterized by extreme formality; he has been socialized to be
obedient to them, and, after marriage, they continue to have considerable authority over him. From childhood, nephews and nieces are
socialized to defer to their uncles and aunts, particularly those who are
likely to be their probable in-laws. The terminology of the kinship
system allows for, indeed anticipates, a smooth transition from an aunt-
uncle/nephew-niece relationship to an "in-law" relationship.

Many Sri Lankans talk about the dowry as a debt from which they
can never extricate themselves. For the parents of the bride, the dowry
is not merely a transfer of wealth, but also a form of social secu-

rity—their son-in-law is expected to provide for them, they collect perpetual interest on this debt. The dilemma for the son-in-law is that the dowry property is deeded to his wife so that while he manages it, she owns it. Although the husband is the family "breadwinner" and is expected to be the head of the household, he remains permanently obligated and in debt to his wife and her family. In family disputes, his wife will look to her family for support and they, in turn, will remind her husband of his debt. Husbands are constantly attempting to establish independent sources of income so that they can be relieved from the burden of the dowry debt. Marriage embeds the newlyweds and their respective families in complex webs of debts and obligations, alliances, and strains. It is, therefore, important that the son-in-law and the wife's family and, conversely (but less so) the daughter-in-law and the husband's family, find the grounds in which to cooperate and recognize their mutual interdependencies.

From this brief description we can see that arranged marriages have a dual function—they provide an initial economic base for the newlyweds, and they function as a sort of social security system for the parents of the bride. An arranged marriage system functions best when parents arrange a marriage between a nephew and their daughter. Arranging a marriage with a non-relative, that is, a stranger to the family, always involves a degree of risk since he may reject and refuse to heed their claims of authority over him. Furthermore, the stranger has no kinship ties that bind him to his wife's family so that in the event of disputes, he is more likely to desert or divorce his wife. This is not an uncommon event. There were, by my count, approximately 27 cases of divorce and desertion by husbands, leaving the wife to support her children. Twenty-two of these cases were a result of outsiders who married into the village and left after most of the dowry wealth was spent.

In love marriages, where the couple self-select themselves solely on the basis of mutual desire, the delicate balance of interests between the husband and his wife's family is potentially undermined. For this reason Sri Lankans view love marriages with dismay, and, if their children should persist in marrying someone despite their parents' disapproval they are unlikely to receive a dowry. By controlling the purse strings, particularly when the children have few opportunities to acquire wealth independent from family resources, parents can perpetuate the dowry-arranged marriage complex.

The above portrayal of an arranged marriage system as a machine that has all the warmth and functionality of an ant colony does not preclude the possibility that passion can be accommodated to the economic interests that sustain arranged marriage practices. Later in this chapter, I will show that Kutali villagers do consider romantic love important in marital choices. I will first present a brief portrait of the village.

KUTALI: A CURIOUS VILLAGE

Kutali is a large rural village with a population of 1,000 Muslims. It is located in the south central district of Moneragala and is bordered on the east by jungle; in the other cardinal directions lie secondary forest growth and Sinhalese hamlets. It is a backward village by Sri Lankan standards—a villager had been attacked by a leopard during my residence, elephant herds often trample their fields, monkeys and birds scavenge their crops. There is no plumbing or electricity, and no villager owns a car or motorcycle. Cobras and vipers can be found in the gardens. The village folk healer specializes in snake bites by cutting through the skin on top of the patient's head with a shard of glass, tapping various herbs in place to cool the heat of the poison. At night villagers walk barefooted, sometimes with a flashlight, but most frequently holding a candle against a half coconut shell that reflects the light. Although Kutali is undergoing rapid social change, a Sri Lankan from 200 years ago would not likely have found the village remarkably altered.

As a Muslim village, Kutali is not only geographically but also ethnically isolated. Consequently, the rate of endogamous (in-village) marriages and cross-cousin marriages is significantly higher than it is for other parts of South Asia. From 1938 to 1982 there was an 80% rate of in-village marriages and a 60% rate of first cross-cousin marriages. Although remarkably few reliable data are available, Trautmann (1981) and Beals (1970) have recorded rates of cross-cousin marriages ranging between 10% and 45% and endogamy averaging about 75% in other south Indian and Sri Lankan villages. The extraordinarily high rate of cross-cousin in-village arranged marriages and the relative isolation of Kutali would suggest that strong social sanctions are in place to suppress love marriages.

In Kutali as elsewhere in rural South Asia, paddy land is the primary source of wealth and the most economically valued component of the dowry. As subsistence farmers, villagers can obtain lands in one of three ways: they can buy it, they can acquire it through the dowry, or they can clear additional forest lands. The first option is exceedingly rare as villagers commit economic suicide by selling their lands, and there are few villagers who have the cash to buy land even were it for sale. The latter option is becoming less viable. The government had recently instituted laws that legislate against the clearing and occupying of forest land without a permit. Stricter government regulations and more efficient enforcement make it impractical for villagers to concentrate their labor on clearing land that eventually will be taken away from them. Consequently, the dowry is the predominant means by which villagers acquire productive arable lands.

Traditionally, villagers supplemented their income by hunting, felling trees for timber, and collecting forest resources such as *areloo*, a nut used as a purgative, and red dye that was sold at nearby fairs. However, stiffer government regulations have reduced the villager's ability to freely exploit forest resources.

With the absence of a nearby industrial base, the villagers have become more dependent on their arable lands for subsistence. Modernization has, if anything, increased the economic value of land. Most factories are located in urban areas so that villagers must migrate if they want to earn a living wage independent of farming. In addition, a civil war has raged in Sri Lanka since 1982 that has claimed approximately 40,000 lives. The civil war is being waged between Tamil Hindu "freedom fighters" called "Tigers" or "the boys" who want to establish a separate sovereign state in the north, and Sinhalese government forces. The civil war has had little direct bearing on the lives of Kutali villagers except to inhibit migration to urban areas.

LOVE MARRIAGES IN KUTALI

In village parlance the term for marriage, *kaliyaanam*, denotes arranged marriages. To refer to love marriages, villagers add the English term "love" to *kaliyaanam*. This usage of the term "love" implies that love kaliyaanam are not true marriages and that they are associated with the corrupting influence of the West. Anthropologists have taken this dualistic conception of marriage as accurately reflecting what people actually do, so that love marriages are usually assumed to be a recent consequence of Western influences. But things are not so simple.

Villagers also acknowledge that love is a necessary precondition for arranging a marriage. Adam Marikar, the retired trustee of the mosque, explained the importance of love in village marital choices as follows:

Anyone who loves a woman will definitely marry that woman because he is going to live with her and not with her father. The man can either elope or persuade the mosque officials to hold the marriage ceremony.

Although it is preferable to have the father's consent, if the father does not agree then it can't be helped. The most important thing is that the Muslim religion strictly prohibits sexual intercourse prior to marriage. If this fact comes to light, then the girl's family will be more interested [in a marriage]

because their reputation is at stake. They will go to the boy's family to discuss
the matter.

However, if the girl's family is poor they can't go to the boy's house for fear that
they will demand too large a dowry. Therefore, they must somehow or other
encourage the boy [to marry the girl] . . . *though parents arrange marriages, the
couple must like each other. . . without affection, no marriage takes place.* [my
emphasis]

All villagers, men and women, interviewed agreed with the gist of
Adam Marikar's analysis. How can love be part of arranged marriage
systems and, at the same time, be construed as denoting an alternative
Western-type of marriage practice?

First, all marriages categorized as love marriages are the result of
the couple themselves deciding to marry against the wishes of one or
both sets of parents. When the parents reject their offspring's choice of
a mate, then the couple's only option for marriage is to oppose their
parents and elope. Of the 18 marriages that I recorded during a 30-
month period in Kutali, four were elopements. The couples did not
receive a dowry and on their return to the village settled down to an
impoverished life without land, depending only on day labor jobs for
their subsistence. When villagers talk of "love kaliyaanam," they mean
these economically devastating marriages.

In interviews with the remaining fourteen newlyweds, ten said that
they married for love, even though villagers categorized these as arranged marriages. All ten of these "love-arranged" marriages were between cross-cousins. Falling in love with a cross-cousin is the optimal
solution to the love versus arranged marriage dilemma. Both the love
interests of the couple themselves and the economic interests of the
parents coincide in these hybrid types of marriages. This is not a matter
of luck but of socialization practices.

Socialization Practices and Falling in Love with a Cross-Cousin

Three primary forms of socialization practices predispose unmarried
adolescents and young adults to fall in love with a cross-cousin: bathing
at public wells, visiting at your cross-cousin's house, and circumcision
rites for males.

Yalman observed an "institutionalized license between cross-cousins
. . . [to] . . . play with each other" (1962:566). Although he meant this for
cross-cousins of the same sex, it also applies, to a lesser extent, to
relations between opposite sex cross-cousins. Village adolescent boys
explained to me that it is "okay" to flirt with their female cross-cousin
(*mathini*) but not their parallel cousin, who is terminologically classified
as a sister (*akka* for elder, *tangachi* for younger). For example, all

bathing is done either at the public wells or nearby river. Unmarried males told me that they looked for places to bathe where a mathini whom they liked was present, for they could flirt with her and passers-by would accept the fact that they were bathing at the same well. However, males said they avoided bathing at wells if their mother, an aunt, or actual or classificatory sister was present for they would feel uncomfortable bathing in their presence. I should add that villagers never bathe nude; males and females both wear *sarongs* (a loose-fitting cotton tube of clothing) tied above the breasts for females and at the waist for males. An 18-year-old boy told me how his female cross-cousin had come to call him "snake charmer" when his sarong accidentally slipped down to his ankles while bathing. On another occasion, a number of teenage boys were chatting on my porch when one of the boy's female cross-cousins walked by with some goods she had just bought at a local shop. The male cross-cousin (*machan*) called out to her, *"nelle saman"* ("good stuff"); she looked over and replied, "Sanghu mark" (Sanghu is the brand name for a maker of top-quality saris). In public arenas such as wells and village streets, conversation with a cross-cousin of the opposite sex is permitted.

Yalman (1962, 1967), de Munck (1993), and Dumont (1983) have emphasized the importance of the brother–sister bond in South Asia. Dumont argues that a brother visits his sister's house after marriage in order to create affinity and alliance between himself and his sister's husband. Since the children of cross-sex siblings are related as cross-cousins, these visits give them an opportunity to play with each other and to begin to think of each other in terms of potential mates. However, brothers and sisters also visit because of sibling solidarity. Trawick (1990:182) for example, notes that brother–sister love is idealized in South Asia and may be the strongest and most enduring affective bond. As noted above, Yalman observed an "institutionalized license" for cross-cousins of the same sex (*machans*) to "play." But when a machan visits another machan, he is also visiting his mathini. All three visiting scenarios offer opportunities for machan and mathini to converse and become acquainted with one another, particularly during their adolescent years.

Circumcision rites provide another institutionalized setting for cross-cousins to acknowledge each other as potential mates. For boys, circumcision usually takes place when they are between 12 and 15 years old. Circumcision rites involve a number of boys of the same age set who are related. An *oosta maama* (circumciser, who, in Kutali, is usually a barber in a town some forty miles away), is called, and an auspicious day is selected for the circumcision. The villagers assemble at the house of one of the families of a boy slated to be circumcised. Islamic devotional songs are sung, foods are passed around, and each boy is sequentially called into the house. The boy is told to sit on a straight-backed chair, he drops his sarong, and an adult male holds the boy's legs firmly around two front legs of the chair. The oosta maama pulls the foreskin forward, holds it with a wooden clothes pin, slices the foreskin off with a razor blade, and ash from the hearth is put on the wound to sterilize it. The boy, by this time in tears and crying for his mother, is lifted up and put down on a mat with a sheet draped over him and pulled up, like a tent, by a string from a roof beam above his penis. The boys rest together in the house for a week. During this week, a boy's mathinis visit, bearing gifts of sweets and inquiring into the health of their "friend." The sweets are called "kaum," which is a popular symbol for vagina so that visit is laden with sexual symbolism.

Each of these three socialization practices encourages and disposes adolescent machans and mathinis to fall in love with each other. But parents sharply discourage actual love relationships. However, this likely enhances the possibility for arousing passionate relations the more. On the one hand, cross-cousins of the opposite sex are encouraged to think of each other as possible mates and to flirt with one another. On the other hand, post-pubescent girls are carefully guarded by their families. There are stringent injunctions against pre-marital sex and the consequence of such relationships, once they come to public light, is that the couple must marry and will receive little or no dowry. Thus, barring unforeseen developments, they are assigned to permanent poverty.

Villagers usually explain the sanctions against pre-marital sex in terms of Islamic doctrine (e.g., "it says so in the Koran"). But this is the ideological grounding and justification for the prohibitions against sex; in pragmatic terms, pre-marital sex symbolizes opposition to parental authority. According to village logic, if a couple cannot control their sexual lust and abide by their parents' wishes, then they are not good dowry investments either. Virginity not only establishes the woman's "honor," but more pragmatically, it symbolizes obedience to parental and religious authority.

The tension between encouraging flirtation and providing strong sanctions against the actual expression of sexuality enhances sexual desire for one's cross-cousin. The "bridge study" of Dutton and Aron (1974) demonstrated that male subjects were more attracted to a woman whom they met under situations of danger than under normal conditions. Reflecting on this and subsequent studies, Aron and Aron state that "potential over arousal is being kept under control," suggesting a "mastery of fear" (1996:46). From this perspective, the emergence of mutual affection between cross-cousins is a result of parental and ritual control over conditions that induce and contain mutual arousal, as meeting at wells, during the post-circumcision week, and at incidental visits at each other's house. This may also be understood in the way South Asians interpret and experience romantic love.

Experiencing Love as Sexual Desire

The literature on romantic love in South Asia has focused on females, and the focus has not been good. Women are viewed as imprisoned by the pervasively patriarchal nature of south Indian culture and as "dangers" to the social order because of their sexuality (O'Flaherty 1980). In Sri Lanka, Obeyesekere (1963, 1981, 1990), Stirrat (1992), and Kapferer (1983) have differently argued that love or, particularly, female sexuality is culturally "controlled," or sublimated, through trance-possession and exorcism. Obeyesekere notes how Sinhalese males "view their women as . . . sexually easily excitable, inducing the male to adultery, and thus. . . [females pose]. . . a threat to the integrity of the family" (1963:326). In this article on pregnancy-cravings and in later in-depth case studies of female trance-possession, Obeyesekere demonstrates how patriarchy and sexual repression of females can become canalized and transformed into erotic fantasies with deities or demons.

Obeyesekere, Kapferer, and those writing on gender issues in Sri Lanka (as well as the rest of South Asia) focus on female sexuality as culturally constructed in terms of a "harlot–virgin" dichotomy. Specifically, female love or sexual attraction becomes interpreted as "dangerous" because it is culturally conceived as leading to unbridled promiscuity and is therefore controlled through socio-cultural processes such as inhibiting mobility, endorsing submissiveness, exorcism, and various expressions of patriarchy (Beck 1989:160–172; Blackburn 1988:232; de Munck 1992; Obeyesekere 1963;1984). The higher incidence of female to male trance-possessors is interpreted as a consequence of these mechanisms. Trance-possession and exorcism provide a way out by privatizing public symbol systems and as avenues for sublimating sexuality.

For Stirrat, female sexuality is controlled by attributing its expression to sorcery or demonic possession. Among Sri Lankan Catholics, priests or other religious specialists may pronounce a young unmarried girl to be a victim of sorcery if she is "in love with the wrong person or refuses an eminently suitable marriage partner" (Stirrat 1992:105). The cultural definition and categorization of women as "more emotional than men," as "source(s) of disorder," and as "a dangerous force which has to be controlled by men" leads Stirrat to an analysis of exorcism as a means to establish "relations of domination": "Once parents have persuaded their errant daughter that she is possessed control has been reimposed" (Stirrat 1992:112). Love, in such cases, is externalized and re-coded as a demonic rather than human expression. Through this symbolic ritual transformation, parental authority is re-established. Love as a "deep motivation" goes against the cultural grain and is channeled to the margins of culture (i.e., exorcism) or constrained through dominational relations.

These analyses are derived from case studies of trance-possession and exorcism, or from tragic tales of love gone bad. Obeyesekere notes that "all of my informants have suffered from severe domestic troubles" and that trance-possessors are a unique minority in Sri Lanka (1990:23, 25). Furthermore, these are all instances of love and lust having penetrated into the public arena. Expressions of romantic love and sexual lust are perceived, like "fire" (agni), as dangerous things when they spill out from the backstage onto the front-stage of the public world. Thus, these and other writers give the false impression that romantic love is viewed as a pathology rather than a valued emotion.

Each of the twenty cross-cousin newlyweds explained to me how they had indirectly made their feelings known to their parents. Wives acknowledged that they had communicated their preference for a spouse to their elder sister or mother, never to their father. Husbands, on the other hand, said they had confided their preference with a village broker (usually Adam Marikar), machan (male cross-cousin), the father of their wife, or a friend, never to their own parents. All informants noted that somehow or other their affections will be communicated to their parents. One woman explained: "I slowly, slowly put it [my affection] to my mother who slowly put it to my father who then approached my father-in-law." A man described how he had selected his wife (with her approval) by approaching her father in private and expressing his desire to marry her. Shortly thereafter, his wife's father had contacted his father and proposed the marriage.

Villagers describe love (arderai or anpu) in terms of bodily desire. Anpu and arderai refer to a passionate emotional brimming over of desire, much like Tennov's description of limerence. Villagers describe love as an uncontrollable and overwhelming desire for a specific other. It is not a sexually indiscriminate but a sexually focused desire that is described as "mad" ("pissu"). A man told me of his son who had a "mad love" for a woman, and fearing that he might commit suicide, he arranged a marriage for his son with that woman. A woman explained how she had a "mad love" for her current husband, even though her parents had begun making preparations to marry her to a well-off cross-cousin. She had told her mother about her love for her current husband, who was poor, and her mother had told her father who canceled the marriage negotiations. She now regrets that move, but it was a "mad love" that couldn't be helped. However, because her love had never come to public light, she and her husband had received a reasonable dowry.

From the villagers' perspective, sex is a natural bodily desire (*acai*); love, like a magnifying lens, harnesses and focuses that desire on a specific individual, so that one feels "mad" or "overwhelmed." Parents acknowledge the potential dangers of such sexual arousal and attempt to guard their daughters so that they do not come in proximity with males. Sexual desire is thought to be catalyzed merely through proximity. As the woman who married the poor villager said, "I was drawn to him like cotton to fire."

In the West, however, love need not be conceived by the lovers as having a necessary sexual component. Hendrick and Hendrick (1986) and Tennov (1979) are among those whose survey results indicate that love, particularly "anxious" and "idealized" love "may squelch sexual feeling" (Hendrick and Hendrick 1986:164). Lindholm (1995:66) summarizes the commonly held view that "to love 'for a reason' is not to love at all. We love because we love, and not because of any advantage that the other has to offer us." This is not the way the villagers conceptualize love; for them romantic, as opposed to familial, love always has a sexual component. It is possible, as Tennov and the Hendricks both suggest, that romantic love in the West always has a sexual component but that it is "backgrounded" due to our idealization of love.

CONCLUSION

Kutali villagers do marry for love and for economic reasons. Economic reasons and parental authority are foregrounded in the arranged marriage-dowry complex, while love is seen as a "silent partner." This is not so different from what we do in the West, except that we foreground love, and the arranged or economic aspects of marriage choices are the silent partners. Parental authority over mate selection is much diminished in the West because of the absence of the dowry and the numerous economic opportunities available to newlyweds. Newlyweds are expected to earn a living independent of their parents' help. But through college, most children are financially dependent on their parents, and parents deploy a number of strategies to ensure that their children will likely marry someone from the appropriate social category. Children from upper-middle and upper-class families in the United States are more likely to attend private universities like Stanford, Chicago, or Princeton where they will meet and probably marry someone like them.

Studies on Western marriage practices demonstrate high rates of social, economic, and psychological similarities among married couples

(Hollingshead 1965). Love is not as blind as it is often portrayed in literature or film. Rather, the person we choose to fall in love with is largely determined by cultural institutions and socialization practices. Arranged marriages may sometimes be loveless and horrible, but often, like marriages in the West, romantic love can exist as a pre-condition for marriage. It is just that in the West, the arranged aspects of marriage act as silent partners, while in South Asia love is the silent partner.

The tragedies that are so much the focus of popular media when it comes to portraying arranged marriage practices should be placed in the context of the tragedies that befall Western love marriages. By exoticizing and often demonizing arranged marriage practices, we are implicitly condemning whole cultures and perpetuating a myth of cultural differences that presume that Western culture is superior to and better than other cultures. If we look a little closer, we recognize that the reasons why we marry are partly reflected back to us in the reverse images of the Other.

REFERENCES

Aron, E. N., and A. Aron. "Love and Expansion of the Self." *Personal Relationships* 3:45–58, 1996.

Bambawale, U., and A. Ramanamma. "Mate Selection in Inter-religious Marriages: An Indian Perspective." *Indian Journal of Social Work* 42:165–173, 1981.

Beals, Alan. "Dravidian Kinship and Marriage." In A. Sjoberg (ed.), *Symposium on Dravidian Civilization*. Austin, Tex.: Jenkins, 1970, pp. 107–141.

Beck, B. "Core Triangles in the Folk Epics of India." In S. H. Blackburn; P. J. Claus; J. B. Flueckider; and S. S. Wadley (eds.), *Oral Epics in India*. Berkeley: University of California Press, 1989, pp. 155–175.

Blackburn, S. H. *Singing of Birth and Death: Texts in Performance.* Philadelphia: University of Pennsylvania Press, 1988.

Caldwell, J.; I. Gajanayake; and B. Caldwell. "Is Marriage Delay a Multiphasic Response to Fertility Decline? The Case of Sri Lanka." *Journal of Marriage and the Family* 51:337–351, 1989.

de Munck, V. "The Economics of Love: An Examination of Sri Lanka Muslim Marriage Practices." *South Asia* 11:25–38, 1988.

———. "The Fallacy of the Misplaced Self: Gender Relations and the Construction of Multiple Selves among Sri Lankan Muslims." *Ethos* 20:167–189, 1992.

———. "The Dialectics and Norms of Self Interest: Reciprocity Among Crosssiblings in a Sri Lankan Community." In C. W. Nuckolls (ed.), *Siblings in South Asia*. New York: Guilford Press, 1993, pp. 143–163.

———. "Love and Marriage in a Sri Lankan Muslim Community: Toward a Reevaluation of Dravidian Marriage Practices." *American Ethnologist* 23(4):698–716, 1996.

Dion, K. K., and K. L. Dion. "Individualistic and Collectivistic Perspectives on Gender and the Cultural Context of Love and Intimacy." *Journal of Social Issues* 49:53–69, 1993.

———. "Culture Perspectives on Romantic Love." *Personal Relationships* 3:5–18, 1996.

Doherty, R. W.; E. Hatfield; K. Thompson; and P. Choo. "Cultural and Ethnic Influences on Love and Attachment." *Personal Relationships* 1:391–398, 1994.

Dumont L. *Affinity as a Value.* Chicago: University of Chicago Press, 1983.

Dutton, D. G., and A. P. Aron. "Some Evidence for Heightened Sexual Attraction under Conditions of High Anxiety." *Journal of Personality and Social Psychology* 30:510–517, 1994.

Gatewood, J. B. "Loose Talk: Linguistic Competence and Recognition Ability." *American Anthropologist* 85:378–386, 1985.

Ghosh, G. "Sociology of Self-settled Marriages in India." *Society and Culture* 2:127–140, 1971.

Goody, J., and S. J. Tambiah. *Bridewealth and Dowry.* Cambridge: Cambridge University Press, 1973.

Gupta, G. R. "Love, Arranged Marriage, and the Indian Social Structure." *Journal of Comparative Family Studies* 7:75–85, 1976.

Hendrick, C., and S. Hendrick. "A Theory and Method of Love." *Journal of Personality and Social Psychology* 50(2):392–402, 1986.

Hollingshead, A. B. "Cultural Factors in the Selection of Marriage Mates." In R. F. Winch, R. McGinnis, and H. R. Barringer (eds.), *Selected Studies in the Marriage and the Family.* New York: Holt, Rinehart and Winston, 1965, pp. 477–489.

Jankowiak, W., and E. Fischer. "A Cross-cultural Perspective on Romantic Love." *Ethnology* 31:149–155, 1992.

Kapferer, B. *A Celebration of Demons.* Bloomington: Indiana University Press, 1983.

Kurian, G. "Marriage in Transition: A Comparison of India and China." *International Journal of Critical Sociology* 3:60–69, 1979.

Lee, G. R., and L. H. Stone. "Mate-selection Systems and Criteria: Variation According to Family Structure." *Journal of Marriage and the Family* 42:319–326, 1980.

Lindholm, C. "Love as an Experience of Transcendence." In W. Jankowiak (ed.), *Romantic Passion: A Universal Experience?* New York: Columbia University Press, 1995, pp. 57–71.

Obeyesekere, G. "Pregnancy Cravings (Dola-Duka) in Relation to Social Structure and Personality in a Sinhalese Village." *American Anthropologist* 65:323–342, 1963.

———. *Medusa's Hair.* Chicago: University of Chicago Press, 1981.

———. *The Work of Culture.* Chicago: University of Chicago Press, 1990.

O'Flaherty, W. D. *Women, Androgynes, and Other Mythical Beasts.* Chicago: University of Chicago Press, 1980.

Schlegel, A., and R. Eloul. "Marriage Transactions: Labor, Property, and Status." *American Anthropologist* 90:291–309, 1988.

Sørensen, B. *Relocated Lives.* Amsterdam: Vrije Univeristaat Press, 1997.

Stirrat, J. *Power and Religiosity in a Post-colonial State*. Cambridge: Cambridge University Press, 1992.

Strauss, C. "Models and Motives." In R. D'Andrade and C. Strauss (eds.), *Human Motives and Cultural Models*. Cambridge: Cambridge University Press, 1992, pp. 1–20.

Tennov, D. *Love and Limerence: The Experience of Being in Love*. New York: Stein and Day, 1979.

Trautmann, T. *Dravidian Kinship*. Cambridge: Cambridge University Press, 1981.

Trawick, M. *Notes on Love in a Tamil Family*. Berkeley: University of California Press, 1990.

van Willigen, J., and V. C. Channa. "Law, Custom, and Crimes Against Women: The Problem of Dowry Death in India." *Human Organization* 50:368–377, 1991.

Yalman, N. "The Structure of the Sinhalese Kindred: A Re-examination of Dravidian Terminology." *American Anthropologist* 64:548–575, 1962.

———. *Under the Bo Tree*. Berkeley: University of California Press, 1967.

Index

About the Editor and Contributors

DUNCAN CRAMER completed his doctorate under Hans Eysenck at the Institute of Psychiatry, London. He is a Reader in Psychological Health at Loughborough University and is a Joint Editor of the *British Journal of Medical Psychology*. His research interests and publications include such topics as mental health, personality, personal relationships, psychotherapy, and counseling. Among the books he has written are *Personality and Psychotherapy* (1992); *Basic Statistics for Social Research* (1997); *Quantitative Data Analysis with SPSS for Windows* (1997) with Alan Bryman; and *An Introduction to Statisitics for Psychology* (1997) with Dennis Howitt.

VICTOR C. DE MUNCK received his Ph.D. in anthropology from the University of California, Riverside. He is a psychological/cognitive anthropologist with a research focus on the construction and management of public and private identities. He has written a book on cultural change and conflict in Sri Lanka, is co-editing a volume on methods, and has written articles on celibacy, Islam in South Asia, sibling relationships, arranged marriage, love, and sex. He is an Assistant Professor of Anthropology at the State University of New York, New Paltz.

LARRY E. DAVIS received his Ph.D. in social work and psychology from the University of Michigan in 1977. His research interests include group dynamics (race relations), romantic relations, family formation, and African American youth. He is a faculty member at Washington University.

DENNIS HOWITT obtained his psychology degree from Brunel University and his doctorate from Sussex University. His major research interests include the social psychological effects of mass media, including violence and pornography, racism, and child abuse. Recent major publications include *Child Abuse Errors* (1993); *The Racism of Psychology* (1994) with J. Owusu-Bempah; *Paedophiles and Sexual Offences Against Children* (1995); and *Professional Abuse of Black Childhood* (1997) with J. Owusu-Bempah.

JOHN ALAN LEE received a D.Phil. in Sociology from the University of Sussex in 1971 and is a Professor of Sociology at the University of Toronto. He has published six books and many articles on a wide range of topics, including romantic love, sexuality, education, police and the law, aging, socio-linguistics, and morality.

CHARLES LINDHOLM is a Professor in the Anthropology Department and University Professors Program at Boston University. He did his original research on love and friendship among the Swat Pushtun of Northern Pakistan, and has published extensively on similar topics. *Charisma,* published in 1990, deals with the political ramifications of idealization. His most recent book is *The Islamic Middle East: An Historical Anthropology* (1996).

GREGORY D. MORROW received his Ph.D. in social psychology from the University of Kentucky in 1988. His research interests include love, factors influencing satisfaction and commitment in ongoing romantic involvements, interpersonal problem solving, and long-distance relationships. He is an Associate Professor of Psychology at Edinboro University of Pennsylvania.

ROBERT L. MOORE received his Ph.D. in Anthropology from the University of California at Riverside in 1981, and his B.A. from Tulane University in 1969. He is an Associate Professor of Anthropology at Rollins College. In 1993–1994 he served on the faculty of Qingdao University in the People's Republic of China as a foreign expert in the Foreign Languages and Cultures Department. He has authored articles on Chinese names and nicknames and on the Chinese concept of "face." He is currently at work on a study of parent–adolescent relationships in contemporary China.

SUSAN M. MOORE holds the position of Inaugural Chair in Psychology at Victoria University of Technology, Melbourne, Australia. She holds a Ph.D. from Florida State University. Her research is chiefly in the area of adolescent risk-taking and health with respect to HIV/AIDS.

Professor Moore has held several major research grants and published more than 50 articles. She has co-authored the books *Sexuality in Adolescence* and *Youth AIDS and Sexually Transmitted Diseases*. She has worked as a school counselor and taught in universities for more than 25 years.

CHRIS O'SULLIVAN has taught Social Psychology at the University of Kentucky and Bucknell University. Most recently specializing in violence in intimate relations, safety, and custody issues, she has served as a research associate to the Center for Women's Policy Studies and as research director at Victim Services. She was a consultant to the National Institute of Justice for a national study of batterer intervention programs and is currently principal investigator of a study on coordination of criminal and family court proceedings in domestic violence cases for the State Justice Institute.

PAMELA C. REGAN is an Assistant Professor of Psychology at California State University, Los Angeles. Her fields of specialization are social psychology and statistics, and her primary research interests are in the areas of close relationships, sexual desire or attraction, and mate selection. She is the author of several articles exploring the actual and perceived causes, manifestations, and consequences of sexual desire.

DOREEN A. ROSENTHAL is a developmental psychologist and an international expert in the field of adolescent sexuality. For the past eight years, Professor Rosenthal has been involved in a program of research on adolescent risk-taking and HIV/AIDS. Her interests include gender and the social construction of sexuality. She is co-author of *Sexuality in Adolescence and Youth AIDS* and *Sexually Transmitted Diseases*, and has published more than 100 articles on adolescent development.

TODD K. SHACKELFORD is an Assistant Professor at Florida Atlantic University. He received his Ph.D. in Psychology from the University of Texas at Austin in 1997. He has co-authored two articles with David Buss on marital (in)stability and its evolutionary underpinnings. His current research interests focus on understanding marital processes and outcomes from an evolutionary psychological perspective. He is especially interested in the topics of marital infidelity and sexual jealousy.

ELISA J. SOBO is a Research Director at the Cancer Prevention and Control Center at the University of California, San Diego. She has authored two books and written numerous articles on her research on HIV/AIDS and conceptions of the body and illness in Jamaica.

MICHAEL J. STRUBE received his Ph.D. in 1982 from the University of Utah. Since then he has been a member of the faculty in the Department of Psychology at Washington University. His research interests include the development of self-concept, group dynamics, interpersonal relations, and decision making.

DOROTHY TENNOV received her doctorate in experimental psychology and philosophy of science from the University of Connecticut. Following a professorship at the University of Bridgeport and publication of her third book, *Love and Limerence: The Experience of Being in Love*, she has focused on a range of topics in both applied and theoretical psychology. These include the utilization of scientific knowledge in strategies for personal planning and increasing personal productivity, the search for human universals in social behavior, especially intra-specific discord, and the effects of incentive structures on the practices of scientists and science-derived professions, e.g., psychological "service provision."

ISBN 0-275-95726-8

9 780275 957261

HARDCOVER BAR CODE